MEXICAN ◇ U.S. RELATIONS
CONFLICT
AND
CONVERGENCE

UCLA CHICANO STUDIES RESEARCH CENTER
ANTHOLOGY NO. 3

Editor: Oscar R. Martí
Series Editor: Carlos M. Haro

UCLA LATIN AMERICAN CENTER
LATIN AMERICAN STUDIES VOLUME 56

Series Editor: Johannes Wilbert

Editorial Committee: Robert N. Burr
John E. Englekirk
Edward Gonzalez
Thomas J. La Belle
Mildred E. Mathias
Stanley L. Robe
Jonathan D. Sauer
Robert M. Stevenson

Carlos Vásquez and
Manuel García y Griego
EDITORS

MEXICAN ◇ U.S. RELATIONS
CONFLICT
AND
CONVERGENCE

UCLA CHICANO STUDIES RESEARCH CENTER PUBLICATIONS
AND
UCLA LATIN AMERICAN CENTER PUBLICATIONS

UNIVERSITY OF CALIFORNIA
LOS ANGELES

ACKNOWLEDGEMENTS

The University of Utah
The Food Research Institute, Stanford University
El Colegio de México
International Security
Proceso
The Academy of Political Science
The Cambridge Journal of Economics

Library of Congress Cataloging in Publication Data
Main entry under title:

Mexican-U.S. relations.

(UCLA Latin American studies ; v. 56) (Anthology ; no. 3)
Bibliography: p. 483
1. Mexico-Foreign economic relations—United States.
2. United States—Foreign economic relations—Mexico.
3. Mexican Americans.   I. Vásquez, Carlos, 1944-
II. García y Griego, Manuel. III. Series. IV. Series:
Anthology (University of California, Los Angeles. Chicano
Studies Research Center. Publications) ; no. 3.
HF1482.5.U5M49   1983   337.72073   83-1878

ISBN: UCLA Chicano Studies Research Center Publications

    0-89551-054-5 (Cloth)
    0-89551-056-1 (Paper)

UCLA Latin American Center Publications

    0-87903-056-9 (Cloth)

Copyright ©1983
The Regents of The University of California, the Chicano
Studies Research Center, and the Latin American Center
at the University of California, Los Angeles.
All rights reserved.
Printed in the United States of America.

This book has been composed in Trump Medieval by
Freedmen's Organization, Los Angeles, California.
Designed by Serena Sharp

To the villages of
Chimayo and Carnuel, New Mexico:
our roots, sources of inspiration,
and many times, sources of strength.

CONTENTS

PREFACE AND ACKNOWLEDGEMENTS ... ix

INTRODUCTION ... 1

PART I. GENERAL FRAMEWORKS: CONFLICT AND CONVERGENCE

   1. Conflicting "National Interests" Between and Within Mexico and the United States ... 29
      James W. Wilkie

   2. The Management of U.S.-Mexico Interdependence: Drift Toward Failure? ... 43
      David Ronfeldt and Caesar Sereseres

   3. Mexico and United States Relations: Interdependence or Mexico's Dependence? ... 109
      Mario Ojeda Gómez

   4. The Future of Mexican-U.S. Relations and the Limits of the Rhetoric of "Interdependence" ... 127
      Carlos Rico F.

PART II. MEXICAN PETROLEUM: A RESOURCE FOR WHOM?

   5. Oil Booms and the Mexican Historical Experience: Past Problems—Future Prospects ... 177
      Lorenzo Meyer

   6. Mexican Oil at the Service of the Bourgeoisie ... 201
      Jorge G. Castañeda

   7. Mexican Petroleum and U.S. Security ... 215
      Richard Fagen

PART III. TRADE RELATIONS: ESCALATING CONFLICT?

   8. The Trade Issue in U.S.-Mexican Relations ... 235
      G.C. Hufbauer, W.N. Harrell Smith IV, and F.G. Vukmanic

9. The Mexican Economy: Recent Evolution
and Future Projections 251
*Centro de Investigación y Docencia
Económicas*

10. The Case Against GATT, 1980 287
Colegio Nacional de Economistas

PART IV. MIGRANT WORKERS: A PROBLEM FOR WHOM?

11. Unequal Exchange in the Binational
Relationship: The Case of Immigrant Labor 309
*Jorge A. Bustamante and
James D. Cockcroft*

12. Labor Market Projections for the United
States and Mexico and Their Relevance to
Current Migration Controversies 325
Clark W. Reynolds

13. America in the Era of Limits: Migrants,
Nativists, and the Future of U.S.–Mexican
Relations 371
Wayne A. Cornelius

PART V. CHICANOS AND THE BINATIONAL
RELATIONSHIP: ACTORS OR SUBJECTS?

14. Chicanos and U.S. Foreign Policy: The
Future of Chicano–Mexican Relations 399
Rodolfo O. de la Garza

15. Notes on an Interpretation of the Relations
Between the Mexican Community in the
United States and Mexico 417
Juan Gómez-Quiñones

16. Mexican Political Actors in the United States
and Mexico: Historical and Political
Contexts of a Dialogue Renewed 441
Carlos H. Zazueta

BIBLIOGRAPHY 483

Preface and Acknowledgments

This book provides a general introduction to a wide range of issues in Mexican–U.S. relations. It draws together several interpretations of contemporary U.S.–Mexican relations in a manner which may be of interest to students of international relations, Latin American and Chicano studies. Several essays were chosen for this volume because they provide concise introductions to key problems in contemporary binational relations, and because they show how these issues are inextricably related. Others are included here because they address specific questions in considerable depth, and in several instances have come to be recognized as important contributions to the debate on the course and character of Mexican–U.S. relations. By including short essays with longer ones we attempt to strike a balance between clear and succinct analyses of general problems, and a more sharply focused and detailed treatment of complex issues.

The sixteen chapters in this anthology were written during the period 1977–82, and come from a variety of sources. Seven have been published previously in English: those by James Wilkie; Richard Fagen; Wayne Cornelius; Clark Reynolds; G.C. Hufbauer, W.D. Harrell Smith, and F.G. Vukmanic; Rodolfo O. de la Garza; and that by a team of economists at CIDE, including José I. Casar, Mario Dehesa, Jorge Mattar, Gisele Pérez Moreno, Gonzalo Rodríguez, Catarina Rock de Sacristán, Jaime Pos and Alejandro Vázquez. By including them here, we have brought together in the same volume, and made more accessible, many views which have marked important turns in the recent discussion about the changing political and economic realities of U.S.–Mexican relations. Wilkie's essay is a revised version of his testimony before Congress in 1977; the remaining chapters were published in working paper form or in specialized journals.

Five chapters were previously published in Spanish and have been translated for this volume: those by Mario Ojeda, Lorenzo Meyer, Jorge G. Castañeda, Jorge Bustamante and James Cockcroft, and by the Colegio Nacional de Economistas. Except for this last chapter, all have been revised, updated, or postscripts added to take into account some of the unforeseen events which have so rapidly altered the political and economic landscape since they were written. Bustamante and Cockcroft's chapter has been revised and expanded considerably from its original Spanish version. The chapter by the Colegio Nacional de Economistas, a series of policy recommendations submitted to the Mexican president in March, 1980, has been left intact to preserve its original flavor and historical value. Without attempting to suggest that these papers are "representative" of all Mexican views, in our selection, we have tried to take into account the diverse range of Mexican perspectives on this topic.

Four of the chapters are published here for the first time. Three of these—the chapters by Carlos Rico, Juan Gómez-Quiñones, and Carlos Zazueta—were written specifically for this book. The first provides an indispensable discussion on the links between intersocietal and intergovernmental relations. The others fill an important gap in the discussion about Chicano participation in U.S.-Mexican intergovernmental and intersocietal relations.

The chapter by David Ronfeldt and Caesar Sereseres, though circulating for some time in manuscript form (and in the process, having started some of the debates that later found their way into print), is also published here for the first time. This paper was prepared at The Rand Corporation as a study for the State Department in late 1977, about the same time that several U.S. government agencies began a major policy review of relations with Mexico. (That review finally culminated in a National Security Council paper known as Presidential Review Memorandum 41 [PRM-41].)*

Several authors asked us to indicate that their chapters reflect personal views and not those of institutions they are associated with, nor official policies of either the U.S. or Mexican government. We take this opportunity to mention that this applies to all of the chapters in this volume.

*Portions of an early draft of PRM-41 were leaked to the press in 1978. See: *The Washington Post*, 15 December 1978, p. A26. Richard Fagen discusses, in his chapter in this volume, the context in which this document was prepared.

The reader may note that in several cases the data cited in these papers is dated. In part this is a result of rapid changes in Mexico and the United States occurring while these chapters were written and this volume edited. The paper by Ronfeldt and Sereseres, written in December 1977, illustrates this point. It predated the establishment—and dismantling—of the Special Ambassador's office at the State Department. Moreover, this chapter refers to a trade agreement negotiated in 1977 which later fell through when Mexico refused to join the GATT in 1980, and to the construction of the gas pipeline, suspended in 1978. We have chosen to publish them without revision, however, because of their historical value. The reader interested in the more recent data should consult those chapters which were written later or updated for publication here. For example, Hufbauer, Smith and Vukmanic and Meyer provide a more recent discussion on two of these points. The value of these papers, such as that by Ronfeldt and Sereseres, does not rest upon the data they present per se, but on how they interpret them, what contributions they make to the debate, and what normative and analytical conclusions they draw. For a more elaborate empirical treatment of the issues, the reader may consult the sources listed in the bibliography appended to this book.

The sixteen chapters in this volume focus on a common set of issues from contrasting perspectives. In selecting them, we sought to include what we consider to be influential perspectives on U.S.-Mexican relations in *both* countries, something a reader seeking an introduction to the topic should take into account. Because several of these views have sparked controversy and shaped the binational debate on these topics, they merit scrutiny. And since in their interpretation of a wide range of issues our contributors frequently disagree, one cannot possibly be in agreement with *all* of the views expressed here. Thus, our selection of readings reproduces part of the recent debate over what constitutes the major problems in the U.S.-Mexican agenda and what should be their respective national policy responses. The objective of this book, then, is not to convert the reader to any one approach to the analysis of Mexican-U.S. relations, but to discuss in some depth the change binational issues have undergone during the past decade and to face some of the questions that these relations, in all probability, cannot avoid.

We would like to thank the many people who contributed to the publication of this anthology. Special thanks to the Chicano Studies

Research Center and the Latin American Center at UCLA; they consistently and patiently supported this effort which, at its inception, was a more modest project. In particular, we would like to thank Dr. Oscar Martí for his conscientious editorial work, Rosa Martinez and Bernadette Monda for their role in pre-production, and the translators who undertook a formidable task—Margarita E. Ayala, Pauline Jinks, and Roberto Sifuentes. We want to thank our contributors, who gave us permission to publish their work, and who were patient with our editorial suggestions. By the same token, we are grateful for the suggestions and criticisms of Juan Gómez-Quiñones, James W. Wilkie, David Mares, and Gustavo Vega.

C.V. and M.G. y G.
East Los Angeles
September 1982

Introduction

Carlos Vásquez and Manuel García y Griego

In the past decade, there has been a fundamental change in perceptions of Mexican–U.S. relations. As late as 1972, dominant U.S. perceptions of Mexico stressed its poverty, dependence upon the United States, and when compared to the rest of Latin America, its political stability. Relations between the two governments centered on problems arising from their nearly 2000-mile common border; and the presence of substantial pockets of Mexican-origin population just north of that border hardly seemed to matter. Thus, Mexico posed no significant challenges to architects of U.S. foreign policy. Indeed, the common difficulty of those concerned with U.S.–Mexican relations was to persuade highly placed U.S. officials, as well as broad segments of the U.S. public, that these relations were important.

During the last ten years, virtually all of these U.S. perceptions changed dramatically. Suddenly, Mexico acquired an enormous oil wealth. It no longer seemed dependent upon the U.S., and other events suggested it was not politically stable. Border issues were submerged as other problems rose to the top of the bilateral agenda, and the presence of a large and growing Chicano population was

---

Carlos Vásquez is a Research Associate at the Chicano Studies Research Center, University of California, Los Angeles. This volume was edited during his tenure as an Institute of American Cultures Research Fellow at the CSRC/UCLA, 1980–82.

  Manuel García y Griego is a professor at the Centro de Estudios Internacionales at El Colegio de México and Coordinator of the Mexican–United States Program. This volume was edited during his tenure as a Tinker Foundation Fellow at the Center for U.S.–Mexican Studies at the University of California, San Diego, 1980–82.
©1983 Carlos Vásquez and Manuel García y Griego

perceived to be relevant both for U.S. domestic politics and for binational relations. During this period, these and other developments augured greater U.S. stakes in relations with Mexico, and in the outcomes of Mexican domestic political debates. By the early 1980s, U.S. policy analysts and broad segments of U.S. society no longer asked themselves the question: Does Mexico really matter? Current perceptions are that it does—that events in Mexico, and Mexican government policies, can no longer be safely ignored.

At a very general level, this change in U.S. perceptions can be attributed to discoveries of enormous oil and gas reserves in Mexico and to other global and binational political events which magnified their importance. One of these events was that in the mid-1970s, Mexico's economy stopped growing, and simultaneously, the government faced new challenges to its traditional control over dissent and the domestic political process. Thus, from the point of view of many U.S. and Mexican observers, the discovery of oil could not have come at a better time. According to this argument, oil offered the Mexican regime an instrument with which to "manage" its domestic crisis, and an "historic opportunity" to escape economic underdevelopment and to revolutionize its relations with the United States. Whether or not this argument is correct is the subject of an on-going debate—part of it reproduced in this volume.

Another set of circumstances which magnified the significance of Mexico's oil finds was the progressive decline in the U.S. position of global dominance, and its sharpened sense of vulnerability to world events not under its overt control. This is reflected by recent challenges to U.S. economic and political predominance by other industrialized countries. Another set of events, and more directly related to the heightened importance of relations with Mexico, was the abrupt interruption in the supply and the sharp increases in the price of oil imported from the Middle East. At this general level, Mexico's oil exports seemed to offer the United States an opportunity to resolve one of its most pressing foreign policy problems. Thus, one would expect Mexican-U.S. relations to be qualitatively more important to the United States now than they were even a decade ago, not only because Mexico has achieved the status of a major oil exporter, but also because some of the problems in the relationship are fundamentally different.

"Change" and "oil" seem to be continuing themes in contemporary U.S.- Mexican relations. Toward the end of the López Portillo Administration, and as this book is going to press, Mexico entered a new financial crisis even deeper than that of 1976-77, a crisis whose most proximate cause was the sudden decline in Mexico's earnings from oil exports. Its immediate consequences—abrupt cuts in government spending, increased borrowing to service Mexico's massive foreign debt, successive devaluations of the peso, the imposition of strict exchange controls, the growth of inflation to levels previously experienced only in other Latin American countries, and the nationalization of the country's banks—are a dramatic testimony to Mexico's new dependence on petroleum exports, symptomatic of a widespread lack of confidence in its currency and, to a lesser degree, its political stability. While all of the chapters in this book were written before this turn of events, many of them express a sharp awareness that oil could not possibly solve all of Mexico's problems and that it could engender new ones. This anthology does not pose the question of what Mexico's most recent crisis means for its political economy nor for its relations with the United States. Careful reading of several chapters, however, provides some material for discussion on the question of whether this crisis is a passing phenomenon or a harbinger of future events. And this volume does identify the major components of change in those relations during the last few years, both in terms of how change occurred and how it was perceived.

In this introduction, we are concerned with two interrelated tasks. One is a general discussion of two major analytical issues that arise in the study of Mexican-U.S. relations. These issues frequently confront the analyst who seeks to describe, organize, and interpret the wide range of topics associated with U.S.-Mexican relations: (1) the distinction between intergovernmental and intersocietal relations, and (2) the emphasis of policy constraints or policy choices in interpreting the behavior of governmental actors. We draw upon the discussion in the chapters to address these problems.

A second task is to discuss the arguments made in the sixteen chapters of this book, the debates in which they engage, and the core set of issues which, according to these authors, constitutes the fundamental problems of Mexican-U.S. relations. In this part of the introduction, we discuss how the papers interpret the changes in U.S.-Mexican relations during the past decade, how many binational issues are interrelated, and how recent developments in this area suggest themes of "conflict" and "convergence." This represents an attempt on our part to show how the different chapters are tied together, to make comparisons and provide material for discussion.

TWO ANALYTICAL ISSUES

INTERSOCIETAL AND INTERGOVERNMENTAL RELATIONS

A perusal of the chapters in this volume may impress upon the reader that U.S.-Mexican relations are associated with a broad range of questions. This book is not unusual in this respect, even though it may give more emphasis to some topics than others. In recent years, students of world politics, as well as diplomats, have reemphasized the importance in international relations of the interaction of national political economies and the actions of nongovernmental actors. By the same token, students of domestic Latin American and Chicano issues have discovered that to obtain a more comprehensive view of their domestically focused concerns, it is helpful to examine the nexus between these and U.S.-Mexican relations.

As intersocietal relations have come to dominate the character and course of intergovernmental relations (and the U.S.-Mexican case is not unique in this respect), making the distinction between the two has become more important. *Intersocietal relations* refers to the relations between the economies and societies of the two countries; the term "nongovernmental relations" is also used in this sense. *Intergovernmental relations* refers to the relations between the executives of the two governments. These two categories are mutually exclusive, but not exhaustive. The terms "transgovernmental" and "transnational" relations are also employed by the contributors to include transnational links that are neither intersocietal nor intergovernmental. Examples of these are relations between the governments at lower levels, and between governmental and nongovernmental actors.

The primary—though not exclusive—concern of this anthology is intergovernmental relations and the formulation of national policy. Because intersocietal relations have a strong influence on relations among governments, we included several chapters explicitly concerned with relations between societies and their influence on national policymaking. Examples are the chapters by Castañeda, Reynolds, the economists at CIDE, and Gómez-Quiñones. These authors discuss some of the domestic political realities of Mexico's oil policies, the demographic and economic restraints on national economic and labor force policies in both countries, the principal problems and probable future of the Mexican economy, and the history of relations between persons of Mexican origin in the United States and Mexico.

POLICY CHOICES AND POLICY CONSTRAINTS

Discussions about *intergovernmental* relations often begin by recognizing that sometimes governments face significant short-term constraints upon their behavior and, by the same token, have some "policy space," or negotiating room, to make some concrete policy choices. Furthermore, policy constraints (and their complement, the range of viable choices) change over time and are the result of a number of factors. A partial list of these would include specific situations and events, domestic and international forces, the resource endowment of their respective countries, their ability to control transnational processes, domestic perceptions about what policy choices are "acceptable," and the relative power potential of the two governments. The discussion regarding choices and constraints, therefore, is not about whether they exist, but about their *nature* and the precise *range* of viable policy alternatives open to governments.

Much of the discussion in this book focuses on how these factors limit or create choices for the U.S. and the Mexican governments. In their discussions, some authors emphasize the *constraints* upon these governments with respect to specific issues. Examples are those by Ojeda, Rico, Cornelius, the Colegio Nacional de Economistas, and de la Garza. Others, for example, those by Castañeda, Zazueta, and Reynolds, are more concerned with demonstrating that in specific areas, the Mexican or U.S. government has a range of viable policy *choices*. Still other chapters, such as those by Ronfeldt and Sereseres; Meyer; and Hufbauer, Smith, and Vukmanic, discuss both the constraints and policy choices available.

Because no analysis can be complete without both, we have included several chapters which survey the dimensions of U.S. and Mexican government "policy space" from different points of view and for different issues. Nevertheless, a discussion emphasizing "constraints" necessarily focuses on different variables and occasionally relies on a different theoretical perspective and normative assumptions than one which emphasizes "choices." The chapters discussing policy constraints to support arguments regarding their nature and implications frequently rely on an extended discussion of existing political and economic realities not amenable to short-term government manipulation. Examples of what are considered to be "realities" vary—they include the dominant contours of domestic public opinion about the nation's destiny, its identity and primary symbols; nongovernmental actors' participation or interference with governmental action; the sensitivities of the two countries and governments to events and policies that originate in the other; and the difficulties of imposing a single and coherent foreign policy upon a set of interested actors in and outside governments. Because of the prominence of intersocietal processes in creating intergovernmental issues in the U.S.–Mexican relationship, a focus on "constraints" is likely to stress the links between domestic and foreign policymaking, and the problem of managing intergovernmental relations. An approach that focuses on policy constraints can also attribute certain immutable elements to the character of Mexican–U.S. relations and stress historical continuity rather than change.

In contrast, the chapters discussing policy choices rely upon a different sort of discussion, although they may also question the belief that a given set of realities imposes genuine constraints upon governmental behavior. Analyses that stress policy choices often rest upon the premise that policy outcomes are not the inevitable result of forces outside of government control. They focus on the *course* rather than the *character* of binational relations, and draw upon another set of concepts: resource complementarities and comparative advantages. Approaches that stress the possibility of choice in intergovernmental relations search for mutualities of interest and identify situations where optimal or positive-sum resolutions, and bargaining, are possible. When these are difficult to find, they stress the importance of dialogue and the need to generate new symbols for an old political discourse. Sometimes the achievement of harmonious intergovernmental relations is seen as a facilitating mechanism for such situations, and therefore as a means for accomplishing national objectives. Because such discussions by definition stress possibilities for change and choice, they necessarily focus on policy goals and normative issues. Such approaches can also attribute a certain malleability to the character of U.S.–Mexican relations. They merely emphasize chance events, the effect of changes in government leaders, on administrations, bureaucratic styles and organization, and stress historical change rather than continuity.

It may be tempting to attach the labels "optimistic" to approaches that emphasize the availability of policy choices, and "pessimistic" to those that stress the existence and determining effects of policy constraints. After all, the first approach stresses what governments can do over what they cannot. Although the emphasis given to constraints or choices may reflect the author's philosophical approach, it is more likely that it indicates his research priorities. The papers in this book focus on a perceived range of viable policy choices and on the persistence of short-term constraints. Whether optimistic or not about the future of U.S.-Mexican relations, all of these chapters reflect attempts to engage the issues with imagination and realism.

TOPICAL ISSUES

The chapters in this book are divided into five interrelated but analytically distinct topics. They are: 1) the character of the U.S.-Mexican relationship and the nature of its problems (general frameworks); 2) energy issues, specifically the export of oil and natural gas from Mexico; 3) other trade-related matters and, in particular, their relationship to the performance of the Mexican economy and economic policies; 4) migration issues, specifically of undocumented Mexicans to the United States; 5) the participation of Chicanos in U.S.-Mexican intergovernmental and intersocietal relations. Each of these areas suggests a number of broad questions; the headings of each section reflect one of the major questions implicit in those chapters.

The literature on Mexican-U.S. relations frequently mentions another area which is also considered in this anthology, although it has not been assigned a separate section: local transborder issues. Such issues arise from the economic and social interpenetration of U.S. and Mexican border communities a systematic treatment of which is beyond the scope of this book. As the chapters in the first section suggest, local transborder issues are extraordinarily varied and complex; to do them justice would have required expanding this volume significantly beyond its present size.

The topical discussion here will follow this organizational scheme, but as will be noted, it is not possible to confine the discussion of each issue exclusively to the papers chosen for inclusion in each section.

GENERAL FRAMEWORKS

The first four chapters treat U.S.-Mexican relations comprehensively. By discussing a variety of topics in a summary fashion, they serve as an introduction for the chapters in the remainder of the book, which treat specific topics at greater length. The first section, then, is concerned with a number of issue areas and with the development of general frameworks to explain, interpret, or manage intergovernmental relations. At one level or another, they seek to interpret the significance of the connection between intersocietal and intergovernmental relations. Wilkie argues that bilateral relations virtually can be reduced to intersocietal relations and the domestic politics of each country; Ronfeldt and Sereseres are more concerned with how the U.S. government manages them; and Ojeda and Rico explore the constraints that they imply for the Mexican government.

The papers by Ronfeldt and Sereseres, Ojeda, and Rico represent part of a debate on the nature of the restrictions and viable policy choices available to the U.S. and Mexican governments in the conduct of their bilateral relations. Ronfeldt and Sereseres characterize these relations by emphasizing the interdependence of the two countries; Rico and Ojeda, by contrast, stress Mexico's dependence. The discussion centers around these and other concepts, such as "sovereignty," "inequality," "asymmetry," "linkages," and "leverage." The debate, however, is not over semantics. The interpretation or characterization that can be ascribed to the relationship has implications for the management of bilateral relations, for likely Mexican responses to the articulation of U.S. interests, and for the Mexican internal debate regarding its foreign relations. There is implied agreement on three propositions: (1) That the asymmetries in power potential between Mexico and the United States are enormous; (2) that Mexico is not defenseless in its relations with the United States; and (3) that Mexican *perceptions* of overwhelming dependence have encouraged agreeable behavior on the part of the Mexican government.

The authors disagree, however, on the nature of the constraints on the U.S. and Mexican governments, i.e., the extent to which the vast asymmetries between the two countries translate into effective power by the U.S. over the Mexican government. Ronfeldt and Sereseres stress the "myth of U.S. bargaining leverage" at the same time that they argue that "government-to-government relations are rarely conducted in terms of who has leverage over whom." Moreover, they criticize Mexican *perceptions* of dependency by arguing that such perspectives use the United States as a scapegoat for Mexican domestic problems, and that they hinder the achievement of mutually shared objectives. The recommendations Ronfeldt and Sereseres offer the Mexican government for improving its relations with the United States include changes in its negotiating style; that it learn to "work" the U.S. government more effectively, much as some "superclients," like Israel, presently do; and that it improve its capacities to negotiate with the United States. (Since their article was written, the Mexican government has made some organizational changes in its contacts with the U.S. government, although much of the description and interpretation of the authors on this point retains its original validity.)

Ojeda and Rico, using different approaches, seek to establish that the United States *does* have considerable leverage over Mexico—and that this imposes certain constraints upon Mexican autonomy and government behavior. Ojeda examines the profile of U.S.–Mexican trade, tourism, border transactions, and foreign investment and indebtedness to arrive at the conclusion that there is a "definite and unequivocal" dependence of Mexico on the United States.

Rico discusses the socioeconomic links between the two countries that can be found in the border region and the significance of Mexico's new-found oil wealth to make his argument. He also suggests that to link issues into "package deals," including the establishment of a "North American Common Market," would favor the United States, not Mexico, and that U.S. government *behavior*—up to 1981—suggested that it did not view Mexican oil as altering, in any fundamental sense, the relative bargaining positions of the two countries. Rico contradicts the notion, expressed in Ronfeldt and Sereseres's chapter, that "issue linkages could represent the keys to managing and improving future interdependence" when he argues that such linkages would generate domestic political conflict in both countries. He posits the North American Common Market idea as the extreme example of such linkages, and concludes: "It would be tantamount to recognizing that the national goals of independence and sovereignty, central ideological tenets of the Mexican Revolution, are out of reach."

The first section, and the rest of the book, reflects some major themes in United States–Mexican relations. The debate over dependence and interdependence suggests two such themes. We have chosen to emphasize and juxtapose two others—conflict and convergence—because the paradox they suggest is at the center of U.S.-Mexican relations. Moreover, behind these themes is a question implicit in each of the papers in this book: Are Mexico and the United States moving toward community, or toward protectionism? This question constitutes the central point of discussion in the chapters by Ronfeldt and Sereseres, and Rico. It also arises explicitly, though not in these terms, in other essays, for example, those by Fagen, Hufbauer, Smith and Vukmanic; Bustamante and Cockcroft; Reynolds; Cornelius; and Gómez-Quiñones.

When we refer to the theme of convergence, we are essentially referring to the concept of community. As later chapters demonstrate, the links between the economies and societies of the two countries are becoming stronger and more complex, largely as a result of trade and capital flows, migration, and the entire gamut of interactions that we refer to as "intersocietal relations." Thus, one of the principal outcomes of the events of the past decade is that without a doubt, the futures of the two economies and societies are tied more closely together. To be more precise, Mexico's future is tied to that of the United States. At another level, "convergence" refers to the *perception*, in some quarters at least, that existing complementarities between the two economies and societies can form the basis for closer political and intergovernmental cooperation. As Rico notes, U.S. conceptualizations of linkage across issue areas have taken several forms, including that of a North American Common Market. Mexican conceptualizations of the same have taken the form of official proposals for package deals in which oil resources are assumed to improve Mexico's bargaining position in areas other than energy.

The theme of conflict refers to a broad interpretation of the concept of protectionism. When the public at large perceives conflict between the United States and Mexico, it usually has in mind the occasional tensions that occur in intergovernmental relations and that find their way into the news media. As various chapters in this book demonstrate, however, this is only the more visible manifestation of conflict. At a more fundamental level, one can note the reemergence and spread of protectionist trends in both Mexican *and* U.S. politics, trends which reflect some resistance to those socioeconomic processes drawing the two countries together. Such resistance, in the Mexican case, is not new; the predominance of national autonomy as a theme in the Mexican political discourse is its most visible manifestation. Nationalist sensitivities to foreign dependence, long perceived in the United States as uniquely Latin American or Mexican characteristics, have also found their way into the U.S. political discourse, in part as a consequence of the progressive decline, in relative terms, of U.S. global influence. U.S. perceptions of vulnerability have extended to the U.S.–Mexican relationship, and are reflected in protectionist responses in such areas as immigration and trade. In part, the debate over dependence and interdependence as characterizations of the binational relationship reflects different positions on whether the closer intersocietal relations increasingly evident in the 1970s augur conflict or convergence in intergovernmental relations for the 1980s and 1990s.

Conflict and convergence, therefore, are not concepts that explain the nature and complexity of U.S.–Mexican relations. They are useful categories that permit us to organize much of what goes on between the two countries, both at the level of intergovernmental and intersocietal relations.

ENERGY ISSUES

The three chapters included in this section outline recent discussion about the political and economic implications of Mexico's export of petroleum and natural gas. As these authors attest, energy-related issues pose significant and subtle political problems for the two governments, as well as for other political actors.

The politics of energy presents a complex set of questions. In broad terms, these fall into three interrelated categories: (1) The significance of oil exports for Mexico's economic future, both in the short and long term; (2) the implications of oil for Mexico's vulnerability and bargaining position vis-à-vis the United States; and (3) the definition of U.S. interests in Mexico's oil. With respect to the first category, the most prominent question seems to be: What is the optimal level of oil exports? The arguments vary, depending on whether the considerations are short or long term, with the former emphasizing the role of oil revenues in overcoming immediate financial constraints upon Mexico's economy. The latter stress a more prudent level of oil exports for three reasons: (a) oil is a nonrenewable resource; (b) there are limits on the amount of oil revenues that Mexico's economy can absorb without falling into the syndrome characteristic of oil-exporting countries; and (c) by exporting more oil, particularly to the United States, Mexico increases its dependence on the U.S. economy. Thus, the issues in the first category mentioned above merge with those in the second and third.

The discussion about Mexico's vulnerability and bargaining position vis-à-vis the United States, and the definition of U.S. security interests in Mexico's oil presents some paradoxes. Depending upon what normative assumptions one makes, the same facts can lead to opposing interpretations. Some authors see oil exports as *exacerbating*, and others as *diminishing*, Mexico's vulnerability and dependence on the United States. As is evident from several authors who touch upon this subject (not only Meyer, Fagen, and Castañeda, but also Ronfeldt and Sereserses, Ojeda, and Rico), each interpretation arises from a different set of implicit definitions about what constitutes "vulnerability," "dependence," "bargaining power," *and* "U.S. security interests."

In general terms, it is agreed that the possession of oil resources and the infrastructure to extract and export them in massive quantities poses a different set of policy choices and constraints on the Mexican government. There is disagreement, however, on what constitutes a "constraint" and a "choice," with authors posing one set of empirical conditions as reflective of a constraint, and others posing the same set of realities in terms of the opportunities presented for choice.

The arguments that emphasize "choice" build upon the indisputable notion that, within certain limits, petroleum resources have increased Mexico's bargaining position vis-à-vis the U.S. government. Rico summarizes and criticizes some of the more extreme expressions of those arguments—those that have found their way into the political discourse. Among the chapters included in this volume, perhaps Castañeda's is the most vocal in arguing that oil gives the Mexican government more "policy space" in addressing both its domestic and foreign policy problems. In his postscript, prepared in 1982, he sustains this argument for a situation when Mexico faces shrinking, rather than expanding, oil revenues.

The arguments that emphasize "constraints" build upon the notion that in *strategic* terms Mexico's oil discoveries have made its domestic affairs qualitatively more important in the eyes of the U.S. government. Meyer argues that an interruption in world oil supplies could pose one of the most significant dangers to Mexico's autonomy and sovereignty. Arguing by historical analogy he laments: "Should that occur, the decision regarding how much oil would be exported to the U.S. would no longer belong to Mexico." Rico pursues this line of reasoning in more abstract terms: "To what extent, then, is power synonymous with possessing something of interest to the globally stronger partner?"

Meyer's history of U.S. intervention in Mexico's internal affairs with respect to oil policy, up to and following the 1938 nationalization of the oil industry, serves an important analytical purpose. It provides the basis for an argument by analogy which, whether viewed as applicable to the present situation or not, partially explains Mexican skepticism toward U.S. pronouncements of good intentions in energy matters. This skepticism shapes the national political discourse on oil policy and Mexico's relations with the United States, and restricts the Mexican government's actions. Meyer also provides a historical context for examining the significance of arguments, such as Castañeda's, about the political feasibility of U.S. military intervention in Mexico.

The implicit debate between Meyer and Castañeda on the paradox of Mexican oil, its perils and opportunities, rests on unexamined assumptions about U.S. interests in Mexican oil. As Fagen's chapter demonstrates, these interests are not as easy to articulate or as easy to pursue as it might first appear. Even if this is true, not only U.S. but also *Mexican* perceptions of what those interest are will influence the binational dialogue and bargaining strategies in this and other areas of the relationship.

Fagen summarizes and critiques the U.S. debate about the national security implications of Mexican oil. He sketches the principal elements in the definition of U.S. stakes in Mexico's petroleum at three levels: (1) oil *supply*, i.e., the volume of Mexican exports to the world market; (2) *marketing* arrangements, i.e., implicit understandings regarding the security of supply; and (3) the *manage-*

ment of export revenues for the amelioration of domestic discontent to a degree sufficient to "keep the lid on the Mexican volcano." In so doing, he notes that U.S. objective interests in Mexican oil can be interpreted in different ways, depending upon which of these levels is emphasized.

Arguments that stress the perils of this strategic resource for the full exercise of Mexican sovereignty rely on interpretations of U.S. interests that focus on the first two sets of concerns. Arguments that rest on the "management of export revenues" build on the premise that "there is substantial congruence between U.S. and Mexican elites" to provide a rationale for U.S. *support* of a Mexican regime which "maintains stability" and does not threaten U.S. interests. In either instance, these arguments accept the view that Mexico's possession of this strategic resource has created a fundamental shift in the importance that U.S. policy makers attach to events in Mexico.

TRADE AND MEXICAN ECONOMIC POLICIES

Since World War II, Mexico's economic policies have emphasized the growth of a consumer and durable goods industry, based on the model of import substitution, and a capital-intensive agriculture largely oriented to the U.S. market. The aggregate results of these policies have been impressive. Since 1950, Mexico's economy has grown in real terms at almost twice the rate of the U.S. economy so that, in spite of an accelerating population growth, GNP per capita has more than doubled. It has been widely perceived in Mexico and the United States that this growth, though shared unequally among Mexico's people, has been a crucial ingredient in keeping political stability and institutional continuity. Wilkie's essay in the first section echoes this perception and stresses that at an aggregate level, living standards have risen throughout most of this century, and that the Mexican system is resilient to political pressures from below, notwithstanding its "cycle of crises."

This pattern of economic development, sometimes called the "Mexican miracle," is not without its critics. One set of criticisms, touched upon by Reynolds, Bustamante and Cockcroft, has to do with the unequal distribution of the benefits of this growth. Following on this theme, Fagen and Reynolds allude to possible social unrest and political instability as consequences of internal inequities. Another criticism can be found in the CIDE essay. The authors note that the Mexican economic development model, *even at the level of aggregate growth*, found internal obstacles that made it impossible to achieve economic growth without massive infusions of finance capital from abroad. Regardless of the precise diagnosis or emphasis, it was evident by the mid-1970s that the Mexican economy had run into serious trouble.

It is in this general context that several events took place which have shaped the debate over Mexico's economic problems, policies, trade, and its relations with the United States. One set of events roughly coincided with the 1976–77 crisis. It includes the 1976 devaluation of the peso, an unprecedented rate of inflation, the flight of capital to the United States, the pattern of slow growth that characterized the U.S. economy—and the discovery of oil. The events of those years constitute a confluence of several factors, internal and external to the Mexican economy, and have evoked many interpretations. The essays by CIDE, Wilkie, Ronfeldt and Sereseres, Ojeda and Castañeda offer contrasting interpretations of what those events mean.

Another set of events relates to the new international and domestic political context in which Mexican economic policy was formulated. During the 1970s, the Mexican government became more involved in Third World politics, in pressing for a New International Economic Order (NIEO), and in the so-called North-South Dialogue. As noted in the essay by the Colegio Nacional de Economistas, Mexico and a number of other nations were seen at that time, according to the *graduation principle*, as *newly industrialized countries* (NICs), and were invited to join the General Agreement on Tariffs and Trade.

Moreover, the Mexican government adopted a new development model that shifted its emphasis from import substitution to export promotion. Significant elements in this model which impact on trade relations are: (1) an emphasis on the export of manufactured goods to the U.S. market; (2) the reduction of protective tariffs, import licenses, and quotas on consumer and intermediate goods in order to enhance the competitiveness of Mexican industry; and (3) a greater emphasis on the domestic production of capital goods. Central to this set of economic policies are the use of petroleum revenues to subsidize export-oriented activities, and the application of *local content requirements* and *export performance requirements* on domestic producers to reduce imports and stimulate exports.

Finally, as noted in the essay by Hufbauer, Smith and Vukmanic, in 1979, the United States made some important changes in its trade legislation which directly affect Mexican efforts to penetrate the U.S. market. These include technical changes that reduce the administrative discretion of the executive branch in resolving trade disputes and give the U.S. private sector a greater role in the timing and control of such conflict. U.S. trade and economic policies, which have undergone some change in the past decade, are themselves a topic of discussion which is only touched upon in these chapters.

The manifold implications of these events can be summarized in four general propositions. First, the Mexican government is counting on improved access to the U.S. market for the growth of an export industry which is supposed to solve acute economic problems. Second, such access is threatened by the conflict between Mexican domestic economic policies and U.S. trade laws (and GATT norms). Third, this conflict is likely to manifest itself in the form of demands for protectionist responses by U.S. producers affected by Mexican competition. Fourth, the framework in which trade matters are handled in the United States is in a state of flux. At present, it will be more difficult for those levels of the U.S. government concerned about the performance of the Mexican economy to intervene in Mexico's behalf. The new political and economic realities of trade in the 1980s pose new problems which carry with them the seeds of conflict in intergovernmental relations.

These new realities pose a number of analytical and policy questions for U.S.-Mexican trade relations: To what extent is the achievement of Mexico's goal of long-term economic growth tied to the increase in export capacity for manufactured goods? This question is important to any discussion of U.S.-Mexican trade relations, even though Mexico's economic strategy is no longer at issue. Are the policy instruments chosen by the government the most appropriate, given the political and economic realities of both countries? Can U.S. interests in areas such as energy, security, and migration mitigate the priority given to domestic and multilateral perspectives and provide the setting for a bilateral trade arrangement? And finally, what are the most probable future trends in trade volume and composition? This short list of questions raises some formidable issues, and a complex debate, part of which is represented in the section on trade, and in the chapters by Ronfeldt and Sereseres and Rico. The appendices to Reynolds's article topically belong in this section.

The chapters by CIDE, the Colegio Nacional de Economistas and Reynolds touch upon the first two questions. The team of economists at CIDE developed a macroeconometric model in 1978 to simulate trends of the 1970s without increasing the country's dependence on foreign finance. The chapter provides technical arguments for the adoption of an export-led industrialization strategy. It also challenges the notions that industrial trade deficits can be corrected by currency devaluations and that reducing import restrictions will promote the competitiveness and export capacity of domestic industry. With respect to the same questions, the chapter by the Colegio Nacional de Economistas defends Mexican development strategies and questions the wisdom of joining GATT at that time. Reynolds, however, argues that some of the causes of the economic malaise of the mid-1970s were policy-induced. Although some of the differences in perspective between CIDE, the Colegio, and Reynolds may be negotiable, the first two emphasize Mexican policy constraints while the last suggests that the Mexican government could have avoided some of the major problems the economy encountered during this period.

The chapters by Hufbauer, Smith, and Vukmanic; Ronfeldt and Sereseres; and Rico focus more specifically on U.S. policy constraints in trade relations. They arise from U.S. multilateral perspectives (see, e.g., the discussion by Ronfeldt and Sereseres on the demise of the U.S.–Mexico Trade Commission), the compartmentalization of issues, the emphasis on the trade principles and norms of the GATT, and the reduced discretion that U.S. agencies have in settling trade disputes. At the heart of this discussion is a political question: To what extent should the U.S. government allow the interests of a particular group to dictate the course of U.S.–Mexican relations? Regardless of the answer, the fact remains that the U.S. government is not free of constraints in exercising control over the resolution of trade disputes.

With respect to the final question, as demonstrated in the chapters by Hufbauer, Smith, and Vukmanic; and Reynolds (appendix 1), the precise course of future trade trends is uncertain for at least two reasons. First, the projection of such trends is based on empirical assumptions concerning a number of variables subject to unforeseen variations, for instance, the performance of the Mexican and U.S. economies, currency exchange rates, the price of oil and other commodities. Second, projections made in the late 1970s were based on expectations of rising oil import revenues and a boom economy—a boom that soured in 1982. Thus, the long-term trends implied by these projections may be artificially high: Mexico may now import less than previously expected as a result of a devalued peso, limited foreign exchange, and exchange controls. Nevertheless, it is still likely that U.S.-Mexican trade will grow substantially in the years ahead, although its volume and composition will fluctuate according to world market conditions and the performance of the U.S. and Mexican economies.

MIGRANT WORKERS

In the United States, the issue of Mexican migration is dealt with largely in terms of its significance for domestic politics. When the issue is discussed in terms of its significance for international relations, the emphasis is on a different set of concerns. The main questions in the chapters included here seem to be: (1) What are the socioeceonomic causes of this labor migration? More specifically, how are they related to Mexican and U.S. patterns of economic growth, of labor supply and demand? (2) What are the international consequences, in broad economic and political terms, of this migration? (3) What are the constraints and policy choices available to the two governments in this issue area? These questions are addressed, with varying degrees of emphasis, in the chapters in this section, and by Ronfeldt and Sereseres, Fagen, and Zazueta elsewhere.

Although the categories and theoretical frameworks implicit in the chapters by Reynolds and by Bustamante and Cockcroft are different, they allude to the same socioeconomic phenomena to explain why this labor migration occurs, and why it can be expected to accelerate in the future. With respect to the "Mexican" causes of migration, the two chapters assign a prominent role to the persistence of a surplus population of workers and to an economy which absorbs "insufficient quantities of labor" in the creation of migration pressures. From that point, the explanations diverge. Reynolds explains these migration pressures as a result of a slow growth in the Mexican economy, and a widening of the gap in per capita income between Mexico and the United States during the 1970s. Bustamante and Cockcroft perceive this migration as a manifestation of U.S. capital domination and Mexico's underdevelopment. Economic dependence on the U.S. is posited as the cause for Mexico's subcapitalization and incapacity to generate enough employment, resulting in an "excessively large reserve army of labor." Although Reynolds and Bustamante and Cockcroft disagree implicitly about the ultimate causes of Mexican labor migration, they are in general agreement about its most proximate causes. Migration is viewed as a response to an imbalance between local supply and demand for labor in both countries, and migration pressures in Mexico are perceived to be directly related to the growing mass of underemployed workers.

It is in their interpretation of the broad political and economic *consequences* of migration where these two chapters differ most sharply. To be sure, both chapters do reject commonly held U.S. perceptions that Mexican migrants constitute an economic burden upon the United States. Where Reynolds and Bustamante and Cockcroft disagree is on the political definition of Mexican migration and its bearing on the relations between the two political economies, and potentially, the two governments. Bustamante and Cockcroft propose that migration constitutes an unequal exchange; one in which the lion's share of the benefits accrues to U.S. capital. The benefits for Mexico, if any, are not discussed. Rather, labor migration, which is seen as a transfer of human capital, is viewed as a Mexican *subsidy* of the U.S. economy. Moreover, U.S. capital benefits from the "superexploitation" of temporary workers, and by the expansion of the U.S. reserve army of labor. Thus, at various levels, Bustamante and Cockcroft argue that the U.S. stands to gain from continued Mexican migration.

Reynolds, by contrast, argues that both the United States *and* Mexico gain from this flow, and that they have much to gain in keeping and possibly expanding this flow in the years ahead. In short, both the United States and Mexico are becoming increasingly complementary in demographic terms. Further, no matter what the U.S. and Mexican governments do over the next few years, Mexico will have a large and growing underemployed population that could lead to social unrest and political instability. (This point is also discussed by Ronfeldt and Sereseres.) On the other hand, the U.S. faces a growing labor shortage, particularly for unskilled occupations, which, if unfilled, will significantly retard the growth of the national economy.

Thus, Reynolds suggests that the two countries are in a positive-sum situation, i.e., both stand to gain from the migration of workers in the next two decades, and recommends a major reassessment of U.S. economic goals to "maximize the mutual benefits from Mexico's economic and demographic growth," while implicitly endorsing a more open U.S. immigration policy.

"Once again," write Bustamante and Cockcroft, "ideological interests enter into contradiction with specific economic interests." This reflects a major theme that runs through the immigration policy debate and U.S.-Mexican relations. Reynolds, as well as Bustamante and Cockcroft, imply that if U.S. political and economic elites acted in their best long-term interests, they would find ways to prevent the adoption of policies which severely restrict the flow of migrant labor. However, according to Cornelius, the *likelihood* that U.S. policymakers will adopt a more open immigration policy is remote. In his chapter, Cornelius explores U.S. public perceptions characterized by anti-immigrant and specifically anti-Mexican biases. After reviewing the history of nativism, he links current anti-immigrant attitudes to the need for scapegoats in U.S. domestic politics, the backlash against the expansion of the social welfare economy, reverses suffered by the United States in its foreign policy, and perceived threats to U.S. security. He argues that such attitudes are likely to harden in the years ahead. The consequences of these perceptions are important constraints on U.S. policy choices with respect to immigration and suggest that the most probable outcome is a restrictionist and punitive policy response. U.S.-Mexican relations, in this scenario, will deteriorate "regardless of other interests which may be at stake in the bilateral relationship."

Absent from these analyses is a thorough discussion of the Mexican side of the equation. Why are Mexican political actors, and the government in particular, likely to respond negatively to U.S. restrictionist or punitive policies? What *are* Mexican interests in this issue area? Though not addressing this point specifically, Zazueta's paper includes a suggestive discussion about the origins of Mexican government policies, and their constraints, with respect to emigration. Bustamante and Cockcroft, in their argument against the Reagan immigration plan of 1981, suggest that the Mexican government should have the welfare of its citizens in the United States and harmonious relations with Chicano groups as priority concerns. Ronfeldt and Sereseres discuss the "safety valve" function of migration for the Mexican political economy. In short, the *costs* of U.S. punitive policies, either in terms of introducing discord into the relationship or affecting specific outcomes in other issues, need to be investigated.

An effort to address at least one of the components of this question appears in Reynolds's chapter. His argument involves a complex set of factors that includes political stability, foreign (U.S.) investment, economic growth, Mexican labor absorption, and migration. Political stability is necessary to allow Mexico to elicit foreign investment for future growth. Rapid growth cannot be achieved without substantial inputs of capital and skilled labor from abroad, as well as access to export markets. The author notes that in the past, and most likely in the future, the United States will figure prominently in all these areas. Rapid growth, moreover, is necessary for the effective absorption of Mexico's surplus labor and insuring rising real wages. These, in turn, are necessary prerequisites both for reducing migration pressures and maintaining political stability. This argument links U.S. and Mexican economic and security interests with continued emigration.

However, as Cornelius and Fagen observe, the definition of U.S. "security interests" implied by arguments such as Reynolds's is not the only one under discussion. Indeed, there is a strong current of opinion in the United States which attributes all sorts of social ills to the presence of Mexican immigrants, and occasionally elevates uncontrolled immigration to the status of a national security threat. Advocates of such positions, as Cornelius notes, argue that Mexican immigration threatens the United States with cultural and linguistic separatism, with the spectre of a Quebec of the Southwest, and with an erosion of national political integrity. Whether such advocates, like former CIA director William Colby, actually believe these arguments is beside the point. What is important to note is that U.S. security interests cannot simply be equated with supporting Mexican regime stability. As Ronfeldt and Sereseres observe, if Mexican national interests require, as is so often assumed, the continued flow of emigration to the United States, U.S. policymakers face a dilemma of defining just how far U.S. security interests extend in this direction.

CHICANOS IN THE BINATIONAL RELATIONSHIP

Two new political realities of the 1970s are at the root of current discussions about the role of Chicanos in the binational relationship. One is that as a group, the Mexican-origin population has a greater capacity to influence political outcomes in the United States than it did a decade ago. Some interpret this development to reflect a new influence in the resolution of issues in the bilateral agenda, particularly U.S. immigration policy. A second reality is that various Chicano leaders and organizations have interacted with political actors in Mexico, the Mexican government, and the Mexican news media. These developments, and the perception that the interests of Chicanos and some Mexican political actors intersect, have attracted attention.

A parenthetical note on the terms used to characterize the Mexican-origin population is needed here. In general, we will employ the same terms used by each author when discussing the arguments in a chapter. Both de la Garza and Zazueta use the term "Chicano" to refer generally to U.S.-born Mexicans (the difference in their definitions involves a legal distinction for dual nationals that need not concern us here). By the same token, both Zazueta and Gómez-Quiñones use the term "Mexican" in a general sense to refer to Mexico and to persons of Mexican origin in the United States, including immigrants and Chicanos. Regardless of the term used, however, when we talk about the role of Chicanos in the binational relationship, we are referring to the activities of organizations, individuals and other political actors who are involved in the advocacy of the "interests" of the Mexican community in the U.S. and which impact in some way upon Mexican–U.S. intergovernmental or intersocietal relations. In this broad sense then, neither the citizenship nor place of birth of the individuals involved matters, nor whether we choose to call them "Chicano," "Mexican," or "Mexican American."

Differences in terminology do reflect more than semantic preferences. The choice of terms employed in the articles by Gómez-Quiñones, de la Garza, and Zazueta implies different conceptions of what the "interests" of the Mexican-origin community are. In his history of transnational political interaction, which he terms "Pan-Mexican relations," Gómez-Quiñones presents the view that in the past, the politics of the Mexican American community in the United States has been closely tied to politics in Mexico. Since the nineteenth century, Mexicans in the U.S. have had an important stake in Mexican politics and, conversely, Mexican political actors (including the Mexican government) have sought support within the Mexican community in the United States. He concludes that Mexican Americans are likely to continue their involvement in the politics of both countries, that such involvement is potentially reinforcing, and that it will eventually extend to the U.S.-Mexican intergovernmental relationship. Implied throughout his discussion is the assumption that a Chicano/Mexican dichotomy is relatively unimportant in political practice when viewed in historical terms.

De la Garza presents a narrower conception of what is meant by politics and the Mexican-origin community. Mexican immigrants are discussed as the *object* of political debate and activity, but are excluded from the discussion of Mexicans as political actors in the United States. Furthermore, he notes that for many and complex reasons, the Chicano population has ambivalent responses to the immigration issue. In his discussion about the growing relationship between Chicano political actors and the Mexican government, he argues that the consequences of this interaction may be mixed, particularly for Chicanos involved in "mainstream American politics." This interaction could, on the one hand, enhance the political future of Chicanos in dealing with U.S. political leaders and institutions; on the other, it could risk their political legitimacy because "the U.S. government may consider such a relationship as potentially threatening to national interests." De la Garza concludes that such future interaction could yield some tangible political rewards for Chicanos, but admonishes Chicano political actors to recognize that their political future lies not with Mexico, but with the United States.

Without addressing the question of where the political future of Chicanos lies, Zazueta suggests that the future relationship between the Mexican-origin community and the Mexican government lies in the context of Mexican domestic politics. He suggests that although the Mexican government could safely ignore Chicanos in the short term, it cannot afford to do so in the medium to long term, and that a mutually beneficial exchange should be encouraged to promote a dialogue. Like Gómez-Quiñones, Zazueta assumes that there is a sufficient community of interests between immigrants and Chicanos to warrant the use of a common political label—Mexicans.

Two chapters, those by de la Garza and Gómez-Quiñones, focus some of their discussion on the role of Chicano political actors in U.S.-Mexican intergovernmental relations. In these chapters, there is considerable disagreement over what that role is likely to mean, both for the Mexican and U.S. governments. De la Garza stresses the obstacles in the path of a Chicano–Mexican alliance, which he discusses in the form of a Chicano lobby for Mexican interests in Washington. He concludes that Chicanos do not meet the technical requirements for establishing such a lobby and suggests that, given Mexico's discoveries of oil—and the implied leverage that flows from this resource—Mexico may not need a lobby, and therefore is not likely to promote it. Gómez-Quiñones argues that whether or not they constitute a lobby, Mexican Americans are as free as any other group to express their opinions and to try to influence U.S. foreign policy. He also argues that they *do* meet, at least partially, the requirements for a lobby, and furthermore, that "Mexico needs a countervailing lobby to the hostile ones."

The discussion in these two chapters about Chicanos as a political pressure group capable of influencing U.S. policies toward Mexico arises from a number of assumptions, some shared, others not. They disagree on (1) the political potential of the Mexican-origin community (de la Garza suggests that it is unrealistic to expect Chicano political actors to significantly affect political outcomes, in the immediate future, on questions that are important to the Mexican government); (2) the degree to which the Mexican-origin population is concerned with issues that are directly related to the bilateral agenda (Gómez-Quiñones suggests that in the present, somewhat as in the past, Mexicans in the United States are concerned about politics in Mexico and U.S.–Mexican relations); and (3) the potential significance of a lobby as one among several levers the Mexican government might choose to develop in order to bargain more effectively with the U.S. government. On the other hand, the authors agree that the cultural identification of Chicanos with Mexico does not automatically translate into support for Mexican government policies, and that the interests of various Chicano political actors may diverge significantly from those of the Mexican government, even in the area of immigration, where they presumably have much in common.

The chapters by de la Garza and Zazueta stress the constraints upon the involvement of the Mexican government in issues which are perceived to be the internal affairs of the United States—even though some Chicano actors may see such involvement as potentially beneficial to Chicano political advancement. For de la Garza, this limits the possibilities for exchange, and puts an obstacle in the path of the development of a Chicano lobby. What, after all, can the Mexican government offer Chicanos? Zazueta suggests that the record of nonintervention in U.S. affairs is not so clear-cut, and that together with a new, more "active" foreign policy, the possibilities of Mexican "interventionist" behavior are greater than they have been in the past, *if* important domestic or foreign policy concerns are at stake. The author examines some activities of the Mexican government in behalf of the Mexican community in the U.S. during the 1920s and suggests that while nonintervention is likely to impose some constraints, that does not mean that the Mexican government need be impotent in defending its interests in the United States. Both authors accept the realist premise that the Mexican government—like any other political actor—is not likely to act in behalf of Chicano interests for altruistic reasons, and that any relationship that develops will have to rest upon mutual interests. But the authors disagree in their conclusions about the possibilities that such common interests exist. De la Garza cites some examples of Mexican government rejection of Chicano overtures as an indication of obstacles; Zazueta argues that major segments of the population in Mexico have been concerned with the defense of Mexicans in the U.S., even if they have responded ambivalently to petitions for repatriation and assistance.

Another topic discussed in these papers, and which is important to the analysis of the role of Chicanos in the binational relationship, is the involvement of the Mexican-origin population in U.S.-Mexican *intersocietal relations.* As Gómez-Quiñones and Zazueta show, for many decades, Mexicans in the United States have maintained complex and enduring links with Mexico—familial, social, cultural, political, and economic. De la Garza also mentions these bonds, though he emphasizes the negative perceptions that Mexicans and Chicanos have about each other, and notes that cultural affinity with Mexico cannot be equated with support for Mexican government policies. Neither Zazueta nor Gómez-Quiñones challenge these arguments. Where they differ with de la Garza is in their emphasis and interpretation of the same realities. Gómez-Quiñones, for example, argues that these negative perceptions are a generalized expression of the conflict among groups within Mexico, although he does not squarely address the issue of Mexican immigrants vs. Mexican Americans. Zazueta links the historical ambivalence of various sectors of Mexican society to Chicanos with their ambivalence toward emigrants and Anglicized "pochos" of northern Mexico. Moreover, both Gómez-Quiñones and Zazueta attribute a positive significance to the Mexican American pursuit of continued links with Mexican society and political groups. De la Garza, however, stresses the risks of closer ties between Chicanos and the Mexican government.

De la Garza does not elaborate on what these risks may mean, but mentions that "by openly seeking Mexico's support or lobbying for pro-Mexican policies, Chicanos might raise the specter of disloyalty," and argues that a Chicano lobby might require an alliance *with* Mexico *against* the United States. These points are not addressed explicitly in the other two chapters of this section, but they merit discussion.

A reading of the chapters in this book will show that it is not unusual for nongovernmental actors to get involved in U.S.-Mexican intergovernmental relations; indeed, as the chapters by Ronfeldt and Sereseres, Rico, Meyer, and Cornelius demonstrate, such involvement is the rule rather than the exception. When, in 1978, several U.S. oil corporations and the Mexican government found themselves in alliance in opposition to the Carter Energy Plan, as Meyer describes, these U.S. political actors were not inhibited by the belief that they were disloyal to the United States. This illustrates the point that the argument alluded to by de la Garza, though not stated explicitly, rests upon a normative assumption: Unlike other political actors, Chicanos do not have the legitimate right to express individual and group interests should these coincide with the position of a foreign government and oppose that of the current U.S. administration.

De la Garza implies that the political realities with which Chicanos must live do not necessarily coincide with the normative assumptions they may accept. In this sense, one possible interpretation of the argument evoking the spectre of disloyalty is that *as a group*, Chicanos are particularly vulnerable in the context of U.S. domestic politics to attacks upon their loyalty and Americanism. This argument recognizes that as political actors, Chicanos need to be cognizant of a unique set of constraints upon their behavior.

In this respect, it appears that the reference made by Ronfeldt and Sereseres to the border region as "the melting pot and the boiling pot of U.S.-Mexican relations" is given a new twist. In the years ahead, intersocietal relations between Mexico and the United States will intensify, and Chicanos will necessarily be drawn into this process. Whether this is or is not accompanied by intergovernmental conflict and heightened national sensitivities to events in the other country, Chicanos are likely to impact upon, and be affected by, U.S.-Mexican relations.

GENERAL FRAMEWORKS:
Conflict and Convergence

I

1
Conflicting "National Interests" Between and Within Mexico and the United States

James W. Wilkie

INTRODUCTION

Historically, U.S.–Mexican relations have involved the diplomatic resolution of common border problems causing temporary tension between the two countries.[1] With the advent of the 1970s, new kinds of tensions reflect structural changes in the affairs of both countries and presage the rise of issues in the 1980s and 1990s that might not be susceptible to traditional diplomatic solutions. In this light, students of Mexico should consider dealing specifically with conflicting "national interests" between and within Mexico and the United States, the dimensions of which are only tentatively sketched here. In short, implications of Mexican developments for the United States represent only one side of the coin—the other side involves the implications and impact of recent developments in the United States as they influence Mexico and in turn react back upon the United States. The resultant symbiotic relationship involves a series of apparently unresolvable dilemmas which have to be worked out within each country before they can be resolved between the two.

James W. Wilkie is Professor of History and University-wide Coordinator of the U.S. Mexus Consortium, University of California, Los Angeles. This paper is based on testimony presented by the author before hearings of the Subcommittee on Inter-American Relationships of the Joint Economic Committee of the U.S. Congress, 1977.
© 1983 by James W. Wilkie

THE TRADITIONAL "DIPLOMATIC APPROACH"

Since World War II, binational border cooperation has been undertaken to resolve a number of matters. Successful negotiations have included U.S.-Mexico pacts to eradicate animal disease (foot-and-mouth disease, 1974; screwworm fly infestation, 1962 and 1966; horse sleeping sickness, 1971), as well as the resolution of historical questions involving nineteenth-century issues (release by the United States of the Chamizal boundary claim, 1967; and release by Mexico of the Pious Fund for support of the Catholic Church in Alta California, 1967). Other successful negotiations have included division of waters (Colorado River, 1945); desalination of water delivered to Mexico (Colorado River, 1965, 1973; Rio Grande, 1966); coastal fishing agreements (1967, 1976); incursion of U.S. citizens into Mexico for stealing archaeological, historical, and other cultural properties for sale in the United States (1970); joint U.S.-Mexican action to suppress the smuggling of marijuana and narcotics into the United States (1970);[2] and provisions for the exchange of prisoners to serve out terms in their own country (1977).

Even the migration of temporary labor was subject to traditional diplomatic negotiations to obtain bracero pacts between 1942 and 1947 as well as between 1951 and 1964. In the early 1970s, Mexico was again pressing for a new bracero treaty but withdrew its demands after the *Washington Post* revealed, upon the eve of President Echeverría's October 1974 meeting with President Ford, that Mexico had discovered huge oil reserves in its southeast. Echeverría apparently feared that any negotiation for a new bracero treaty would eventually involve exchange for oil sales to the United States at preferential rates detrimental both to Mexico and his OPEC friends.

STRUCTURAL ISSUES TO THE FORE: ORIGINS

Mexican presidential regimes have more often than not paralleled in style and thrust of governmental policy their counterpart regime in the United States. Thus, in spite of different ideologies and problems in and between the two countries, the presidency of Calles came to accept the tone of conservatism espoused by the presidency of Coolidge, e.g., cutback of land reform and protection of U.S. oil rights. The presidencies of Roosevelt and Cárdenas came to be compared as involving "new deals" for the "people," as Roosevelt and Ambassador Josephus Daniels quashed a move within the Democratic administration to bring Mexico to its knees in retaliation for expropriation of U.S. land and oil rights. President Avila Camacho cooperated closely with Roosevelt in the World War II effort, laying the basis for the "era of good feeling" between Presidents Truman and Alemán. As a symbol of good will, these presidents even exchanged captured flags from the Mexican-American War. Differences about the conduct of the cold war to the contrary, Presidents Eisenhower and Ruiz Cortines governed under the image of father to citizenries enjoying economic stability; and Presidents Kennedy and López Mateos simultaneously offered a shift to social concerns for their respective countries, each appearing as a social reformer after years of emphasis on economic growth. Under the presidencies of Johnson and Díaz Ordaz, troops were called out in both the United States and Mexico to repress students who objected to their country's respective international policies—U.S. students refusing to die for nothing in Vietnam's civil war and Mexican students refusing to support Mexico's bid for international recognition by hosting the Olympics.

In a new era of world politics, most recently, Presidents Nixon and Echeverría set out to reorganize giant bureaucracies to make them more responsive to presidential control. Echeverría sought to follow the Johnson upheaval (accepted by Nixon) giving the federal government new and vast influence over education, health, and public welfare activities. Even with all of Echeverría's shortcomings, at least he tended to foster world law in contrast to Presidents Johnson and Nixon. They tended to violate international and national law and waged a war to protect their own pride—neither wanting to be the first president to lose a war. Not only was the Vietnam War a major cause of U.S. inflation, but it lapped over into Mexico which sells to and imports from the United States over two-thirds of its international trade. At the same time, Echeverría's big-spending policies were undertaken partly to offset an internal depression caused by his administration's initial slowdown in public expenditure to turn away from economic growth and toward greater social justice. Under recent U.S. presidents, and under Echeverría, the United States and Mexico each underwent "legal revolutions," both countries legislating a deluge of unworkable and ill-advised laws to excessively control and regulate the private sector. Not only have the laws been incomprehensible in the main, but they have enmeshed all concerned in useless paperwork and red tape hardly "managed" by swollen bureaucracies.

Although the analogy between U.S. and Mexican presidential regimes should not be pushed too far, it is clear that Mexico's problems did not all originate under the strange and unstable presidency of Echeverría (perhaps less strange and more stable than those of Johnson and Nixon, if we are to judge by the chaos each left behind). Briefly put, the essence of governmental policy in both countries has followed remarkably similar lines, as in the case of Presidents Johnson and Díaz Ordaz who preferred force to reason. It is easy to justify a policy when leaders of similar inclinations (and close neighbors at that) are taking similar actions. It has often been said that Mexican presidents have been selected to meet the demands of their times, but it could also be argued that they are influenced by their times, and by their neighbors in the United States, as they seek to resolve dilemmas in national development.

STRUCTURAL ISSUES IDENTIFIED: TEN DILEMMAS

Within the context of similar policy orientations, however, Mexico and the United States each face a series of issues that are not subject to traditional diplomatic solution.

MEXICAN DILEMMAS

1. *Mexico's "national interest" to encourage tourism vs. "national interest" to develop industrialization.* Mexico's biggest foreign exchange earnings come from U.S. tourism to Mexico, a tourism predicated upon "bargain prices" and "quaint" living style that is uniquely Mexican. Yet Mexico's drive for industrialization has tended not only to raise the cost of living but also to introduce a modern, mass-produced life style (making Guadalajara little different from Kansas City, if we may exaggerate the

point). Industrialization is increasingly costly as it becomes more technologically oriented to keep up with advances—the earlier and easier stages having passed. And the Mexican middle class appears determined to adopt the latest U.S. styles that are advertised on live television broadcasts of U.S. football games (consumerism being geared to import economy). Ideally, tourism and industrialization should go side-by-side, but in practice industrialization may cause tourists to someday lose interest in Mexico. (Echeverría attempted to limit tourist stays to less than 30 days but, as Mexico priced itself out of the tourist market, he permitted a return to the traditional 180-day tourist authorization to enhance Mexico's drawing power.)

2. *Labor intensive vs. capital intensive economic activity.* Mexico cannot afford the U.S. practice of displacing workers with automated equipment because it does not have a system of unemployment insurance to cover the social costs of such economic advancement. Yet Mexico must displace workers to provide, for example, efficient automated telephone communication for Mexico City which struggles to accommodate its overpopulation. (In contrast to the United States, however, the government of Mexico does provide work for college graduates by creating a never-ending stream of well-funded government study commissions.)

3. *Need for U.S. investment vs. loans.* With Mexico's capital needs outstripping domestic resources and imports exceeding exports, Mexico under Echeverría (1970-1976) sought to regulate private investment. At the same time, it placed a greater emphasis on gaining more foreign credits, mainly from the United States, especially as Mexico saw foreign investment levels decline and domestic capital flee in the face of governmental caprice. However, the loans won by Mexico were not as efficiently used as planned, negating any hoped-for gains from public sector control over private foreign funds—private sector efficiency tends to be more productive and less inflationary in its national impact.

4. *Need for diversified trading partners throughout the world to achieve "economic independence" and insulation against U.S. recessions vs. reliance on its U.S. neighbor, especially during times of economic crisis.* Echeverría's planned trade diversification was damaged by a world economic slump, caused by OPEC price rises that compounded the problems of his mid-1970s recession, thus making Mexico more dependent upon its closest trading

partner. At the same time as Mexico's social and economic experiments caused internal recession of production and flight of capital to the United States, Mexico found itself to be also in need of imported goods and capital from the United States. Ironically, recession meant less diversification of trade partners.

5. *Need to modernize agriculture (i.e., to expand food production for Mexico's cities and to expand exports) vs. need to distribute land.* Under the official Partido Revolucionario Institucional (PRI), land distribution served as the major test of "revolutionariness" for each leftist-oriented president since the 1930s. By periodically passing the test in order to assure that at least about half of the agriculturally employed population always holds land under the land reform law, the PRI has attempted to justify its continued one-party rule for "permanent revolution." Lands are granted in community-held form, which has never prospered and does not show much prospect of doing so. After the rhetoric of Echeverría (who did not distribute as much land as his two immediate predecessors but who did try to distribute the better lands located in northwest Mexico), the government is again talking of the criteria of efficiency in production instead of the "worker's right to own the land he works."[3]

6. *Need for open U.S. border as an escape valve for excess labor vs. need to retain ambitious rural workers in Mexico.* Too often the escape value drains the best rural workers out of Mexico, resulting in a long-term accumulation of a less competent rural labor pool. Ironically, while Mexican governments demand protection of the rights of Mexicans working in the United States, they have closely curtailed the rights of U.S. citizens to work in Mexico.

UNITED STATES DILEMMAS

1. *U.S. "national interest" to have a cheap reserve labor pool vs. "national interest" to close the frontier to "excessive" immigration from Mexico.* Although the U.S. government now feels that temporary labor is not in much demand, in the past it has felt differently and may do so again in the future. In the meantime, the illegal influx of laborers, many of whom remain permanently, appears to threaten minimum wage provisions and places an added burden on U.S. health and welfare functions.

2. *Need to expand exports to Mexico vs. need to control imports from Mexico.* Perhaps because Mexico has so many high barriers to protect its industry (which is often also subsidized by the Mexican government), the U.S. government generally has felt justified in initiating sudden changes in import quotas and taxes (most recently on items such as shoes). These sudden U.S. changes do not allow Mexico to develop stable national plans and they encourage the kind of unstable Mexican reactions criticized unfairly in 1976 by seventy-six U.S. Congressmen.[4] Although it could be argued that Mexico's protectionism is best met by U.S. protectionism, Mexico's industry is so penetrated by U.S. investment that it can therefore be considered to be an extension of the U.S. economy—and it is thus considered by many Mexican observers of all political shades.

3. *U.S. "national interest" to have a healthy, stable neighbor on its southern border vs. "national interest" to keep Mexico politically and economically dependent as the United States seeks to retain its role of world leader.* With Echeverría's plan to make Mexico a leader and conscience of the "Third World" against U.S. "abuse of power," and with Echeverría at one point apparently unable to defeat rural and urban guerrillas, the U.S. military probably drew up "contingency plans" for sending troops to Mexico. When I lectured at the U.S. National War College in 1973 and again in 1974, U.S. officers attempting to qualify for new promotions repeatedly asked me if it were not in the "national interest" of the United States to send troops to Mexico. My response was: It is in the U.S. "national interest" to have stable friends where intervention is not necessary. Although it appeared to be in the U.S. best interests to intervene in Mexico in 1916-1917, intervention accomplished nothing (as in Vietnam) and withdrawal permitted Mexico to gain its own experience with success and mistakes that would eventually make it into one of the most stable countries in Latin America. Had the United States continued to intervene militarily in Mexico as it did in Haiti, in the Dominican Republic and in Nicaragua, we could expect to see the same kind of dismal results. Has the United States not yet learned that it cannot create the "great society" in the United States, let alone force it on others?

4. *U.S. foreign aid vs. a "special relationship" with Mexico.* Although the Alliance for Progress did not "fail"—it could never

have succeeded in the short time allotted—and Mexico did not receive much assistance because it proudly believed that it could handle its own development, it has been suggested anew that foreign assistance can solve Mexico's problems.[5] Mexico's oil wealth will certainly obviate the need for U.S. or any foreign "experts" poking around the country telling Mexico how to "recover" or "takeoff." Mexico can justifiably argue that if it were accorded a true "special relationship" owing to its 2,000-mile border with the United States, its economy would not be subject to the whims of the U.S. Congress. The U.S. Congress has most recently dealt a serious blow to the recovery of Mexico's tourist industry by limiting the number and conditions under which U.S. citizens can attend tax-deductible foreign conventions. In addition, by imposing controls on meats, fruits, and vegetables, the U.S. executive agencies work a tremendous hardship on Mexico, as in the case when suddenly certain grades of tomatoes are prohibited from import to the U.S. market after they have been planted and harvested.

Clearly the dilemmas enumerated here move beyond the traditional realm of diplomatic negotiation. How can conflicting international issues be resolved if conflicting national issues for both countries have not been articulated? How can the United States treat Mexico fairly if it does not understand Mexican politics?

THE POLITICS OF "CRISIS" IN MEXICO

It is common in the United States to denigrate the idea of government by "permanent revolution" in Mexico, not only because U.S. tradition is based upon evolution, but also because the U.S. left likes to talk of Mexico's "frozen revolution." However, "revolution" in Mexico is a code word for development. Although massive social and economic change has taken place, it has come unevenly and under the constraints of one-party politics. This situation has led to calls for change within the political system, particularly following a change in administration.[6] Thus, after the crisis of the Echeverría administration was identified in 1976, the country's new leaders turned away from trying to lead the Third World, and, as they slowed down land reform, they sought an "alliance for production" in order to ease inflationary pressures caused by too little output in the face of heedless government expenditures. Confidence in the Mexican system has been subsequently restored as the new president, José López Portillo, ended the practice of governing mainly by rhetoric. The official party rallied, as it has before, to provide a periodic new image in order to assure its continuance in power.

Moreover, crises seem to be endemic to the Mexican system, particularly when viewed from the United States. Every few years Mexico appears to undergo a "final crisis" of the revolution that began in 1910. But what happens in Mexico is that the revolutionary family, governing Mexico under a one-party system, is able to—within the wings of right, center, and left of the party— resolve these crises, pull the family together by working the problems out from within, and keeping the party in power. In 1940, the presidential transition that threatened to lead to a bloody civil war was eased when outgoing President Cárdenas balanced his 1938 expropriation of the foreign-owned oil industry with the choice of a successor who would avoid controversial programs, thus calming unrest in Mexico and restoring U.S. confidence. We saw similar "crises" when activist presidents, for example, placed so much emphasis on economic growth in the 1950s that a series of general strikes occurred in 1958 and 1959, a series that threatened to bring the Mexican political system down. By shifting Mexico's developmental emphasis toward more social benefits for the people, President López Mateos was able to push himself to the top of the Mexican political system.

Since each president holds power for six years and can never be reelected, at the end of six years political innovation has died out as the outgoing president seeks only to implement his "solutions" to problems identified when he took office. To renew the political system, younger generations compete to identify crises and thus determine Mexico's course for the following six-year presidency. New leaders, then, push themselves to the top by successfully identifying a crisis and convincing enough Mexicans that theirs is indeed the most serious crisis. Viewed from outside, this political system seems unstable; from inside, this system works rather smoothly to maintain the party of permanent revolution in power. In this process the problem Mexico faces is that of distinguishing between real and apparent crises.

The most recent crisis, an artificial one, came in 1976 at the end of the Echeverría administration. It had to do with presidentially-generated land invasions in northwestern Mexico. Although the massive redistribution of land in the 1930s has led President Cárdenas to claim that he had distributed all land and ended the need for further reform, after decline of land reform in the 1940s and 1950s, President López Mateos underlined his shift to social programs by discovering new lands to distribute. This discovery involved not renewing certificates of inaffectability, originally granted by Cárdenas, the "great leftist president of Mexico," who had realized that Mexico would have to feed its urban population by protecting large cattle ranches from land reform. Cárdenas, who distributed more land than any other president, granted certificates of inaffectability that ran up to thirty years. Beginning with López Mateos, presidents have not been renewing these certificates of inaffectability, thus "finding" land they can distribute to communal farmers.[7]

For a time observers believed that Mexican land reform did not involve crisis because reform was quite productive. Now it does not appear as productive as once thought because the private sector was selling much of its produce to communal farmers who had guaranteed sales to the Mexican government. This distorted the data as to who was producing how much food.

On the one hand, land reform makes sense in Mexico because Mexico does not have an unemployment insurance system and land reform provides labor-intensive jobs. On the other hand, Mexico must feed itself, and it is estimated that by around 1990 Mexico will not be able to do so. For example, Mexico is already importing wheat, milk, and corn. It is working itself into a long-range position of dependence upon the United States for imports of food.

In spite of the Echeverría-generated land crisis intended to call attention to the plight of the rural poor, "permanent revolution" has involved more than a myth: Non-monetary poverty data for Mexico declined rapidly during the 1960s even in Mexico City where it had not declined during the 1950s. The national data (see table 1) shows that percentage decline reached its fastest rate ever (25.1 percent) between 1960 and 1970, a fact obscured by the largely irrelevant debate over Mexican income distribution. Though income may have become relatively more concentrated, the middle classes and masses feel themselves to be better off in absolute

TABLE 1.—SHARE OF MEXICO'S POPULATION LIVING ILLITERATE, ILL-FED, ILL-CLOTHED, ILL-HOUSED, AND IN SOCIAL OR GEOGRAPHIC ISOLATION, 1910-1970

Census year	Average percent
1910	56.9
1921	53.1
1930	50.0
1940	46.6
1950	39.4
1960	33.1
1970	24.8

Source: James W. Wilkie, La Revolución Mexicana (1910-1976): Gasto Federal y Cambio Social (México: Fondo de Cultura Económica, 1978), p. 370.

terms. And it is the increase in their consumer purchasing power that helped fuel inflation. Although first-time visitors may be appalled at Mexico's poverty, anyone who has traveled regularly through Mexico during the last twenty years can see today's relative affluence. The problem in Mexico does not involve so much redistributing income as it does slowing down the mad rush for consumer goods and the "better life" which is putting a tremendous strain on the ability to produce or import goods when capital accumulation is needed to build Mexico's economic infrastructure. Disillusion with consumerism led the Echeverría government to sympathize with the Club of Rome's "no growth" philosophy precisely in order to emphasize social justice instead of economic investment. Ironically, the masses may be demanding the growth which will allow them to buy the goods that will change the face of Mexico so that it is less desirable for needed foreign tourism.

Many officials in the López Portillo government inaugurated in 1976 recognized the crisis in production. To begin with, they talked about an end to land reform. Once again they argued that land reform cannot continue because it works against the interests of the urban folk who demand their right to eat inexpensively—in contrast to the worker who has demanded the right to the land he works. The government of López Portillo moved away from the Third World activism that was sponsored by Echeverría. It recognized that it must resolve internal problems, and to their end, undertook a bureaucratic reorganization as has the United States beginning with President Carter.

CONCLUSION

"Crisis" in Mexico may be real or imagined; either way it tends to obscure the dilemma that Mexico's social and economic development is tied to that of the United States. In a sense U.S. events condition events in Mexico. This concept is crucial to U.S.-Mexican diplomatic relations. While the two countries have been successful in the past in working out problems on the diplomatic front, new problems are not diplomatic at all. They involve economic relations between the two, including the immigration of Mexicans who cannot find work. As we have seen, problems arise in no small measure because of erratic U.S. policy toward Mexico, whereby the United States imposes arbitrary controls on agricultural exports from Mexico and disrupts Mexican export plans after crops have been planted. Mexico cannot make economic long-term plans if the United States lacks meaningful policies toward a Mexico that depends on U.S. markets for its goods.

The United States must first of all understand that in Mexico the concept of permanent revolution (open-ended revolution under the aegis of the state) does not mean revolution in a violent or communist sense. It is rather a code word for development. Under a one-party system, Mexico has created one of the most stable political systems in Latin America and has kept political abuse of power to a minimum.

If the United States recalls that Mexico lives by "crises," it will come to expect them, especially under activist presidents, with the realization that crisis will subsequently subside as the less active president who follows will begin to solve Mexico's problems by seeking moderation. This means that the United States must not simply sit back and say that Mexico is facing the final crisis or that it is sliding into "communism," as seventy-six U.S. Congressmen claimed in 1976. It means that the United States must be concerned with helping Mexico to maintain its own identity. One way to do this would involve stimulating Mexican economic activity with such programs as allowing all American tourists who go to Mexico to import into the United States tax-free as many goods as they would like. This would be a great boon to the Mexican tourist economy, and it would help to expand employment in production of Mexican arts and crafts.

If the United States wants to avoid new generations of Mexicans "disrupting" the U.S. labor market and social welfare system, it could help Mexico by removing most of the tariff and import controls and permitting Mexico to sell whatever it can in the United States, hence opening the door to economic expansion in Mexico. Change within Mexico and the United States means that there are few "solutions" to common problems. With the articulation of the dilemmas in the development of each country, it is clear that actions on either side of the border involve uncomfortable side effects that may well distort major "national interests" of both countries.

Perhaps the advent of Mexico's new petroleum bonanza (since 1976) will help the United States finally recognize that the special relationship of the U.S.-Mexico border requires fair economic treatment from the northern side. In return for access to Mexican oil and natural gas, the United States may have to eliminate unjust trade policy that limits Mexican economic imports into the United States. In the long run, the U.S. "national interest" will be best served by helping Mexico to develop its own national interests.

Notes

1. See Lyle C. Brown and James W. Wilkie, "Recent United States–Mexican Relations: Problems Old and New," in *Twentieth-Century American Foreign Policy*, eds. John Braeman, Robert H. Bremner, and David Brody (Columbus: Ohio State University Press, 1971), pp. 378–419.

2. See Lyle C. Brown, "The Politics of United States–Mexican Relations: Problems of the 1970s in Historical Perspective," in *Contemporary Mexico*, eds. James W. Wilkie, Michael C. Meyer, and Edna Monzón de Wilkie (Berkeley: University of California Press, 1976), pp. 471–93.

3. For further discussion, see James W. Wilkie, "Pulling, Hauling Mark Mexico's Land Reform," *Los Angeles Times*, 26 December 1976, p. VI-3.

4. "Open Letter to President Ford from 76 United States Congressmen of Both Parties Denounces Mexico's Slide to Communism under President Echeverría," *New York Times*, 16 August 1976, reprinted from the *Congressional Record*, 10 August 1976, p. E4499.

5. For quantitative assessment of the alliance, see James W. Wilkie, "The Alliance for Progress and Latin American Development," in *Statistics and National Policy* by James W. Wilkie (Los Angeles: UCLA Latin American Center Publications, 1974), pp. 409-31. On foreign aid for Mexico, see John Parke Young, "Why Not a U.S. Marshall Plan for Mexico?" *Los Angeles Times*, 8 December 1976, p. II-7.

6. For development of this concept, see James W. Wilkie, "Mexico: Permanent 'Revolution', Permanent 'Crisis'," *Los Angeles Times*, 5 December 1976, p. VIII-17.

7. However, the 1981 Mexican Law for Agricultural and Livestock Development has provided anew for the issuing of certificates of inaffectibility to protect from land reform certain lands used for cattle raising or for the growing of feed grains and other crops.

2
The Management of U.S.-Mexico Interdependence: Drift Toward Failure?

David Ronfeldt and Caesar Sereseres

PREFACE

This "think-piece" provides part of the written component of a research project on U.S.-Mexico relations that was contracted to The Rand Corporation by the Department of State.

The piece is intended to contribute to binational dialogue on the future of U.S.-Mexico interdependence. It discusses perspectives found among policy-oriented elites in Mexico as well as in the United States.

The piece examines factors affecting the ways in which the U.S. government may cooperate with Mexico to manage the complex issues confronting the two nations. It does not aim to provide substantive recommendations for resolving specific issues.

This study is being published here as an "historical document" with no revisions to the original draft and only minor editing. Since 1977, the draft has circulated widely in Washington, D.C. and Mexico City as a working note containing preliminary findings from a project supported by the U.S. Department of State. The views and conclusions expressed in this draft are those of the authors and should not be interpreted as reflecting official opinion or policy.

Readers wanting to see further views of the authors on this subject are referred to: Ronfeldt and Sereseres, *Treating the Alien(ation) in U.S.-Mexico Relations* (Rand, P-6186, August 1978); and Ronfeldt, Richard Nehring, and Arturo Gándara, *Mexico's Petroleum and U.S. Policy: Implications for the 1980s* (Rand, R-2510-DOE, June 1980).

© 1983 by David Ronfeldt and Caesar Sereseres

I. DRIFT AND DISORGANIZATION IN U.S.–MEXICO RELATIONS

The improvement of U.S.–Mexico relations deserves to be a high priority objective on the national agenda. The United States can no longer afford to take settled relations with Mexico for granted. U.S.–Mexico relations are neither bad nor lacking in political goodwill, but they have deteriorated in recent years. At the same time, changing domestic situations in both nations have given rise to important new interests and incentives for building improved relations.

Developments since the late 1960s have jarred customary views of Mexico and U.S.–Mexico relations. We are accustomed to dealing with a relatively passive Mexico . . . a Mexico that has little we need . . . a Mexico that lacks bargaining leverage with the United States . . . a Mexico that cooperates in a "special relationship" with the United States . . . and a Mexico that can normally be neglected. We are also accustomed to dealing with a politically and economically stable Mexico . . . a Mexico where the myth of revolutionary legitimacy is strong . . . a Mexico that has great institutional continuity . . . a Mexico ruled by a highly cohesive and durable elite known as the "revolutionary family" . . . a Mexico with great capacity for co-opting dissidents and managing domestic conflicts . . . a Mexico that is one of the very few quasi-democracies left in the Western Hemisphere . . . and a Mexico that is making steady economic progress through the success of the Mexican Revolution.

New uncertainties emerged in virtually all these areas by the mid-1970s. The "special relationship" has lost favor in Mexico as an overall principle for guiding U.S.–Mexico relations. The discoveries of major petroleum and gas reserves have given Mexico a new strategic significance to the United States, but other issues are not inviting. In particular, the immigration of undocumented Mexican workers, and the clandestine influx of heroin, have aggravated serious socioeconomic problems in the United States. Meanwhile, political divisions, financial disarray, and demographic pressures in Mexico have strained the stability of its postrevolutionary institutions. Suffering from untenable deficits in the balance of payments and trade, Mexico has required exceptional loans from U.S. and international banking agencies.

While this complex bundle of issues is increasingly referred to as "the Mexican problem," its significance transcends U.S.-Mexico relations. As George Ball concludes in his *Diplomacy for a Crowded World*, "The problems one can predict between the United States and Mexico foreshadow those we will face with many other countries. They are problems for which we are not prepared—psychologically, intellectually, emotionally, or in terms of concrete plans and programs."[1] Indeed, three bilateral issues—energy, migration, and drugs—rank very high on the U.S. agenda of global problems that require presidential attention.

Reflecting a growing uneasiness about the future of bilateral relations, Presidents Jimmy Carter and José López Portillo agreed in March 1977 to coordinate policies on major issues and to fashion new mechanisms for managing interdependence. Presidential commitment will prove essential if new measures are to take effect. As an initial step, the careful cultivation of a new sense of high level trust and direction, including collaborative discussion of problem issues, should prove more useful than fast-paced (and inherently unilateral) U.S. efforts to resolve those issues. It remains to be seen, however, whether Mexico-related issues can compete with the major policy concerns confronting the U.S. government at home and abroad.

At the very least, emerging public discussions about bilateral problems will lead increasingly and inevitably to new discussions of controversial domestic conditions in both countries, in particular, arousing sensitive public reactions within Mexico and in the U.S. Southwest. For example, an election-timed letter to President Gerald Ford, signed by 76 U.S. Congressmen in 1976, erroneously warned that Mexico was heading toward communism behind a "cactus curtain." That unfortunate letter, and the caustic Mexican reaction, indicated that the potential for public misunderstandings has grown on both sides, and that bilateral issues and domestic controversies easily intermingle.

The purpose of this paper is to contribute to binational dialogue regarding the management of future U.S.-Mexico interdependence. *While the specific issues alone suggest a problematic future for U.S.-Mexican relations, equally serious are the lack of a central policy concept and of an organizational interface that can motivate dialogue and provide overall direction in bilateral relations.*

While recognizing the importance of private sector interests, this paper focuses on *government-to-government relations* according to the following areas of concern:
- The complexity of the *major bilateral issues* is described in Section II. While most have proven quite resistant to resolution, linkages between some issues raise the possibility of trade-offs. However, differing priorities and domestic linkages have created obstacles to a willingness to resolve the issues in both countries.
- The evolving nature of the *special relationship* is discussed in Section III. This central principle in U.S.-Mexico relations may need revision if it is to provide a sense of direction to policymaking encounters within and between the two governments. Whether Mexico is and should be considered "special" by the U.S. government involves sensitive issues for U.S. multilateral policies.
- The structure of *the organizational interface* between the two governments is treated in Section IV. The ways in which the two governments are organized for dealing with each other affects the treatment accorded to specific issues. The prevailing compartmentalization of the issues in both countries, and Mexico's weak representational and lobbying presence in the United States, have tended to hinder the prospects for negotiations and bargaining.
- Perspectives on *dependency, leverage, and bargaining* are the concern of Section V. Common mythologies of great U.S. leverage and of negligible Mexican influence have served to restrain dialogue, and even to create preferences for preserving the status quo and for avoiding bargaining over issue resolution.

In our final thoughts, we move *from a present sense of drift and disorganization, to a prophecy of failure* in the management of future U.S.-Mexico relations. Interdependence between the United States and Mexico is acute and growing. Yet neither government seems prepared to establish ways for managing this interdependence. Numerous ideas have been floated regarding policy measures that might strengthen interdependence. These ideas range in scale from narrowly selective tariff adjustments to co-sponsored border development programs. However, the prevailing tendencies in bilateral relations continue to result in isolated piecemeal efforts at issue resolution, often undertaken without significant consultations, frequently without much effect, and sometimes with unintended consequences that further strain relations. In both countries, we find widespread doubt that either government can surmount the policymaking constraints which we identify below.

II. BILATERAL ISSUES AND LINKAGES

Few economies and societies are as tangled together as those of the United States and Mexico. Of the major bilateral issues—illegal immigration, U.S. access to Mexican oil and gas, trade and protectionism—not one has a simple solution. Some issues, especially migration and drugs, are serious for the United States but Mexico may well prefer the status quo to possible solutions. Most issues have controversial aspects. A few seem intractable. Many interact with each other. Some issues link to major domestic U.S. interests and policies, as well as to domestic factors of potential political and economic instability in Mexico, which in themselves have become an issue in recent years. Trends in virtually all issue areas reveal that Mexico's great dependency on the United States will probably increase.[2]

FINANCIAL STAKES: INVESTMENTS AND CREDITS

The United States has an enormous capital investment in Mexico, affecting private and public sector relations in both countries. The book value of U.S. direct investment approximated $3.2 billion at the end of 1975, representing some 80 percent of the $4 billion estimated as total foreign direct investment. About 75 percent of the U.S. investment was in the manufacturing sector. During the past decade, U.S. and multinational corporations purchased numerous Mexican businesses and concentrated in the fastest-growing, most profitable sectors of Mexico's economy—a fact that has aroused some resentment among Mexicans.

While Mexico needs foreign investment to create jobs and exports, the government has advanced numerous laws to restrict and guide its impact, while also seeking to stimulate domestic private investment.[3] Foreign investment is not permitted in basic industries including petroleum, basic petrochemicals, gas distribution, nuclear energy, electric power, railroads, telecommunications, most transportation, and forestry. State enterprises control these areas (although some are heavily indebted to foreign banks). In many other areas, the law requires "Mexicanization," that is, Mexicans must hold 51 percent equity interest. Recent laws specify cost-benefit criteria for evaluating the merits of a proposed foreign investment, and require increased domestic benefits from technology transfers. In general, the intent is to protect domestic industries, strengthen domestic participation in joint ventures, and halt "denationalization" of the business economy.

Implementation of these laws has proven quite pragmatic. Yet their initial appearance created widespread uncertainty among foreign businessmen, while in general the policies of the Echeverría administration also lost the confidence of domestic businessmen. The ensuing withdrawal of investments and capital flight contributed significantly to the peso devaluation/flotation in late 1976. Since the change of administrations, Mexico's private sector has promised to support the new president's plans. But President López Portillo has received greater confidence and support from U.S. and other foreign investors who have rescued Mexico's economy from its greatest monetary crisis in decades.

The economic crisis confirmed that the United States had enormous financial as well as capital stakes in Mexico. Indeed the United States has recently provided greater support to Mexico's monetary system than to any other developing country. At the time of the peso devaluation, the total foreign debt of Mexico's public sector approximated $20 billion (with the private sector debt summing another $7–8 billion). U.S. commercial banks held more than $10 billion of this debt, while the U.S. Export-Import Bank, the World Bank, the Inter-American Development Bank, and other U.S.-supported institutions accounted for additional billions of exposure. Apart from the foreign debt, the current account deficit in Mexico's balance-of-payments for 1975 rose dramatically to $4.2 billion, most of it with the United States. This deteriorating situation owed largely to a trade deficit, a tourism decline, and to a great increase in borrowing and spending by the Echeverría administration to expand the public sector's role in Mexico's economy.

While an estimated $2–4 billion left Mexico during a near-panic in 1976, U.S. and foreign financial institutions committed large credits to avert a continuing crisis after the peso devaluation. Initial steps included drawing rights for $1.2 billion from the International Monetary Fund (IMF), and a Eurocredit loan of $800 million from a consortium of sixty-four banks, including U.S. banks. In addition, the U.S. Treasury and Federal Reserve offered $600 million in short-term drawings to the Bank of Mexico. Although this stabilization effort rescued Mexico's economy during 1976-77, its longer-term financial stability will require additional billions from international and domestic sources.

The IMF agreement, by requiring Mexico to abide by an austere stabilization program for three years, has restricted the economic and political flexibility of the Mexican government. However, following an appeal to the U.S. government, the Mexican government did gain exemption of the state oil company, Petróleos Mexicanos (Pemex), from the limitations on public sector borrowing. This frees Pemex to seek large credits for petroleum development. President López Portillo meanwhile warned about a potential "South Americanization" of Mexico's politics if the United States should prove unresponsive to Mexico's economic needs. Indeed, concern had spread that the original IMF requirements might seriously strain political cohesion among Mexico's governing elites.[4]

PETROLEUM

U.S. interests in Mexico's oil and gas reserves have strategic significance and may provide Mexico with some bargaining leverage. With the development of new on-shore and off-shore oil fields, the present cautious estimate of nearly 20 billion barrels of proven hydrocarbon reserves (including oil and mixed gas) may soon rise to 30 billion barrels, and possibly to the 60 billion figure frequently cited in foreign reports. Pemex has compared fields in Tabasco-Chiapas and the Gulf of Campeche to the Alaskan and North Sea finds respectively.

Pemex plans to double both crude production and refining capacity and to triple its petrochemical output during the current presidential *sexenio*, 1977-82. Accordingly, petroleum production will rise from 1.1 million barrels daily at present, to 2.2 million barrels daily by 1982. Exports, mostly in crude form, will increase from 200 thousand barrels daily at present, to 1.1 million barrels daily by 1982. The United States and Israel buy most current exports. While Pemex production already exceeds its schedule, the Central Intelligence Agency recently released an estimate that Mexico could produce 2.2 million barrels daily by 1980, and possibly double that figure by 1985. Other recent appraisals show similar optimism.

According to Pemex projections, Mexico stands to earn more than $20 billion from exports during the *sexenio*. Revenues close to $1 billion in 1977 may rise to $6–8 billion annually by 1982. Meanwhile, petroleum development will require some $15 billion in investments, including $5 billion for equipment imports.[5] The Pemex program may generate about 50,000 new jobs, and at least 100,000 more in areas indirectly related to petroleum production.

The expansion program will require foreign financial and technological support. To raise the $15 billion for investments, Mexico aims to mix domestic with foreign capital on a one-for-one basis. Mexico will not accept foreign financing that is conditioned on direct participation in the state oil industry. Nonetheless, Pemex has a long history of obtaining credits from U.S. and European financial agencies. Recent measures include loans negotiated in the Eurodollar market and with the U.S. Import-Export Bank, as well as the sale of "petrobonds" secured by the Mexican government.

While Pemex is deservedly proud of its technological achievements at near self-reliance, it remains partially dependent on U.S. and other foreign companies for specialized equipment and services that all oil companies require to some degree from outside contractors. Mexico's petroleum development will surely require large purchases of equipment and services from U.S. suppliers. Foreign consulting service contracts are arranged through the Mexican Petroleum Institute. Private foreign investment, to a level of 40 percent participation, may enter the secondary petrochemical industry sectors through the Institute.[6]

By declining for the present to join the Organization of Petroleum Exporting Countries (OPEC), Mexico expects to preserve its freedom of action, to acquire some bargaining power, and to avoid possible sanctions under the U.S. Trade Law of 1974, while still obtaining high prices for its oil exports. Mexico is discussing oil sales in exchange for foreign products and technical cooperation with Brazil, Canada, France, and the Soviet Union. Mexican officials have objected publicly to signs of U.S. pressures for special petroleum access.

Mexico's petroleum policy is a politically delicate issue. Mexican nationalism is symbolized by the 1938 expropriation of foreign oil companies, and by the sanctity of Pemex as the nation's sole producer and supplier. The prospect of large-scale petroleum development has excited public concern that voluminous exports will increase Mexico's dependency on the United States and possibly jeopardize Mexico's sovereignty and security. Conservationists in Mexico advocate dedicating the oil mainly to the manufacture of fertilizers, plastics, and other petrochemicals that meet growing domestic needs, while preserving the reserves for future generations.

NATURAL GAS

Pemex has discovered major gas deposits in Tabasco-Chiapas and in several northern states, including Baja California. The Tabasco-Chiapas oil fields alone may contain 20 trillion cubic feet of mixed gas, compared to the 26 trillion cubic feet estimated for Prudhoe Bay, Alaska. Pemex plans to produce 3.6 billion cubic feet of natural gas per day by 1982.

Pemex and six U.S. interstate pipeline companies are negotiating an agreement to construct a 750-mile pipeline from the Tabasco-Chiapas fields to the Reynosa-McAllen border area. The pipeline would be built during 1978-79 at a cost over $1.5 billion, financed by Pemex and foreign sources, and providing employment for thousands of Mexican workers. Initial exports of one billion cubic feet per day would rise to two billion cubic feet per day by 1980-81. Mexico seeks to charge prices substantially higher than for U.S. regulated gas, thereby arousing objections in the U.S. Congress that have slowed the final negotiation of U.S. loans.

Whereas oil constitutes a national problem for the United States, gas represents more of a problem for specific states. The Mexican gas would be distributed over various U.S. pipelines, with some 175-300 million cubic feet daily going to California. Governor Jerry Brown and President López met in April 1977 in Baja California to discuss future gas acquisitions that could ease

California's looming shortages. During February 1977 President López Portillo agreed with President Carter to supply gas on an emergency basis for sixty days to ease winter shortages in the northeastern states.

Mexico wants its gas sales to result in U.S. purchases of other products. However, critics in Mexico protest that the pipeline will increase dependency on the United States.

GENERAL TRADE AND PROTECTIONISM

While Mexico's economic growth depends greatly on U.S. economic conditions and on bilateral trade, the two countries conduct their trade without benefit of a general treaty or agreement. The last formal instrument, the Reciprocal Trade Agreement of 1942, expired by mutual consent in 1950, largely because of Mexico's concern to protect its import substitution policies and maintain its freedom of action. For similar reasons Mexico also declined in 1947 to join the General Agreement on Tariffs and Trade (GATT), but it has recently become interested in the Multilateral Trade Negotiations (MTN) relating to GATT. While the United States has extended "most favored nation" status to Mexico through informal understandings, the trade interplay has stayed highly complex, focusing mainly on specific items and restrictions.

Each country has sought increased access to the other's markets for agricultural and manufactured goods. Mexico, though accounting for only some 3 percent of U.S. imports and 5 percent of U.S. exports, has nonetheless constituted our fourth leading trade partner. The United States is Mexico's leading trade partner, accounting for some 60 to 70 percent of imports and exports in recent years. For example, figures for 1973-1976 show that Mexico's annual imports from the United States ranged $3-5 billion, while U.S. imports in turn ranged $2-3.5 billion. Mexico's main exports have consisted typically of cotton, coffee, sugar, tomatoes, cattle, shrimp, fluorspar, zinc, and various electronic and electrical goods. U.S. exports have consisted largely of capital goods (equipment and machinery), and increasingly of grain foodstuffs. Imports by Mexico's public sector have grown faster than for its private sector. Mexico restricts the importation of luxury and consumer goods.[7]

Mexico has historically incurred a trade deficit with the United States, which was largely offset by tourism and border commerce until 1975. Mexico's shift in policy emphasis from import substitution to export diversification helped encourage export growth in the early 1970s. However, this growth faltered as a result of industrial recessions in the United States and abroad, the decline in world commodity prices, financial and political difficulties in Mexico, as well as a downturn in foreign investment and tourism. While Mexico's public sector in particular continued to increase its imports, the trade deficit enlarged to an alarming $3.6 billion in 1975, of which some $2 billion was with the United States.

Restrictive measures were adopted in the mid-1970s by both Mexico and the United States to protect their respective employment and balance-of-payments situations. Both countries have recently sought to simplify their tariff, quota, and licensing systems—but while barriers have gone down in some product areas, others have gone up. On balance, Mexico has benefitted from the U.S. Trade Act of 1974 and the Generalized System of Preferences (GSP), although its competitive-need ceiling restricts the volume of certain exports.

Protectionism has been the source of most complaints. The principal U.S. trade problems have concerned Mexico's import licensing requirements, which apply to over 60 percent of all import categories in its tariff code, and Mexico's refusals to allow U.S. access to local markets for some items that Mexico exports on a competitive basis to U.S. markets. Other complaints have focused on Mexico's official pricing policies, inordinate "red tape" delays, defaulting of some negotiated contracts, and the "dumping" of certain items, most recently sulfur, copper, and cement. Mexico has defended its protective licensing policies, and rejected reciprocal market access, for purposes of maintaining local employment, even though the inefficiencies and costliness are recognized.

Mexico has protested principally about the lack of long range, unimpeded access to U.S. markets, without threat of sudden marketing order restrictions that have especially affected Mexico's exports of winter vegetables, as well as beef, textiles, and shoes. Tomatoes, a significant earner of foreign exchange, have been a sensitive item affecting U.S. growers in Florida and

Southern California.[8] Mexico has complained about U.S. applications of voluntary quota reductions without sufficient prior negotiation, and about U.S. non-tariff barriers, including health and safety regulations, that discriminate against agricultural items in particular. Mexico has also objected to the United States as representing a middleman in triangular trade with countries like Canada and Japan.

Regarding current developments, President López has placed U.S. trade concessions at the top of his negotiating agenda, mentioning agricultural products in particular. The special bilateral trade agreement signed in December 1977 represents a significant step that will open U.S. markets to $63 million in Mexican products, and Mexican markets to $36 million in U.S. goods. During the negotiations, handled within the MTN framework in Geneva, Mexico proved willing to make concessions concerning its import licensing system, and became the first developing country to reach a bilateral agreement with the United States within a multilateral framework.

While the foregoing agreement mainly concerned tropical products, Mexico aims to increase its manufactured exports as well. The peso devaluation should increase Mexico's comparative advantage. However, results are mixed so far, and it is not clear that increased export opportunities will lead to new production and employment. One problem is that Mexican businessmen expect higher profits than their American counterparts and are not particularly efficient and competitive in many product areas.

In the past few months, Mexico's trade deficit has diminished, and future prospects seem excellent for large exports of petroleum, gas, and eventually of phosphates. However, Mexico's population growth and agricultural disorganization are expected to lead to growing importation of basic foodstuffs, while U.S. business protectionism may impede increased Mexican exports of agricultural and manufactured products.

THE IN-BOND INDUSTRIES

Chronic high unemployment in northern Mexico, intensified by the 1964 termination of the U.S. *bracero* agreement, stimulated the Mexican government in 1964 to initiate the Border Industrialization Program (BIP).[9] U.S. and Mexican officials hoped the program would alleviate the growing potential for social unrest in northern Mexico.

Mexico passed new laws in 1965 to attract U.S. investments in manufacturing for the U.S. market. These laws allowed the duty-free entry of foreign materials and components for use by assembly plants (maquiladoras) located within a zone two kilometers deep along the border, provided that their total output was exported. In 1972, Mexico modified the laws to allow the in-bond plants to locate anywhere in Mexico's interior, where unemployment was often higher and wages lower than along the border. The new laws also provided for some in-bond production to be sold inside Mexico. The program exempts the plants from the new foreign investment law, which requires 51 percent Mexican equity in foreign-invested enterprises.

The Mexican program depends on U.S. import policies that grant U.S. plants access to special items 807.00 and 806.30 of the U.S, Tariff Schedule. Item 807.00 enables U.S. components and materials to be assembled abroad (in any country) and returned as duty-free products to the United States—with import taxes levied only on the value added from the non-U.S. portions of the assembly operations, including non-U.S. components. These tariff items have permitted hundreds of U.S. businesses to remain cost competitive by moving their labor-intensive assembly operations to low-wage locations abroad. For many U.S. businesses, pressured by rising wages and inflation-recession at home, the only alternative would have been to close shop.

Though not among the first countries to take advantage of the U.S. tariff items, Mexico became the major beneficiary by the mid-1970s. The number of plants in Mexico grew to a peak of 586 in 1974. Then, rising wages in Mexico, combined with further inflation-recession in the United States, drove numerous plants to reduce their operations. More than a hundred closed shop entirely, some moving to countries where wages were lower and better regulated. However, by late 1977 Mexico's in-bond program began to revive, in response to the peso devaluation, the moderation of local wage-hike demands, and the U.S. economic recovery.

Illustrating the program's dimensions, figures for 1975 estimated the total number of plants at 447, with only 22 located in Mexico's interior. U.S.-owned subsidiaries of major U.S. corporations accounted for about 90 percent of the plants. Most of these engaged in electronic assembly, apparel industry, and food processing. Many operated a twin-plant system, with a plant on each side of the border. In 1975 the total value of U.S. imports from Mexico under the special tariff items amounted to slightly over $1 billion, representing about 30 percent of total U.S. imports from Mexico. The dutiable value added was $468 million, or 46 percent of the total in 1975—rising to $520 million in 1976. Figures for 1977 still show 447 in-bond plants, now including 43 in Mexico's interior, and direct employment of about 76,000.

The in-bond program stirs ambivalent reactions in Mexico. Critics contend that the maquiladora system increases dependency on the United States and mainly benefits U.S. businessmen, while also strengthening powerful political conservatives in northern Mexico. Moreover, the critics assert, the system has not produced spin-off industries in Mexico, nor otherwise advanced its technological development and alleviated unemployment. In fact, the maquiladora system has encouraged migration northward. Unemployment remains chronic among young males and heads of household, while 90 percent of the plant employees are women, mainly single in the 16–24-year-old bracket. Nonetheless, expansion of the maquiladoras represents a very significant alternative available to the Mexican government for creating new jobs.

Within the United States, organized labor has demanded elimination of item 807.00, contending that the in-bond industry programs damage the U.S. economy by exporting U.S. jobs to foreign countries and exposing U.S. workers to low-wage competition.[10] However, their opposition seems directed mainly against the in-bond establishments in Western Europe, the Far East, and the Caribbean Basin, since salaries and wages paid there fail to enter the United States. Those paid in northern Mexico largely return to the United States through border transactions and imports.

THE BORDERLANDS

The borderlands comprise a special zone with its own special problems. Here two distinct cultures and disparate economies make contact in a semi-arid land some two thousand miles long, a couple of hundred miles wide, including parts of four U.S. and six Mexican states, and populated by some six million citizens from both countries. At times the borderlands seem far from the heartlands of either nation. The U.S. side has a strong Chicano subculture, while the Mexicans often consider their norteños a special breed. The U.S. side contains what some label the "poverty belt" of the American Southwest, yet Mexicans tend to see the border as a land of hopeful opportunities.[11] Washington and Mexico City each field numerous agencies to regulate border activities, yet neither federal capital has much effective control.

Border issues involve far more than illegal immigration. Citizens of both nations direct crime and violence at citizens of both nations. Officials of both governments, charged with border control operations, sometimes mistreat citizens of both nations. Juvenile delinquency, pollution, flood control, and disaster relief concern officials on both sides. While U.S. border cities seek to attract Mexican shoppers, Mexico counts on tourist transactions and border industrialization to create thousands of jobs and help balance Mexico's trade deficit with the United States.

The borderlands are renown for their clandestine trade in "undocumented alien goods," roughly valued in the billions of dollars. The smuggling of weapons and contraband consumer goods (appliances, televisions, automobiles, cigarettes) into Mexico may have entailed a currency outflow of some $500 million to $1 billion in 1976—up from an estimated $250 million in 1970. However, as discussed above, narcotics trafficking may return double the amount into Mexico.[12] Adding to this the estimated $1–3 billion in remittances from undocumented workers we see that the unofficial balance of clandestine payments runs significantly in Mexico's favor—though it escapes becoming direct government revenue.

The federal governments have attempted to organize special programs for border development, though without much success in recent decades.[13] Mexico's President Adolfo López Mateos initiated a Programa Nacional Fronterizo in 1961 that engaged in some beautification projects for a few years. Bilateral cooperation in the Border Industrialization Program (BIP), begun in 1965, proved vastly more effective. Presidents Lyndon Johnson and Gustavo Díaz Ordaz also founded the U.S.–Mexican Commission for Border Development and Friendship (CODAF) in 1966; it raised high hopes until its termination in 1970.

Since then, the two governments have not joined to organize a new bilateral development program along the border. The Mexican government has shown increasing concern about its apparent lack of central control over the border economy, which means increasingly integrated with the U.S. economy. The creation of customs-free zones in the northern states signified recognition by Mexico City that it could not effectively regulate border commerce and contraband smuggling. On the positive side, the new governor of Baja California, Governor Roberto de la Madrid, considers his state to be Mexico's "most important outpost" along the 2000-mile border, and wants Baja to represent a model of good relations with the United States. In particular, he seeks U.S. cooperation to develop fishing, agriculture, tourism, and assembly plants, and thereby to alleviate unemployment along the California border.[14] A close personal friend of President López Portillo, Governor de la Madrid could play a very influential role in shaping U.S.-Mexico relations at their territorial contact point, the border.

Meanwhile, in the United States, recent Title V legislation, falling under the responsibility of the Department of Commerce, has entailed creation of the Southwest Economic Development Region as a kind of "Appalachia program" for the four U.S. border states. In addition, the Carter administration has proposed the establishment of a border management agency that would absorb the fragmented, poorly coordinated operations of the Bureau of Customs, the Immigration and Naturalization Service (INS), and possibly the Coast Guard. Government officials have begun to recognize that law enforcement perspectives alone will prove inadequate to deal with the social and cultural complexities of the borderlands, which represent both the melting pot and the boiling pot of U.S.-Mexican relations.

TOURISM

Tourism represents Mexico's second largest industry and a leading source of foreign exchange, next only to petroleum. During the early 1970s, tourism in Mexico grossed about $2 billion annually and employed some 350–450 thousand individuals. In good years, three to four million tourists a year visit Mexico's interior for several days, 87 percent of them from the United States. Millions more visit border cities on brief excursions and business transactions.

Mexicans own most of the tourist industry, and the Mexican government itself is making large investments to develop new sites and facilities. Mexico is counting on tourism to remain a leading source of income and foreign exchange to help offset balance-of-payments deficits.

Aided by the peso devaluation, the tourism industry is now recovering from a temporary decline that began in 1974. Late that year, American Jewish leaders organized an effective tourism boycott in protest against Mexico's vote in the United Nations supporting a Third World bloc resolution to condemn Zionism as racist. The boycott cost Mexico millions of dollars in revenue. Economic recession in the United States, and reports of tourist deaths and political unrest in Mexico, further inhibited U.S. tourism.

The image of Mexico's political stability has historically affected the volume of tourism. Thus after anti-U.S. disturbances in the late 1950s and early 1960s led to drops in tourism, the Mexican government moved to take greater security precautions in the future. For example, the government quelled the student-led disturbances in 1968 partly to assure the staging of the Olympic games.

At present, Mexico's tourism leadership reports that the recent decline in U.S. tourism accounts significantly for the recent increase of illegal migration to the United States.[15] Accordingly, thousands of the migrants are displaced workers from hotels, restaurants, stores, and other businesses that rely on tourism for sales and income. As one remedial measure, Mexican officials request doubling the $100 limitation on goods with which Americans may return duty-free from Mexico. Mexicans have also objected to a change in U.S. tax laws limiting the deductibility of conventions held outside the United States.

Mexican tourism to the United States has expanded significantly. Close to a million Mexican tourists visited the United States annually prior to the peso devaluation and their expenditure of nearly $1 billion in 1976 proved a drain on Mexico's balance of payments. These expenditures, though representing only 2 percent of total tourist spending in the United States, added vital commerce to U.S. border cities.

THE MIGRATION OF UNDOCUMENTED WORKERS

The most impassioned issue historically is the illegal immigration of Mexicans seeking work in the United States. Millions of

Mexican nationals (estimated between two and eight million) reside illegally in the United States on a permanent or temporary basis. About a million or two cross the border surreptitiously each year. Hundreds of thousands—over 900 thousand in 1977, compared to about 90 thousand in 1967—are caught and returned to Mexico. Other hundreds of thousands return seasonally to their families and communities. On balance the ebb and flow of illegal migration from Mexico probably adds an annual increase of several hundred thousand to the U.S. population, which presently totals about 215 million.

The migration pattern stems from the huge wage differentials between the two countries and from the shortage of jobs in Mexico. Unemployment-underemployment there runs about 30 percent and job creation lags far behind population growth. Moreover, Mexico's gross domestic product of $80 billion runs a mere $1,300 per capita, while the $1.5 trillion U.S. economy offers an alluring $7,000 per capita as well as millions of job opportunities.

The migration incentives may increase. At present, the floating devaluation of the peso and economic recession in Mexico increase the attractiveness of earning U.S. dollars. In the future, Mexico's population, growing at one of the world's highest rates (about 3.5 percent a year), may nearly double by the year 2000 (from the present 65 million to 120 million) and its labor force may triple in size, while job opportunities fail to keep pace. Birth control measures have spread among some urban, middle class sectors but not among rural populations where the growth rate remains highest, and the jobs scarce.

Some U.S. domestic interests claim that the presence of Mexican aliens represents an economic threat. Accordingly, the aliens take jobs away from less skilled Americans. They put Americans on unemployment and welfare rolls. They depress wage scales. They undercut union organizing efforts. They remit millions, perhaps billions of dollars in detriment to the U.S. balance of payments. They consume more in welfare and educational services than they pay in taxes. They generate crime, corruption, and a multi-million dollar smuggling racket. They are creating the potential for a new wave of civil rights problems in the 1980s–1990s.

Contrary to those views, recent field research indicates that removal of the aliens would resolve none of those issues, and that the aliens may contribute more to the U.S. economy than they take out. Accordingly, the aliens often take the lowest-paying, least-skilled, dirtiest jobs in agriculture, canneries, packing houses, restaurants, hospitals, garment and construction industries— while Americans collect unemployment or welfare. Aliens enable some industries to survive that otherwise might succumb to rising wages or cheaper imports. Aliens pay far more in taxes than they consume in social services. Aliens are carefully law-abiding to avoid detection and deportation. Indeed, costly policing measures could not stem the crossings from Mexico, whose economic stability depends significantly on migration opportunities as a "safety valve."[16]

In a plan made public in mid-1977, the Carter administration recommended amnesty and permanent resident status for some aliens, temporary resident status for others, civil penalties for employers who knowingly hire illegal aliens, large expenditures on border enforcement, and economic cooperation for developing labor-intensive projects in source countries.[17] The H-2 certification system, which allows employers to request temporary foreign workers through the Department of Labor, will also be reviewed. As part of the border enforcement plan, the Immigration and Naturalization Service has requested the addition of 2000 personnel (about a third being Border Patrolmen), helicopters, vehicles, and ground sensors at an initial cost of $90 million. The Carter administration has ruled against a new bracero-like program or mass deportation for the present.[18]

The López Portillo government has quietly objected to the Carter plan. While Mexico prefers the unmanaged status quo as a "safety valve," its government officials have proposed alternatives: a temporary worker program that would avoid the abuses of the bracero system, as well as U.S. trade preferences and tourism measures that would generate employment in Mexico.

DRUGS AND NARCOTICS

Drug abuse has become a major problem in the United States, entailing an estimated $14 billion in social costs, and involving some 400-600 thousand heroin users.[19] About 85-90 percent of the heroin available on American streets originates in Mexico, which is also a major source of marijuana and pharmaceutical drugs, as well as a transit point for cocaine from South America. Heroin production in Mexico expanded rapidly after 1972, following effective U.S. campaigns to eradicate smuggling from France and Turkey. This multi-million and possibly billion dollar "growth industry" in Mexico reportedly involves some 25,000 acres of opium poppies, distributed among twice as many small plots in remote mountain areas, and employing some 250-500 thousand individuals in cultivation, processing and distribution. While U.S.-Mexico drug cooperation began in the 1950s, Mexico agreed to a greatly enlarged effort in 1969 following the near-closure of the border by the U.S. government with "Operation Intercept." At first directed mainly against marijuana and presently against heroin, U.S.-Mexican cooperation has included an opium-poppy eradication program, intelligence and route interdiction operations, and joint efforts to apprehend and prosecute drug traffickers. Mexico has spent millions of dollars on civilian and military programs ($35 million in 1976) with loss of life and equipment, to cooperate with the United States. Mexico has also become a high priority of the International Narcotics Control Program administered by the State Department, in collaboration with the Drug Enforcement Administration (DEA). In 1976, these programs provided $11 million for helicopters, herbicides, technical assistance and liaison advisers to Mexico.

U.S.-Mexico cooperation may prove successful in the long run. Nonetheless, U.S. accusations of official corruption in Mexico have hampered cooperation. In turn Mexican critics have charged that some activities of U.S. agents, and their collaboration with local military and police units, constitutes one more form of U.S. intervention in domestic affairs. Mexican officials see a contradiction between U.S. pressures to be "tough" on drugs but later "soft" on prisoners of U.S. citizenship. These aspects have publicly embarrassed the Mexican government, which has pointed out that the solutions to the U.S. drug problem ultimately reside within the United States.[20]

MEXICO'S STABILITY

Recent events in Mexico have surprised many observers. At first, the large student-led disturbances of 1968 seemed an exceptional event of exaggerated importance. However, the subsequent emergence of rural insurgency, urban terrorism, peasant unrest, divisiveness between certain business and government elites, doubts about the viability of the governmental party (the PRI-Institutional Revolutionary Party), rumors of increased military participation in politics, the largest turnover of government officials since 1940, and a striking presidential rhetoric of reform in the presence of a severe balance-of-payments deficit, slowing economic growth rates, rising unemployment, and one of the worst income distribution patterns in Latin America, all stimulated questions on whether the regime of former President Echeverría would preserve institutional continuity. His closing acts in office, to expropriate commercially valuable lands in northern Mexico and to permit devaluation of the peso, temporarily converted these questions into fears of an imminent institutional crisis.

In this setting, the inauguration of President López Portillo aroused great popularity and widespread relief throughout Mexico and in the United States. The International Monetary Fund, the U.S. government, and U.S. as well as other banks, meanwhile, assisted in restoring some balance to Mexico's economy. And the domestic unrest and violence subsided.[21] Thus the fears of instability soon returned to the status of questions, tempered by forecasts that new oil income will rescue Mexico from its socioeconomic problems.

The progress of post-revolutionary Mexico is frequently termed an economic "miracle" supported by the "genius" of the Mexican political system and by the "myth" of revolutionary legitimacy. While one set of intellectual critics or another has often predicted crisis and collapse, Mexico's institutions have always preserved their stability. Most observers regard the recent political troubles as being transitory to the inherent resilience of the permanent revolution. Such troubles merely reflect the belated and temporary passing of trends that have already coursed elsewhere around the world. Accordingly, the renewed prophecies of institutional crisis deserve to be dismissed.

A SPECULATION

The prospects for stability and continuity appear reasonably good, though not as good as before 1968. No one has made a convincing argument that Mexico has entered an institutional crisis. Even so, our own judgment concludes that Mexico is, or will be, experiencing an institutional transformation that may engender unrest and struggle.

In traditional conceptions, the Mexican government is ruled by a "revolutionary family" or coalition of elites, headed normally by the existing president. This family has carefully included new post-revolutionary generations along with the original inheritors of the 1910 Revolution. The president has relied mainly on two institutional pillars. The most important is the PRI party, given its remarkable capacities for mobilization, control and co-optation.[22] The second pillar is the army, given the sparing use of its limited, but occasionally critical, capacities for maintaining order and repressing dissent on behalf of the chief executive.[23]

This traditional conception may need revision. The president remains the government's leader. The revolutionary family still shows great discipline but may be headed toward a post-revolutionary separation. Generational changes within the elite (including the military officer corps), replacement of the unifying experiences of 1910 by the divisive experiences of 1968 as a benchmark of generational identity, and recent divisiveness between private business and public sector elites, represent changes that augur poorly for intra-elite cohesion.[24]

The post-revolutionary state, meaning the presidency and the federal bureaucracy, is replacing the revolutionary family as the centerpiece of the political system.[25] At the same time, the PRI party seems to be awakening as the main institutional pillar of the government. Its capacities for mobilization and conflict management show declining effectiveness, even as political reforms broaden the opportunities for alternative parties and groupings. Meanwhile, the government's reliance on the military has grown; and moreover, the military education system is expanding to cover Mexico's political, economic, and foreign policy experiences.

Neither extreme of a military coup or a new revolution seem likely in Mexico's future. Broader military participation in government would not be surprising.[26]

BILATERAL-DOMESTIC ISSUE LINKAGES

The more sensitive bilateral issues affect the potential for instability in Mexico. The migration of Mexican undocumented workers eases the effects of population growth, land scarcity, unemployment-underemployment and poverty conditions. The migration returns new capital and some light technology into Mexico, thereby representing a beneficial rural aid program that may be superior to most U.S. economic aid programs abroad.[27] U.S. efforts to reduce illegal immigration would alarm Mexican officials, who fear strains on their economic and political institutions. Demographic pressures already aggravate rural unrest. According to dire predictions, a closure of the U.S. border to illegal immigration would stimulate social unrest in Mexico's northern cities and induce requirements for military operations. Such a trend could increase military participation in Mexico's politics.

The drug business threads the political, economic, and criminal fabric of the northwestern states of Sinaloa, Sonora, Durango, and Chihuahua. Marijuana and opium poppy cultivation have proven profitable for impoverished peasants in some violence-ridden areas, as well as for some politically powerful and privileged individuals. As the government manages to control drug agriculture and trafficking, it will need to generate alternative livelihoods for the affected rural populations. Meanwhile, rural guerrillas and urban terrorists, as well as ordinary criminals, have traded drugs to procure weapons smuggled from the United States. The Mexican government has expanded the army's presence in these areas in order to control both the drug business and social unrest.

The petroleum discoveries promise national profit and progress. Yet over the short-term the politics of developing the oil and gas resources may exacerbate divisiveness between some elite factions. Internal debates—regarding how energy income is used, in what public and private sectors, for what kinds of programs, and to what diplomatic ends—may sharpen differences between capitalist- and socialist-minded elites, raising tensions over pro- and anti-U.S. dispositions. Mexican critics already complain that government policies will increase dependency and vulnerability relative to the United States. Intragovernmental disputes may also attend the reorientation of Pemex, away from its historical role as an essentially political institution, toward becoming an efficient economic enterprise. Over the longer run, mounting income from energy production will not spell salvation for Mexico's vast problems—especially those found in rural areas.[28]

The major bilateral issues also link to important U.S. domestic interests and problems. These range from the national scale, as in regard to energy, drugs, labor employment, and the status and rights of the Chicano population—to more regionally focused issues, like those affecting tomato growers in Florida and tuna fishermen in Southern California. The linkages are often so deep that the traditional dichotomy between foreign and domestic affairs becomes artificial in the case of U.S.-Mexico relations.[29] Thus, while Mexico may seek attention in terms of foreign affairs issues, the U.S. Congress in particular seems more likely to approach Mexico-related issues from an essentially domestic perspective.

For both countries, the strength of the bilateral-domestic linkages means that the discussion of bilateral issues typically converts into controversial discussion of the other country's domestic conditions. This sometimes leads to identification of the neighboring country as the scapegoat or potential solution to the original country's inability to arrive at a domestic solution. For example, U.S. interests sometimes blame Mexico for U.S. drug and employment problems, while other U.S. interests see Mexico as a solution to energy needs. In turn, Mexicans sometimes blame the United States for Mexico's financial and economic problems.

The illegal migration issue will prove especially sensitive. Whatever U.S. policy stance one may favor, discussion will inevitably focus on agrarian conditions in Mexico. Thus U.S. critics will blame the Mexican government for allowing such conditions to evolve, and may insist that Mexico bear the burden of resolving the migration issue. Individuals favoring sympathetic or accommodative policies toward the illegal migration will point to those very same conditions in Mexico, but may advocate the U.S. assistance programs and toleration of the migration as a safety-valve for Mexico's growing numbers of jobless and landless individuals. In any case, such discussions are found to arouse sensitivities in Mexico. As one reaction, some Mexicans may take a human rights perspective that criticizes the domestic U.S. treatment of Chicanos as well as illegal Mexican migrants. Public bitterness could result on all sides, with some individuals even arguing that the United States has reasonable cause to seek expanded involvement in Mexico's socioeconomic development processes despite Mexican sensitivities. Thus, congressional deliberations regarding undocumented workers and related aspects of the Carter proposals may well aggravate U.S.-Mexico tensions—similar to the emotionalism aroused by the proposed Panama Canal treaties.

APPROACHING THE ISSUES

The complexity of the issues and their linkages make possible various policy approaches. The traditional approach is to treat each issue separately. However, a comprehensive, linkage perspective suggests alternative approaches such as a sequential strategy, by treating specific issues in a deliberate negotiating order; or a trade-off strategy, by exchanging U.S. trade preferences for preferred access to Mexican oil exports, for example; or a "package" program, such as a Marshall-like plan for Mexico's rural areas.

Some U.S. and Mexican officials have shown a new sensitivity to issue linkages in bilateral relations. In Mexico this sensitivity appears at the highest level, where President López Portillo takes the position that:

> ... There are no isolated problems; everything is part of everything else.
>
> If, for example, we want to solve the problem of undocumented workers, we must understand that the problem lies in Mexico's economic situation. This will improve if we achieve a better balance in our very unfavorable trade relations with the United States.[30]

In another interview regarding worker migration, he stated:

> We see it as a problem of commerce, a problem of finance, a problem of development, a problem of demography . . . We cannot resolve it as a police problem.[31]

Within the United States, linkage perspectives are found mainly in the State Department. Otherwise, they are a rarity, for there is normally little time to frame neat analytical packages. The U.S. government must ordinarily deal with issues as they arise—and that often depends on which congressman or private interest proclaims the loudest.

The most likely approach to the preceding issues may turn out to be continuous, unresolved dialogue, until some specific crisis or difficulty obligates remedial measures. This seems likely for both countries not only because of the complexity of the issues. Other contributing factors, discussed in the next sections, are the lack of a central bilateral policy concept, the compartmentalized nature of the organizational interface, and a sense of dependency that inhibits bargaining.

III. THE "SPECIAL RELATIONSHIP"

A mutually agreeable central policy concept or rationale does not exist to guide and symbolize relations between the United States and Mexico. It might be useful—it may even become a necessity—to formulate a new, mutually agreeable rationale to take the place of the rhetoric of "special relationship." Otherwise, the policymaking biases inherent in broader U.S. multilateral and regional concepts will foster the continued neglect of U.S.-Mexico relations.

DEMISE OF THE SPECIAL RELATIONSHIP

The United States has traditionally promoted a "special relationship" with Mexico, and Mexico has not rejected the idea. U.S. and Mexican leaders recognize that *a bond* known as the special relationship does, even must, exist by dint of geography and history as neighbors. Thus President John F. Kennedy once stated in Mexico City that geography had made us neighbors, tradition has made us friends, and economics had made us partners. In that sense, U.S.-Mexico relations are so intertwined as to be implicitly special, and in that sense the uniqueness of the relationship cannot perish. Nonetheless, *the policy* traditionally known as the special relationship has lost meaning on both sides of the border, particularly in Mexico.

Some Mexicans have come to regard the policy idea as being worn out, inactive, even defunct. Others believe it never really existed. That is, whenever Mexico has tried to invoke the special relationship by seeking a preferential adjustment of some global or regional U.S. policy measure, Mexico has seldom found a special responsiveness.

The meaning and origins of this vague concept are not clear. No explicit definition has ever been offered. Traditional elements would appear to be a relatively open and unfortified border, close consultation over problem issues, and some advantageous treatment for Mexico in trade and migration matters. The special relationship idea was meant to signify that, despite vast asymmetry, mutual dependency would enable Mexico to become strong and independent. Furthermore, bilateral cooperation would be based on mutually valued principles, such as respect for sovereignty, nonintervention, and equality.

The special relationship notion has proven to be more symbol than substance. It has not served to clarify whether or how to resolve specific problem issues. Nor has the concept entailed a framework for perceiving possible linkages and trade-offs among the issues. These were left to be compartmentalized within the U.S. and Mexican bureaucracies.[32]

The idea of a special relationship between the two neighbors gained prominence in recent years—but achieved little more than rhetorical significance. Rooted in World War II experiences, when U.S.-Mexico relations were extremely cooperative, the idea was overshadowed by U.S. regional concepts involving the Alliance for Progress in the 1960s. Then, in the 1970s, the New Dialogue suggested a broad "special relationship" with Latin America. Mexico was sometimes mentioned as representing a special-special relationship within the region.

For its part, Mexico resisted this regionalization of specialness, ostensibly because it might increase regional dependence on the United States, but also because it might stimulate new competition for preferential relations with the United States. In recent years there has been a proliferation of U.S. "special relationships" with emerging regional powers, such as Brazil, Iran, and Saudi Arabia (plus the unsuccessful claim of other countries for their own special relationship, as in the case of Venezuela). With so many rivals for special relationships, Mexico saw its own as having relatively diminished stature even as a symbol, and seemed particularly sensitive to the appearance of a growing special relationship between the United States and Brazil in the mid-1970s.

Prior to the recent petroleum discoveries, U.S. interests and objectives in Mexico did not seem to warrant much special attention. Treating the special relationship mainly in procedural terms, the United States continued to provide ready, high level access to Mexican officials. Moreover, U.S. officials continued to avow that Mexico deserved preferentiality in relations. The United States steadily remained disposed to discuss the initiation of major economic and technical assistance programs for Mexico. Yet Mexico remained adamant in refusing large-scale bilateral aid from its neighbor, partly for reasons of image. Indeed, following flood damage in 1977, Mexico was reluctant to request even temporary disaster relief—and the United States was reluctant to offer it because of concern for offending Mexican sensitivities and pride. (Nonetheless, some recent signals indicate that in Mexico, the new administration might be receptive to special development funding programs which fall outside the traditional AID assistance framework.)

In substantive terms, successful negotiation of the Chamizal issue in the early 1960s, and of the salinity issue in the early 1970s, served to symbolize and sustain the generally good bilateral relations.[33] Apart from such border issues, no serious bilateral differences, of a structural or diplomatic nature, arose during the 1940s–1960s to challenge the basic acceptability of the special relationship idea and its apparent benefits to Mexico. But Mexicans have focused on other experiences in recent years to mark the violation and demise of the special relationship, typically perceived to involve a sudden unilateral action by the United States without warning or consulting Mexico. These experiences included Operation Intercept (the sudden near-closure of the border in 1969 to pressure the Mexican government to take measures against narcotics trafficking), the 1971 enactment of the 10 percent import tax surcharge without exempting Mexico (or Canada), protectionist trade measures that took the form of marketing orders and non-quota tariffs, and in 1976 changes in the U.S. Immigration and Nationality Act lowering the number of Mexicans allowed to immigrate yearly. The 1971 surcharge was particularly galling to the Mexicans (and it also marked an end to Canada's belief in a similar special relationship with the United States).

Although waning over these past few years, confidence exists in Mexico that the United States has the resources and imagination to resolve bilateral problems. Accordingly, it is only a question of political will and attention. As Mexicans have been quick to claim, perhaps the United States was too preoccupied with developments elsewhere to attend properly to Mexico in the early 1970s. This lenient view holds that various developments—including U.S. efforts to build new relations with distant, former enemies rather than resolving problems with old friends and allies, the new U.S. strategy to replace bilateral with multilateral approaches to economic problems in the Third World, U.S. balance of payments problems, and the proliferation of new special relationships—ultimately reinforced tendencies to neglect U.S.-Mexican issues.

One of Mexico's leading foreign affairs analysts, Mario Ojeda, has described the U.S. neglect of Mexico in regional-strategy terms.

> Thus . . . by the end of the 1960s, with the coming to power of a new government in Washington, once that it was clear that social revolution in Latin America was not going to explode so easily as had been thought; once that the first signs of a relaxation of the Cold War were in sight; and once that it was clear that the government of Fidel Castro had moved from a policy of supporting Latin American guerrillas to a less belligerent attitude, Mexico's strategic value for Washington decreased in relative terms. As a result of this, the "special relationship" was shelved by Washington, and the Mexican government lost a great part of its past capacity to negotiate with the United States.[34]

A different but nonetheless popular Mexican viewpoint has held that the United States has had no interest in seeing the development of a strong and independent nation next door—and therefore would do nothing special to advance Mexico's development.

Under these circumstances Mexico turned to pursue an unusually active, internationalist policy in the 1970s, suited to a new vision as a potential medium power and leader among Latin American and Third World nations. The growth of the European Economic Community (EEC) and Japan and the relaxation of U.S.–Communist bloc tensions were seen to provide new opportunities for economic diversification. Mexico was prompted as well by economic stagnation and political dissidence at home, and by concern for casting a new international and domestic image to Mexico's policies. Beginning in 1971, therefore, Mexico sought to diversify its markets and obtain new capitalist partners for trade and investment. Mexico further began to advocate a familiar redistributive line for the Third World and to oppose U.S. positions in Third World and other multilateral forums.

International activism thus gained official favor in Mexico over the now rather quiescent "special relationship." Bereft of bargaining power in the bilateral relationship, Mexico hoped to locate distant new allies and issues, especially in the EEC and the Third World, that would help reduce dependence on the United States while at the same time giving Mexico some claim against it.

Despite the Third World rhetoric voiced by some Mexican government officials in international forums, Mexican officials remained fairly cooperative and uncontroversial when dealing privately and bilaterally with U.S. officials. Indeed in this period Mexico did virtually nothing by way of demanding a new framework for bilateral relations or new resolutions to problem issues.

With the decline of the special relationship idea and the lack of any replacement, charges of dependency, neocolonialism, and neoimperialism have spread as a currency of recent Mexican political discourse toward the United States. In the absence of a concept of mutual dependency, latent perspectives of unilateral dependency and vulnerability have come to the fore within Mexico. The spread of such viewpoints has reflected generational changes within Mexico's political institutions, where rising young nationalists have found the new dependency concepts useful for calling attention to certain problem areas and for trying to put the United States on the defensive.[35]

CONSEQUENCES FOR MEXICO'S FOREIGN POLICY

Third World activism did gain some new political prestige for Mexico in Latin America, in Third World and in other multinational forums. Moreover, the decay in the climate of bilateral relations did come to trouble U.S. policymakers sufficiently to make them ready to pay attention and give Mexico higher priority. For Mexico, these gains may have been worth the effort.

Mexico's strategies have not been as successful in achieving other major objectives. Mexico's bargaining leverage with the United States has not increased. Drift and disorganization characterize bilateral relations more than ever—even though relations may be described as "good" in the traditional diplomatic sense. Mexico's efforts at economic diversification have brought meager results. Instead recent government policies have led ironically to an increase in economic and financial dependency on the United States and to the discovery that Mexico has very limited trade options outside the United States.

Mexico has never conceded that its future may lie more with North America than with its Latin American brethren—though this may prove to be a lesson of recent experiences. Several times in recent decades Mexico has offered to serve as a mediator in U.S.-Latin American relations. There has been concern that a U.S. policy which lacked understanding of Latin America would have grave repercussions in Mexico.[36] Nonetheless, at present Mexico appears disinterested in playing a significant role in the formation of a special Caribbean Basin policy by the United States.

In recent years Mexico has campaigned hard to strengthen its status and role in the Latin American system. Yet its opportunities in Latin America are severely restricted by the prevalence of rightist military dictatorships in South America, from which Mexico has received numerous exiles and escapees of liberal and radical political convictions, and by the poor prospects for economic integration and regional trade and investment. Moreover, other Latin American countries have tended to regard Mexico as a peripheral member of the region, too closely meshed with the United States. Mexico has recently provided leadership for organizing new Latin American institutions, notably the Latin American Economic System (SELA). But so far these are weak entities.

Thus, Mexico's Latin American options have not significantly enhanced bargaining leverage with, nor independence from, the United States. Once again Mexico appears to be an exception to Latin America—with almost nowhere else to turn but directly to the United States.

Mexico's new president, José López Portillo, has proven friendlier toward the United States and less Third World in orientation than was his predecessor. Although the new president is not abandoning the recent policy image favoring a new international order, he has given relatively less emphasis to it. Efforts to expand and institutionalize relations with other Latin American countries and groupings are continuing—but again with less emphasis. A turn toward a Mexican isolationism, or toward an extreme focus on bilateral relations with the United Sates, might cost Mexico what little foreign bargaining capacity it has. In any case, he is likely to proceed cautiously toward the United States if only for the sake of appearance. His preferred option would probably be a revitalization of the special relationship.

FUTURE CHOICES FOR THE UNITED STATES

The United States has essentially three choices for designing a new policy concept regarding U.S.-Mexico relations. The choices are not ideal. Each reflects different aspects of current views about U.S. interests and objectives, about the value to be placed on good relations, and about willingness to resolve specific issues. A likely outcome may be some blend of the three perspectives.

Toward A New Special Relationship

One alternative would be to revitalize the "special relationship" by giving it new meaning and possibly calling it by some other name. Thus the United States could emphasize shared interests in issue resolutions, convey symbols and standards for the conducting of relations, and offer a presumption of preferentiality in those relations in part because the traditional U.S. dichotomy between foreign and domestic affairs is so artificial in the case of U.S.-Mexico relations. It may not be necessary to specify whether or how particular problem issues should be resolved.

A series of principles might be identified on which to base the management of U.S.-Mexico interdependence. Some pertinent principles might be as follows:

- assurance of U.S. interests in seeing the development of a strong, independent Mexico;
- public and private awareness of each other's sensitivities about sovereignty, nonintervention, and equality, so as to avoid the appearance of policy imposition;
- a border whose openness symbolizes neighborliness, along which no fortifications are installed, and which allows constant, easy trade, communications, and exchange;
- recognition that the relationship as well as its consequences are national in scope and not limited to the border states;
- ready access to each other's top decision makers and close consultation whenever problem issues arise;
- an assumption of mutually shared responsibility for creating most problem issues, combined with an assumption of mutually shared responsibility for dealing with them—that is, an "organic" view of the relationship;
- an absence of precipitative punitive actions, as well as consultative forewarning of measures that may have an adverse impact even though they be directed at a third party or be multilateral in nature;
- preferential treatment in selected areas where mutual benefits can be realized.

Beyond such principles, the building of close, cooperative relations might be rationalized in terms of protecting each other's economic vulnerabilities in the changing world context. U.S. access to Mexico's petroleum reserves and Mexican access to U.S. commerce, financial, and labor markets may represent implicit stakes in the economic relationship. There is a likelihood, however, that many Mexicans would not *publicly* accept an "economic security" rationale unless it brought sizable concessions from the United States. "North American interdependence," including Canada, and some reference to the defense of democracy, might also provide additional rationales.[37]

There are serious constraints, symbolic as well as substantive, to building close, cooperative bilateral relations. Mexico and the United States are very different countries with very different interests, needs and identities at stake. Most Americans probably feel their country already has too many problems to become deeply enmeshed with Mexico's. Most Mexicans fear and resent encroachment from the Colossus of the North, and many nationalists do not want or trust a close U.S. embrace. Nor do they want to appear publicly to be collaborating.

Even so, earlier experiences suggest that a special bilateral concept may have considerable appeal and utility. In its absence, U.S.-Mexico relations will likely be neglected, or else will fall prey to other mythologies (the special relationship itself being a kind of mythology) about the Mexican Revolution and the history of U.S.-Mexican relations.

An Ad Hoc Approach

Some Americans and Mexicans entertain that the best approach would be to have no particular U.S.-Mexico policy at all, and certainly not one that is avowedly special and thereby seems paternalistic. Accordingly, any new policy should be left quite undefined—so as not to inhibit mobility and flexibility in bargaining. Each issue must be treated separately. Relations are so complex as to defy a priori technocratic planning. One risks becoming overly fascinated with the predefinition of the relationship. A special new blueprint for U.S.-Mexico relations could even be dangerous, especially for Mexico. Ambiguity and a lack of definition may be essential to successful government in Mexico and to manageable U.S.-Mexico relations.

This ad hoc perspective may appeal most to those who prefer freewheeling diplomatic negotiations and who wish to avoid any possible signs of U.S. paternalism. Yet there are arguments against adopting this approach *in toto*. The symbolism of specialness seems unusually important in the case of U.S. relations with

Mexico. In withholding such symbolism, an ad hoc policy concept would likely lead to the triumph of multilateral, regional, or parochial U.S. interests in the treatment of bilateral issues. In American eyes, if Mexico is not special then it tends to be regarded as just another Latin American country, easy to neglect and entitled to relatively little attention. Mexico is typically considered an exception even among U.S. specialists on Latin America, who typically prefer to attend to South America where the main ideological struggles occur. Multilateral trade negotiators, who oppose the emergence of regional trading blocs and who generally resist preferential trade arrangements, have no reason to make any exceptions for Mexico. An ad hoc perspective would likely facilitate the influence accorded to domestic U.S. interests in dealings over bilateral issues.

Apart from such potential impact on U.S. interests, the ad hoc approach also appears unsuitable as a basis for dialogue with Mexico. An empty concept, especially if it contained little symbolic assurance of beneficial U.S. intentions toward Mexico, would likely arouse Mexican cynicism and suspicions about U.S. bargaining efforts. Indeed, an ad hoc approach that became an excuse for drift and neglect might well serve to strengthen anti-American radical elements in Mexico, on both the extreme right and left, who would be interested in destabilizing Mexico's internal conditions. At the same time, the absence of special symbolism might well raise the burden placed on organizational mechanisms to achieve solutions to the specific problem issues.

Unilateral Protectionism

A unilateral turn toward a defensive and protectionist policy concept may appeal to certain U.S. sectors regarding certain problems such as drugs, migration, and trade. Such a concept would be tantamount to identifying Mexico more as a threat and contaminant, with the open border representing more a liability than an asset. The open border, Mexico's safety valve for political stability, would lose much of its porous nature. Mexico would be treated as a scapegoat for domestic U.S. problems. Law enforcement might become a leading rationale. Mexico would be blamed for exporting its problems.

Despite possible short-term benefits in controlling drugs and migration, and in protecting some domestic U.S. industries and labor markets, this policy perspective would prove quite risky. In the first place, it might well become a self-fulfilling prophecy, by contributing to the potential for increased political instability in Mexico, as well as by serving as a terrible affront to Mexican nationalism. Were serious instability to occur, the United States would be faced with the dilemma of determining up to what point it could tolerate an unstable Mexico. Pressures for some kind of U.S. involvement (if only for a militarized border security system on the U.S. side) would probably arise if the political situation deteriorated.

A protectionist approach would surely alienate Mexico from serving as a key ally for the United States as we move into the uncertain energy context of the 1980s. More so than in case of an ad hoc policy, Mexican elite coalition balances would be disturbed by a U.S. protectionist policy, thereby strengthening those groups not in favor of friendly and open relations with the United States. Indeed, severe U.S. protectionism could serve to induce new elite alignments in Mexico, including alignments of extreme left with extreme right-wing nationalists. For those and more moderate circles as well, U.S. behavior would be taken as further proof that it will not allow a strong, independent Mexico on its borders—and will always work to keep Mexico weak and divided.

While a *protectionist* approach would not provide incentives for Mexico's friendship and cooperation, it might appear tempting for some U.S. sectors to test as a hard bargaining tactic. For example, threats to increase trade protectionism or border security might be viewed as leverage to obtain U.S. access to Mexican energy reserves, or to make Mexico develop an effective population stabilization program. Nonetheless, such risky and offensive tactics would not attack the heart of the bilateral problems. Their management ultimately depends on the building of cooperation rather than barriers between the two neighbors, and on U.S. and Mexican capacities to determine internal solutions to their own internal problems without seeking foreign scapegoats.

IV. THE ORGANIZATIONAL INTERFACE

Neither government seems well organized to bring about changes in the relationship. The compartmentalization of issues on the U.S. side, and the penchant for "closet diplomacy" on the Mexican side, seem better designed for maintaining the status quo. A new organizational approach, one that would allow the consideration of linkages and trade-offs across issues, and that would have strong executive support above entangled domestic interests, may improve the prospects for protecting good relations and managing interdependence in the future.

COMPARTMENTALIZATION OF U.S.–MEXICO RELATIONS

The organization of the U.S. government encourages the compartmentalization of relations and the separation, if not isolation and fragmentation, of individual bilateral issues. The organizational interface with Mexico is characterized by counterpart-to-counterpart relations that tend to reinforce particular institutional perspectives and interests on most bilateral problem issues. The U.S. Department of State deals directly with Mexico's Ministry of Foreign Relations, Agriculture with Agriculture, Treasury with Treasury and the Bank of Mexico, the special trade representative with Treasury, Commerce with Industry and Commerce, and Justice with Mexico's attorney general. Such a structure is natural for large bureaucracies.

While policies thrive on generalities, bureaucracies thrive on details. At working levels, the constant reinforcement of bureaucratic perspectives and the dispersal of issue responsibilities among varied offices lead to technical, administrative definitions of the issues. Consideration of issue linkages and trade-offs is inhibited. Negotiations and bargaining become difficult to initiate. The proposal of "package" deals is prevented. Split responsibilities in most issue areas may lead to serious coordination problems as well as jurisdictional rivalries, for example between DEA and Customs agents regarding drugs.[38] The alien issue alone involves elements of Labor, HEW, Justice, INS, the Border Patrol, State, the Domestic Council, and Congress, not to mention labor unions, employer organizations, Catholic and Chicano groups, and the police and other private and state-level agencies. The "special relationship" means virtually nothing at the level of specific issues.

So many issues involve trade and finance that Treasury, Commerce, and their Mexican counterparts tend to dominate relations. The strong domestic linkages of many issues also strengthen the roles of these agencies, as well as of private pressure groups.[39]

The U.S. Department of State and Mexico's Ministry of Foreign Affairs may be kept informed of working discussions and decisions. But they generally have low involvement and marginal influence in these matters. Thus State Department may end up having to explain, defend, and implement decisions in which it had little participation. Indeed, it spends considerable time trying to restrain other departments from taking steps that may appear blunt and insensitive to Mexican officials.

At times, there may be deliberate circumvention of the State Department and the Foreign Ministry as coordinating organs. In one case a U.S. agency, concerned about safeguarding professional, technical treatment of the issues for which it was responsible, pursued a strategy of relating almost exclusively with its Mexican counterpart in order to strengthen the latter's role in that issue area independent of its Ministry of Foreign Relations, which was studiously ignored. The officials involved wanted to prevent the intrusion of political and ideological criteria that would alter their technical-administrative definition of the issues.

U.S. administrative compartmentalism and jurisdictional jealousies are not the only organizational constraints to approaching bilateral issues. Advocacy by multilateralists, regionalists, and domestic lobbies have all played havoc on the organizational relationships between the United States and Mexico. Within the U.S. government, these perspectives and pressures have reinforced compartmentalization, fostered a technical focus on specific issues, and contributed to the avoidance of issue linkages and tradeoffs. U.S.–Mexico relations get trapped amidst strong U.S. domestic interests and broader multilateral and regional perspectives, especially in regard to trade issues.[40] The overall result has diminished the attention assigned to enhancing good bilateral relations.

MEXICO'S PENCHANT FOR "CLOSET DIPLOMACY"

The Mexican foreign policy process tends to be secretive. Thus the Mexican government has preferred to deal with the United States in a style that resembles "closet diplomacy." That is, reflecting a self-conscious effort to maintain an image of independence from the United States, Mexican authorities have generally preferred to deal only with the highest levels of the U.S.

government (usually secretarial or presidential), on a basis of quiet, informal, loosely structured, personal consultations, usually at the initiation of the Mexicans, and focused on a specific issue rather than on the broader relationship or issue linkages. This approach enables the Mexicans to raise some matters, such as linkage to Mexico's political stability, that they would prefer not to discuss with lower U.S. functionaries or in public. Congress, the U.S. media and many interest groups tend to be regarded in general as potential pressures on the U.S. executive that are not amenable to Mexican diplomatic style and whose actions are likely to have adverse consequences for Mexico. This approach also helps to give Mexico's president a free hand independent of outside pressures and interest groups, which are few in any case in Mexico's foreign policymaking processes.

The classic tendency is to wait for an issue to reach near-crisis proportions and then rely on special access to the executive branch or to individual congressmen who have shown an interest in Mexico. This tendency stems in part from the fact that, at the working level, Mexico has not been well organized for representing its interests with the United States on a daily basis. The Mexican embassy has not been actively suited for either gathering information or handling the complexity of U.S. government processes in Washington, D.C. Mexico has not made use of lobbyists. Mexico has not developed skills for dealing with the congressional and administrative processes of the federal government. Mexico has preferred to deal mainly with the White House, and secondarily with the Department of State, where it does maintain steady contact. Mexico has frequently ignored other agencies, and has neglected opportunities for monitoring and influencing bills and laws as they take form within the U.S. government; for example, by early presentation of Mexican views regarding marketing-order restrictions within the Department of Agriculture, Mexico has lacked the bureaucratic follow-through that may gain them occasional breakthroughs on smaller issues.[41] There has been deficient coordination in Washington between officials in Mexico's embassy and those dispatched on missions from Mexico City.[42]

Mexico's representational capabilities in Washington do not even compare favorably with those of their Latin American brethren. The embassies of Argentina, Brazil and Venezuela seem to understand better how to "work the U.S. system," especially in legislative matters. Panama and Venezuela have used their U.N. missions skillfully to spread public relations materials. Even a small country, Nicaragua, has contracted effective U.S. lobbyists to defend its interests with Congress and the executive branch.[43] Elsewhere, the Japanese embassy recently confessed to being mystified by the complexities of U.S. domestic politics and thus hired two U.S. law firms to provide background analyses for Japanese diplomats.

Mexico has the ability to make a number of improvements in its institutional capacity to provide effective representation in Washington. Such improvements would surely benefit the prospects for managing interdependence and for gaining quiet, early attention to specific issues. Until such improvements are made, it will probably continue to be said that the best representation of Mexico's views in Washington comes from the U.S. embassy in Mexico City.

From an institutional perspective, Mexico's bilateral as well as multilateral efforts have been quite dispersed among various ministries. This dispersal is to be reduced somewhat by the administrative reorganization, which, for example, will bring the concentration of trade and investment responsibilities in the new Ministry of Trade and Commerce, placing that ministry in a comparatively strong position. New efforts are also to be made at establishing interministerial committees for purposes of liaison and counsel at working levels, and for purposes of reducing intersecretarial rivalry. However, it is not clear that these institutional changes in Mexico City will have much effect on Mexico's capacities to deal directly with the United States. These could probably be raised more effectively by improving Mexico's representational capabilities in Washington, D.C.

In the meantime, Mexico's diplomatic and administrative capabilities will continue to depend very much on individuals, especially those few who combine technical competence along with personal status and connections in both Mexico and the United States. The absence in Mexico of a professional foreign service may affect the availability and preparation of skilled diplomats and negotiators who are knowledgeable about the United States. However, Mexico's recently expanded commitment to multilateral approaches and organizations, a turn that may have risen in part from frustration at trying to negotiate with the thicket of U.S. compartments involving international trade and financial issues, is serving to produce new personnel who are quite experienced at dealing with the United States.

SOME LESSONS FROM PAST COOPERATIVE MECHANISMS

Since World War II, the United States and Mexico have periodically established special mechanisms in order to overcome bureaucratic and political barriers to expanding cooperation.[44] Some special bilateral mechanisms in recent years have included: the International Boundary and Water Commission, the U.S.-Mexico Trade Commission, the Commission on Illegal Immigration to the United States, and the U.S.-Mexico Commission for Border Development and Friendship. Experiences with them suggest that little faith is to be placed in the establishment of special bilateral mechanisms.[45]

The International Boundary and Water Commission (IBWC) is considered the prize example of U.S.-Mexico cooperation. Established in 1889, the commission has facilitated the resolution of numerous boundary disputes, the Chamizal settlement, and the resolution of the Colorado River salinity dispute. The mission of this bilateral mechanism was based on the mandate to deal with "all problems on the land and water boundary susceptible to an engineering solution." Successful negotiations by special interagency task forces operating within the framework of the IBWC have proven successful largely because of the technical nature of the problems (meaning "nonhuman" problems). Other essential factors were the presidential-level interest in the Chamizal and salinity issues, the provision of sufficient interagency staff, and the low profile, nonpublic nature of the negotiations.

Similar efforts to establish mechanisms of cooperation in other issue areas have not proven as successful. The U.S.-Mexico Trade Commission, established in 1965, fell into disuse in 1973, as it became clear that the commission had no authority to negotiate and could only make recommendations. Difficulties occurred because the Mexican perspective focused on demands for bilateral concessions and preferences, while the Americans conceptualized discussions primarily in multilateral terms. The Mexican government broke off trade discussions when it recognized that its expectations for bilateral preferences could not be met. Differing conceptual approaches, the absence of the authority to negotiate and bargain, and the lack of high-level support led to the demise of the U.S.–Mexico Trade Commission and its replacement by informal ad hoc trade meetings that were often ritual in form.

Since the early 1970s, the governments of the United States and Mexico have made efforts to discuss illegal immigration. On two occasions, commissions were created to "study" the problem.[46] On both occasions, the appearance of "bilateralism" masked what were also unilateral efforts at public relations, meant to symbolize that both governments were trying to do something about the problem. In practice the commissions exhibited minimal coordination with low expectation that solutions would result from meetings between U.S. officials and their Mexican counterparts. There existed no authorized framework for real negotiation. There was little exchange of information, and no authority from the respective presidents to discuss alternative proposals. This supposedly bilateral commission, in the words of one State Department official, amounted to "nothing more than expensive public relations" between the two countries. Indeed, it was never clear whether there was one joint bilateral commission or two separate national commissions operating independently within their domestic constraints.

The U.S.–Mexico Commission for Border Development and Friendship (CODAF) was established in 1966 by joint agreement between Presidents Lyndon Johnson and Gustavo Díaz Ordaz for the express purpose of improving relations and settling bilateral problems along the border. Its demise was facilitated by several factors. In the first place, CODAF's roles were left undefined, and this led further to confusion over its "study" versus its "action" functions. CODAF's roles also overlapped with the bureaucratic prerogatives of other U.S. agencies, and included an unclear relationship to the Department of State. Then there were congressional restrictions placed on funding CODAF, and presidential attention declined after its creation and especially after the change of presidency in 1969. Finally, there was a lack of cooperation between the two countries apart from the exchange of information during periodic meetings of their representatives. In short, CODAF may have been a good idea. But without the presidential commitment and resources that had allowed the establishment of CODAF, it fell prey to organizational jealousies, congressional indifference, and the pressures of domestic interests.

Lessons may be drawn from these experiences. (1) The United States must first set out to resolve its own problems of coordination before effective negotiation and cooperation with Mexico can take place. (2) The first step toward cooperation is to develop an organizational and conceptual consensus between the two countries *before* substantive discussions take place. (3) Presidential attention and authority must be forthcoming and sustained, backed by an NSC directive or cabinet resolution. (4) The U.S. effort should be headed by an individual of high stature who has extensive bureaucratic knowledge and clout. (5) The *technical* aspects of the issues must be isolated from the *political*, as the basis for negotiations. (6) The United States must be willing to accept a bilateral and preferential framework. (7) The public nature of the dialogue must be minimized.

Such lessons could prove useful to guide the creation of new future mechanisms.[47] However, the dominant tendency within both governments favors avoiding the establishment of new mechanisms. There is widespread doubt that such a special body could be effective once created. Since no clear solutions exist for key problems in trade and migration areas, formal government-to-government negotiations might only lead to public impasse and bitterness. Moreover, apart from illegal migration, no single issue relating to Mexico has seemed sufficiently urgent and critical to require a special coordinating body within the U.S. government.[48]

The initial meeting between Presidents Carter and López Portillo in January 1977 did result in the creation of three bilateral consultative groups organized according to economic, social and political themes. These were directed to examine individual policy issues and possible options, prior to a future presidential meeting. Although the working groups held several meetings in mid-1977, their activities now appear to be suspended. On the positive side, the group meeting helped each government to identify the other's players and to form personal contacts. One meeting laid useful groundwork for the trade agreement signed in December 1977. On the other hand, these working groups were not allowed to consider the recent proposals by the Carter administration to prevent the hiring and entry of undocumented workers. The full text of the plan was provided to the Mexican government only days prior to its public release in August 1977.

V. BARGAINING, LEVERAGE, AND DEPENDENCY

A profound sense of dependency pervades Mexico's relations with the United States. The great asymmetry of power potential, and presumptions about the imbalance of influence and leverage, have inhibited Mexico from seeking to bargain and negotiate with its superpower neighbor. In addition, dependency-related beliefs within the United States have tended to amplify, and even exaggerate, the sense of influence and leverage that the United States could exert on Mexico, if need be.

Dependency is not entirely a myth. But in policy terms it is limited and negotiable. There are few, if any, ways in which the United States could inflict damage on Mexico without also harming itself. Mexico could learn better to work the U.S. system—much as some U.S. "superclients" do. Indeed, it is in U.S. interests that Mexico improve its capacities to bargain and negotiate with the United States.

THE EXAGGERATION OF DEPENDENCY

While the idea of the "special relationship" has lost favor, newer "dependency" perspectives have spread in both Mexico and the United States, particularly among policy oriented intellectuals. Accordingly, Mexico is locked structurally to the United States as a weak, dependent client-state.[49] Thus Mexico's historic yearning for a national independence is ultimately contradicted by recognition that Mexico's economic health is unwillingly linked to the U.S. economy. The evidence lies in the scale of Mexico's indebtedness to U.S. banks, reliance on the U.S. economy for imports and exports, penetration by U.S. investors in the most dynamic business sectors, and requirements for U.S. technology and tourism. Other evidence is said to lie in the manipulability of some Mexican leaders, the military weakness of Mexico, and contamination of the social fabric with U.S. cultural styles.

It is often argued by Mexicans and Americans alike that Mexico's dependency confers potentially overwhelming influence and leverage on the United States. Accordingly, reliance on U.S. trade, tourism, credits, debt financing, investment, technology, an open border, and favorable media treatment makes Mexico vulnerable to a broad range of potentially powerful instruments of control. U.S. capacity to limit imports and credit, or to curtail migration and deport aliens, represents especially great leverage.

By contrast, Mexico has virtually no effective leverage with the United States. Two significant "exports," narcotics and undocumented workers, do not represent viable foreign policy instruments. And Mexico's trade and economic policies can have relatively minor impact on the health of the giant U.S. economy. In sum, there are numerous ways in which U.S. activities could damage Mexico, but there is essentially no way in which the Mexican government could deliberately pressure its neighbor.

Many Mexicans have expressed a belief that the United States does not want, and will not allow, the development of a strong and independent neighbor. That is, U.S. security and sectors of the U.S. economy make it imperative that Mexico's course remain subordinate and closely tethered to the United States. Thus there is little that Mexico can do on its own behalf should its actions adversely affect fundamental U.S. interests. The United States can depend on bilateral relations to remain within manageable, agreeable bounds. Mexico is thought to have flexible leeway only on secondary issues.[50]

Government-to-government relations are rarely conducted in terms of who has leverage over whom. Nonetheless, the mere prospect of U.S. leverage has weighed heavily on the Mexican mind and served to condition agreeable behavior. Even though U.S. leverage may rarely be applied, the perception of dependency has constrained Mexico's freedom of action. Dependency perspectives, motivated more by nationalism than by socialist inclinations, are not necessarily inimical to the United States or to its capitalist economic practices. Nonetheless, the philosophical bases do affect pragmatic behavior. The old special-relationship idea exaggerated what the U.S. government might do for Mexico. But the existing dependency perspectives exaggerate that Mexico's internal problems stem basically from U.S. foreign relations, and that the global order must be changed in order to remedy domestic problems in Mexico. Furthermore, dependency perspectives tend to foster resentment and distrust, thereby hindering communication and cooperation. Falling prey to the dependency syndrome tends to inhibit bargaining and to blind individuals to the possibilities for managing issues and building interdependence in the face of great asymmetry.

MYTHS OF U.S. LEVERAGE

Barring reformulation of a central policy concept for U.S.-Mexico relations, Mexico's current generation of leaders may be tempted to ply modified dependency perspectives in their dealings with the United States. On the one hand, this may represent a tactic for making U.S. officials defensive and apologetic toward Mexican sensitivities. But on the other hand, by subscribing to the dependency syndrome, Mexico's leaders risk succumbing to self-fulfilling theories of their own ineffectiveness.

Some theoretical presumptions may be mythical. In the first place, the dependence of Mexico on the United States constitutes an organic or symbiotic relationship that entails significant constraints on U.S. behavior. The two countries are so deeply linked that the U.S. government is unlikely to exploit many potential levers. Punitive or discriminatory U.S. options would arouse U.S. domestic repercussions against continuation of the leverage attempt. For example, Operation Intercept in 1969 did secure Mexico's agreement to a joint anti-narcotics campaign—but it also aroused irate opposition among businessmen on the U.S. side of the border, who suffered from the disruption of Mexican tourism and commerce. Major deportations of undocumented workers would likely arouse opposition from segments of U.S. agricultural, manufacturing, and service industries. Such measures would also antagonize the Mexican American community, especially in the U.S. Southwest. In addition, many U.S. businesses might complain against U.S. measures affecting tourism, investment, or trade.

The exercise of leverage is further constrained by U.S. concerns for Mexico's stability. U.S. policymakers are sensitive not to endanger stability in Mexico and to help sustain a government there that can manage internal affairs. The United States has shown that it does not want an unstable, violence-ridden, or unfriendly country as a neighbor. This inhibits potential resort to pressures, especially in economic and financial areas, that might damage domestic stability in Mexico, especially at a time when its stability seems less secure than in the past.

In sum, the United States actually lacks instruments to hurt Mexico deliberately without also harming its own interests—a true mark of interdependence. Mexico may not be able to escape from dependency, but neither can the United States escape from interdependence.

PREFERENCE FOR STATUS QUO: AVOIDANCE OF BARGAINING

The most workable option so far, for both Mexico and the United States, has been to treat the issues one by one, in isolation from each other. As a result of sensitivities on both sides, trust has been placed in maintaining a general fabric of relations in which the issues are not deliberately threaded together, and in which negotiations and bargaining are avoided.[51] Ritual dialogue has proven safer than attempts at substantive reciprocity. Preserving the relationship has taken precedence over resolving the issues.[52]

Mexican and U.S. officials have been generally reluctant to link issues, implicitly or explicitly. Until the recent meeting between Presidents Carter and López Portillo, neither government was proposing package deals or sequential trade-offs (for example, to exchange Mexican oil exports for U.S. acceptance of other Mexican products or of a labor program agreement). The feeling in both governments is that, because the issues and people who deal with them are so disparate, failure would ultimately result from attempts to design an encompassing institutional framework or to arrange broad gauge resolutions. On the U.S. side, private domestic interests as well as bureaucratic responsibilities militate for keeping the issues separate.

In Mexico there is a tendency to suspect that possible U.S. or even Mexican initiatives to link issues would lead to risky tit-for-tat bargaining games, or even to U.S. encroachment, with Mexico ending as the loser. There is a belief that Mexico, by working to keep the issues separate, may better determine which issue comes to the fore. Mexican officials worry about taking actions in one issue area that might lead to indirect, adverse effects in another issue area.

While Mexico has hesitated in the past to negotiate issue linkages, Mexican officials have frequently viewed the United States as linking issues for purposes of pressure or retaliation. For example, a U.S. cut in Mexico's sugar quota in 1966 was said to represent retaliation against Mexico's lenient policy toward Cuba. More recently, the U.S. press announcement of major Mexican oil discoveries, nine days prior to a meeting between Presidents Echeverría and Ford, was viewed as a prelude to a U.S. proposal for trading oil and immigration preferences. Furthermore, Mexico's concern in 1976 regarding delicate negotiations with U.S. and international financial agencies evidently led Mexico to refrain from objecting to disadvantageous changes in the U.S. Immigration and Nationality Act. Mexico has been quite defensive about indications of U.S. bargaining maneuvers that seemed designed to secure access to Mexico's oil—while Mexico in turn seemed reluctant and cautious about using its oil resources as a bargaining instrument.

Some Mexicans are even doubtful that their government has the capacity to negotiate favorable agreements that resolve single issues, let alone issues linked in a larger policy package. So beyond making motions that symbolize "good" relations, they ask, why negotiate at all? In this view, it is preferable to cope with the disadvantageous but nonetheless familiar status quo, especially in regard to illegal immigration, than to risk bargaining for major changes that might ultimately benefit the United States, at the expense of Mexico.

U.S. diplomatic style also makes it very difficult for Mexico to negotiate. Accordingly, when Mexico enters negotiations, it seeks to present a single, centralized face toward the United States. But the United States presents numerous conflicting agency faces that seem to immobilize its negotiating capacity.[53] The Mexicans feel that there is no central location to go for a decision —unlike the case in their own country, where the presidency is clearly the hub of decision-making. This condition is said to have advantages for the United States. For example, when the State Department does not care to negotiate, then it can blame others for the lack of decisive action. However, when the State Department aims to negotiate, it may have great difficulty in organizing a unified position. According to Mexican complaints, the U.S. government has too many commissions and meetings to negotiate effectively, and cannot take special interests into account before beginning negotiations. Thus regarding such issues as trade and migrant labor, the United States keeps raising domestic impediments. Therefore, Mexicans raise the question, why negotiate with a party that cannot negotiate? Partly because of this perspective, Mexican officials have preferred secretive informal diplomacy, and have often regarded the U.S. Congress and media as obstacles to good relations.

Given this preference for informality and secrecy, a common Mexican line of analysis holds that the creation of a special high level post or agency within the U.S. government, or the formation of a special bilateral commission for U.S.-Mexico relations, whether focused on single or various issues, would likely produce superficial results. Such a major undertaking would likely stir new conflicts within the U.S. government and still not allow determination of a unified U.S. position before negotiations began. A public mechanism would also prove rigid and cumbersome for the Mexicans, depriving them of flexibility and requiring them to "play" at negotiations with U.S. government agencies that still lacked decision-making authority. In addition, establishment of a formal mechanism would create difficult problems of coordination among bureaucratic *feudos* within the Mexican government.

Such pessimism reinforces Mexican preferences for a piecemeal approach, that is, for being satisfied with the benefits of little achievements in some areas, such as trade, while defending the status quo in general—especially in regard to illegal immigration.

MEXICO'S NEGOTIATING STYLE

Despite a lack of general confidence, Mexico is reported to have negotiated quite skillfully with the United States on specific issues, where Mexican negotiators have adopted a resolute, pragmatic stand, and have displayed thorough technical preparation. Examples include the negotiations over the salinity dispute and, more recently, over a fisheries agreement, financing for Pemex programs, and a trade agreement.

The history of U.S.-Mexico relations has led to the development of a distinctive Mexican negotiating style, one that has in fact been very patient and tolerant toward the United States. One prominent trait is to emphasize the moral and juridical aspects of an issue. This fits within the broader foreign policy view that:

... the best, if not the only, way of maintaining Mexico's international prestige and authority is to defend firmly and perseveringly the basic principles underlying her foreign policy, placing them above circumstantial considerations of temporary values.[54]

Thus engagement of the U.S. government in the salinity negotiations depended largely on a protracted campaign that the issues were moral and juridical in nature, not simply technical as the U.S. government initially maintained.[55]

A second, more recent trait has emphasized the multilateral and international aspects of an issue. This helps Mexico to avoid settlements within a bilateral framework that might appear to favor the United States.[56] The U.S. commitment to settle the salinity problem through special bilateral negotiations was prompted in part by U.S. concern regarding a Mexican fallback proposal to engage in an international juridical action that, in the U.S. view, might turn into a lengthy and potentially acrimonious dispute.[57] The recent bilateral trade agreement was negotiated mainly in Europe, within the framework of broad multilateral trade negotiations.

Mexico's style often contains proud expressions about Mexico's national sovereignty, appeals to the reputed shame or guilt of U.S. behavior in long-past historical incidents, as well as accusations that make the United States a "scapegoat" for Mexico's internal problems. Such characterizations have sometimes helped Mexico to shape a psychological climate that induces U.S. sensitivity and responsiveness.

References to the necessity of Mexico's political and economic stability have constituted a persuasive element of Mexico's negotiating style. For example, following termination of the bracero agreement in 1964, combined Mexican and U.S. concern for Mexico's economic stability led to establishment of the Border Industrialization Program in 1965. More recently, President López Portillo has carefully warned about the risks of a "South Americanization" of Mexico's political system, should the United States prove unresponsive to Mexico's financial needs.

In sum, Mexico's style has produced successful results in some negotiations regarding some specific problem issues. Yet these tend to be the exception rather than the rule. A general lack of confidence and expertise still makes many Mexicans hesitant to promote bilateral negotiations affecting the broad range of relations.

EXPERTISE AND BARGAINING CAPACITY

A Mexico that does not understand the United States is not in the best U.S. interests. Few important countries have remained so aloof as Mexico from the American political process, and relied so strongly on personal, private, high-level contact for promoting selected government interests. If relations are to improve, Mexico in particular will need to strengthen its negotiating capacity.

Mexico could learn better how to work the U.S. system, much as other friendly countries succeed in doing at times. Some "superclients" like Israel, Iran, Cuba, as well as Finland, have succeeded in gaining "reverse leverage" and freedom of action on selected issues in their respective bargaining relations with the United States and the Soviet Union. While power relations are largely conditioned by resource differentials, the capacity of a lesser country to bargain and exercise leverage is also heavily influenced by psychological and perceptual factors that belie dependency, an ability to identify and make critical issue linkages, tactical knowledge of bureaucratic policymaking processes in the stronger power's government, and tight centralism and continuity in foreign policy decision-making within the weaker nation's government.[58] While Mexico has fallen short on all but the last account, improvements may be emerging on all accounts.

Despite proximity, the Mexicans have lacked general knowledge and training for dealing with the United States. The United States has only recently become a fit subject for academic study in Mexico's universities. Indeed, prior to the mid-1960s, specializing in the United States was somehow considered anti-Mexican, likely to make one pro-American, and thus subject to criticism by "nationalists" and leftist intellectuals. Although a school of international relations was established at the National University in the early 1950s, at present a major research focus on U.S.-Mexico relations does not exist. The most important research center is El Colegio de México, where a small group of academicians, some of them advisers to the government, has concentrated on the analysis of Mexico's foreign policy. The recent establishment of the Centro de Investigación y Docencia Económicas (CIDE), which publishes a monthly newsletter analyzing U.S. politics and foreign policy toward Mexico and the rest of Latin America, represents an innovative effort. Within the Mexican government, a new Institute of Diplomatic Studies "Matías

Romero'' was recently established as a base for some researchers and for training individuals and groups that may be sent on missions abroad. But at present the institute remains in the formative stages. Experience in foreign affairs is further hampered by the low continuity of office-holders from one administration to the next and by shifts in issue responsibilities from one office to another.

Mexico's rejection of U.S. assistance programs in the 1950s and 1960s may have deprived it, ironically, of gaining experience in how best to negotiate with the U.S. government. These economic and military aid programs were regarded in the United States as important instruments for U.S. influence and leverage abroad. But in fact many nations, ranging in size from Iran to Guatemala, used them as training and testing grounds to become quite skillful at bargaining for U.S. programs and concessions. As a result, these were sometimes larger or more advantageous than what the U.S. government originally planned to provide. Some recipients learned to ply arguments and tactics that successfully played upon the varied U.S. bureaucratic interests and rationales. In addition to acquiring familiarity with U.S. bureaucratic processes, the aid recipients also formed a range of personal contacts as reference points. While Mexico had reasons for declining or minimizing participation in such aid programs, one unexpected cost appears to be Mexico's comparatively less developed skill at diplomatic gamesmanship.

At present, Mexico is working to overcome these deficiencies in training and expertise. In particular, one notices the advancement of a new generation of elites who have worked extensively in various international banking and financial institutions.[59] In addition, the creation of international affairs offices in various ministries may also help gradually to strengthen Mexico's institutional capacity for dealing with the United States.

The centralization of foreign policymaking in Mexico's presidency may constitute an asset for influencing and bargaining with the United States. Tight centralization of decision-making around one leader and his principal advisers sometimes helps to close access points for a foreign power, thereby making it difficult for that foreign power to influence internal coalitions and mobilize in-country allies. Tight centralization sometimes enables the leading decision-maker to orchestrate issue linkages and trade-offs, and to take a firm negotiating stand that may involve a convincing demonstration of willpower. The capacity for influence and leverage often increases as the central decision-making leadership gains experience through continuity in office. These are lessons to be observed in the cases of Iran and Israel vis-à-vis the United States, and in the cases of Cuba and Finland vis-à-vis the Soviet Union.[60]

RECENT DEVELOPMENTS

Since the advent to office of Presidents Carter and López Portillo, the United States and Mexico have expressed new interests in negotiating improved, closer relations. Oil and alien migration issues have mainly motivated U.S. interests, with population pressures in Mexico being recognized as having long-range potential significance for U.S. security. Economic difficulties at home, and fear of possible U.S. measures to increase border security, have mainly motivated Mexico's interests.

Departing from Mexico's recent diplomatic style, President López Portillo has proposed examination of the "total picture." In his view, specific bilateral issues, for example, relating to trade and worker migration, should be assessed not according to individual national interests, but rather according to their impact on the U.S.-Mexico relationship as a whole. Moreover, the assessment should recognize the interconnections among issues in the relationship. Mexico, he has suggested, might be willing to consider a "package" approach to some issues. Indeed, Mexico has begun to clarify just what specifically it would like the U.S. government to do about improving relations. Mexico also appears newly receptive to the idea of a Marshall-like plan for developing rural areas where poverty and unemployment cause labor migration to the United States. In the area of energy, however, the Mexican government is finding it easier and less constraining to deal with the U.S. private sector than with the U.S. government regarding the development of Mexico's petroleum and gas fields.

Although Mexico has lacked resource leverage since World War II, the newly discovered oil and gas reserves give Mexico renewed strategic significance to the United States. Mexicans are very sensitive to the potential risks as well as benefits that may extend from the renewed strategic significance of their territory. On the negative side, some Mexicans claim that petroleum development will only increase national dependency on the United States. On the positive side, the observation is pertinent that:

> Whatever may be the strategic value of Mexico for the United States, it is well to remember that historically this value has increased in times of world and hemispheric political crises, and has consequently decreased in periods of world and regional political stability. One can conclude, then, that Mexico increases or diminishes its bargaining capacity with the United States according to these changes.[61]

Thus in view of the worldwide petroleum situation, Mexico's oil may represent an important bargaining chip, if the Mexican government so desires, and if Mexico's domestic economic and political conditions permit its use as such.[62] While Mexico has not yet determined how best to make use of this instrument, it will have to be careful not to exaggerate its leverage potential and not to adopt hard-bargaining tactics that offend the United States.

Issue linkages could represent the keys to managing and improving future interdependence. It is important to understand—and both governments do understand—that causal interactions connect many bilateral issues, such that a move in one issue area often affects others. The perception of linkages also raises a possibility of bargaining for trade-offs that may allow mutual gains.

Whether to link or separate issues is a fundamental question for negotiators in both countries. In general terms, the functioning of bureaucracies depends upon the technical separation and compartmentalization of issues. The linking of issues represents an essentially political act that often confounds bureaucracies and requires handling at the highest levels of government, namely the White House or the Cabinet. Perceiving this significance of issue linkages, wily leaders of some foreign governments have posed issue linkages precisely in order to demand attention from the White House, or else to impel middle-level officials to make a favorable response that fulfills their bureaucratic responsibility to keep issues from going to higher levels.

In recent years, the Kissinger approach made grand use of linkage politics. As a result, the bureaucracy often played marginal roles on key issues whose management was centralized and privatized within the White House. However, the change of administrations has brought a new perspective into power, represented in particular by participants from the Trilateral Commission. The trilateralists have advocated isolating the issues, giving their elements a technical definition, and avoiding issue linkages. This approach has in effect returned the issues to the bureaucracy. Thus, ironically, Mexico has moved toward a linkage perspective just as the United States has chosen to usher it out. Nonetheless, Mexico's promotion of the linkage perspective may help it to work higher levels of the U.S. government as other U.S. allies have succeeded in doing.

VI. A PROPHECY OF FAILURE

Some recent signs suggest a hopeful future for U.S.-Mexico relations. Numerous ideas are floating, in the respective governments and elsewhere, regarding possible policy measures to ameliorate bilateral problems. These ideas presently include selective trade accommodations and large co-sponsored development programs. The $99 million trade agreement signed in December 1977 represents a fruitful outcome to earlier discussions between Presidents Carter and López Portillo. It provides some evidence that an atmosphere of mutual concern and cooperation may be emerging between the two administrations. In addition, the recent formation of a bilateral consultative mechanism, as well as separate U.S. efforts to create the Southwest Economic Development Region, a border management agency, and an interagency task force on immigration, will all help institutionalize attention to U.S.-Mexico relations, and to provide contact points for Mexican officials as well as for the growing Chicano population in the American Southwest.

The lessons of history promise a hopeful future. Despite predictions of imminent crisis in times past, Mexico's political and economic systems have always managed to maintain their remarkable resilience, owing in part to the skill of Mexico's leadership and the patience of its peoples. Past crises never proved so serious as observers sometimes feared. Nor did U.S.-Mexico relations ever turn irreconcilable. Thus, even though difficulties within Mexico and in U.S.-Mexico relations may sharpen, they will not necessarily result in crisis or failure.

Now as in the past, a convincing case cannot be made that Mexico and/or U.S.-Mexico relations are necessarily entering a critical phase that will require unusual measures. Now as in the past, skillful leadership within Mexico and the United States could make obsolete any prophecy of failure.

While acknowledging that unqualified pessimism seems unwarranted, we nonetheless choose to pose a prophecy of "failure." This prophecy of failure extends from the prospect that, in the absence of joint presidential attention, the dominant issues will be approached in a bureaucratic and protectionist manner within each government. Indeed, apart from the December 1977 trade agreement and loans after the 1976 peso devaluation, we are not aware of any serious bilateral measures being taken to surmount the policymaking constraints identified above. In the area of government-to-government relations, impasse and cosmetics seem the most likely outcome. A combination of factors—Mexico's penchant for defensive closet diplomacy, its preference for the status quo in key areas, the pathology for avoiding displays of close cooperation with the United States, and a sense of dependency that inhibits bargaining—all lead to doubt that Mexico possesses the will and capacity to develop a strategy that will be effective in Washington. Another combination of U.S. factors—the priority given domestic and multilateral perspectives, the compartmentalization of issues, the absence of a bilateral policy concept, and the assumption of great leverage—all instill further doubt that the U.S. government possesses the will and capacity to manage and promote interdependence with Mexico. The main areas of exception to such doubts would be the protection of existing investments and efforts to secure access to Mexico's oil and gas resources.

Even with presidential attention, the more divisive issues will still entail great symbolic and substantive difficulties. As one U.S. official remarked to us, effective policy coordination can only take place at the presidential level—but by the time a Mexico-related issue gets to the White House, it is usually too late to adopt a bilateral framework. There is even a risk that once a U.S. president directs his attention to settling U.S.-Mexico issues, Mexico will not be prepared to respond. For one thing, an eager United States could overwhelm Mexico with plans and data.

Mexico may simply give an appearance of favorable response, while it seeks to keep the United States at a distance and to isolate Mexico's domestic problems from public debate in the United States.

Preserving a sense of neighborly relations, in part through appeal to transcendant symbolism, should prove much easier than managing the substance of specific issues. Public discussion of substantive bilateral issues would only lead to exposure of controversial domestic problems, which both governments would rather avoid.

The illegal immigration issue, assuming priority on the U.S. agenda, involves the most sensitive human and symbolic questions. Thus it could become a "lightning rod" for the entire U.S.-Mexico relationship, unless carefully handled within Congress as well as within the executive branch. The congressional structure, like the federal bureaucracy, tends to fragment issue elements among various committees and sub-committees. But unlike the case with the executive branch, the public nature of congressional deliberations is highly exposed to media propagation. Spirited congressional debate is inherently contradictory to Mexico's diplomatic style, which traditionally seeks to avoid the arousal of U.S. public passions while dealing mainly with the executive branch.

Current efforts by the Carter administration to legislate a program package to deal with the undocumented worker will eventually require the cooperation of the Mexican government. Not only will the Mexican government find it difficult to assess the economic and political implications of the current proposals, but the uncertainty about the actual consequences of such a policy package may well compel the Mexican government to take a strictly defensive posture in order to buy time and hopefully forestall unilateral decisions by the United States.

What would some elements of "failure" look like? First, bilateral issues would translate into increasingly controversial discussion of each other's domestic conditions, especially concerning social issues. In addition, issues presently regarded as separable and economic in nature would begin fusing together as sociopolitical issues, thereby becoming less amenable to traditional diplomacy. This would especially affect the border areas, where present demographic and economic trends augur serious future problems, and where the influence of Washington and Mexico City often seems remote. Furthermore, possible instability resulting from "failure" of the Mexican Revolution cannot be discounted.

Virtually all trends indicate that socioeconomic interdependence will grow and grow, and that neither the United States nor Mexico can, or should, escape from having close, interdependent relations. Mexico might conceivably try to diminish U.S. dependency by using the oil resources—the "wild card" in Mexico's game—to expand business protectionism and economic nationalism at home. But such a move would risk retarding economic growth, while leading to increased technology imports from the United States, as well as stirring protectionist U.S. countermoves against Mexico's agricultural exports. On the other hand, should the United States manage to curtail labor migration at the border, economic necessities would likely drive Mexico to require increased U.S. investment and trade. Thus an initial U.S. measure to put boundaries between the two countries would only result in the expansion of other linkages.

The critical question is not whether U.S.-Mexico interdependence will be close and consequential. The critical question is whether U.S.-Mexico interdependence will be cooperative and manageable for their respective governments and for the private sectors.

Notes

1. George W. Ball, *Diplomacy for a Crowded World* (Boston: Little, Brown and Company, 1976), p. 250.

2. Sources regularly consulted regarding most issues include: *Comercio Exterior de México*, a monthly publication of the Banco Nacional de Comercio Exterior, S.A.; *Review of the Economic Situation of Mexico*, a monthly publication of the Banco Nacional de México, S.A.; and the *Quarterly Economic Review of Mexico*, published by the Economist Intelligence Unit, Ltd., London.

An earlier and still informative discussion of a range of bilateral issues is Lyle C. Brown and James W. Wilkie, "Recent United States–Mexican Relations: Problems Old and New," in *Twentieth-Century American Foreign Policy*, eds. John Braeman et al. (Columbus: Ohio State University Press, 1971), pp. 378–419.

3. The regime of former President Luis Echeverría, noted for its nationalistic bent, promulgated important new codifications, consisting of the Law to Promote National Investment and Regulate Foreign Investment, the Law on the Transfer of Technology, and a Law on Patents and Trademarks. These created a set of new

institutions, notably the National Commission on Foreign Investment, the National Registry of Foreign Investments, and the National Registry of Technology Transfer.

4. Cabinet changes in Mexico in December 1977, eliminating two top economic advisers, reflected internal controversies regarding IMF constraints on government budgetary policies.

5. These publicized dollar figures should be regarded as rough conversions from estimates in pesos. For example, Pemex currently estimates its investment program at 310 billion pesos. The total Pemex budget will amount to some 900 billion pesos. The estimate for export earnings runs about 450 billion pesos.

6. Pemex also exports technology abroad, including two petrochemical plants to be constructed in the United States.

7. These import restrictions in turn motivate significant smuggling operations.

8. See Thomas G. Sanders, *The Modern Agricultural Sector of Sinaloa and Mexico's Population Growth*, Fieldstaff Reports, North American Series, vol. 3, no. 1 (1975). Sanders has produced a wide range of useful and informative Fieldstaff Reports from Mexico.

9. The standard U.S. work is Donald W. Baerresen, *The Border Industrialization Program of Mexico* (D.C. Heath Company, 1971). Some critical but interesting material appears in "Hit and Run: U.S. Runaway Shops on the Mexican Border," *NACLA's Latin American and Empire Report* (July-August 1975).

10. Donald W. Baerresen, "Unemployment and Mexico's Border Industrialization Program," *Inter-American Economic Affairs* (Autumn 1975): 79-90, stipulates that elimination of item 807.00 would severely harm Mexico's program and stimulate U.S. investors to transfer assembly operations to other foreign countries—without necessarily increasing U.S. employment. However, a calculated increase in U.S. import duty rates, combined with retention of item 807.00, would stimulate U.S. investors to shift overseas assembly operations into Mexico, and would benefit employment in both the United States and Mexico—while still leading to a decline in the total value of U.S. imports under item 807.00.

11. The U.S. Bureau of Census classifies nearly 30 percent of the Mexican American population located in the region as living below the poverty level. Regarding the adverse effects of the Southwest rural economy on Chicanos, and the related impact of undocumented workers, see Vernon M. Briggs, *Chicanos and Rural Poverty* (Baltimore: Johns Hopkins University Press, 1973); and Briggs, "The Mexico-United States Border: Public Policy and Chicano Economic Welfare," monograph (University of Texas at Austin, 1974).

12. Both U.S. and Mexican officials in the field along the border see some contradiction between Mexico's antidrug cooperation with the United States and the lack of similar U.S. cooperation to halt contraband flowing into Mexico.

13. Meanwhile, state and municipal organizations joining both sides of the border—including the Commission of the Californias, the Arizona-Mexico Commission, the Good Neighbor Commission of Texas, and the binational Border Cities Association—have served as useful communications networks outside the federal framework.

14. See Frank del Olmo, "The Border: A Promising *Sexenio*," *Nuestro* (December 1977):54-55.

15. See the interview with Mexico's Director of Tourism, Guillermo Rosell de la Lama, *San Diego Union*, 9 May 1977, p. B-3.

16. Recently published studies on illegal migration to the United States include: Jorge Bustamante, "Impact of Undocumented Immigration from Mexico on the U.S.-Mexico Economies," in *Fronteras 1976* (Proceedings of a Conference on the International Border in Community Relations, San Diego, California, November 19-20, 1976), pp. 28-50; Wayne A. Cornelius, *Mexican Migration to the United States: The View from Rural Sending Communities* (Cambridge: Migration and Development Study Group, Massachusetts Institute of Technology, June 1976); David S. North and Marion F. Houston, *The Characteristics and Role of Illegal Aliens in the U.S. Labor Market: An Exploratory Study* (Washington, D.C.: Linton and Company, Inc., 1976); *Domestic Council Committee on Illegal Aliens: Preliminary Report* (Washington, D.C.: U.S. Department of Justice, Office of Policy and Planning, December 1976); Joyce Vialet, *Illegal Aliens: Analysis and Background* (Washington, D.C.: Congressional Research Service, Library of Congress, February 1977).

17. Some controversial legal aspects of the Carter plan are discussed by Arturo Gándara, *The Chicano/Illegal-Alien Civil Liberties Interface* (Rand Corporation, P-6037, November 1977).

18. We would like to raise a potentially controversial idea not seen elsewhere. Our idea amounts essentially to legitimizing and controlling the illegal migration, on a pay-as-you-go basis, by charging an official fee for a temporary work permit.

For example, the fee might be set in accordance with the going rates for smuggling and deportation. At present, smugglers charge about $200 to transport an individual into the United States. The INS estimates that apprehension and deportation cost about $223 per individual. These considerations suggest institutionalizing a system whereby a certain number of temporary work permits (say for six months) may be "rented" by individuals who are required to pay a flat rate (say $200), which is refundable upon relinquishing the work permit by its expiration date. The permit could be used for identification purposes with prospective employers. If the individual does not relinquish the permit and return to his/her country with the valid time period, he/she would forfeit the security deposit.

While other elaborations come to mind, our basic point is to propose discussing the potential usefulness of converting the illegal migration phenomenon into a legal public enterprise that pays for itself. Any surplus funding might be dedicated to economic development projects along the border; other uses are also imaginable.

19. *White Paper on Drug Abuse, A Report to the President from the Domestic Council Drug Abuse Task Force* (Washington, D.C., September 1975).

20. A brief overview of U.S.-Mexico drug cooperation efforts and problems is provided in *The Shifting Pattern of Narcotics Trafficking: Latin America, Report of a Study Mission to Mexico, Costa Rica, Panama, and Colombia* (House Committee on International Relations, U.S. Congress, Washington, D.C., May 1976).

Useful material appears in Richard B. Craig, "*La Campaña Permanente:* Mexico's Anti-Drug Campaign" (Paper presented at the Annual Meeting of the Latin American Studies Association, Atlanta, Georgia, March 25-28, 1976). The paper provides findings from extensive field research in drug-producing areas of Mexico.

21. Economic growth is not a sure sign of political stability—the violent disturbances in 1968 and prior incidents in 1967 occurred during years of relatively good economic performance in Mexico.

22. On methods of control and co-optation, see David Ronfeldt, *Atencingo: The Politics of Agrarian Struggle in a Mexican Ejido* (Stanford: Stanford University

Press, 1973) updated and published in translation as *Atencingo: La política de la lucha agraria en un ejido mexicano* (México: Fondo de Cultura Económica, 1975). Also see Evelyn P. Stevens, *Protest and Response in Mexico* (Cambridge: Massachusetts Institute of Technology Press, 1974).

23. This cursory, simplified description draws on the standard U.S. bibliography on Mexico. It includes works by Roger Hansen, Frank Brandenburg, L. Vincent Padgett, James Wilkie, Martin Needler, Robert Scott, and numerous others whose full citations are readily available.

Recently revisionist writings from Mexico have emanated mainly from El Colegio de México and the Instituto Mexicano de Estudios Políticos, and include works by individuals too numerous to summarize briefly.

24. Peter S. Smith, "Continuity and Turnover within the Mexican Political Elite, 1900-1971," in *Contemporary Mexico: Papers of the IV International Congress of Mexican History*, eds. James W. Wilkie et al. (Berkeley: University of California Press; México: El Colegio de México, 1976), pp. 167-86, finds that private business and public sector elites come from dissimilar socioeconomic and educational backgrounds.

25. In the original formulation by Frank Brandenburg, *The Making of Modern Mexico* (Englewood Cliffs: Prentice Hall, 1964), the "revolutionary family" was said to consist of a top level, composed of the president and his inner council, a second level consisting of important interest group leaders, and a third level corresponding to the government bureaucracy and related formal organizations. What seems to be evolving now, more than ten years after Brandenburg's formulation, is that the formal administrative apparatus is surpassing the interest groups in policymaking importance.

26. On the continuing residual political roles of the army, see David Ronfeldt, "The Mexican Army and Political Order Since 1940," in *Armies and Politics in Latin America*, ed. A.F. Lowenthal (New York: Holmes and Meier, 1976), pp. 291-312. Also see Guillermo Boils, *Los militares y la política en México, 1915/1974* (México: Ediciones "El Caballito," 1975).

27. Cornelius, *Mexican Migration*.

28. Venezuela's large oil revenues have made little impact on its rural conditions.

29. The frequent artificiality of the foreign-domestic dichotomy receives a valuable discussion by Bayless Manning, "The Congress, the Executive, and Intermestic Affairs: Three Proposals," *Foreign Affairs* (January 1977): 306-24.

30. From an interview reported in *Christian Science Monitor*, 14 September 1977.

31. From an interview by Frank del Olmo, *Los Angeles Times*, 26 April 1977.

32. A view in Mexico claims that the "real" special relationship consists of U.S. financial loans and opportunities for U.S. businessmen. In other words, the respective private sectors have attained a more authentic special relationship than have the two governments.

Another depiction of the "real" special relationship consists essentially of the U.S. private sector and the Mexican government.

33. For ex-Secretary of State Henry Kissinger, successful negotiation of the salinity issue reportedly demonstrated that dialogue could be useful and thereby helped give him cause to initiate the New Dialogue with Latin America in general.

The broader point that Mexico has often been the anvil of U.S. diplomacy toward Latin America, a point made originally by Frank Tannenbaum in 1948, is reiterated by Robert E. Quirk, "Mexico and the United States," in *The Caribbean: Mexico Today*, ed. A. Curtin Wilgus (Gainesville: University of Florida Press, 1963), pp. 193-98.

34. Translated from Mario Ojeda, *Alcances y limites de la politica exterior de México* (México: El Colegio de México, 1976), p. 94.

Another good source is Olga Pellicer de Brody, *México y la revolución cubana* (México: El Colegio de México, 1972), and her article, "Mexico in the 1970s and its Relations with the United States," in *Latin America and the United States: The Changing Political Realities*, eds. Julio Cotler and Richard R. Fagen (Stanford: Stanford University Press, 1974). Useful background and analysis also appear in Richard R. Fagen, "The Realities of U.S.-Mexican Relations," *Foreign Affairs* (July 1977):685-700.

35. The observation that younger elite generations push themselves to the top of the political system in Mexico by taking advantage of new rhetoric and new problems and issues is presented by James W. Wilkie in his statement before Hearings of the Subcommittee on Inter-American Relationships of the Joint Economic Committee, *Recent Developments in Mexico and Their Economic Implications for the United States*, 95th Cong. (Washington, D.C.: U.S. Government Printing Office, 1977). [Editors' note: See the paper by the author included in this volume.]

36. See Jorge Castañeda, "Revolution and Foreign Policy: Mexico's Experience," *Political Science Quarterly* (September 1963): 391-417.

37. The demise of democratic governments in Latin America has made Mexicans all the more wary about the potential for political instability and authoritarian rule in their country as well—"South Americanization," President López Portillo called it. Mexico's political system is not a liberal democracy. Nonetheless, as the renowned Mexican political analyst Daniel Cosío Villegas has stated in *American Extremes* (Austin: University of Texas Press, 1964), p. 52:

> The United States can be sure of one thing as far as Mexico is concerned. This country, poor and sluggish if you will, lives for one reason alone, with one sole end: to achieve, to practice, and to live liberty and democracy. All our history is but one long effort to achieve this end. And if there is one way of definitely alienating the friendship and admiration of Mexico, it is by convincing it that only here, in Mexico, may a Mexican live as he likes.

38. While mechanisms exist in Washington for coordination among federal agencies, mechanisms for federal-state coordination are lacking. Title V legislation and related activities under the Department of Commerce will bring changes in this area.

39. This fits with a broader projection of U.S. domestic agencies into foreign affairs. See Manning, *op. cit.* from footnote 29. According to Joseph S. Nye, Jr., "Independence and Interdependence," *Foreign Policy* (Spring 1976):130-61.

> These miniature foreign offices that domestic agencies have developed for dealing with the international aspects of issues with which they are concerned are not merely bureaucratic nuisances. They are needed in the man-

agement of interdependence issues that are both domestic and foreign. As the entire government becomes involved in "international" affairs, it becomes more difficult to reserve a separate section of the agenda for the State Department (p. 138).

40. Differences between the Office of the U.S. Special Representative for Trade Negotiations (SRT) and the Department of State provide an illustration. In recent years SRT has encouraged Mexico to adopt a multilateral trade perspective. The Mexican government has generally preferred (not being a member of GATT) to seek special bilateral arrangements with the United States. SRT has generally resisted efforts by the State Department and the Mexican government to discuss "special" trade concessions.

41. For example, for over a year the Mexican government sought to obtain a quota-free status for *cajeta*, a product made from goat's milk. The lack of follow-up consultations, and pressures, in part from the Mexican embassy, resulted in prolongation of a decision that would mean additional foreign exchange earnings for Mexico. In the words of one U.S. Treasury official, "The U.S. Government expects other countries to 'work' the U.S. system to their own interests. Mexico is not very effective at 'working' the U.S. system."

42. Examples of deficient coordination also occur between the U.S. Embassy in Mexico City and U.S. officials dispatched from Washington agencies—but to a lesser degree.

43. A general assessment that does not mention specific countries is Roger E. Sack and Donald L. Wyman, "Latin American Diplomats and the United States Foreign Policymaking Process," in *Appendices: Commission on the Organization of the Government for the Conduct of Foreign Policy*, vol. 3 (Washington, D.C.: U.S. Government Printing Office, 1975), pp. 243-47.

44. In the aftermath of a 1943 wartime meeting between Presidents Roosevelt and Avila Camacho (the first time that a U.S. president had officially entered Mexico and only the second time that the presidents of the two countries had met face-to-face), a Mexican-North American Commission on Economic Cooperation was set up to study problems and coordinate programs that required the cooperation of the two nations. The commission requested opinions from technicians and industrialists and made recommendations for bilateral policies. As a result, ". . . American technicians and experts . . . swarmed into Mexico and began, with the enthusiastic cooperation of their Mexican counterparts, to tinker with Mexican social and economic mechanisms." From Howard F. Cline, *The United States and Mexico*, rev. ed. (New York: Atheneum, 1968), p. 273.

45. Neither the Interparliamentary Group nor the existing drug "cooperation" program are seen as significant models of bilateral mechanisms for resolving issues. The periodic meetings between members of the respective legislative bodies are primarily symbolic and procedural, not substantive. The Mexicans have often used their congressional contacts to convey concern on such matters as the 1971 tax surcharge, Operation Intercept, the Chamizal, water salinity, and the recent letter signed by seventy-six U.S. congressmen about "communism" in Mexico. The Mexicans believe that their contacts have been quite useful for resolving the issue at hand. Nonetheless, Congress is not the place to base any new mechanism.

The drug "cooperation" program is seen in Mexico largely from the perspective of tacit threat bargaining in the aftermath of Operation Intercept. The Mexicans were provided with two choices in 1969: (1) continue to minimize antidrug efforts and cooperation with the U.S. and be open to periodic border closures that disrupted border economies but not the flow of heroin into the U.S., or (2) commit sizable resources for an antidrug campaign and establish open cooperation with the U.S., especially DEA, by facilitating antidrug intelligence activities and operations in Mexican territory.

Other examples of organized cooperation include the Mixed Commission on Scientific and Technical Cooperation.

46. Mexico created a special Intersecretarial Commission headed by its Ministry of Foreign Affairs. The U.S. efforts were called the Special Study Group on Illegal Immigrants from Mexico, headed by the Department of Justice, and subsequently the Interagency Committee on Mexican Migration to the United States, headed by the State Department.

The establishment of the Domestic Council Committee on Illegal Aliens was a separate, more important measure taken in response to U.S. domestic pressures.

47. The establishment of a comprehensive bilateral mechanism has been proposed from various directions in recent years including in our initial version of this paper.

Similar suggestions appear in James D. Theberge and Roger W. Fontaine, *Latin America: Struggle for Progress, Critical Choices for Americans*, vol. 14 (Lexington: Lexington Books, 1977), p. 113; and in testimony by Clark W. Reynolds, in "Hearings before the Subcommittee on Inter-American Economic Relationships," pp. 37-56.

48. At present, the Soviet Union is the only country for which the State Department contains a policy "Czar."

49. Throughout the hemisphere, a voluminous literature has blamed U.S. imperialism and Latin America's dependency for underdevelopment in the region. However, the best-selling, innovative analysis by Carlos Rangel, *Del buen salvage al buen revolucionario* (Caracas: Monte Avila Editores, 1976), maintains that these perspectives are largely incorrect and mythical, and that the burden of responsibility falls on local national elites. How one state learned to manage dependency and bargain with multinational corporations is analyzed by Franklin Tugwell, *The Politics of Oil in Venezuela* (Stanford: Stanford University Press, 1975).

50. In this spirit, Ojeda, *Alcances y límites*, has observed:

> ... The United States recognizes and accepts Mexico's need to dissent from American policies in all matters that are fundamental to Mexico, even though they may be important but not fundamental for the United States. In exchange, Mexico offers its cooperation in all matters that are fundamental or even important for the United States, even though they are not fundamental to Mexico (p. 93).

Ojeda goes on to say that:

> In consequence, the United States seems to have been willing to tolerate a dissident position on Mexico's part if this helps foster the internal political stability of the country. ... (pp. 93-94).

51. Similar patterns prevail in U.S. relations with its other neighbor, Canada. U.S. ambassador to Canada, Thomas O. Enders, "Canada and the United States:

The Framework and the Agenda," *Department of State Bulletin* (9 April 1976): 508-13, states cogently that five points of reference govern bilateral relations, including:

> Fourth, try to deal with each issue on its own terms. In the past, we've generally tried to avoid tradeoffs on unrelated questions. Of course, few decisions have been made in the Canadian Cabinet or in the U.S. administration without asking how the rest of the relationship was going. But both of us have felt that to link various issues, at different stages of ripeness, with different regional constituencies and different supporting interests would make them less solvable, not more. Some now on both sides of the border are urging us to start linking issues. That would be wrong. Across-the-border bargaining could easily produce frustration and quite possibly brawls. But it is obvious that we can avoid linkage only if we can show that good progress can be made in the case-by-case approach (p. 512).

The other points of reference are: first, consult before taking action; second, build in predictability; third, debilateralize where appropriate by using multilateral frameworks; and fifth, go for expansionary solutions by avoiding zero-sum approaches to problem issues.

52. A very good discussion of these points, as well as of others in preceding sections, is Donald L. Wyman, "Interdependence and Conflict in United States-Mexico Relations, 1920-1975," in *Diplomatic Dispute: U.S. Relations with Iran, Japan, and Mexico*, Donald Wyman et al. (Cambridge: Harvard Center for International Affairs, 1978). Wyman reaches many conclusions similar to our own.

53. At one point during the salinity negotiations in the early 1960s, the United States reportedly fielded so many positions that a State Department negotiator asked Mexico's forgiveness for not being able to adopt a single position.

54. Castañeda, "Revolution and Foreign Policy," p. 417.

55. See *La salinidad del Río Colorado: una diferencia internacional* (México: Secretaría de Relaciones Exteriores, 1975).

56. The U.S. government prefers to "debilateralize" issues in its relations with Canada as well as Mexico. See the speech by Enders, "Canada and the United States."

57. U.S. views are expressed in Herbert Brownell and Samuel E. Eaton, "The Colorado River Salinity Problem with Mexico," *American Journal of International Law* (April 1975):255-71.

58. Studies of bargaining and leverage practices between big and small powers are scarce in quantity and quality.

Significant contributions include the neglected work by Richard W. Cottam, *Competitive Interference and Twentieth Century Diplomacy* (Pittsburgh: University of Pittsburgh Press, 1971); as well as Robert O. Keohane, "The Big Influence of Small Allies," *Foreign Policy* (Spring 1971):161-82; and Robert O. Keohane and Joseph S. Nye, *Power and Interdependence: World Politics in Transition* (Boston: Little, Brown and Company, 1977). Annette Baker Fox, *The Politics of Attraction* (New York: Columbia University Press, 1977) includes extensive material on Mexico.

59. However, their experiences as economists and bankers lead them to neglect the social dimensions of problem issues.

60. The analysis of leverage/bargaining practices in these and other cases will be discussed in David Ronfeldt and Edward González, "Superclients and Superpowers: A Comparison of Iran-U.S. and Cuba-U.S.S.R. Relations" (in preparation).

The experience of Finland may be instructive for Mexico, since it too borders on a superpower. George Maude, *The Finnish Dilemma: Neutrality in the Shadow of Power* (New York: Oxford University Press, 1976).

Even more instructive comparabilities exist in Canada-U.S. relations. There too the "special relationship" is out of favor. The organizational interface is highly compartmentalized. Conflict management takes precedence over problem resolution. Issue linkages and bargaining are avoided. And both sides are very wary about establishing special institutional mechanisms. Very interesting material, potentially useful for comparing U.S.-Mexico and U.S.-Canada relations, appears in the following sources: John Sloan Dickey, *Canada and the American Presence: The United States Interest in an Independent Canada*, Council on Foreign Relations (New York: New York University Press, 1975), especially the final chapter; C. Robert Dickerman, "Transgovernmental Challenge and Response in Scandinavia and North America," *International Organization* (Spring 1976):213-40; Kal J. Holsti and Thomas Allen Levy, "Bilateral Institutions and Transgovernmental Relations Between Canada and the United States," *International Organization* (Autumn 1974):875-901; and Peyton Lyon, "The Canadian Perspective," in *Canada-United States Relations*, ed. H. Edward English, *Proceedings of the Academy of Political Sciences* 32 (1976):14-26. Also see Keohane and Nye, *Power and Interdependence*; and Wyman, "Interdependence and Conflict."

61. Ojeda, *Alcances y límites*, p. 94.

62. An interesting, wide-ranging discussion appears in Edward A. Williams, "Oil in Mexican-United States Relations: Contextual Analysis and Bargaining Scenario" (unpublished manuscript, 1977).

3
Mexico and United States Relations: Interdependence or Mexico's Dependence?

Mario Ojeda Gómez

Most analysts of contemporary international politics agree that, in general terms, the sovereignty of the nation state erodes through time as it engages in international commerce, finances, investments, and communication. The political-juridical concept of sovereignty, as conceived by its original proponents, reflected the socio-economic and political reality of its time, the result of the centuries-long process of national integration. For those theorists, and for others who followed in their steps, the most important charactcristic of sovcrcignty was thc suprcmc and indcpcndcnt authority of the king or the state, limited only by national borders and the sovereignty of other states.

This political-juridical concept of sovereignty has prevailed up to the present. The United Nations Charter, for example, is based on the principle of states' legal equality and grants an equal vote to each member-nation in the General Assembly.[1] This sanction given by the United Nations to the principle of juridical equality among states does not reflect the political reality of the world today. The actual distribution of power among nations is very different. To establish this, we only need to recall that the world is

---

Mario Ojeda Gómez is the General Academic Coordinator of El Colegio de México. This is an English translation of a paper presented at El Primer Congreso Nacional sobre Estudios Fronterizos, Monterrey, Nuevo León, México, January 1979. Translated by Roberto Sifuentes and Manuel García y Griego.
©1983 by Mario Ojeda Gómez

made up of rich and poor countries. We can see from this that the principle of juridical equality of the states is but a norm, and in truth, a goal.[2]

When the founding fathers of the concept of sovereignty developed their theory, theirs was a different political world. They were facing a new historical development, the birth of the European nation-state. With the collapse of the Holy Roman Empire, the first integrated and independent kingdoms emerged, ruled by sovereigns who exercised political control over their territories and populations.[3] Their authority flowed from having emerged victorious over both the Empire and the feudal lords, that is, they secured independence from both within and without. What remained to be resolved was the mutual recognition of this fact by the other monarchs.[4] This helps explain their concern for regulating the relations among sovereigns and coincides with the birth of international law.

Moreover, the centralized kingdoms supplanting the feudal system developed within a socio-economic context that took centuries to gestate. This context was the nation, an economically self-sufficient community, socially and culturally homogeneous.[5] This *de facto* system of economic self-sufficiency did not result from autarchic policies or a self-sufficient economic base. It reflected scarcities caused by economic backwardness, limited technological diffusion and slow international commerce. Nevertheless, self-sufficiency provided a high degree of cohesiveness and economic independence for the nation-state of that era.

The Industrial Revolution and the concomitant growth of international commerce began to erode the sovereignty of the European nation-state. Countries started to specialize in the production of certain goods, which were sold to other nations and in turn generated the impetus to buy goods from other countries. Thus, self-sufficiency began to give way to interdependence—or to dependency—since many products were either necessities no longer produced or new industrial products not domestically produced. With the passing of time it became necessary to export more, so as to import goods which were not produced internally.

While this was happening in Europe, the inhabitants of the great "vacuums of power," Africa, Asia, and what today is known as Latin America, to whom the concepts of nation-state and sovereignty were alien, were conquered by the offspring of the first centralized European kingdoms and thus incorporated into the division of labor created by the growth of international commerce. Here we note that from the very beginning, so-called economic interdependence appeared in an asymmetrical form—a context of inequality.

During the nineteenth century the European colonial metropolises exported not only manufactured goods, but also capital. This marks the beginning of the final phase of the internationalization of the world economy.

At this point we can make several observations. First, it is evident that sovereignty or full independence of the state does not exist today in its original form, given the erosion of the political and economic base which provided its support. Second, although the original independence of the state has been supplanted by a growing interdependence among industrialized nations, the process is marked by inequalities. Finally, the nations on the periphery of these industrialized economies cannot be considered as part of the above-mentioned process of growing interdependence. These nations were incorporated into the international economy in a subordinate role and their position can be best described as "dependent." This thesis will be developed in the following section.

Up to this point we have attempted to delineate the origin and meaning of the concepts of independence, interdependence and dependence. These terms, particularly interdependence, have become fashionable again, notably in the writings of analysts from the United States.

During the early 1970s, when the industrialized economies began to suffer from inflation and recession, and particularly with the so-called "energy crisis" caused by the 1973 Arab oil embargo, the concept of interdependence regained currency among analysts of international relations. Several scholars began to utilize the concept to explain not only the level of world co-penetration resulting from a growing interrelation among nations, but also the reciprocal effects and mutual influences that domestic developments within a nation have on other countries.[6] To illustrate this, one might consider a process we are presently witnessing, that is, how inflation itself has become internationalized through international commerce and finance.

Many analysts have gone as far as suggesting that the organization of world power has been altered to the extent that all states, including the great powers, are interdependent and equally vulnerable among themselves. This no doubt is a distortion of the concept arising from a wrong-headed, and perhaps literal interpretation of "interdependence," which strictly speaking means "mutual dependence." "Dependence" literally means "subjection" or "subordination." We need only common sense to note that the contemporary organization of world politics is not one of "mutual subordination."

Having stumbled upon this contradiction, some analysts prefer to label the phenomenon "asymmetric interdependence," thereby suggesting that "mutual dependency" is not the same for all states.[7] This seems to be closer to the truth, though to some extent it is a semantic contradiction. The term "interaction," used by Jorge Bustamante to describe this relationship, and strictly meaning "reciprocal influence," is a better representation of reality. This term permits one to qualify the nature of the relationship, depending on the degree to which domestic processes have an external influence, or how some political actors affect others.

One could make a case for the use of the term "co-penetration" (mutual penetration), since it permits one to establish gradations in the relationship, but to avoid further semantics we shall use the term "interdependence," modified by the adjective "asymmetric."

When viewed in this context, we might note that during the last decade there has been a notable evolution in the organization of world politics. The bipolar arrangement that emerged from World War II, i.e., the concentration of power in the United States and the Soviet Union, gave way to another which tends to be multipolar or pluralistic and takes into account the relative distribution of world economic power. China, France, Germany, Japan, and to a lesser extent Great Britain and Italy have gained a measure of political independence once they achieved post-war economic recovery. From a military perspective the organization of world politics is still bipolar, given that only the United States and the Soviet Union have the capability to engage in an intercontinental nuclear conflict, either as a preventative or as a postmortem strategy.

Moreover, we might note that the oil-exporting countries have also advanced their standing in international politics as a result of their control, to a significant extent, of a product with great worldwide demand, given its relative scarcity, and strategic, economic, and military importance.

For most other countries, the gap in terms of political and economic power between them and the rest of the world has either remained the same or widened. What *has* occurred is that the cold war has thawed somewhat and this has allowed these countries a greater degree of flexibility and some diversity in their international relations.

The impression—and in some cases incautious optimism—left in the minds of some analysts by the growing international multipolarity, due to the thawing of the cold war, and more specifically the Arab oil embargo, caused them to prematurely conclude that the interdependence among the large industrial countries could be used to describe the relations of these countries with middle powers who are not necessarily oil exporters. This was the case of the United States-Mexico relationship. In this vein, and even before Mexico became a significant exporter of oil, several authors (particularly North Americans), impressed by the effects the domestic policies of each country has on the other, concluded that the Mexican-U.S. relationship fits a framework of interdependence. Some scholars attribute a broad socio-economic meaning to the concept of interdependence, referring generally to the impact or repercussions which events or domestic policies have on the other country (domestic linkages).[8] Other scholars perceived it as the bargaining leverages at the disposal of either one of the two governments.[9]

Though the degree of interaction between the United States and Mexico has reached a point where events in either society and policies adopted by either government affect the other, the central thesis of this article is that the type of interdependence is asymmetric, and biased in favor of the former. In other words, relations between Mexico and the United States function within a structure of dependency, of Mexico's dependency on the United States.

As a counterexample to this thesis, one could note that a high rate of population growth in Mexico combined with a strategy of economic growth that has not emphasized labor-intensive development has increased domestic unemployment and underemployment, which have had important effects on the migration to the United States. This does not mean that transnational socioeconomic effects are felt with equal intensity in Mexico and in the United States, nor that the extent to which some industrial sectors or specific regions are thus affected are equal in both countries. For example, the present recession and inflation of the Mexican economy have had a slight impact on the United States, limited to certain segments of the U.S. economy or to certain regions of the country, such as the border cities. On the other hand, the effect that recession and inflation in the United States have on Mexico is unquestionably serious, not only because it is felt through a variety of channels, but also because it tends to affect the general economy of the country.

The asymmetry of the interdependence between the two countries is also evident when we examine the negotiating position that each of the governments assumes relative to the other, that is, the leverage that each can exert during negotiations. To elaborate on this point, we will consider a number of indicators which permit one to sketch an outline of the magnitude and relative importance that the bilateral relationship has for each of the two countries.

We will begin with the obvious. On one side we have the United States: the richest and most powerful country in the world with a territory of more than eight million square kilometers, rich in natural resources, with a population of more than 200 million, a GNP that exceeds one trillion dollars and an average per capita income that surpasses eight thousand dollars. On the other side we have Mexico: a middle power, a developing country with a territory of two million square kilometers, well-endowed in natural resources, rich in variety but mostly poor in abundance, with serious social deficiencies, a rapidly growing population of 67 million people, a 1977 GNP of 70 billion dollars and an average per capita income of 1,100 dollars. This means, in principle, that Mexico is the weaker partner in the relationship.

In addition to the fact that Mexico is the weaker element in this equation, Mexico also depends more on the United States than the United States depends on Mexico. In other words, the relation between the United States and Mexico is much more important for Mexico than for the United States.

For example, with respect to commerce, the United States is Mexico's most important trade partner. There is a large gap between the U.S. and the country in second place. In 1975, the United States absorbed 60 percent of Mexico's exports and provided 62 percent of its imports.[10] Japan, the second-ranking trade partner, provided only 4.4 percent (imports and exports added) of Mexico's international commerce. Even when blocs of countries are grouped together, trade proportions are modest. The European Common Market and the Latin American Free Trade Association participated with 14.5 percent and 7.3 percent respectively (imports and exports added).[11]

In contrast, Mexico's importance to the United States in international commerce is secondary. The fact that Mexico occupies fourth place in the world as a client of the United States and fifth as a supplier should not confound us. Although Mexico occupies these rankings, it is only because of the high degree of diversification in U.S. international commerce. Actually, Mexico absorbed 4.7 percent of U.S. exports in 1975 and provided 3.1 percent of U.S. imports (see table 1).

This does not mean that from a U.S. perspective Mexican trade is negligible. On the contrary, Mexico has constantly maintained a deficit in its balance of trade with the United States which has meant that during the 1970s the United States accumulated a trade balance of more than ten billion dollars in its favor.[12] But, while this is a favorable transaction from the U.S. point of view—giving Mexico some leverage[13]—one should not draw the conclusion that the United States is more dependent on Mexico, when it is in fact the opposite. We should underscore what has already been noted: that commerce with Mexico is only marginal (4.7 percent of the total exports and 3.1 percent of the imports) to the United States, while for Mexico, commerce with the United States is of fundamental importance (60 percent imports and 62 percent exports). But this difference in relative importance of commerce for each country can be better appreciated when we consider the composition of exports and imports. It can be said in general that (excluding oil), Mexico exports non-essential goods to the United States, their demand and prices fluctuating; moreover, they can easily be substituted in other markets. By contrast, Mexico imports capital goods and essential agricultural products from the United States; their acquisition cannot be interrupted without seriously affecting the country's economy and the supply of basic foodstuffs.

Tourism is yet another indicator of dependence. Even considering that the balance in this commercial transaction is favorable to Mexico, the relative importance of tourist-generated income

TABLE 1.—RELATIVE IMPORTANCE OF NATIONS AS TRADE PARTNERS
TO THE UNITED STATES IN 1975
Millions of dollars

	Volume of goods bought from U.S.	%	Volume of goods sold to U.S.	%
Canada	$ 21,743	20.2	$ 22,170	22.8
Japan	9,563	8.8	11,425	11.7
West Germany	5,194	4.8	5,400	5.5
Mexico	5,141	4.7	3,066	3.1
Great Britain	4,527	4.2	3,773	3.8
Others	61,423	57.3	51,106	53.1
Total	$107,591	100.0	$ 96,940	100.0

Source: U.S. Department of Commerce, Bureau of the Census, *Statistical Abstract of the United States, 1976.* Washington, D.C., GPO, 1976, pp. 842–845.

for each country's economy again demonstrates the disparity of the so-called interdependence.

In 1976, the number of United States tourists visiting Mexico (not taking into account the border traffic) was 2,671,851.[14] The corresponding number of Mexican travelers visiting the United States was 1,920,000 according to U.S. sources[15] and 1,817,873 according to Mexican sources.[16] These latter numbers are high when we take into account that with the devaluation of the Mexican peso that year the number of travelers had decreased from that of 1975, when 2,079,075 Mexicans visited the United States.

The first impression that these figures give us is that this exchange is disproportionate given the sizes of the populations in each country. The number of U.S. travelers to Mexico represents 1.2 percent of the total population of the United States, while the number of Mexican travelers to the United States represents 2.8 percent of the Mexican population. These numbers are more significant still when we consider that the average per capita income is eight times greater in the United States than in Mexico.

Moreover, the income that Mexico acquired from U.S. tourists visiting the country was $670 million.[17] Mexican tourists, on the other hand, spent $298 million in the U.S.[18] Therefore, the balance left by tourists favors Mexico by $372 million.

Nevertheless, these figures should not confound us; one should note that the United States was the most important contributor to tourism in Mexico (approximately 85 percent), while Mexico was the second-most important contributor to tourism in the United States, with Canada the first. In addition, tourism in Mexico has traditionally played a strategic role in the Mexican economy, serving to compensate its trade deficit. Even so, this role has declined in importance as Mexico's favorable tourist balance of trade has stopped growing as a result of the rapid growth of Mexican tourist expenditure abroad.[19]

For the United States, Mexican tourism has been of lesser importance for the country as a whole, even though for certain regions such as the border cities it has been of major importance. This can be seen clearly when we consider the extraordinary number of Mexicans who legally cross the border annually;[20] this is significantly larger than the number of U.S. citizens going south (see table 2). In truth these expenditures (tabulated as part

TABLE 2—LAND BORDER CROSSINGS
INTO THE UNITED STATES BY
U.S. AND FOREIGN CITIZENS (1975)
Millions of crossings

	Foreigners	U.S. citizens	Total
Canadian border	43.6	34.8	78.4
Mexican border	97.5	60.9	158.4
Both borders	141.1	95.7	236.8

Source: U.S. Department of Commerce, Bureau of the Census, *Statistical Abstract of the U.S., 1976*. Washington: 1976, table 171, p. 107.

of border transactions) left Mexico a favorable balance of $394 million ($1,453 million income, $1,059 million outflow) in 1977; though less than the 1976 balance which was $558 million ($1,609 million less $1051 million). This drop after the peso's devaluation suggests that the devaluation caused its most serious damage on the Mexican side of the border.

Given the importance which U.S. tourism has for Mexico, it follows that any restrictions applied by Washington or by U.S. private groups significantly reduce Mexico's income derived from tourism which, in turn, increase the nation's external debt. A concrete example of policies adopted by Washington which have affected tourism in Mexico has been the limits applied to tax-deductible conferences that can be attended outside of the United States, and the 50 percent cut in the amount of duty-free liquor each tourist can bring back into the United States. A specific example of a situation where a U.S. private group applied pressure on Mexico was the 1975 American Jewish boycott. It is also clear that the United States has on occasions been affected by measures adopted by the Mexican government. A good example of this is the devaluation of the Mexican peso, limiting the growth of Mexican tourism to the United States and the income earned through border transactions. Nevertheless, the impact was marginal since income did not drop, it merely stagnated, with the only significant impact felt in border cities.[21] In any event, it was the Mexican, not the U.S., border cities which were most seriously affected.

Another point of vulnerability is in the fact that U.S. tourism to Mexico is more sensitive to publicity campaigns and to prices in Mexico than Mexican tourism to the U.S. Besides, the tourist markets that compete with Mexico are diverse (the Caribbean, Hawaii, etc.). In contrast, 85 percent of Mexican tourism abroad goes to the United States, which underscores the greater rigidity of the Mexican tourist with respect to the destination. This may be because the average Mexican travelers are not typical tourists. Their main reason for traveling abroad seems to be for the purchase of clothes and other articles, medical check-ups, gambling casinos, and other forms of luxury consumption difficult to find in other countries nearby.[22] Thus, while the total expenditures of Mexican tourists abroad dropped from $423 to $396 million between 1976 and 1977, the expenditures of Mexican tourism in the United States remained constant at $298 million notwithstanding the devaluation of the Mexican peso.

Another index of Mexican dependency is direct investment by the U.S. The value of these investments in 1975 has been estimated at $3.2 billion, 72 percent of the total foreign direct investment.[23] Overall, direct foreign investment is not crucial to Mexico. In past years, it constituted only 5 percent of national domestic savings deposits, 8.8 percent of the savings of the private sector. In addition, the proportion contributed by foreign enterprise to the GNP in the same period was only about 13 percent.[24] However, from the perspective of its impact on the Mexican economy, the role of direct foreign investment is very important. Foreign investment has concentrated on strategic and dynamic sectors of the Mexican economy such as on manufacturing. It has been estimated that close to 65 percent of U.S. investment in Mexico is in manufacturing. Within the industry itself, foreign investment has tended to concentrate on the most dynamic and strategic branches. Studies have shown that from among the top 938 corporations measured in terms of the value of capital investment and production, 26 percent were owned by foreign capital. By focusing on the top 100 corporations in the country, we can show that 47 percent belong to foreign capital.[25] The significance of foreign investment in Mexico is enhanced when one considers that it holds a controlling interest in those industries utilizing advanced technology. It has been estimated that 53 percent of the capital goods industry is owned by foreigners.[26] To this we might add the indirect control of licenses and patents on technology in industries owned by national capital. Finally, we should not forget the effect of the inflow of new foreign investment on reducing the balance of payments required to service the external debt.

Direct investment in Mexico is only of marginal importance to the United States. This does not mean that it constitutes a transaction of negligible value. After all, in comparison with other developing countries, Mexico has provided a large and constantly growing market, domestic political stability, a favorable investment climate in spite of the regulation of foreign investment. However, the value that the U.S. receives in profits and royalties from Mexico is relatively small compared to the income earned from foreign investment in other countries. During 1975 the United States received close to $9.5 billion in profits and $4.3 billion in royalties worldwide. Mexico provided 1.6 and 3.2 percent respectively.[27]

On the other side of the coin, though not new, Mexican investment in the United States has acquired added importance as of 1976. That year marked an extraordinary flight of capital before and after the peso devaluation of August 31. That year the flight of capital was estimated as approximately $4 billion, going mostly to the U.S. To date, where this capital was invested is not known, but one may assume that most of it ended up in bank accounts or in real estate. Also unknown are the profits and what is done with them, that is, whether they are reinvested in the United States or other foreign countries, or whether they return to Mexico.[28] In 1975, however, Mexico was not receiving income earned from investments in the United States. Although only one percent of payments fell into the category "other types of investment," this amount came to the sum of 100 million dollars.[29]

Lastly, another important indicator of Mexican dependence on the U.S. is its external debt. The relative positions of the United States and Mexico are of creditor and debtor, respectively. More importantly, the United States is Mexico's principal creditor. As of the end of 1977, Mexico's public external debt amounted to $23 billion.[30] To this we can add the several billion dollar debt of the private sector. Of the total, 70 percent was contracted from U.S. public and private sources.[31]

We should note some additional information regarding the debt structure pertinent to our analysis. The growth in Mexico's external debt, both public and private, has shown a marked trend towards increasing reliance on the private sector, the banks, and the United States—a "Northamericanization" of the external debt. This trend, and the consequences of the increasingly important role of the United States as creditor of the external debt have still to be understood.[32]

It has been argued that loans from private banks are less likely to have strings than those secured through public bilateral or multilateral lending institutions. It is widely known, however, that the U.S. government has become increasingly involved in the regulation and limiting of foreign credits extended by U.S. private banks.[33] It has also been argued that, in a sense, international creditor institutions are the hostages of the debtor countries, given that they must often extend new credit to assure a stable economy and thus insure that the borrowing country is in a position to service and liquidate the old debt. Finally, it has been argued that because banks are in the business of lending money, they are the most interested parties in providing additional credit, and in seeking to avoid a situation where a foreign government may have to suspend payment.

These arguments are overstated. Notwithstanding all of the above considerations, occasional International Monetary Fund intervention for "disciplining" the debtor nation to assure financial stability and unbroken debt service cannot be avoided. Mexico is in this predicament at this time because of the enormous influence that the International Monetary Fund, the World Bank, and the Inter-American Bank have.

The previous analysis of four major indicators of dependence—commerce, tourism and border transactions, direct foreign investment and foreign debt—should be sufficient to clarify the central point of this paper: that there is a definite and unequivocal dependence of Mexico on the United States. Consequently, instead of considering new indicators of dependence, we will consider recent examples illustrating Mexico's vulnerability to pressures from the United States.

The first example, "Operation Intercept," was described by then-President Richard Nixon as "shock treatment" designed by the U.S. government to induce the Mexican government to take drastic measures against the production and smuggling of drugs entering the United States. The strategy of "Operation Intercept" was to require the strict and scrupulous inspection of all persons crossing the border into the U.S. by customs officials. As a result, border traffic came almost to a halt, and people on both sides of the border reduced their border crossings, seriously cutting into border tourism and the economies of border cities. Operation Intercept ended when Mexican authorities agreed to take measures against the production and traffic of drugs.[34]

The second example is the 10 percent surcharge approved by President Nixon in August 1971 on all imports to the United States. At that time, Mexico and Canada were the only countries that separately sought to bilaterally negotiate an exemption to the surcharge, on the basis of their geographic position and their rank as trade partners. Their proposals were rejected and they, with the rest of the world, had to live with the surtax. However, these two were among the countries that suffered the most from the surtax, due to the volume of their exports to the U.S.

The third example is the tourist boycott of Mexico initiated by Jewish groups in the U.S. as a result of Mexico's vote on the United Nations resolution which associated Zionism with racism. This boycott decreased U.S. tourism in Mexico and caused some damage to other areas of the economy.[35] Consequently, the Mexican government saw itself forced to send its Minister of Foreign Relations to Israel in order to reduce tensions and, with the same objective in mind, former President Echeverría invited a number of leaders from the U.S. Jewish community to Mexico City.[36] As a result, the effects of the boycott ameliorated somewhat for a time, though they were renewed by the criticism that the Mexican government made of the Israeli commando raid at Entebbe.[37] The matter was settled when the administration of López Portillo came to power. Perhaps the sale of Mexican oil to Israel was significant in this rectification.[38]

The final example is that of a letter sent by 76 U.S. members of Congress to President Ford, and reproduced as a paid advertisement in *The New York Times* on August 24, 1976. The letter sought to "warn" Ford that Mexico might become a "new Cuba." Its effect on Mexico is difficult to measure. It obviously fed the intense fears that were already contributing to the flight of capital from Mexico; fears that were reinforced by an internal World Bank memorandum leaked to *The Wall Street Journal* which noted Mexico's need to devalue its currency. The letter also served to confirm rumors rampant in Mexico regarding the regime's stability and which even predicted a *coup d'etat*. The letter had not only an economic but also a politically destabilizing effect.

It would be incorrect to leave the impression that Mexico is totally defenseless in its dealings with the United States. Mexico can under some circumstances attenuate to an extent the effects of unilateral actions taken by the United States and even benefit sometimes as a result.

To begin with, one should note that Mexico has special strategic value to the U.S. This value is a limitation upon its complete autonomy, but also carries some weight in negotiations on other matters. As a consequence of Mexico's strategic significance as an immediate neighbor, its economic, social and political stability are important to Washington.[39] Thus, though some political groups, or even official bodies of the U.S. government, have at times demonstrated an interest in destabilizing a specific administration, the overall view which has traditionally prevailed in the State Department is that of reinforcing and maintaining the Mexican regime in power, though under certain conditions.

One might also note that Mexico is an intermediate power in international affairs. Certain characteristics, such as being twelfth in population in the world, fifteenth in gross domestic product, having an intermediate level of development and a large market, are important in reinforcing Mexico's international bargaining position.

All of these characteristics are, as the theorists would say, international power factors. They are not, in the strictest sense, bargaining leverages which the Mexican government can employ at will in diplomatic exchanges.

For the first time in decades, Mexico seems to have an important negotiating instrument at its disposal, not only relative to the U.S., but with respect to the world in general—oil. As a result of its being a non-renewable resource, its relative scarcity, general demand, and economic significance, oil is—as the Arab countries have demonstrated—an important political tool. Yet, its effectiveness as a negotiating instrument depends upon the relative weight that the exporting country possesses as a supplier in the market of the importing country.

The case of Mexico as an oil exporter to the U.S. is illustrative in this respect. Up to now Mexico has been a marginal supplier to the U.S. market (less than 5 percent of all imports); its influence upon the U.S. has also been marginal. It would be an altogether different matter if Mexico were to become a major supplier to the U.S., as Saudi Arabia is or Iran was until recently. Such a prospect would imply political dangers. An important supplier of oil to the United States becomes ipso facto an important link in the latter's national security which, at the same time, limits the exporting country's bargaining position. Because of this oil can be a two-edged sword. Mexico should utilize its oil with great care and discretion, keeping uppermost in mind that it can be a weapon of international dimensions.

Notes

1. Félix Barra García, "La intervención tradicional y las nuevas formas de intervención," Facultad de Ciencias Políticas y Sociales, UNAM, 1971, unpublished B.A. thesis, p. 19.
2. *Ibid.*
3. *Ibid.*, p. 92.
4. George Schwarzemberger, *La política del poder* (México: Fondo de Cultura Económica, 1960), p. 75.
5. Barra García, *op. cit.*, p. 97.
6. For example, see Robert O. Keohane and Joseph S. Nye, *Power and Interdependence; World Politics in Transition* (Boston: Little & Brown, 1977); and Philip H. Trezise, "Interdependence and Its Problems," in *International Journal* 29 (Fall, 1974). For a critique of the view of interdependence expressed by authors from developed countries see the first part of Guy F. Erb and Valeriana Kallab (eds.), *Beyond Dependency* (Overseas Development Council, 1975).
7. See Annette Baker Fox, *The Politics of Attraction: Four Middle Powers and the United States* (New York: Columbia University Press, 1977).
8. David Ronfeldt and Caesar Sereseres, "The Management of U.S.-Mexican Interdependence; Drift Toward Failure?" in this volume. A similar reference is made by Stanley Ross of the University of Texas at Austin (comments made at the *Mexico Today* Symposium, New York University, New York City, November 8, 1978). For a contrasting view, see Calvin P. Blair, "Mexico: Some Recent Developments and the Interdependence Relationship with the United States," in U.S. Congress, *Recent Developments in Mexico and Their Implications for the United States; Hearings before the Subcommittee on Inter-American Economic Relationships of the Joint Economic Committee* (Washington, D.C.: Government Printing Office, 1978), pp. 355–361.
9. See, for example, the previously cited works of Ronfeldt and Sereseres, and Fox.
10. The year 1975 was chosen as base since the following years have been very atypical because of the devaluation of the peso in 1976.
11. Banco Nacional de Comercio Exterior, *México 1976* (México: Banco Nacional de Comercio Exterior, 1976), table 4, p. 227.

12. Samuel I. del Villar, "Conflicto de intereses en el mercado México-estadunidense de energéticos," El Colegio de México, November, 1978. Unpublished manuscript.

13. Traditionally, Mexico has traded with the U.S. with relative success insofar as exports are concerned, making note of the fact that it is one of its principal buyers. Consequently, to maintain its import capacity in the U.S. market, Mexico needs to sell more to the United States.

14. Banco de México, *Encuestas turismo receptivo* (México: Subdirección de Investigación Económica y Bancaria, 1978), p. 6. (Cuaderno 1976-77).

15. U.S. Department of Commerce, *Mexico: A Study of the International Travel Market* (Washington, D.C.: Department of Commerce, 1977), p. 3.

16. Banco de México, *Encuestas turismo egresivo* (México: Subdirección de Investigación Económica y Bancaria, 1978), p. 37. (Cuaderno 1970-77).

17. Banco de México, *op. cit.*, (1976-77), p. 6.

18. *Ibid.*, p. 19.

19. The balance of trade in 1974 was $507 million in Mexico's favor though it declined since, the devaluation of the peso notwithstanding. Nevertheless, it was expected that this amount would be surpassed in 1978, given that during the first eight months of that year, the favorable balance was about $401 million according to preliminary figures. See the official notice in *Proceso*, no. 111 (December 18, 1978):32.

20. Apparently, many cross legally into the U.S. but later work in that country without the necessary documentation. See Jorge Bustamante, "Commodity Migrants: Structural Analysis of Mexican Immigration to the United States," in Stanley Ross (ed.), *Views Across the Border: The United States and Mexico* (Albuquerque: University of New Mexico Press, 1978).

21. See the statements of Representative Gillis W. Long and Senator Lloyd Bentsen during the Congressional hearings cited above. U.S. Congress, *op. cit.*, pp. 85 and 87 respectively.

22. The distribution of tourist expenditures by Mexicans in the United States is, on the average, 31 percent in the purchase of souvenirs and gifts, 18 percent in entertainment, 29 percent in room and board, and 13 percent in secondary transportation. See: U.S. Department of Commerce, *op. cit.*, p. 18.

23. Blair, *op. cit.*, table 3, p. 361.

24. Bernardo Sepúlveda and Ali Chumacero, *La inversión extranjera en México* (México: Fondo de Cultura Económica, 1973), pp. 54-55.

25. Ricardo G. Cinta, "Burguesía nacional y desarrollo," in *El perfil de México en 1980* (México: Siglo XXI, 1972), vol. III.

26. *Ibid.*

27. Blair, *op. cit.*, table 4, p. 361.

28. Nevertheless, the Mexican Secretary of the Treasury recently stated in a speech before the Partido Revolucionario Institucional (PRI) that the flight of capital has been overcome. See: *Excélsior*, December 13, 1978.

29. Blair, *op. cit.*, table 4, p. 361.

30. Banco de México, *Informe Anual; 1977* (México: Banco de México, 1978), p. 91.

31. Rosario Green, "La dependencia financiera de México frente a Estados Unidos: algunas consecuencias." Unpublished manuscript, El Colegio de México, December, 1978, p. 1.

32. *Ibid.* In the past, the greater part of the public external debt had been contracted through international public institutions, principally the World Bank and the Inter-American Development Bank.

33. *Ibid.*

34. For a review of the details and consequences of "Operation Intercept," see "Secuelas de la intercepción," in *Comercio Exterior* 19 (November, 1969):864.

35. The gross income due to tourism in 1974 was $842 million. This dropped in 1975 and 1976 to $800 and $835 million, respectively. It is difficult, however, to attribute all of this decline to the Jewish boycott, given that by that time Mexican tourist services had become expensive due to the over-evaluation of the peso.

36. See *Excélsior*, December 5, 8 and 11 of 1975, respectively.

37. *Moment, the New Magazine for America's Jews*, published in Newton, Mass. 2 (September, 1976):3.

38. *The New York Times*, March 11, 1978.

39. I have analyzed this importance in another study. See: *Alcances y límites de la política exterior de México* (México: El Colegio de México, 1976), pp. 87–94.

4
The Future of Mexican–U.S. Relations and the Limits of the Rhetoric of "Interdependence"

Carlos Rico F.

INTRODUCTION

The last few years have witnessed the emergence of a tendency in the United States, and in some Mexican circles, to discuss the relations between both countries—at least at the level of political discourse—by employing what I term the rhetoric of "interdependence." Such rhetoric confounds the discussion on both sides of the border regarding the fundamental realities of the relationship and its possible future. Whatever merit the arguments may have, they cloud one of the basic characteristics of these relations—their profound asymmetry.

This paper analyzes some of the shortcomings central to the rhetoric of interdependence, focusing on a specific set of asymmetries, i.e., those that affect the bargaining power of the U.S. and Mexican governments in their bilateral dealings. This emphasis on governmental bargaining power defines and limits the objective and scope of our critique. I have, nevertheless, decided to follow such an approach for two reasons. It allows the introduction of order and clarity into the discussion of a very complex set

---

Carlos Rico F. is on leave from his position as Senior Researcher at the Institute of U.S. Studies, Centro de Investigación y Docencia Económicas (Mexico City). He has taught at the Universidad Nacional Autónoma de México, at the Universidad Iberoamericana (Mexico City), and at the Latin American Graduate School of Social Sciences (FLACSO). He has also taught in Chile, Guatemala, and Peru. He has published numerous articles in Mexico and the United States, on U.S. foreign policy, U.S.–Latin American relations, and U.S.–Mexican relations. Translated by P.M. Jinks.
© 1983 by Carlos Rico F.

of phenomena. Moreover, the subject itself is not without importance. It could be argued that the future shape of U.S.-Mexican relations will be to a large degree defined by forces beyond the control of both governments, stemming from the basic reality of the relationship, that is, the capitalist nature of both socioeconomic formations. But even if one agrees with such an argument, when we try to analyze the political dimensions of this question, as well as the likelihood of considerable levels of friction and conflict being present in the short and medium run, a precise evaluation of the power of both governments is central to the problem of outlining the probable future of this relationship. Thus, by clearly defining their relative bargaining capacity, one could clarify, for example, the extent to which the Mexican government can exercise autonomy in practice, as a consequence of the availability of petroleum resources. This would help us to gauge realistically the degree to which Mexico controls its own future.

A full evaluation of the bargaining power of both governments is outside the scope of this paper. I will only try to show how a consideration of this aspect of the relationship highlights the shortcomings of the rhetoric of interdependence. Discussion is developed in three steps. In the first section of this paper, the specific manner in which the rhetoric of interdependence has been employed with respect to Mexican-U.S. relations will be described. Mexican and U.S. policy makers, academics, and political leaders have used this rhetoric, paradoxically, to support views of future relations that in some ways are incompatible. Though both views have sought for different reasons to negate Mexico's dependence upon the U.S., the dominant views in the U.S. have employed the rhetoric to support policy proposals that would tie the economies and societies of the two countries more closely together, while Mexican views have employed it to support projections of Mexico's future as an independent capitalist power. This first section identifies some of the analytical problems that flow from this use of the rhetoric of interdependence.

In the second section, an attempt is made to clarify, at a conceptual level, some of these analytical problems. When the term interdependence is employed rhetorically, what is actually meant is that mutual "sensitivities" exist between Mexico and the

United States. Alternative meanings and uses describe interdependence in terms of "vulnerabilities" and the profound asymmetries that characterize U.S.-Mexican relations at two levels. One level is that of nongovernmental relations (those between the two economies and societies); the other is that of intergovernmental bargaining power.[1] Central to these alternative meanings of interdependence are the links between nongovernmental and intergovernmental relations.

In the last section, alternative approaches are applied to one of the key issues between Mexico and the United States—relations at the border. This serves two purposes: testing the rhetoric of interdependence in a specific case, and evaluating the potential impact of the asymmetries on the relative bargaining power of the U.S. and Mexican governments. The concept of interdependence is not just rhetoric; it has a basis in reality, closely related to a set of phenomena which, to a great extent, derive from the foreign domination of Mexico's economy and society. The existence of transnational links and mutual "sensitivities" between Mexico and the U.S. is not rhetorical; what *is* rhetorical is the image of a harmonious future relationship which the mere incantation of the term conveys.

THE RHETORIC OF INTERDEPENDENCE AND MEXICAN-U.S. RELATIONS: A CRITIQUE

How has the rhetoric of interdependence been employed in Mexico and the U.S.? What political purposes has it served? Answers to these questions can help us understand why these views are referred to as the *rhetoric* of interdependence. They also serve to identify some analytical problems arising from this rhetorical use of the concept whose resolution will shed some light on the probable future of the Mexican-U.S. relationship.

MEXICAN VIEWS

First I will describe the basic outlines of those Mexican evaluations for the future of the relationship that are based, implicitly or explicitly, on the rhetoric of interdependence. However, before considering the political benefits apparently sought by those who have taken up this rhetoric on the Mexican side, it is necessary to clarify one point. Although the use of the term *interdependence* is far less widespread in Mexico than in the United States, the denial of Mexican dependency, implicit in the concept, has come to be restated in recent years as an important element of the political discourse of Mexican politicians. In this sense, it is perhaps appropriate to ascribe a more general scope to the arguments of Mexican politicians who explicitly adopt the term, like the leader of the Mexican senate, Joaquín Gamboa Pascoe,[2] and the former Secretary of Foreign Relations, Santiago Roel, who said, "I can state that Mexican sovereignty has remained uncompromised in a relationship of perfect interdependence with the United States."[3]

Interdependence is useful to characterize dealings between equals, in contrast to *dependence*, or *dependency*.[4] Thus, the rhetoric of interdependence seems to be utilized by Mexican officials to justify a closer relationship with the United States—particularly to those sectors of the Mexican public where Mexican foreign policy has helped legitimize the alleged progressive nature of the regimes of the "institutionalized revolution."[5] If the way some of the symbols central to the ideology of the Mexican Revolution—such as oil—are manipulated makes the Mexican side resort to new rhetorical forms, then interdependence can also be used to disguise one of the developments which most clearly contradict some of the basic tenets of this ideology—the foreign dependence which is a necessary result of the development model followed by those regimes that claim to inherit the Revolution.

Although not always employing the term *interdependence*, various recent projections made in Mexico about its future and that of Mexican-U.S. relations rest upon precisely this use of the rhetoric that interests us. Perhaps the clearest example can be found in those public expressions that indicate a belief in an independent and dynamic future for Mexican capitalism. The Mexican press presents many references by both national and international spokesmen in this respect. Thus, in the words of the Swedish Secretary for Foreign Trade, Mexico is ". . . a nation that has already left underdevelopment behind and [which] soon will become a great power. . . ."[6] Another observer notes that Mexico is "destined to play an important part in the world economy by virtue of its oil resources."[7] The phrase, "by virtue of its oil resources," leads us to a discussion of the common ingredient upon which the Mexican visions of interdependence are largely based. In fact, if one were to judge from the repeated references in other Latin American countries[8] and the public statements of Mexican officials of ministerial rank,[9] one would gather that oil is becoming the central element of—as one influential Mexico City newspaper editorialized—a "qualitative change in Mexican-U.S. relations."[10]

On the Mexican side, oil constitutes the key ingredient supporting the conviction that the United States now depends more on Mexico. It is the element most emphasized in Mexican views of interdependence, when considering the Mexican government's bargaining chips in its dealings with the U.S. government.[11] Thus, the argument is made that Mexico can take advantage of the negotiating power afforded by its hydrocarbons in order to wrest U.S. concessions in other areas. This idea, for example, took the concrete form of a proposal for a "package deal," made by Mexico's president José López Portillo during his Washington visit in February 1977. In this view, oil is the key factor that would assure Mexico that its experience of U.S. domination would be supplanted by negotiations conducted on an equal footing.[13] According to these arguments, in exchange for Mexican cooperation in energy, the U.S. government would grant concessions in other areas[14] with relations as a whole becoming increasingly harmonious.

The Mexican projections of relations with the U.S. are particularly interesting. In them Mexico's future as an independent capitalist power is not only the necessary outcome of an increase in Mexican bargaining power, but the basic prerequisite of any attempt to overcome potential friction. These projections are at odds with the predominant ones in the United States. To show to what extent such visions of the future differ, one need only recall the unfavorable reaction by members of various official and semiofficial Mexican circles when the idea of a North American community—summing up the principal U.S. views—was made public. We shall group the arguments of Mexican observers against a North American market into six propositions. The idea of a common market is first a step toward making Mexico a part of the United States rather than a partner. In this sense the proposal has been called a "sophisticated provocation" of Mexico.[15] Second, despite benevolent statements which emphasize the general concerns of the two (three?) parties to be met by such a "community," the most articulate proposals reek of oil. Rather than viewing these proposals as a general package of cooperation, Mexican observers saw them as vehicles for the United States to obtain access to Mexican energy resources.[16] Third, those versions of the proposal which emphasize the exchange of goods and services are actually mechanisms to "recycle" Mexican "petro-pesos." Mexico would be encouraged to import indiscriminately, including products that in many cases may not be necessary.[17] Fourth, the free flow of the factors of production (e.g., labor), a basic requirement for the economic assumptions of the model, is not a viable possibility in the face of short- to medium-term U.S. political realities. Fifth, to apply the theory of comparative advantages under such restrictions could lead Mexico to specialize in those products that it has sought to escape from in the last twenty-five years.[18] Finally, there is no "complementarity" of interests between buyers and sellers.[19] Thus, while U.S. exponents of the interdependence rhetoric have largely been favorable to the common market idea, the Mexican exponents of the same rhetoric have largely rejected it—though for varying reasons.

As can be seen from this discussion, those Mexican definitions of the country's future and of relations with the United States, based on the denial of Mexican dependency that the rhetoric of interdependence usually embodies, emphasize the dimension I have chosen as the focal point of our analysis—governmental bargaining power. In this case, the shortcomings of rhetoric stem from its failure to realistically gauge such power. To evaluate the degree to which Mexico's energy resources have decreased their dependence on the U.S. and improved their bargaining position, it is not enough to simply point out that "the possession of energy resources obviously increases a nation's power."[20]

There is no question that within certain limits the availability of energy resources can increase the Mexican government's bargaining power with the U.S. government. However, it is necessary to define where those limits lie, not only with regard to the specific subject of trade in hydrocarbons, but also in the context of the relationship as a whole. Linking the different issues and levels of relationship would not necessarily benefit Mexico's bargaining position. Indeed, a number of writers have emphasized the opposite.[21] At the level of relations between societies and economies, specific asymmetries exist which favor the weaker part. If such asymmetries are sufficiently costly for the dominant party, one might expect it to attempt to link together the different levels of relationship to insure that decisions made in the weakest area will reflect the realities of the relationship's global context and its overall superiority.

This would be true for the Mexican–U.S. relationship, where for various reasons its different components have been handled on an ad hoc basis.[22] In this perspective one should expect that the U.S. government—not the Mexican—would stand to gain from a linkage across issue areas, if it could achieve such a linkage at little cost in other spheres such as domestic politics.

The question is not whether the availability of energy resources provides an increment of bargaining power to the Mexican government; rather, it asks to what extent does the new bargaining element compensate for the global realities of the relationship? From this point of view, the elements normally considered as favorable to Mexico—e.g., the strategic, as well as economic value of energy—suggest the degree of opposition the Mexican government would face if it adopted policies that affected U.S. interests considerably. To what extent, then, is power synonymous with possessing something of interest to the globally stronger partner? The approach mentioned earlier of promoting "package deals" could easily become a double-edged sword.

Even in the limited sphere that Mexican views emphasize and which I have chosen as our focal point, that of governmental bargaining power, incantations of interdependence do not solve the problem of realistically evaluating those factors that will undoubtedly affect the relationship's future. The need for a more complex set of concepts and assumptions should be clear after this discussion. In the second section of this paper I will try to develop them after describing some shortcomings in the use in the U.S. of the rhetoric of interdependence.

Before proceeding with our argument it is necessary to briefly state other realities that go beyond the direct consideration of governmental bargaining power and which are usually underestimated or even neglected by those who postulate as a possibility the development of an independent Mexican national capitalist economy. Closely related to the above points are (a) the extent to which the Mexican economy has already become integrated to the U.S. economy; (b) the extent to which the internationalization of capital and the worldwide recomposition of the reserve army of labor permeating global capitalism are present in the case of Mexico; and (c) the consolidation of increasingly powerful social classes and groups that have benefited from Mexico's past economic development strategy.

UNITED STATES VIEWS

If we change our focus to the debate taking place north of the border, we note that the imprecision characterizing the rhetorical use of "interdependence" supports arguments and proposals to a great extent incompatible with those discussed in the south.

Our discussion of U.S. views will concentrate on the period between former Secretary of State Henry Kissinger's remarks to the Seventh Special Session of the U.N. General Assembly in 1975 and the Carter Administration. During those years, the rhetorical use of interdependence constituted one of the key terms in Washington's political discourse when responding to the new realities in world politics since the late sixties. Indeed, this concept seems to have had broad appeal among the more internationalist and liberal sectors of the U.S. policy-making establishment.

The general use of the rhetoric of interdependence had some clear political benefits for those groups in international and domestic politics. With regard to the former, the constant invoking of interdependence seemed to have become an important political instrument for negotiations between the center and the periphery of international capitalism during the last decade. This is evident from the statements made by U.S. representatives in numerous appearances before international forums. Typical of these might be the words of Terence Todman, former Assistant Secretary of State for Inter-American Affairs, who emphasized the existence of ". . . a world where scarcity of food and natural resources, and global economic forces affecting us all, have made all nations increasingly interdependent, regardless of their differing ideological systems or levels of development," a world whose present economic problems "go beyond national borders and in Latin America and the United States have become increasingly dependent upon each other." The moral that Todman drew from these facts is particularly relevant:

... In such an interdependent world—in such a complex, precarious world—our only security lies in working together in a spirit of equality and mutual respect, knowing that a nation like the U.S. is as dependent on the success of our efforts and on the respect and good will of our sovereign neighbors as they are on the cooperation of the U.S.[23]

The message is clear. It is a denial of the existence of conflicts and contradictions between the different countries within the capitalist system. This creates an image of the system as an "organic whole" which emphasizes the importance of every country and of its particular role. Carrying out the different functions by each of the national economies in the international division of labor is hailed as a constructive development for the participants as a whole. Rather than conflicts of interest, this view stresses complementarities, or mutualities of interest.

Moreover—and this is a point which has both foreign and domestic political dimensions—the rhetoric of interdependence has served to rationalize an approach of the United States in which a number of countries are assigned "priority attention." This strategy acknowledges the importance of such countries according to, among other things, gradations of U.S. "dependence" upon them relative to the rest of the economies that make up the international system.

With regard to U.S. domestic politics, the rhetoric of interdependence was used to combat isolationist and protectionist tendencies with two arguments. First, the continued worldwide projection of the U.S. is unavoidable, given that the country depends on foreign supplies, raw materials, and on the "health" of the international economy as a whole. Second, the free flow of goods, labor, and capital assures the highest level of economic efficiency and welfare for all members of the world economy. Thus, because the U.S. now depends more on the rest of the world and on the operation of a more or less open international economy, the U.S. government must maintain an active international role.

The rhetoric of interdependence thus acquired special relevance for international and domestic reasons, to those bilateral relations with some priority for U.S. diplomacy, and which possess the minimum characteristics necessary to refer to them plausibly through the use of this rhetoric. It should surprise no one that appeals to the rhetoric of interdependence proliferated in the U.S. official political discourse about Mexico during those years.[24] Indeed, even if the term interdependence or the statement that "the United States needs its neighbor"[25] is not new to Mexican-U.S. relations,[26] they appeared with increasing frequency in the mid-1970s when new oil wealth was discovered in Mexico.

Instances of the political benefits in U.S.-Mexican relations derived from a rhetorical use of the term interdependence are not difficult to find. In this case, it was evident that an effort was being made to substitute interdependence for the so-called special relationship idea in U.S. (and Mexican) official characterizations of relations during the post-war period. The reasons behind such an effort were clearly expressed on numerous occasions. A paper prepared at The Rand Corporation in 1977 pointed out:

> With the decline of the special relationship idea and the lack of any replacement, charges of dependency, neo-colonialism, and neo-imperialism have spread as a currency of recent Mexican political discourse toward the United States. In the absence of a concept of mutual dependency, latent perspectives of unilateral dependency and vulnerability have come to the fore within Mexico.[27]

In this context, the reference to "North American interdependence" was seen as a potential component of the rationalization of a new special relationship that would resolve some anomalies, such as the fact that "Mexico has never conceded that its future may lie more with North America than with its Latin American brethren —though this may prove to be a lesson of recent experience."[28]

Used in the context of U.S.-Mexican relations, the rhetoric of interdependence shared the basic characteristics we have already discussed at a more global level. Interdependence was presented not only as a source of mutual benefit, but also as something inevitable almost by definition. The interests of the different participants in the relationship were defined as complementary rather than competitive, stressing that there were no contradictions between their economies.[29] Interdependence, to paraphrase former U.S. Vice President Walter Mondale during a visit to Mexico, came to mean a more balanced and more profound, mature relationship in which there would no longer be a domination of one country by another, but the presence of sovereign nations seeking common aims.³⁰ This perception showed that "in spite of the economic differences and in spite of the contrasting cultural traditions, there are no two nations on earth whose present and future are so closely intertwined."³¹

The rhetoric of interdependence thus had some important consequences. One was that it obscured the relationship of domination at the core of Mexican–U.S. relations. More significantly, it also provided support for policies which would further intertwine more closely the destinies of the two countries. This second aspect of the rhetoric of interdependence bears close scrutiny.

Summarized, the views associated with the rhetoric of interdependence (a) see the process of de facto integration of the Mexican economy into its U.S. counterpart as a consequence and proof of the existence of a series of complementarities between the two economies; (b) perceive this de facto integration as inevitable, a "natural" consequence of the current realities of this geographic area; and (c) foresee a future relationship between the two governments that is increasingly free of friction, largely because of the integration mentioned above. The logical policy proposal that follows from this would stress elements of "community." Though not always stated explicitly, the chief proposals congruent with the views associated with the rhetoric of interdependence are those which have been discussed in some U.S. circles regarding the possibility, in the not-too-distant future, of advancing toward the integration of Canada, the United States, Mexico, and some countries of the Caribbean into one sole economic (and perhaps eventually political) unit. These proposals cover a wide variety of alternatives. One specific example limits its focus to the labor market,³² while others postulate the supposed benefits of a bona fide North American Common Market. Thus, the rhetoric of interdependence is an integral element in the formulation of policy proposals which stress a future relationship of "community."

Given that these proposals are, as I have already pointed out, quite varied, it is somewhat artificial to group them under one heading. In fact, arguments which favor such proposals have been made by groups representing practically every faction in the U.S. political spectrum. Examples range from the present Republican majority leader in the Senate, Howard Baker,³³ and President Ronald Reagan,³⁴ to the Democratic governor of California, Edmund G. Brown, Jr.,³⁵ the Senate Finance Committee,³⁶ and the Energy and Natural Resources Committee.³⁷

A greater economic integration between "major trading partners *isolated* on a continent"[38] (emphasis mine) characterized by Pete Domenici, Republican senator from New Mexico—was proposed as a mechanism for the resolution of conflicts between the participating countries.[39] The president of the Dow Chemical Co., Paul Oreffice, made explicit the possible ingredients of a Mexican-Canadian-U.S. "Big Deal."[40]

> ... a recognition of the problem faced by the United States may lead to a flow of oil and gas from its neighbors ... a recognition of Mexico's problems may lead to the free flow of the needed Mexican labor into the United States [and] recognition of Mexican agricultural problems may lead to [a] better market for U.S. and Canadian agricultural products.[41]

The proposals for a North American community, though varied, constitute an element of the U.S. political debate.[42] Whether one provides additional elements[43] for Oreffice's basic scheme or follows the idea along its more general lines, the argument is still fairly simple. In economics, it is a variant of the theory of comparative advantages. In the politico-ideological dimension, it constitutes an appeal to the complementary character of Mexican and U.S. interests, in a word, to the rhetoric of interdependence.

If we try to make a first evaluation of these ideas, additional shortcomings of the rhetoric of interdependence come into view. The most relevant for our analysis seem to be two. First, even if the process of de facto integration is recognized, it does not necessarily follow that the result is equally beneficial for all participants. This is clearer if we abandon the simplistic assumption of the existence of only two partners (the Mexican and U.S. economies) and concentrate on the several economic and social groups affected on both sides of the border. As I will try to show later in this paper, the consequences for these different groups may be quite varied. The second shortcoming is based on the characterization of future Mexico-U.S. relations as a harmonious and natural development of the North American community. This view is also questionable with regard to the idyllic image of no friction and conflict at the intergovernmental level. At this level both governments would face innumerable domestic political problems as they increase the de facto integration that characterizes the recent relations between Mexican and U.S. economies and societies.

In this instance, criticism of the rhetoric of interdependence highlights a set of issues different from the Mexican views of the same rhetoric, even if both are necessary to a realistic evaluation of governmental bargaining power. In the analysis of the shortcomings of Mexican expressions of the rhetoric, we treated both the U.S. and Mexican governments (and to a point, both social formations) as "unitary rational actors."[44] When one eliminates that simplistic assumption, additional complexities arise.

After our discussion of Mexican views, a clear picture should emerge of problems faced by the promotion, at an intergovernmental level, of the de facto integration of the Mexican economy into its U.S. counterpart. These domestic political problems are hardly understandable from the perspectives dominant in the U.S., which project a positive characterization of interdependence as if it should necessarily be shared by Mexico. Nevertheless, an open acceptance of this approach would have serious implications for the Mexican state. It would be tantamount to recognizing that the national goals of independence and sovereignty, central ideological tenets of the Mexican Revolution, are out of reach.[45] These arguments remind us how difficult it would be for the Mexican government to handle this type of proposal because of the country's own political and economic realities. They are also suggestive of the extraordinary complexity that the bargaining process would assume.[46]

The problems that such a scheme would entail for the U.S. government are often underestimated in discussions regarding the integrationist proposals. These include the degree of bureaucratic and domestic political conflict that could result. This conflict would arise from a number of sources, including (a) the extreme complexity of Mexican-U.S. relations which not only presents innumerable points of potential friction between both social formations, but also makes necessary, within the U.S. itself, the participation of numerous governmental actors in the definition of any global policy; (b) the degree to which nongovernmental actors can affect the initiatives taken at the governmental level. Rather than auguring a relationship free of conflict, the proposals under discussion could, in fact, open up a Pandora's box not amenable to the political will of those governing, and, because of the social, political, and economic realities of the relationship, result in exactly the opposite effect. Both of these points will be developed in the second section of this paper.

These are some of the complexities of the Mexican–U.S. relationship that are not addressed by the rhetoric of interdependence. Its inability to deal with these basic realities reflects analytical and methodological deficiencies in the concept. In the next section, we will summarize the principal criticisms. Such criticisms are numerous and derive from different theoretical and political perspectives, from those that start with dependency to those that point out that an increase in the links between the economies and societies of nation-states can increase the possibilities of intergovernmental conflict. These critics openly question the assumptions of reciprocity and relative equilibrium which accompany the concept in its rhetorical usage, stressing how, in situations of inequality between participants, the phenomena that the rhetoric of interdependence normally refers to may become a mechanism for perpetuating and reinforcing such inequalities. Since the focus in this paper is on governmental bargaining power, the criticisms of the rhetoric of interdependence that interest us most are those that emphasize its tendency to confuse different levels of the relationship. Specifically, the rhetoric mixes together what should remain analytically separate: the links between societies and economies, on the one hand, and the effects they have on the relations between governments, on the other. This is a key point in our attempt to clarify the concept in the next section.

INTERDEPENDENÇE—A CONCEPTUAL CLARIFICATION

To clarify the meaning of interdependence as far as it is useful for evaluating governmental bargaining power we have to be explicit about our methodological needs. We are concerned with the links between socioeconomic and political realities. This is an interplay between related but analytically distinct sets of phenomena: those objective socioeconomic conditions that constitute the basis of governmental action; and the political capabilities of governments to use the opportunities provided by those realities. These two sets of phenomena correspond to the two shortcomings emphasized in previous criticism of the rhetoric of interdependence as it has been used in both Mexico and the United States.

Taking into account these specific methodological needs, the following discussion is based on a review of some of the U.S.

literature on the connection between interdependence and power. Such literature questions the supposed mutual benefits which, according to the rhetoric, naturally and necessarily arise from such interactions, in relation to governmental bargaining power.[47] Criticism of the rhetoric of interdependence will not be based on the theoretical or methodological perspective common to the studies based on the category of *dependency* developed since the end of the sixties in Latin America.[48] Rather, emphasis on *relations between governments* is the main reason for restricting ourselves to the ideas of such authors as Robert Keohane and Joseph S. Nye, Jr. Among its many merits, such literature offers a series of concepts which, once cleared of the ambiguities of everyday usage, can have a fairly precise operational application, at least with reference to the problem of power. Moreover, a clear and precise use of these concepts does not seem to necessarily conflict with dependency views, such as that which stresses that ". . . international relations are asymmetrical relations between societies at different stages of development which result in situations of subordination and superordination that are reciprocally conditioned."[49]

It is necessary to make two other clarifications before turning to the chosen approach. In the first place, the term "power" needs to be defined. Throughout this paper this concept is used in its most elementary sense: Robert A. Dahl's intuitive idea that *A* has power over *B* when *A* can make *B* do something *B* would not otherwise do.[50] This definition would prove insufficient if we wished to study governmental bargaining power or its domestic dimensions in all their complexity. However, the simplicity of the concept of power we are using enables us to rank and schematize more clearly the elements directly connected to the various sources of governmental bargaining power, particularly where the economies and societies are articulated in such a complex manner.

Second, given that the analytical framework on which we base our argument shares the same term employed by the rhetoric which it questions, the discussion in this section can be read as a classification of alternative meanings of the word interdependence. At the most general level, that of rhetorical use, the concept of interdependence refers to mutual sensitivities between the economies and societies of the various countries that make up the world community of nations, and more specifically, the international capitalist system. At this level of generality, interdependence simply refers to the extent to which events that take place in one country influence events that occur in another.[51] This point of departure is common both to the academic attempts to clarify and develop the concept, such as those we shall refer to below, and to the rhetorical applications of the same. The latter, however, do not go beyond this first level of analysis.

The literature that we are reviewing, however, starts with the idea of sensitivity and proceeds to develop levels of meaning of interdependence on the basis of two notions: vulnerability and control. For the first term, analysis remains at the nongovernmental level, while the second focuses on the manner in which the relations between societies and economies impact upon the political and administrative capacities of governments—their relative bargaining power.

We shall explore some of the issues involved in the evaluation of potential vulnerabilities. Such vulnerabilities can be assessed by identifying those asymmetries that prevail in the governmental sphere on the basis of two criteria. The first is concerned with the alternatives available to each party. Should a particular link between two countries be broken, what can each government do to find a functional replacement? An asymmetrical relationship exists when alternatives are relatively costly for one government, but not for the other. Secondly, how much does the elimination of certain ties cost each participant? The answers to these two questions define their relative vulnerabilities. In their simplest form they would show that the most vulnerable party is the one with the lesser number of alternatives and for whom the cost of ending the linkage would be higher. Joseph S. Nye Jr., clarifies the difference between this notion and that of sensitivity in the following manner:

> Sensitivity means liability to costly effects imposed from the outside in a given situation—in other words, before any policies are devised to try to change the situation. Vulnerability means continued liability to costly effects imposed from the outside, even after efforts have been made to alter or escape the situation.[52]

The example most often cited as proof of U.S. dependence on foreign countries—the degree to which the U.S. economy depends on the import of certain goods or raw materials—affords us an opportunity to illustrate some of these basic points.[53] The first implication of the argument just presented is the need to distinguish, as regards imports, between those which arise from the nonexistence of a particular product or the almost total impossibility of producing it at home and those imports which take place because of price considerations.

One might argue that in the first situation the economy of the importing country is more vulnerable than in the second, when it has options. U.S. economic dependence on the import of a certain product does not necessarily indicate increased vulnerability to interruption in its supplies—at least in the short to medium run. Other elements to consider are how many suppliers there are for the product in question and the kind of relationship the importing country has with each one of them. Regarding the cost of terminating such relationships, one should note the position of the suppliers for whom cutting off exports could turn out to be more difficult than for the importing nation itself. The economic and strategic importance of the imported product and the availability of substitutes are additional factors to be considered, as well as the capacity of the importer to endure the interruption of supplies (e.g., through the use of strategic reserves) for a longer time than the suppliers, who depend on exports.

Vulnerability is "a matter of degree and varies with the costs and time involved in developing alternatives."[54] For example, if the economic cost incurred by giving up cheaper sources of the material in question is tolerable, and the process of substitution of suppliers relatively simple, the vulnerability of the importing country will not reach its levels of sensitivity.

Through this example, one can see how the approach we have summarized would assess each of the participant's degree of dependence, and therefore, how it would characterize the level of asymmetry in the relationship. From this asymmetry follows not the sensitivity but the *vulnerability* of one national economy and society with respect to events that take place in another.

At the level of intergovernmental relations, the assessment of the inequalities in the different parties' bargaining power takes as its point of departure the asymmetries that characterize the particular links between societies and economies as the basis of the relationship. However, we need to add a new element here: *the degree of control* that each of the governments in question can exercise over the different nongovernmental channels through which these connections are expressed. This can be assessed at two levels: (a) the simple technical capacity to exercise control, and (b) the political capacity to behave as a unitary rational actor in relation to the subject at hand.

Technical capacity may be developed further by comparing the extent of direct control by the U.S. government in the operations of the U.S. transnational corporations and trade flows across U.S. borders. In the former, the relationship of asymmetry that exists at the nongovernmental level is clear, both for the relations between the head office and the subsidiaries and for those between the Mexican and the U.S. economies. This follows not only from the limited impact the activities of each subsidiary have on the whole firm, but also from the subordinate role that subsidiaries play in the global corporate strategy of the firm. But, as pointed out above, the relative position of the governments is defined not only by the patterns of asymmetry that characterize the relationship at the level of the societies and economies, but also by the degree of control that each has over nongovernmental actors and channels. From the point of view of the U.S. government, even though it could potentially influence the activities of the head office in the U.S., and of the subsidiaries operating outside its territory (by means of the extraterritorial application of its laws),[55] this control is not as immediate or direct as that which it can exercise over the flow of trade across its borders. It may well be the case that even if the asymmetries present in a given instance of trade relations are not as clear as those which characterize the relationship between subsidiary and head office, their value in terms of governmental power could be considerably higher.

We now turn to the second factor which defines the potential for governmental control. The capacity of the United States to behave as a unitary rational actor basically rests upon two factors. The first is the degree of complexity in the relationship, defined as the number of participants and interests, in which both governmental and nongovernmental participants operate. The second is the importance that the central organs of the U.S. executive branch—that is, the White House—attribute to the need to articulate and impose on the various participants a single, coherent policy on a specific issue or on the relevant bilateral relationship as a whole.[56]

The relation between the levels of transnational linkage of nongovernmental relations and the power of the governments involved can be considered at different levels of analysis: sensitivity, vulnerability, and control. These are illustrated in exhibit 1. From this exhibit, it is evident that as we advance from one level of analysis to another, the phenomena that are initially associated, in a strict sense, with the mere sensitivity between economies and/or societies become clearly identified as sources of power, distributed unequally, at the level of intergovernmental relations.

This concludes our review of the literature. It would not require much effort to see how the application of these concepts would modify substantially the image which the rhetoric of interdependence attributes to the realities of the Mexican-U.S. relationship. As an illustrative case study, in the next section we shall use this conceptual clarification and the three levels of analysis mentioned above to examine one of the areas most often appealed to by interdependence theorists: border relations.

THE BORDER: A CASE STUDY[57]

That Mexico and the United States share a border of nearly two thousand miles defines a first and fundamental set of connections between the two social formations. The Mexican-U.S. border offers some unique opportunities for observing the kinds of phenomena that we have discussed. In the rest of this essay, I will discuss these connections on the basis of the notions of sensitivity, vulnerability, and control. But before analyzing some of the basic characteristics of the Mexican-U.S. border using the scheme developed in the last section, the importance of border issues in the more general context of the bilateral relationship must be stressed. Such importance is evident from the border's role in the dynamics of some of the main components of these relations: drug smuggling, fruit and vegetable trade, the flow of undocumented workers, etc. Moreover, one can also note that border problems have been important in Mexican-U.S. government relations. In the post-war period, many subjects that entered bilateral policy discussions and were seen as issues by both governments fell under the heading of *border problems*. Even if limiting oneself to a brief review of current Mexican-U.S. relations,[58] border questions still stand out on the Mexican-U.S.

EXHIBIT 1.—LEVELS OF ANALYSIS OF "INTERDEPENDENCE"

I. Sensitivity (between societies and/or economies)
What happens in one country affects events in another.

II. Vulnerability (between societies and/or economies)
Asymmetries with regard to:
a) alternatives available to the participants
b) costs of a break in the connections for each participant

III. Power (intergovernmental relations)
Asymmetries, as in II, plus government control over nongovernmental channels and actors (governmental and nongovernmental)

post-war diplomatic agenda. Indeed, a number of writers perceive the U.S.–Mexican border as constituting the principal source of differences between the international problems of Mexico and those of the rest of Latin America.[59]

For these reasons border questions not only present some clear examples of practically all potential sources of interdependence cited by those authors who subscribe to this perspective[60] but can also be considered in and of themselves as very important components of U.S.–Mexican relations. We now turn to the analysis of such questions on the basis of the notions developed in our previous section.

SENSITIVITY

The Mexican–U.S. border offers many instances of how events that take place in one country affect those in the other. At the most elementary—physical and geographic—level, the two countries share resources, such as the Rio Grande and the Colorado River, which play an important economic role on both sides of the boundary. Although this is not a unique example, the problem of the salinity of the Colorado clearly illustrates a sensitivity of what takes place on the other side of the border.[61] A second example is the simultaneous effect that different natural phenomena, hurricanes, for instance, have on both sides of the border. This raises interesting questions, such as what effects do attempts by citizens to modify weather conditions have on the other side of the border. Another is that of cross-border pollution; though its origins are complex (industrial growth, the movement of firms seeking to escape stricter pollution controls to the border, rapid growth of border cities, etc.[62]), these phenomena are still at the level of mutual sensitivities.

It is not hard to find other examples of linkage and articulation at this same level in which the border plays a central role. Witness, for example, its function in the easing of the movements of speculative capital, and even of physical goods. These occur occasionally when it becomes evident to certain parties that such movements would protect their interests. Examples can be found in the sale of certain Mexican products, such as cattle, whose importation to the U.S. is not limited by quotas,[63] during times when the currency exchange rate was unstable. In such instances, geographical contiguity itself would favor a trend toward the speculative conversion of pesos into dollars. Witness also the border's impact on the governmental capacity to apply economic policies (e.g., the imposition of strict foreign exchange controls on the Mexican side).

In all these instances, the way in which events that take place on one side of the border may affect those on the other is clearly shown. The very same examples could also be considered from the perspective of some of the issues raised in discussing the shortcomings of the rhetoric of interdependence. At this point, we are interested in those shortcomings not directly related to the evaluation of governmental bargaining power. In particular, I would like to recall the idea that those sensitivities described may be the expression of processes in which the assumption of differentiated roles by the two economies and societies have quite different economic, social, and even political consequences for each of them. In a sense our contention that those phenomena to which the rhetoric of interdependence makes reference can be considered as expressions of a process of U.S. domination over Mexico rests on precisely such an assumption.

Up to this point I have referred to border issues in a quite general way. By proceeding to more specific topics it may be possible to observe more clearly the complexity of the problems which arise as a result of the transborder connections between social formations and illustrate our argument regarding the different consequences of the roles assumed by each of them in the process. An example of more specific topics is the type of economic and social development that has characterized the principal border cities. By focusing our attention at this level we are not overstating the importance of the activities these urban centers have for the border relationship as a whole. For example, in 1970, Tijuana, Mexicali, Ciudad Juárez, and Nuevo Laredo accounted for 80 percent of the border transactions and together with Matamoros, they received 70 percent of all foreign visitors to the region. More than 65 percent of the Mexicans who visited the United States crossed through the same ports.[64] These cities, in many cases, are becoming veritable socioeconomic enclaves whose activities depend almost entirely on the U.S. economy.[65]

In this instance, U.S. domination is expressed through a complex process in which the very economic growth of the border cities renders their increasingly complex dependence on the U.S.

economy more acute. The Mexican border economy, in turn, has markets for its products, locations for the labor-intensive stages of production, and an important reserve of workers that can even be used on the U.S. side of the border when the economy of the southwestern states makes it necessary or profitable. The border, moreover, permits the U.S. to limit somewhat the import of acute social problems—e.g., the high unemployment rates—which also characterize the dependent growth of these cities. The contrasting effects of the differentiation of roles for each country alluded to by the rhetoric of interdependence can now be seen more clearly. Calvin P. Blair describes what he calls border symbiosis:

> The Mexican city typically furnishes some workers to the agriculture and service trades of the U.S. side. It also acts as an entrepôt for goods moving into the Mexican interior, serves as an assembly point for location of one of the "twin plants" which produces for U.S. markets and draws to its tourist attractions large numbers of U.S. and Canadian travelers who reside temporarily on the U.S. side of the border, in the past, accounting for anywhere from 10 percent to 90 percent of the retail sales of individual establishments. The sister city on the U.S. side provides similar entrepôt and expenditure stimuli to its Mexican counterpart, and it often contains the other half of the "twin plants."[66]

The subordinate role of the most important Mexican border cities in this relationship can even be likened to that of the subsidiaries of foreign firms. We will focus on the latter when we discuss "production sharing" agreements, though it is pertinent to note here that the relations between the components of such firms project their influence over the Mexican border urban centers as a whole.

Up to this point our discussion has emphasized *Mexican* sensitivities to events that take place on the U.S. side. We will now turn to a brief discussion of some examples of the opposite situation. Some of these examples arise as a consequence of the sensitivity of U.S. commerce and economic activity along its southern border to the Mexican domestic economy, a fact that is particularly evident in times of Mexican economic and financial instability. For instance, it was reported that during the Mexican economic crisis of the fall of 1976, retail sales in U.S. border towns experienced a drop between 50 and 75 percent.[67]

But perhaps the most important sensitivities that the border represents for the U.S. can be found at another level entirely. In effect, geographical proximity defines a considerable U.S. interest in Mexico's political and economic stability—at least as long as the Mexican government is not perceived as a threat to U.S. interests. At this level, the fact that they share a common border delineates more clearly a potential relationship between Mexico's internal affairs and the domestic economic and social problems of the United States. An article in *Business Week* late in 1977 pointed out that during the coming decade, Mexico's economic and political problems would spill over into the United States, since "Mexico's problems won't stop at the border."[68]

By the same token, such phenomena as Mexican labor migration, which most evidently result from the links between the economies and societies of the two countries, attribute a direct strategic significance to the border—at least as perceived by some U.S. officials. In this regard, one might refer to a statement by former CIA director, William Colby: "The most obvious threat [for the U.S.] is the fact that there are 60 million Mexicans today and there are going to be 120 million of them by the end of the century." According to Colby, this will result in a voluminous Mexican immigration—impossible to restrain—something of the order of 20 million Mexicans by the end of the century, because no matter what is done to reinforce the Border Patrol, "it will not have enough bullets to stop them."[69] Although these assertions wildly exaggerate the migration phenomenon, they do exemplify in a dramatic fashion the perception in the U.S. of Mexico as the only underdeveloped country in the world that can itself introduce underdevelopment into the U.S. society.[70]

VULNERABILITIES

As with sensitivities, the study of the Mexican-U.S. border affords an opportunity to view the consequences of the profound asymmetry—as defined in the second section of this paper—which characterizes this bilateral relationship. It is not hard to find examples of the vulnerabilities that define Mexican-U.S. border relations. A study of border transactions on the basis of the criteria of asymmetry developed above sheds some light on the determinants of Mexican vulnerability. A first indication in this sense is provided by the relative importance of this activity for

TABLE 1.—MEXICO: NORTHERN BORDER
TRANSACTIONS
(Millions of dollars)

Year	Income	Expenditures	Net income
1970	878.9	585.0	293.9
1971	966.9	612.5	354.4
1972	1054.0	649.3	407.7
1973	1207.7	695.0	512.7
1974	1372.9	819.2	553.7
1975	1541.6	957.7	583.9
1976*	1609.7	1051.5	558.2

*Preliminary data.
Source: Banco de México, Indicadores Económicos 6 (March, 1978):64, 88.

the whole economies of both countries. Border transactions represented, by the late seventies, the second-most important source of foreign exchange for Mexico. This amounted to 18.1 percent of the income in the current account. For the United States such activities only amounted to 0.5 percent of its income from the export of goods and services.[71] It is necessary to point out that though the net exchange of these transactions continues to be in Mexico's favor, between 1965 and 1972 Mexican expenditures increased at a rate of 12.4 percent, while income only did so at a rate of 11.4 percent, marking an increasingly unfavorable trend that has continued to the present (see table 1).[72]

The figures in table 1 permit us to evaluate the relative costs that a suspension of border transactions would have for the whole of the U.S. and Mexican economies. The asymmetry is obvious. Thus, we should not be surprised that when the U.S. government has decided to use the suspension of these transactions to apply pressure in other areas of the relationship, it has proved to be an effective bargaining chip. A dramatic example of how the U.S. was successful in securing an immediate and desired Mexican response can be found during the so-called "Operation Intercept" of late 1969.[73]

Instances of asymmetry that seem to favor Mexico can also be found. An interesting example of such a situation can be seen in a proposal by the San Diego Gas and Electric Company and the Southern California Edison Company to purchase electricity from the Comisión Federal de Electricidad of the state of Baja California. A joint study demonstrated the feasibility of connecting their respective systems. Nevertheless, the existence of such examples, whose impact on the U.S. economy as a whole is obviously less relevant than that of border transactions for its Mexican counterpart, does not alter the fundamental asymmetry that characterizes the relative importance of border issues for both countries. Such asymmetry can be more clearly perceived if we focus on specific examples. A particularly illustrative one is that of the maquiladoras (also known as assembly plants, in-bond industry, and production sharing schemes) which even if not restricted, legally or otherwise to this area, are usually set up on the northern border of Mexico. Of the "total number of plants in 1974, 94.3 percent were located in the border area; Tijuana, Ciudad Juárez, and Mexicali alone were host to 53 percent of the plants" (see table 2).[74]

In order to assess more realistically the relevant asymmetries and vulnerabilities some basic background on the more general nature of the phenomenon must be provided. Production sharing across international boundaries is not limited to assembly plants on the U.S.-Mexican border. Rather, it constitutes a new type of activity by transnational corporations that no longer limit themselves to the market of the countries they operate in, and that respond to the world market—which in this case fundamentally means the U.S. market.[75] One of the effects of the increased economic competition between the U.S. economy and other centers of world economic power since the late sixties has been to seek greater levels of "efficiency." In some cases this has been achieved through diversification of the production process, and by locating its labor-intensive segments in those regions where labor productivity and wages are most favorable to the firm.[76] In this process, the ties that unite the activities which take place in one country or the other are even more direct than was the case in other issues we have described. Peter F. Drucker has expressed the notion that production sharing is neither an exporting nor an importing activity in the traditional sense (even if it is still treated as such in trade statistics), but instead represents a de facto economic integration through the linkage of different stages of the process of production.[77] In fact, the phenomenon of production sharing is linked to global forces which seem to be leading to a new international division of labor. In the words of a German industrialist, this global phenomenon would combine "the advanced method of administration, capital and techniques of the investor nations with the work force and natural resources of the receiving nations."[78]

Thus, it is the production process itself that is becoming internationalized and integrated. No matter where its different stages are geographically located, they still are controlled by the head office. In this case, the economic activity does not only depend on the market conditions of the developed country to which these products are exported, but on the constant assessment of the firm's decision-makers regarding the possibility of reducing operating costs by relocating segments of the production process. Clearly, there is a marked asymmetry in the decision-making power of the subsidiary on the one hand and the central office on the other, regarding not only the activities of the firm as a whole, but even those specific ones performed on the Mexican side.

If one considers the principal cost differentials that lead firms to locate in specific areas, it will be easier to comprehend what kinds of connections may occur between events on both sides of the border. First among these are wage differentials, together with the relative levels of productivity and the economic or technical difficulties of mechanizing the labor-intensive processes exported.[79] Others may include the availability of certain production inputs in the locality; its tax laws; its location, particularly its relative proximity to large markets; and even favorable laws (or the nonenforcement of unfavorable laws) in such areas as air pollution.

In all of these cases, links extend beyond any specific bilateral context. Indeed, the phenomenon is worldwide. As a consequence, there is a peculiar competition among countries interested in becoming export platforms to provide an environment characterized by lower wages to encourage such firms to introduce segments of their production processes based on wage differentials. Thus, the incentives for such firms not only take wages in the United States into account, but also wages in other real or potential export platforms, as well as other factors such as transport

TABLE 2.—GEOGRAPHICAL DISTRIBUTION OF IN-BOND MANUFACTURING IN MEXICO

	1974		1976	
	Number	Percentage	Number	Percentage
(Total)	455	100.0	448	100.0
Location of plants				
Border	429	94.3	406	90.6
Tijuana	99	21.8	93	20.8
Ciudad Juárez	85	18.7	81	18.1
Mexicali	57	12.5	69	15.4
Others	188	41.3	163	36.4
Interior of country	26	5.7	42	9.4

Source: Secretaría de Programación y Presupuesto. Data cited in *Comercio Exterior*, April, 1978, p. 411.

costs. This makes it difficult to evaluate the asymmetries since this view limits itself to Mexican–U.S. relations.

This also highlights the problem of relative vulnerabilities as measured by evaluating the kinds of alternatives available to the participants. In this "complex system in which the export of all kinds of goods and services is intertwined with the export of capital, the relocation of productive installations in different parts of the globe, and the internationalization of the production process itself,"[80] Mexican alternatives are closely related to the function that proximity to the U.S. market plays in making this kind of activity possible. Since wage levels in Mexico are higher than those in other real or potential export platforms (table 3), Mexico's competitiveness in production sharing activities is helped by other factors, such as labor productivity and geographical proximity to the United States. Considerably lower transportation costs play a central role in the existence of maquiladora activities in the Mexican case. This factor apparently cannot be functionally extended to the markets of other industrialized countries—at least,

TABLE 3.—UNSKILLED LABOR WAGE LEVELS IN EXISTING OR POTENTIAL EXPORT PLATFORMS (1979)

Typical wage level (in dollars per hour)	Countries
.20–.30	Haiti, Indonesia
.30–.50	Taiwan, Philippines, Korea
.50–.80	El Salvador, Costa Rica, Singapore, Dominican Republic
.80–1.20	Hong Kong, MEXICO
1.20–3.00	Italy, Japan, Great Britain
3.00–4.00	United States, France
4.00–5.00	West Germany, Holland
5.00–6.00	Belgium

Source: Calculated on the basis of Flagstaff Institute data provided to the author by the director, Richard L. Bolin.

not as regards this kind of production. Thus, Mexican alternatives in this regard are quite limited.

Similar results are obtained if one uses our second criterion of vulnerability, i.e., the costs implied for each of the parties by a potential constriction of these linkages. For Mexico, a cutback in these activities would have deleterious effects. The function of production sharing has extended beyond that of job creation, the objective that originally gave birth to the Border Industrialization Program in 1965,[81] and now extends to the generation of foreign exchange and affects the balance of payments. The Mexican journal, *Comercio Exterior*, sums up the situation in an article which points out that ". . . from 1971 to 1977, the income derived from assembly activities recorded an average annual growth of 30 percent. Similarly, while this amounted to 3.2 percent of the income in the current account of the balance of payments in 1971, in 1976 it had reached 7.2 percent of the same."[82]

Up to this point we have emphasized the Mexican side of this question. But, to what extent are there asymmetries unfavorable to the U.S. side? The basic factor is the existence of alternatives; as mentioned above, the Mexican government is not the only one in the periphery which promotes production-sharing activities. Geographical proximity and consequently lower transport costs seem to be the only cost differentials in relation to which such alternatives are limited. In all others the situation seems to be quite favorable to the U.S. side. If one considers for example wage levels, the considerable range of alternatives that exist is clearly shown in table 3. As was mentioned earlier, the production sharing industry located in Mexico does not merely compete with wages in the U.S., it also competes with wages elsewhere. This gives U.S. firms a great deal of flexibility, and restricts their vulnerability to developments that could take place on the Mexican side.

This flexibility seems to help determine the volatile and unstable nature of this activity. A brief consideration of other factors that also help condition such instability may also help, showing how in this case the fulfillment of differentiated roles on both sides of the border has different consequences in each of them.

The behavior of the border assembly industry in the 1974-1975 recession illustrates these contrasting effects on events that take place on each side of the border.[83] Production sharing is vulnerable to market variations in the U.S. and to wage hikes in Mexico. The implications of the supposed interdependence thus can be seen, in this concrete instance, to be starkly different for the parties in this relationship. Vulnerability to the changes in the U.S. market for assembled goods is very different in its social consequences from a vulnerability to the wage levels of Mexican workers.

CONTROL

Having explored some of the asymmetries in Mexican–U.S. border relations, we can see how they can represent a potential source of governmental bargaining power in the context of bilateral negotiations, be they in connection with specific issues or a "package deal." This brings us to the third level of our analysis—power in intergovernmental relations. To evaluate its possibility of realization we will consider the problem of governmental control over those channels that link the two economies and societies that we have briefly reviewed. Following the scheme developed in the second section of the paper, I will deal with the technical and political capacity of governments to behave as unitary rational actors in relation to these issues. Given the patterns of asymmetry we have already described—which point to a clear superiority on the U.S. side—we will concentrate on the U.S. government.

As regards the technical capacity of the U.S. government to employ the asymmetries we have described as instruments of pressure, recent events in Mexican–U.S. relations make it unnecessary for us to go very far back in history to find examples. In fact, if episodes such as Operation Intercept in 1969 afford us some lessons, it would be that the general perception of Mexican vulnerability that we have described has a strong basis in the case of border relations.[84] This is the only possible conclusion to be derived from the efficacy of U.S. government action—described by then-president Richard Nixon as shock treatment designed to persuade Mexico to collaborate in the fight against drug traffic from Mexico to the United States. Operation Intercept consisted of procedures instituted temporarily which virtually closed the border to north-bound traffic. In this instance, it was demonstrated clearly how the degree of control exercised by the U.S. government over on-going border transactions is more than enough to transform the asymmetries and vulnerabilities I have described to effective sources of power.

A similar picture can be drawn for specific cases such as production sharing, analyzed above. An adequate starting point for the discussion of this example would seem to be the evaluation of the extent to which the continued existence of transborder connections of this type may be dependent on U.S. government decisions. There are two sides to this problem. On the one hand, one might stress how this phenomenon is linked to the declining competitiveness of some sectors of the U.S. economy, pointing out that it is rooted in more than the U.S. legislation that facilitates it.[85] This would seem to favor the Mexican side of the relationship. The other side of this coin would stress the role that U.S. governmental policies play in facilitating the operation of the nongovernmental forces we described above. Donald W. Baerreson links our previous discussion with this problem:

> This *vulnerability* [of the Mexican side] is *an inevitable consequence of the Border Program*, which for its success has *depended primarily upon continuance of certain United States import policies* and upon United States financing, technology, and markets.[86]

Of particular relevance in this regard are U.S. tariff items 806.30 and 807.00. The same author points out some of the potential consequences of their abolition:

> A few companies in the Border Program operate without using items 806.30 and 807.00, but for the great majority of companies, these tariff provisions are an important and often essential element for successful operation. According to the opinions of the factory managers and owners, it seems reasonable to estimate that elimination of these provisions (with no change in import tax rates) would reduce present participation in the Border Program by at least 75 percent.[87]

This example enables us to suggest some of the political complexities involved in the problem of governmental control. On the one hand, modifying the tariff laws is exclusively within the domain of the U.S. government. On the other, it would not appear to be a useful instrument of pressure over the short run, not only because it would take a substantial amount of time to eliminate tariff items such as 806.30 and 807.00, but also because doing so would involve other actors, such as the U.S. Congress. Nevertheless, this is not the only instrument that the U.S. government has to exercise some control over the production sharing industry. As in the case of Operation Intercept, the executive branch can always set up obstacles of a purely administrative nature to bar the entry of assembled goods for such time as necessary for the Mexican government to adopt a desired set of policy responses.

I now turn to the U.S. government's political capacity to behave as a unitary rational actor in these matters. As developed in the second section of this paper, such capacity depends in the first place on the degree of complexity in the relationship defined as the number of participants both governmental and nongovernmental that are at work. As regards governmental participants three different instances have to be considered: (a) the executive branch itself, (b) Congress, and (c) state and local authorities.

In the first case the capacity of the U.S. government to control those channels of the relationship in which there are Mexican vulnerabilities can be studied in bureaucratic/political terms. The most important actors in the executive branch can be identified in a number of ways. One is to examine who participated in the binational working groups created as part of the Mexico–U.S. consultative mechanism, which represented the highest level of on-going negotiation between the two governments during the Carter Administration. These working groups were involved with trade, energy, finance, industrial development, migration, tourism, law enforcement, and border issues. The U.S. participants in the latter group included representatives from the Departments of Commerce, Treasury, Health, Education and Welfare (now the Departments of Education and Health and Human Services); Housing and Urban Development; and State. Also involved were representatives from the President's Domestic Council and the International Communications Agency.

Even as we stick to those interpretations closest to the paradigm of bureaucratic politics, one can see the wide scope of conflict and disagreement present in these complex combinations. The principal concern for some of these U.S. agencies is domestic unemployment; for others it is strictly law enforcement, inflation, the ability of the U.S. to compete abroad, etc. Not only do their specific objectives vary, but so do their preferred solutions, both in relation to the problems of the border itself, and for the relationship as a whole. Moreover, we should note that the Departments of Commerce, State, and Treasury, and other agencies were represented not only in the border issues group but also in a number of other working groups in the consultative mechanism.

If we now take up the case of the legislative branch, the emerging picture is similar. Border relations between Mexico and the U.S. constitute a clear example of the process by which foreign policy issues have reached Congress as a result of the emergence of so-called intermestic issues.[88] Thus, although on many occasions Congress treats problems traditionally considered as domestic issues, these have ramifications for U.S. foreign policy to a far greater extent than before.

This process tended to crop up in the U.S.–Mexican relationship before it did elsewhere, largely as a result of the content of the Mexican–U.S. intergovernmental negotiating agenda itself. In recent years, congressional interest in Mexico has grown and through a series of mechanisms it has sought to influence the policy of the executive branch toward Mexico. For example, Congress has been one of the organs of the U.S. government which paid closest attention to the debate over North American economic integration. A growing interest in "Mexican issues" by Congress is demonstrated by its attention to energy-related problems, its hearings and public debates over such issues, and the frequent visits to Mexico by an increasing number of legislators.[89]

Border issues have attracted particular interest. There is a large number of legislative committees and subcommittees whose jurisdictions include issues such as those we have reviewed in this section. This number would be even larger if to these issues we add others such as drug smuggling and the migration of undocumented workers.[90] Moreover, congressional interest in U.S. policies toward Mexico has deep historical roots, and intervention in the making of such policies is a jealously guarded prerogative of U.S. legislators. It should surprise no one that some actions which have most impacted upon relations with Mexico were initiated by the legislative branch. To the highest levels of the U.S. government, this introduces an additional element of complexity in the "management" and control of its policy toward Mexico. Indeed, some of the problems examined in detail here undoubtedly represent specific issues in which Congress's tendency to "respond in ways that protect the short-term interests of highly organized domestic groups" can express itself.[91]

A third element adding to the burgeoning number of government actors and to the extreme complexity of the formulation of

U.S. policy toward Mexico should be mentioned. This is the participation of various state and local governments. While a discussion of this question is beyond the scope of this paper, it may be noted that these agencies not only influence the outcome of issues that explicitly and obviously fall within their jurisdictions; they also affect some of the central issues of the relationship, including those discussed in this paper.[92] Some of the potential implications of such influence can be grasped if we remember such things as, for example, the fact that in the case of the U.S., bilateral relations assume a very different character and significance when viewed from the Southwest than when viewed from Washington. Border region politics add another dimension: U.S. regional politics. One set of important actors in this arena has been the governments of the principal border cities. The pursuit of their interests provides us with an example of the complex relations that crop up between U.S. regional, state, and federal politics on the one hand and Mexican-U.S. relations on the other. Differences among regions with regard to the impact of such developments as a U.S. economic recession can alter how the objective conditions of the relationship are defined, since they would result, for example, in different regional attitudes toward such issues as undocumented migration.

Up to this point in our discussion of the actors expressing divergent or even contradictory views and policy proposals to those of the highest levels of the executive, we have limited ourselves strictly to governmental agencies. Let us now consider the influence of nongovernmental actors, which demonstrates the close linkages between domestic and foreign policy issues; at least for those which figure prominently on the Mexican-U.S. intergovernmental negotiation agenda. In these areas, the governmental agencies responsible for executing policy are increasingly less isolated from civil society. This greater contact with nongovernmental forces imposes limitations on coherent U.S. government responses to virtually all of the issues we have discussed. The number of private interests that have a stake in the outcomes of bilateral issues is quite large.

A glimpse of the complexity of nongovernmental participation in matters affecting this aspect of U.S.-Mexican relations is offered in a recent article by Milton H. Jamail which discusses "voluntary organizations along the border."[93] The author identifies several types of organizations:

1. Semi-voluntary organizations which, notwithstanding their official status and state financing, do most of their work through volunteers; and operate basically at the state level. Examples: the Arizona–Mexico Commission, the Commission of the Californias, the New Mexico–Mexico Commission, and the Texas Good Neighbor Commission.
2. Local voluntary organizations, including community organizations, social service agencies, and binational groups which deal with the problems of the twin cities, such as the Inter-City Group in the area of El Paso and Ciudad Juárez.
3. Region-wide voluntary organizations such as the Organization of United States Border Cities and Counties, the United States–Mexico Border Health Association, and such educational groups as the Border State University Consortium for Latin America and the Association of Borderlands Scholars. All of these draw their membership from throughout the border region.
4. Business associations such as those composed of assembly plant firms (Committee for 806.30 and 807.00, Inc.) and vegetable exporting interests whose membership straddles the border (West Mexico Vegetable Distributors Association) or can be found exclusively on one side, such as the several associations of vegetable growers in Florida.
5. National organizations that have programs with a focus on border issues. Examples: American Friends Service Committee, Partners of the Americas, Sister Cities International.
6. Single issue groups such as the Presbyterian Church (USA) Task Force on Mexico-United States Relations and Migration of the Undocumented, and the San Diego–Tijuana based Servicios de Solidaridad Transfrontera which deal with issues related to undocumented workers.

To this long list of voluntary organizations Jamail adds the extended network of what he calls *informal relations*, through which border city interests are coordinated, and which can involve "bank presidents, activist groups, city officials, law enforcement personnel, or members of the educational community."[94]

As many observers have noted, both the high level of integration into the U.S. economy that the border region as a whole has reached, and the resulting complex set of transborder social interactions have helped to give rise to this multiplicity of nongovernmental actors at all levels. The resulting process was called by Richard Fagen "politics of the borderlands."[95] At times, some of the interests have formed strong transnational alliances which have influenced the policy direction taken by officials of either or both of the governments involved. At other instances, the very fact that the border is the physical point of contact between the two social formations has sharpened those frictions and tensions that characterize the relationship as a whole. Thus, the capacity of the nongovernmental actors to generate conflict and to promote transnational alliances is considerable, with their interactions eventually reflected at the level of intergovernmental relations.

The in-bond industry can be used again to illustrate some of these real or potential developments. It is clear that retaining items 806.30 and 807.00 in the U.S. tariff laws is not just convenient for Mexico's balance of payments; it is also in the interest of certain sectors of U.S. industry. One of the main obstacles to the operation of this form of transnational capitalism is import trade barriers on assembled goods. At least in this area, the objective interests of the Mexican government and these U.S. firms converge, not only at the level of intergovernmental relations, but also at that of U.S. domestic politics. This, of course, does not eliminate the possibility of heightened domestic conflict over this specific issue extending beyond localized environments. This possibility stems from the deterioration of the U.S. economy in the last decade, and from the growing volume of off-shore assembled goods. One should not forget that organized labor has been sharply critical of this development.[96]

Thus far, our analysis of governmental bargaining power in relation to border issues has shown two opposing conclusions. On the one hand, the existence of asymmetries and vulnerabilities in nongovernmental relations between Mexico and the United States provides the latter with a considerable number of potential sources of bargaining power. On the other hand, the realization of these potentials by the highest levels of the U.S. government is made difficult by the complexity of border problems which results from the number of governmental and nongovernmental interests at work.

Because of this complexity, the only way to guarantee a minimum of coherence in the actions of different U.S. government agencies is for the highest levels of the U.S. government to assign a relatively high priority to Mexican issues. In other words, discussion should proceed from the question of the extent to which the U.S. government has the power, to the question of the extent to which it *needs* to control and manage the different channels of nongovernmental relationship. This largely depends on whether or not the U.S. needs to use its bargaining chips to achieve the desired Mexican responses to specific border issues, or to the global context of the relationship. Regarding the former, an assessment of the need to apply pressure on specific border issues would depend on conjunctural factors. It would be difficult, however, to identify any such need at present.

The need for the U.S. government to use the potential sources of power to achieve desired Mexican responses in the global context of the relationship would, in turn, depend on a more complex set of considerations. It is noteworthy that the level of priority given by the U.S. government to Mexican issues has increased considerably in the last decade, a trend that has become more marked since 1977. This increased priority seems to be closely related to the leading role of Mexican energy resources in reactivating the search for new forms of political discourse in Mexico-U.S. relations, described in the first section of the paper. In any case, oil and gas have clearly stimulated U.S. interest in Mexico. But—as can be seen from these remarks—a discussion of those considerations that may lead the U.S. government to use the potential sources of power in the global context of the relationship falls outside the limits of the case study we have tried to develop. In fact such a discussion will constitute the basic component of the concluding remarks, where the relevance of the analysis developed in the study of Mexican-U.S. relations at a more general level and predictions for the future will be assessed.

CONCLUDING OBSERVATIONS

In this paper I have tried to identify the principal shortcomings of the rhetoric of interdependence by exploring some of the implications of general statements such as those which argue that "it is obvious that the United States needs Mexico, as Mexico needs the United States,"[97] and by clarifying some of the concepts employed by this rhetoric.

The arguments could be summarized in four propositions. First are the processes that have given rise to the phenomena of interdependence. Rather, as we saw in the case of border production sharing activities, and probably in many others, these can be explained better as manifestations of the de facto integration of "Mexican" activities into the workings of the U.S. economy. In some of the examples chosen one might even argue that the activities described have stronger links to the economy of the U.S. than to that of Mexico itself.

Second, one of the major themes that has emerged from our analysis could be characterized as the paradox of dependency. This paradox arises from the fact that while many of the activities and interactions we have discussed not only express but reproduce and exacerbate Mexican dependency, they are, at the same time, of vital importance for the present Mexican model of development.

Third, it is clear that the dynamics of this process do not show a mutual dependence, but rather U.S. domination of Mexico. Notwithstanding the rhetoric, the types of nongovernmental linkages in the areas we have studied reflect a profound asymmetry which provides the U.S. government with an impressive set of potential pressure points with respect to the Mexican government. Indeed, we have described a whole series of mechanisms which, if the highest levels of the U.S. government were in a position to manage, could be applied individually or jointly, depending upon the degree to which they wanted to make the Mexican government feel the significance attributed by them to a particular issue. More interesting is that these could be applied without having to make any explicit reference to the issue in question. Thus, the mechanisms which U.S. government officials have to manage interdependence are subtle and discreet.

Finally, this potential power of the U.S. government is not without its obstacles. As has been pointed out, these do not stem from a lack of technical capacity to control those nongovernmental links I have been describing. But to exercise these potential sources of bargaining power, the U.S. government would face some domestic political costs, insofar as it would have to impose a single policy not only on the number of government actors involved but also on a range of private interests which may or may not be in agreement. These difficulties would be greater if such a policy were to link many different issues into a package deal. For this reason, one would not expect that the U.S. government would pay this price unless it was absolutely necessary. What would make such a policy necessary?

This question seems to have, as regards governmental bargaining power, two types of answers. One would be the Mexican government's acquisition of a bargaining power of such magnitude that the U.S. government would be forced to make major concessions in specific areas, that is, to behave like a reliable partner. Another would be the impossibility of achieving central U.S. foreign policy goals through other means. Either of these challenges would force the U.S. government to pay the domestic costs necessary to make its counterpart behave in a suitable way.

A discussion of the possible use of the sources of power available to the U.S. government as, metaphorically speaking, carrots or sticks, would have to take into account (a) the need to do so, and (b) the domestic political costs involved in the different alternatives to be considered. As regards their use as carrots in the context of a package deal made necessary by an increase in Mexican bargaining power, we have already recalled the relative increase in the importance assigned by Washington to Mexican issues during recent years. This new level of priority can only be evaluated by comparing it to that received by other countries and regions which compete for the attention of the central policy makers, and by weighing it against the requirements imposed by the complexity of the relationship.

In any case, the U.S. government's behavior in the last few years suggests that it remains to be convinced that the Mexican government has any new bargaining power. Such an evaluation may have been reinforced by the deterioration of the Mexican balance of payments, leading to a situation where it may become as important for the Mexican foreign trade sector to sell oil as it is for the economy of the United States to buy it. Be that as it may, the U.S. government has yet to adopt a more coherent approach in its dealings with Mexico.

In the end, U.S. attempts to formulate a more coherent policy may result not so much from an enhanced Mexican bargaining power as from some of the basic realities of the relationship itself, such as the de facto linkage among the main issues on the Mexican–U.S. agenda. This bilateral relationship poses some difficulties for both governments which seek to concentrate on only one of the many bilateral connections—e.g., energy—without taking into account possible effects in the political, economic and social spheres. Put in other terms, for the U.S., Mexico is not just another oil-exporting country. The nearly two thousand miles of common border, whose implications we have discussed, elevate the risks of narrowly defined policies for the U.S. government. Nevertheless, it is important to realize that if a more coherent policy were to result from this kind of consideration, its basic outlines would be defined not through a process of bilateral negotiations—as would be the case if the need for it derived from an increase in Mexican bargaining power—but on the basis of U.S. unilateral decisions and evaluations of the domestic and international costs and benefits involved.

In considering the possibility of the potential bargaining chips analyzed as sticks to be applied on an ad hoc basis, we can start by making a quite general consideration. It could be argued that the domestic political costs would be higher in the case of package deal negotiations and lower if the objective of U.S. action was only to penalize the Mexican government through the use of some of the potential sources of power available. The basic reason for this would be that the use of the points of pressure provided by the existing asymmetries as instruments of punishment could be limited in the scope of interest affected (which could be chosen unilaterally by the U.S. government) and in its duration. If such an evaluation is realistic, this second kind of use of the points of pressure we have described would seem to be more likely than any package deal, *if* the U.S. government felt the need to let its displeasure over a given Mexican policy (foreign or domestic) be felt by its counterpart. A discussion of the concrete instances where such a possibility may arise is beyond the scope of this essay. Nevertheless, some of them can be pointed out. An increase in friction in bilateral relations as a result of the complex political process exemplified in the previous section, the possibility of considerable changes in the conduct of the Mexican government, or objective changes in the domestic and international underpinnings of U.S. foreign policy might open the door to a U.S. attempt to articulate a coherent policy to circumscribe Mexican government behavior. Three points have to be remembered. First, the U.S. government has an interest in Mexican political stability—which has led to a certain tolerance for Mexican actions legitimizing the regime in power. Second, it has a stake in the maintenance of the basic outlines of Mexican economic arrangements. Third, it is possible that considerations such as these may impose some limits, at least as regards their most extreme expressions, on the uses of the sources of power as instruments for penalizing the Mexican government.

What does all this tell us about the prospects for Mexican-U.S. relations in the eighties? If the analysis developed in this paper is correct, one can see that the events of the coming decade are likely to be very different from the normative futures suggested by exponents of the rhetoric of interdependence. Rather, we see a future of recurring diplomatic conflict which would accompany —if present trends continue—the intensification of the de facto integration process of the Mexican economy into the U.S. economy. Such conflict will serve to remind us of the extraordinary complexity of the relationship at a nongovernmental level. It will also reactivate the interest of and the priority assigned to these issues by the U.S. government on a recurring basis. In any case, reality will differ greatly from the images derived from any rhetorical incantation of Mexican-U.S. interdependence.

Notes

1. The terminology used in this paper is based on the work of those authors who have developed the field of transnational relations. Three basic levels and channels of contact between social formations will be identified: (a) transnational relations in which at least one of the participants is a nongovernmental entity; (b) transgovernmental relations in which those entities that interact are neither the highest levels of government nor those agencies specifically and formally charged with the execution of foreign policy; and (c) intergovernmental relations in which the participants are the highest levels of government. See, for example, the introduction and conclusion in Robert Keohane and Joseph Nye, Jr. (eds.), *Transnational Relations and World Politics* (Cambridge: Harvard University Press, 1971); Keohane and Nye, Jr., "Transgovernmental Relations and International Organizations," *World Politics* 26 (Autumn 1974); and Keohane and Nye, Jr., *Power and Interdependence: World Politics in Transition* (Boston: Little, Brown and Company, 1977). See also the articles published in *International Affairs* 52, no. 3 (July 1976). Particularly useful in this issue is the article by Susan Strange, "The Study of Transnational Relations."

2. See, for example, Joaquín Gamboa Pascoe's comments before several U.S. Congressmen in Washington. *Excélsior*, 4 June 1978.

3. The statement was made at a 4 May 1978 press conference. Reproduced in *Department of State Bulletin* (June 1978):58.

4. We are using these concepts in the sense proposed by James A. Caporaso in the introduction to the Special Issue of *International Organization on Dependence and Dependency in the Global System* 32 (Winter 1978). In general, dependency refers to the insertion of the lesser developed countries into the global capitalist

system, while dependence refers to the external reliance of one nation-state on another.

5. Olga Pellicer de Brody, *México y la revolución cubana* (México: El Colegio de México, 1970), is the standard work in which these ideas are developed.

6. "México se convertirá en una gran potencia, señala Jean Olf Carlson," *Excélsior*, 29 January 1980, p. 23.

7. "México jugará un papel importante en la economía mundial: *Les Echos*," *El Día*, 31 January 1979.

8. "El crudo limitará la dependencia de México," *Excélsior*, 17 October 1978, p. 18A.

9. The Mexican Secretary of Patrimonio y Fomento Industrial, José Andrés Oteyza, was quoted as saying that "oil and gas will afford us the financial self-determination to obviate economic policy schemes imposed from outside; they will provide an opportunity to make a great leap forward." "El petróleo permitirá eliminar imposiciones políticas externas: Oteyza," *Excélsior*, 9 November 1978, p. 4.

10. *Uno Más Uno*, 17 February 1979, p. 3.

11. See, for example, Mario Ojeda, "México ante los Estados Unidos en la coyuntura actual," *Foro Internacional* 18 (July–September 1977): 32–53.

12. "Hidrocarburos: el poder mexicano," *Proceso*, 4 December 1978.

13. *Hanson's Latin American Letter*, 21 October 1978 [Washington, D.C.].

14. Kenneth E. Hill, *North American Energy: A Proposal for a Common Market Between Canada, Mexico and the United States* (New York: Blith, Eastman, Dillon, and Co., 1979), p. 3.

15. Statement made by Jesús Puente Leyva, then-chairman of the Comisión de Energéticos of the Mexican Chamber of Representatives. "Provocación el mercomún que propone EE.UU.," *Excélsior*, 19 April 1979.

16. For a discussion of common market proposals that emphasize energy see Hill, *North American Energy*; the arguments of Herbert E. Meyer in his article, "Why a North American Common Market Won't Work Yet," *Fortune*, 10 September 1979, p. 118; and the comments of the Interpress Service reproduced in "La propuesta de Estados Unidos para la creación de un mercado común norteamericano sería inaceptable para México," *Uno Más Uno*, 21 January 1980, p. 14.

17. See Jesús Puente Leyva's statement, *Excélsior*, 19 April 1979.

18. This is one of the principal concerns, arising from the obvious differences in the industrial capabilities of both countries, which have been referred to, for instance, by Mexico's Undersecretary for Foreign Trade, Héctor Hernández, "Es impossible el mercomún E.U.-México-Canadá," *Uno Más Uno*, 31 August 1979. See also Hill, *North American Energy*, and particularly, Meyer, "Why a North American Common Market," and Interpress Service, "La propuesta de Estados Unidos para la creación de un mercado común," p. 14.

19. This line of reasoning was developed by the present Mexican Secretary of Foreign Relations, Jorge Castañeda, in a book originally published in 1956. See *México y el orden internacional*, 2nd ed. (México: El Colegio de México, 1981), pp. 179–184. New proposals such as the common market have breathed new life into an old Mexican debate on Pan Americanism, to which Castañeda's arguments were directed.

20. George Grayson, "Mexico's Oil Boom," *Foreign Policy* 29 (Winter 1977–78):67.

21. Robert Keohane and Joseph Nye, Jr., "Introduction: The Complex Politics of Canadian-American Interdependence," in *Canada and the United States: Transnational and Transgovernmental Relations*, edited by Annette Baker Fox et al. (New York: Columbia University Press, 1976).

22. *Ibid.*

23. Terence A. Todman, "Latin American Development in an Interdependent World," *Department of State Bulletin*, 3 October 1977, pp. 440-41.

24. For a discussion see Carlos Rico F., "Las prioridades de la administración Carter y su política hacia México," in *Perspectivas actuales de las relaciones entre México y Estados Unidos*, ed. Edmundo Hernández Vela S. (México: Universidad Nacional Autónoma de México, 1980), pp. 77-102.

25. This was pointed out by out-going U.S. Ambassador to Mexico, Joseph John Jova. See *Excélsior*, 4 February 1977, p. 9A.

26. See, for example, references to a speech by then U.S. Secretary of State Henry Kissinger, 11 June 1976, in Secretaría de la Presidencia, Departamento Editorial, *3000 kilómetros de frontera* (México, 1976).

27. See the article by David Ronfeldt and Caesar Sereseres in this volume.

28. *Ibid.*

29. Thus, to paraphrase the former ambassador to Mexico, Patrick Lucey, Mexican and U.S. interests are not incompatible. On the contrary, they uniquely complement each other. Speech delivered by Lucey to the Cooper Union Foundation, reproduced in a special bulletin from the Agency for International Communication, U.S. Embassy, Mexico City, 16 October 1978, p. 12.

30. Speech delivered by U.S. Vice President during his visit to Mexico in January 1978, reproduced in *Department of State Bulletin* (March 1978):11.

31. Lucey, speech delivered to Cooper Union Foundation.

32. See, for example, the paper by Clark W. Reynolds in this volume.

33. "Proponen un mercomún hemisférico los legisladores republicanos de Estados Unidos," *Uno Más Uno*, 1 August 1979, p. 15.

34. *Uno Más Uno*, 16 November 1979.

35. "Las diferencias México-Estados Unidos tienen solución: Brown," *Uno Más Uno*, 7 July 1979, p. 5.

36. "Mercomún entre México, Canadá y Estados Unidos, propone un comité de senadores," *Uno Más Uno*, 8 June 1979, p. 14.

37. "Senadores de Estados Unidos por la alianza energética con México y Canadá," *Uno Más Uno*, 27 April 1979.

38. "Mercomún entre México, Canadá y Estados Unidos," *Uno Más Uno*, 8 June 1979, p. 14.

39. "Las diferencias México-Estados Unidos tienen solución," *Uno Más Uno*, 7 July 1979, p. 5.

40. As referred to in *Hanson's Latin American Letter*.

41. "¿Mercomún norteamericano?" *Uno Más Uno*, 17 July 1979.

42. The discussion of such proposals seems to have extended to groups such as the Organization of American States (OAS). See references and replies to a statement made by OAS Secretary Alejandro Orfila in Lima, Peru. "Pugna la OEA por la integración económica de Estados Unidos, Canadá y México," *Excélsior*, 16 April 1979.

43. According to Margaret L. Lawson, there is room for concrete proposals in areas such as aerospace products, concrete, agricultural machinery, electronics, building materials and petrochemicals. See "The North American Neighborhood," *Christian Science Monitor*, 6 November 1979.

44. See Graham Allison, *Essence of Decision* (Boston: Little-Brown, 1971).

45. Of particular interest are statements made by Víctor Manzanilla Schaffer, then-chairman of the Foreign Relations Committee, Mexican Chamber of Representatives, "No debemos integrarnos a un sistema tripartito con Estados Unidos y Canadá, afirma Manzanilla," *Excélsior*, 9 February 1979.

46. This would hold because the Mexican observers cited above view such a future as incompatible with the country's present political realities. Some, though not all, would even echo the unqualified assessments of the Interpress Service or of Herbert Meyer, who was quoted, in the *Uno Más Uno* article of 21 January 1980, as suggesting that a "common market would seal an irrevocable situation of dependency, which—though already existing—would reduce to a minimum the efficacy of any defensive policy." The latter argues, in his article "Why a North American Common Market," (p. 122), that the U.S. would inevitably dominate such a common market, however carefully its rules might be set up or smoothly its diplomats act, or however well the economies of the other members behave.

47. See note 1.

48. To include the category of *dependency* in our analysis, taken as a structural conditioner of the economies of the periphery of the capitalist system, undoubtedly would increase our understanding of the phenomenon that interests us. Thus, we could not only explain the basically unidirectional sense in which such peripheral economies have been affected by the dynamics and expansion of those in the center, but we would link the fulfillment of their specific functions, not to the efficiency of the whole, but the backwardness of some and the dynamism of others. Such a category would also enable us to concentrate our attention on the structure of internal domination linked to the fulfillment of this function, as well as the articulation of the dominant groups in the center and in the periphery. Nevertheless, for the purposes of this essay, it is not necessary to consider these additional questions. This is because attention is centered on the strict level of relations between governments and not on that of the relations between social classes and groups to which the analysis of dependence inevitably returns us. See for example Ruy Mauro Marini, *Subdesarrollo y revolución* (México: Siglo XXI Editores, 1971); Fernando Cardoso and Enzo Faletto, *Dependencia y desarrollo en América Latina* 4th ed. (México: Siglo XXI Editores, 1971). An attempt to develop this approach for the Mexican case is Lorenzo Meyer, "Cambio político y dependencia," *Foro Internacional* 13 (1972):101-138. Among others, these works offer a lesson that the concept of dependency also has different meanings and uses.

49. "Comentario a Pellicer de Brody," made by Edelberto Torres Rivas, in *Relaciones políticas entre América Latina y Estados Unidos*, eds. Julio Cotler and Richard R. Fagen (Buenos Aires: Amorrortu Editores, 1974).

50. Robert A. Dahl, "The Concept of Power," *Behavioral Science* 2 (1957): 201-05. A short, but powerful critique of this "one dimensional view" of power

can be found in Steven Lukes, *Power: A Radical View* (London: Macmillan Press, Ltd., 1974).

51. Oran R. Young, "Interdependencies in World Politics," *International Journal* 24 (Autumn 1979).

52. Joseph S. Nye, Jr., "Independence and Interdependence," *Foreign Policy* 22 (Spring 1976):133.

53. Kenneth N. Waltz, "The Myth of National Interdependence," in *The International Corporation*, ed. Charles Kindleberger (Cambridge: MIT Press, 1977), pp. 211-12.

54. Nye, Jr., "Independence and Interdependence," p. 134.

55. Jack Behrman, *National Interests and the Multinational Enterprise* (Englewood Cliffs, N.J.: Prentice-Hall, 1970), pp. 88-127.

56. This aspect of our analysis has been developed in "Method and Madness, Looking for a Typology of Issue-Areas in U.S. Foreign Policy Making," unpublished manuscript, Department of Government, Harvard University, 1981.

57. An earlier draft of these ideas was presented in Carlos Rico Ferrat, "La frontera mexicano-norteamericana; la retórica de la 'interdependencia' y el problema de las asimetrías." (Paper presented at the First National Symposium on Border Studies, El Colegio de México and the Facultad de Filosofía y Letras of the University of Nuevo León, January 24-27, 1979).

58. See James W. Wilkie, "Conflicting 'National Interests' Between and Within Mexico and the U.S.," in this volume.

59. Mario Ojeda, *Alcances y límites de la política exterior de México* (México: El Colegio de México, 1976).

60. Peter J. Katzenstein, "International Interdependence: Some Long-term Trends and Recent Changes," *International Organization* 32 (Winter 1977), p. 1023. See also Edward L. Morse, "Transnational Economic Processes," in *Transnational Relations and World Politics*, ed. Joseph Nye and Robert Keohane (Cambridge: Harvard University Press, 1972).

61. The literature on this subject is abundant. See, for example, the papers of David A. Gantz; J.F. Friedkin; S.E. Reynolds; César Sepúlveda; and Alejandro Sobarzo included in *Pollution and International Boundaries*, ed. Albert Uton (Albuquerque: University of New Mexico Press, 1972). These essays provide a good view of the terms of the debate regarding the effects of salinity in the Mexicali Valley.

62. See, for example, Joaquín Telloz, "Sources of Atmospheric Pollution at the U.S.-Mexican Border;" and Bill Enríquez, "International Legal Implications of Industrial Development Along the Mexico-U.S. Border," in *Pollution and International Boundaries*.

63. A discussion of what occurred in the months following the August 1976 devaluation appear in "Weak Peso Drives Mexican Cattle to U.S.," *New York Times*, 3 January 1977, p. 33.

64. Joaquín Xirau Icaza and Miguel Díaz, "Nuestra dependencia fronteriza," *Archivo del Fondo* (Fondo de Cultura Económica) 48 (1976):88.

65. An historical treatment of this process in Ciudad Juárez appears in Oscar J. Martínez, *Border Boom Town: Ciudad Juárez Since 1848* (Austin: University of Texas Press, 1978).

66. Calvin P. Blair, "Mexico: Some Recent Developments and the Interdependence Relationship with the United States," in *Recent Developments in Mexico and Their Economic Implications for the United States, Hearings before the Subcommittee on Inter-American Economic Relationships of the Joint Economic Committee* (Washington, D.C.: Government Printing Office, 1977), p. 357.

67. Earl Gottschalk, "Shopkeepers North of the Border Suffer from Devaluation of Money in Mexico," *Wall Street Journal*, 14 December 1976, p. 40.

68. "Mexico's Problems Won't Stop at the Border," *Business Week*, 19 December 1977.

69. *Hanson's Latin American Letter*, 17 June 1978.

70. For an analysis of U.S. public and official perceptions of Mexico in the late seventies see Olga Pellicer, "La política de Estados Unidos hacia México: la nueva perspectiva," *Foro Internacional* 19 (1978): 193-215.

71. Banco de México, *Indicadores Económicos* 6 (1978):30-68; U.S. Department of Commerce, *Survey of Current Business* 58 (1978):28.

72. Xirau Icaza and Díaz, "Nuestra dependencia fronteriza," p. 88.

73. Ojeda, *Alcances y límites*, p. 154.

74. "La industria maquiladora: evolución reciente y perspectivas," *Comercio Exterior* (April 1977):410-411.

75. Raúl Trajtenberg, *Transnacionales y fuerza de trabajo en la periferia: tendencias recientes en la internacionalización de la producción* (México: Instituto Latinoamericano de Estudios Transnacionales, 1978).

76. Isaac Minian and Pedro Vuskovic, "Nuevas tendencias en las formas de integración de los países subdesarrollados a la economía mundial." (Paper presented at the CIDE seminar, Barcelona, Spain, June 5-10, 1978).

77. Peter F. Drucker, "The Rise of Production Sharing," *Wall Street Journal*, 15 March 1977.

78. Enid Baird Lovell, *Nacionalismo o interdependencia: las alternativas* (Buenos Aires: Editorial Paidós, 1973).

79. It is beyond the scope of this paper to treat the economic issues involved in the creation of the production sharing industry. For a discussion of this see Isaac Minian, *Progresso técnico e internacionalización del proceso productivo; el caso de la industria maquiladora de "tipo electrónico,"* Cuaderno de CIDE, no. 1 (México: CIDE, 1977).

80. *Ibid.*, p. 2.

81. Donald Baerresen, *The Border Industrialization Program of Mexico* (Lexington, Massachusetts: Lexington Books, 1971), pp. 3-8.

82. "La industria maquiladora," *Comercio Exterior*, p. 412.

83. "Border Crisis 1975: Workers Strike, Shops Move On," *NACLA Latin America and Empire Report* 9 (July-August 1975): 16-23.

84. Ojeda, *Alcances y límites*.

85. For a development of this argument see Virginia Moori Konig, "Pérdida de competitividad de la industria manufacturera norteamericana," *Cuadernos semistrales de Estados Unidos: perspectiva latinoamericana*, no. 4 (1978): 287-317.

86. Baerresen, *The Border Industrialization Program*, p. 115, emphasis added.

87. *Ibid.*, p. 65.

88. Bayless Manning, "The Congress, the Executive and Intermestic Affairs: Three Proposals," *Foreign Affairs* (January 1977).
89. Donald L. Wyman, "The United States Congress and the Making of U.S. Policy Toward Mexico," Working Papers in U.S.-Mexican Studies, no. 13, La Jolla, California: Program in U.S.-Mexican Studies, University of California, San Diego, 1981.
90. *Ibid.*, p. 13.
91. *Ibid.*, p. 60.
92. For examples of this, see "Coinciden JLP y (Texas Governor) W. Clements: debe cambiar el status de los indocumentados," *Uno Más Uno*, 25 January 1979; "Jueces de Los Angeles piden que se legisle para proteger a indocumentados," *Excélsior* 9 July 1978, p. 19A; "Carter, dispuesto a negociar el gas; deben reanudarse tratos; cuatro gobernadores," *Uno Más Uno*, 14 February 1979, p. 1; "[Edmund G.] Brown insiste sobre la venta de gas," *Excélsior* 14 October 1978, p. 1.
93. Milton H. Jamail, "Voluntary Organizations Along the Border," in *Mexico-United States Relations, Proceedings of the Academy of Political Science*, ed. Susan Kaufman Purcell (New York: Academy of Political Science, 1981), pp. 78-87.
94. *Ibid.*, p. 85.
95. Richard Fagen, "An Inescapable Relationship," *Wilson Quarterly* 3 (Summer 1979).
96. Peter Baird and Ed McCaughan, "Hit and Run: U.S. Runaway Shops on the Mexican Border," *NACLA Latin America and Empire Report* 9 (1975):24-28.
97. Statement by Patrick J. Lucey, former U.S. Ambassador to Mexico, published in *Excélsior*, 26 October 1977, p. 22A. See also the statements made by then Deputy Assistant Secretary of State for Inter-American Affairs, Sally Shelton, reproduced in *Proceso* 12 December 1977.

MEXICAN PETROLEUM:
A Resource for Whom?

II

5
Oil Booms and the Mexican Historical Experience: Past Problems—Future Prospects

Lorenzo Meyer

Since 1976, Mexico's oil policies have changed dramatically. After the discovery of new petroleum deposits in the early 1970s, Mexico decided to become a relatively important exporter of oil and petroleum by-products. This change reflects a break with the past—with the second to fourth decades of this century. During that period, Mexico experienced its first oil boom. We would be committing a serious error and failing in our responsibility to future generations if we now ignored some of the lessons we should have learned then. The objective of this essay is to show that those lessons are still valid today.

Mexico ceased to be a significant oil exporter more than half a century ago. When this country expropriated the oil industry in March of 1938, it simply accentuated this. With a single stroke, Mexican oil was eliminated from the channels of international

---

Lorenzo Meyer has been a professor at the Center for International Studies of El Colegio de México since 1970, and is the author of several books, including *Mexico and the United States in the Oil Controversy, 1917-1941* (1972) and two volumes in the series *Historia de la Revolución Mexicana*. He is the co-author of a forthcoming book titled *México frente a los Estados Unidos: Un enfoque histórico*, to be published in 1983 by El Colegio de México.

This is a translation and 1981 updating of the article, "El auge petrolero y las experiencias mexicanas disponibles: Los problemas del pasado y la visión del futuro," which first appeared in *Las perspectivas del petróleo mexicano*, published by Centro de Estudios Internacionales, El Colegio de México, México, 1979. Reprinted with permission. Translated by Manual García Griego.
© 1983 by Lorenzo Meyer.

commerce dominated then by the same powerful foreign companies which had created and developed Mexican oil production during the first decades of the century. Then, only 40 percent of oil production—18.7 million barrels in 1937—were exported, a relatively low proportion considering that in 1921, 190 million barrels, or 99 percent of the oil produced, was destined for export. Nevertheless, the loss of export markets in 1938 had an immediate effect on the Mexican economy, as a result of its declining balance of payments. When World War II began, the Allies applied an oil embargo against the Axis powers, which further diminished the volume of Mexican oil exports. By the end of the war, Mexico was exporting only 5.5 million barrels annually—a mere 13 percent of what had already become a modest level of production.

During the post-war period, the newly nationalized industry dedicated itself almost completely to supplying the domestic market. This was no easy task, since the demand was growing quickly. Although a small amount was exported, it must be borne in mind that some oil and refined products were also imported to supply the needs of the northern sections of the country. After 1944, Mexico occasionally experienced a negative oil trade balance, and by the early seventies, its role as an oil exporting country seemed to be a thing of the past.

In 1976, this role was transformed almost overnight. The global energy crisis had coincided with a Mexican domestic crisis—the end of the twenty-year "stabilizing development" model during the Echeverría administration. Both forced the Mexican government, despite the skepticism of many, to reevaluate the level of available proven oil reserves and to undertake a policy which rapidly increased investment and expanded exports in the oil industry. Beginning in 1978, Mexico reentered the world oil market with an export volume of 250,000 barrels per day, which increased sharply to more than 1 million barrels per day in 1980. This decision placed Mexico in a position reminiscent of the early period of the industry, and for this reason we must now recall some of the experiences of the past.

Although the lessons of the past do not constitute a blueprint for dealing with present events, it has never been prudent to dismiss them. Those who forget history, observed George Santayana, are condemned to repeat it. To be sure, every social—and particularly political—process has a set of unique characteristics which, strictly speaking, cannot be duplicated. All historical lessons, therefore, are incomplete. Nevertheless, since each new chain of events preserves important aspects of the past, it is useful to consider the collective memory—history—as one additional factor when formulating policies that would change the present, and above all, alter the future. And without a doubt, today we face some of the same circumstances which shaped the history of Mexican oil vis-à-vis the rest of the world up to the middle of the twentieth century.

The struggle to nationalize the oil industry entailed a long process. It began formally in April 1916, with the presentation of a report by the Technical Commission on the Nationalization of Oil to then-president Venustiano Carranza. The report concluded that ". . . we believe that it is just and proper to return to the nation that which belongs to it, the richness of the subsoil, coal, and oil."[1] This objective might be said to have been assured by the early fifties, when the foreign companies formerly engaged in oil production and their governments finally ended their efforts to return to Mexico and accepted PEMEX as the only agency responsible for oil production and distribution[2] and that a meaningful foreign presence in those areas was impossible.

This process was significant because of the conflicts it engendered. So acute were these that in large measure they determined the nature of the relations between the Mexican Revolution and the rest of the world and even the character of the Revolution itself. At given times, such as 1917–20, 1925–27, and 1938–40, the most serious threats to the new regime and the principal obstacles to its programs did not come from within, but from without —from the pressures exerted by powerful oil interests and from governments acting in their behalf. On the other side of the coin were those instances when the Mexican government enjoyed considerable support from without, such as when government policy was relatively compatible with foreign interests. Two memorable examples would be the times when the Bucareli and Calles-Morrow agreements were negotiated in the 1920s. In any event, it cannot be denied that Mexico's oil policy choices of the decades 1910–50 had significant impact. Some of their consequences are still being felt.

The major decision of the last few years has been in the direction of dealing with the disastrous balance of payments problem by substantially increasing the volume of oil and petroleum byproducts exported. Everything seems to indicate that this decision will be crucial for Mexico's future—not only in the economic, but in social and political spheres. Apparently, the present political system cannot overcome the economic obstacles its own development model has created. If this is so, then the political demands generated by Mexico's unemployment and inflation, as well as the pressures of population growth (urban concentration, the inability of Mexico's industry to absorb the growing labor force) could take the present regime—itself the product of the Revolution—beyond its capacity to insure a minimum degree of national consensus and a minimal level of control over the principal political actors.

The respite oil gives to the present political system as a consequence of Mexico's transformation into an oil exporting country entails some risks. Some, but not all, are different from those in the past. And it is just here that the lessons of history are pertinent.

CHANGES AND CONTINUITIES

Among the factors that must be taken into account when trying to compare Mexico's situation as oil producer and exporter until nationalization, and again since 1976, one stands out: Mexico's dependence upon the United States, the country's major oil purchaser. Although Mexico's relations with the United States have changed somewhat in the two periods compared, its dependence on the U.S. has remained a basic constant. Many indicators support this observation; for instance, the concentration of foreign trade. On the eve of the 1938 expropriation, the U.S. received 56 percent of all of Mexico's exports and provided 62 percent of its imports. The situation has changed in the direction of increased concentration of foreign trade. In 1980 the country sold 61 percent of its exports to and bought 62 percent of its imports from the United States.

Another indicator is direct foreign investment in Mexico. Since before the Revolution, U.S. participation prevailed. It did not change when the governments of the Revolution were consolidating, nor has it materially changed since then. The U.S. proportion of foreign direct investment is presently about 80 percent. In the past, such investment was concentrated in the well-known mining and petroleum "enclaves," which have since disappeared. Today's direct foreign investment is concentrated in the new leading sectors of the Mexican economy—more than 70 percent can be found in industry.

The foreign public debt, whose servicing was postponed by the Revolution and which was later settled for a fraction of the original amount, has since reappeared. By the end of 1981 it had mushroomed to almost $50 billion, more than half of which is owed to U.S. lending institutions or to other institutions where U.S. influence predominates.[3]

Other indicators could be mentioned, but these are sufficient to sustain the argument that notwithstanding the elimination of enclave economies through nationalization or the Mexicanization of key industries (the oil industry among them), the economic dependence of Mexico vis-à-vis the United States persists.

An economic dependence relation is only part, though significant, of a broader dependence relation which includes political aspects. The latter constitutes another set of historical continuities. Even before the Revolution and certainly since then, Mexico has sought, in its dealings with the U.S., more maneuvering room than other Latin American countries. Nonetheless, after World War I and a U.S. confrontation with England and Germany over Mexico, there could be no doubt that Mexico was left without any recourse and within the U.S. sphere of influence. The world powers recognized it as such. Moreover, the alliance between Mexico and the U.S. during World War II and the subsequent effects of the Cold War afforded Mexico few opportunities to exhibit a modicum of independence. Nevertheless, Mexico took advantage, as far as it could, of many opportunities to keep some distance from the United States, though still remaining within the latter's sphere of influence.[4] In this vein one may note that the formulation of the Revolution's oil strategy took place in the context of this general dependence and of attempts to diminish it. The new oil strategy should be developed in the same context.

Another historical continuity to bear in mind is Mexico's limited importance as an oil producer in the global context. Between the downfall of Porfirio Díaz and the consolidation of Obregón's power, Mexico's high level of oil production was constantly increasing. When it reached a level of 157 million barrels, 25.3 percent of world production in 1921, Mexico was second only to the United States among the world's oil-producing nations. This peak did not last; production started to fall off in 1922, and by 1926 the decline was catastrophic. Two years later Venezuela surpassed Mexico's level of oil production, and Middle Eastern developments further diminished the importance of Mexican petroleum. From 1928 on, Mexico became a marginal producer of oil.

One might note that in 1973, Mexico barely produced 1 percent of the world's oil output and held only 0.6 percent (3.6 billion barrels) of the world's proven reserves. The picture changed somewhat with the September 1981 announcement that proven reserves had increased to a level around 72 billion barrels (approximately 9 percent of world reserves). This increase, notwithstanding its importance in placing Mexico considerably above Venezuela, did not constitute a qualitative change in a global context. At the beginning of 1978, Mexico produced 1.22 million barrels daily, 250,000 of which were exported, a level which doubled by the end of the year. The plans announced by PEMEX in March 1978 were that 2.2 million barrels of oil would be produced daily by 1980, which in fact occurred. Thus, by 1981 Mexico was exporting 1.5 million barrels per day—a tripling of the 1978 volume. Even so, the amounts produced and exported are only a fraction of the global output. In short, no matter how important oil's impact on Mexico may be, in an international context this nation will never have the means to significantly influence the world petroleum market as it did between 1918 and 1923, unless, of course, a tremendous crisis were to suspend the flow of oil from the Middle East, particularly from Saudi Arabia. For the immediate future and under normal conditions, the world will impose market conditions on Mexico, not the reverse. And in large measure, the natural market for Mexican oil is the United States.

Finally, one should examine the change and continuity of Mexico's economy and society over the period considered. It is in these that one finds significant and new developments. Until World War II Mexico had an agrarian society on the threshold of industrialization. The possibility of exhausting the nation's oil reserves did not loom large in reality, nor was the importance of oil quite as evident in Mexico as it was in the industrial societies of the time. But at the present time a Mexico without oil or gas is inconceivable.

The nation consumes over one million barrels of oil daily, and directly or indirectly this represents 85 percent of total energy consumption. Hydroelectric power plants are few; nuclear plants do not yet exist; and coal does not seem to be a viable alternative source of energy. As it is, coal is used only in such industries as steel—where no substitute is available. In sum, petroleum is a much more important raw material today than it was in the past. This presents us with a dilemma between national consumption and foreign export—and unless current estimates of proven reserves are revised significantly, the dilemma will become increasingly acute as we approach the end of the century.[5]

OIL AS A STRATEGIC MATERIAL AND MEXICO'S BARGAINING POSSIBILITIES

Once the United States resolved its problems in Southeast Asia in the early seventies, foreign policy concerns became a matter of lesser priority for Washington. As the Republican administration was replaced by the Democrats, Washington shifted its attention to the energy problem created by the 1973 oil embargo and the increase in the price of oil imports. The Carter Administration presented the problem of solving the energy crisis to the U.S. public as nothing less than the "moral equivalent of war." The securing of petroleum and its by-products in the short term, and the discovery of petroleum substitutes in the long term, have emerged as a preponderant, almost dominant concern of the present U.S. government's national interest. With Reagan and the relative oil glut in the world market of 1981, the energy crisis has now lost some of its sense of immediacy. Nevertheless, this definition is still applicable and has important implications for Mexican petroleum policy: from here on anything that involves the importation of energy supplies is a matter of priority importance to Washington.

The situation presently facing Mexico is not new. In 1915 the U.S. produced 300 million barrels of oil (about ten times the production of Mexico at that time), almost 65 percent of total world production. U.S. domestic consumption absorbed almost all of this, and by 1916, the need to substitute the oil which the U.S. exported to the Anglo-Franco alliance became a priority concern.[6] Fuel imported from Mexico became indispensable for the maintenance of an adequate equilibrium between domestic needs and the demand of the alliance.[7] Between 1915 and 1918 Mexican oil production doubled, and in the latter year, the Constitutional Congress of Querétaro adopted the fourth paragraph of Article 27 of the Constitution, which returned subsoil deposits to the public domain. The hitherto unquestioned control of a strategic material by U.S. and British corporations was thus challenged by Mexico. For many years the nation had to face the consequences of that decision.

The strategic nature of Mexican petroleum was doubly significant. On the one hand, a number of U.S. and British interests pressed the U.S. government to occupy militarily the Mexican oil producing regions arguing that German agents could sabotage the Mexican oil fields. (The British were arguing from experience, since they had destroyed the Rumanian wells on the advent of their occupation by the Central Empire.)[8] On the other hand, and in spite of the inability of Carranza's forces to withstand an invasion of Mexican territory, it was clear that the Mexican forces *did* have the means to destroy their own oil wells before foreign troops could take them over. Given the primitive roads of the region, an invading force could have taken hours—even days—to reach all of the strategic points of the production complex.[9] Moreover, the occupation of the petroleum region would have meant doing to Mexico what the Germans had done with Belgium, which would diminish the credibility of the U.S. position. Finally, going to war with Mexico would have required the withdrawal of a significant number of troops from the European front.

It was the strategic nature of oil itself that stopped the United States from resorting to invasion as a means of resolving the problem created by the adoption of the new Mexican Constitution of 1917. This strategic importance also led the U.S. to provide covert aid to General Manuel Peláez so that he might keep most of the petroleum-producing region out of Carranza's control.[10] Though it did not take place, the threat of an invasion to protect and maintain the foreign control of resources considered vital for the U.S. economy and national security was one of the constant pressures on Mexico from 1916 to 1920. In 1917, the U.S. War Department drafted and readied WPD 6474-408, a plan to occupy the Mexican oil region as quickly as possible.[11] In the final analysis, even if the invasion did not take place, Carranza found it impossible to enforce the section of Article 27 which applies to petroleum. On February 19, 1918, when he issued the executive order requiring oil companies to secure a concession from the government to confirm their activities, these corporations, with the support of the Department of State, simply refused to comply. Its sovereignty questioned, the Mexican government had to back down and accept, for tactical reasons, the fact that foreign enterprises would continue to produce oil as before. The enforcement of the Constitution would be postponed for a better time.[12]

If the past is at all instructive with respect to the influence that Mexican oil—or any other strategic natural resource—can have on negotiations with Washington, it shows that if carried out intelligently, i.e., if they appeal to the mutualities of interest between both countries, such negotiations can result in the U.S. accepting conditions it might otherwise ordinarily reject. But it is also clear that if Mexico's policy contemplates the possibility of denying its neighbor access to these resources, U.S. responses may include any action necessary to force Mexico to behave in accordance with the former's national interests. If in 1938 the United States did not use force to prevent the expropriation of the oil industry which President Cárdenas initiated, it was due in large measure to the fact that Mexican oil was no longer of strategic importance. By that time U.S. oil production had passed the billion barrel mark while Mexican production had dropped to 56 million; indeed, Mexico was simply one of many secondary oil producers. Moreover, at that time the United States needed Mexican cooperation in other and more important strategic areas. Oil could not be allowed to become an obstacle to a general agreement between the two countries.

Mexico's level of oil production is currently a fraction of the world total, and it is not therefore as strategic for the United States as it was in the final stages of World War I. However, it would not be too bold to suggest that, given the inability of world oil reserves in general, and U.S. in particular, to meet U.S. oil demands, a not-too-remote possibility, Mexican oil and gas can once again acquire the strategic value that they had in the past. Should this occur, whether we like it or not there will be the ever-present danger that Mexico will again be pressed to subordinate its own national interest to that of its neighbor. As Richard Fagen has noted in his chapter included in this volume, a Middle East crisis could result in Mexican oil becoming a strategic resource for the United States. Should that occur, the decision regarding how much oil would be exported to the U.S. would no longer belong to Mexico.

THE NATURE OF MEXICAN-U.S. NEGOTIATIONS AND THE POSSIBILITY OF ALLIANCES WITH U.S. PRIVATE INTERESTS

In early 1978, Mexico's petroleum policy faced a dilemma. An ambitious project was being threatened which involved the construction of 1,350 kilometers of gas pipeline from the fields in Cactus, Chiapas to the northern border at Reynosa, Tamaulipas at an approximate cost of $1 to $1.5 billion. The original idea was to export up to 2 billion cubic feet of gas daily to six U.S. companies at a price eight times higher than that of the Mexican domestic market. This would have provided Mexico with an income of $3 million per day, gradually rising to $5 million. The problems began when the U.S. government decided to oppose the plan because it would have involved the importation of gas at a cost of $2.60 per thousand cubic feet—Canada was exporting gas at a mere $2.16 per thousand cubic feet, and the U.S. price for natural gas produced domestically was lower still. The U.S. petroleum corporations headed by Tenneco Interamerican, Inc., indicated that they were willing to pay a higher price for imported gas than that which they received for gas produced domestically because this would provide an opportunity to engage in the construction of one of the world's great gas pipelines and, furthermore, by exacerbating the difference between domestically and foreign-produced gas, they would have one more argument with which to pressure Washington for a higher official domestic price for intrastate gas.

The Mexican officials responsible for the gas negotiations apparently counted on the political clout of the U.S. oil companies in Washington. Thus reflecting its confidence on this chance alliance, the Mexican government did not wait for final approval from the U.S. government before beginning construction of the pipeline. To the dismay of both the Mexican government and the oil companies, the Secretary of Energy did not approve the negotiated price of the gas, and in early 1978 the project came to a sudden halt, leaving PEMEX in a difficult position.[13] As a consequence, it became necessary to find a domestic justification for the gas line to the northern border: to supply northern Mexico with gas, and export the remainder. In any event, it should be noted that Mexico's domestic price for gas was still much lower than that offered by the U.S. government at that time.

Mexico had fallen, perhaps unconsciously, in the midst of a struggle connected with one of the major domestic political problems then facing the United States, and found itself allied with the group that opposed the energy plan President Carter presented to Congress in 1977. One of the bones of contention in this struggle, in which billions of dollars were at stake, was that the gas industry and its supporters in Congress wanted price controls removed from the so-called "new gas" or newly-discovered gas deposits in the United States. Supporters of the industry argued that the global price of oil was following a steady upward trend, and the results of the negotiations with Mexico served to reinforce this point. This helps explain the opposition of the Secretary of Energy to the terms of the agreement between Mexico and the oil companies. Moreover, the Energy Secretary wanted a gas line between Alaska and the continental United States. The problems created by a refusal of the Mexican deal were therefore secondary, particularly since the supply of gas in the United States exceeded domestic demand.

In its dealings with the U.S. government, Mexico can and should make better use of the enormous range of implicit alliances made possible by the variety of interest groups in that country. This has already occurred in the past, although care should be taken in deciding with whom and under what circumstances such alliances are made, and how far these arrangements go. It is particularly inadvisable, without first weighing the alternatives and having some good reasons, to confront the executive branch of the U.S. government when something of such high priority, as the Carter energy plan, is at stake. The manner in which the proposed gas sale was handled, together with the reaction of public opinion leaders in Mexico, led the Mexican government to adopt the position (at the end of 1977 and early 1978) that the price of gas was not negotiable. Such a firm and clear position would have been laudable under different circumstances. By then much of the construction of the pipeline, one of the longest in the world, was under way. For this reason, the Mexican government's policy space had shrunk dramatically by then: either the gas was to be consumed internally or burned off.

As it turned out, PEMEX successfully negotiated an agreement later, and in 1980 it sold to the U.S. 300 million cubic feet of gas per day—one seventh of what had been contemplated earlier. Moreover, it did not express any interest in selling any larger quantities; instead, it encouraged the domestic consumption of gas.

There is a lesson to be learned from this. PEMEX will continue to sell petroleum products to the U.S., but in any event, it will be necessary to exercise more caution in the future. It is particularly important to keep in mind that the position of the powerful oil companies (this time, ironically, on the side of Mexico) is not always met with approval in Washington. This is especially true when, as in this case, that position goes against clearly established administration policy. Given that the Mexican historical experience had shown that the oil companies generally enjoyed the full support of the U.S. government when they operated in Mexico, it is easy to understand why PEMEX officials had such confidence that the position of the oil companies would prevail. This view, however, must be qualified: the position of these companies is favorably received in Washington as long as it does not directly conflict with other more powerful interests or with what is considered to be in the national interest.

There are at least two instances in Mexico's experience where such conflicts arose, and the position of the oil corporations did not prevail. The first occurred in December 1925 when President Calles promulgated a law for the enforcement of the petroleum clause of Article 27. For a year, the companies—in violation of this law—did not show any signs of submitting to the same. Instead, they countered by arguing that the regulations were retroactive because, among other reasons, their licenses to pump oil, which had been granted in perpetuity, were being limited to a period of fifty years, and their property rights to land acquired or leased prior to the effective date of the 1917 Constitution were not recognized unless they had actually begun to draw petroleum from those lands prior to May of that year. (The latter was known as the "positive act.")

The U.S. executive initially supported the position of the oil companies as it had in the immediate past. International tensions mounted to a point where it was feared that the U.S. might use force to prevent Calles from interfering with the activities of the rebel companies.[14] But by mid-1927, for domestic reasons both Congress and U.S. public opinion had turned against the position being adopted with respect to Mexico, and the U.S. executive branch changed its policy accordingly. For his part, Calles did not interfere with the now illegal extraction of petroleum.

The United States sent a new ambassador to Mexico, Dwight Morrow, who brought a more conciliatory position to the bargaining table. By early 1928, Morrow had worked out an informal agreement with Calles. Mexico made some changes in its petroleum law, relinquishing some of the limits that had been imposed upon the definition of acquired property rights, and the United States accepted some of the terms to which the companies had objected. Foremost among the latter were the "positive act" and the requirement that the oil companies exchange their titles, which conveyed absolute property rights, for "confirmed concessions" granted by the government. From a practical standpoint the real interests of the companies were not at all affected; from a legal standpoint there was a significant change—the new titles no longer conferred absolute subsoil rights. For this reason the companies protested before the U.S. government. They were able to count on the support of the major newspapers of that country, which decried the weakness of the State Department in its dealings with Mexico. The U.S. stood firm, however, and in the end, with much grumbling the oil companies accepted the change in their titles. The conciliatory approach taken by the U.S. reflected a need by that government to reach a general agreement on the various outstanding issues facing both countries at that time, and a new U.S. foreign policy toward Latin America.[15] For the first time, it had become clear that the pressure exercised by the oil companies had its limits.

The second incident occurred as a result of the expropriation of the oil industry in 1938. While on the one hand the oil companies rejected the legality of the expropriation itself,[16] the U.S. government, on the other, merely conditioned the measure to the "prompt, adequate and effective" payment of what the Mexican government had taken over. Since Mexico was in no position to effect payment on those terms, the difference in the positions adopted by the companies and the U.S. government did not immediately surface, and both pressed Cárdenas simultaneously.

The situation changed dramatically when the Cárdenas Administration ended and Mexico found itself—to the great surprise of many—shoulder-to-shoulder with the United States, fighting the Axis powers. The interests of the United States now required effective cooperation from Mexico in both economic and strategic areas. With respect to the former, the U.S. needed Mexican raw materials and labor. With respect to the latter, it needed permission to fly aircraft over Mexican airspace to the Panama Canal Zone; it needed Mexican cooperation for the surveillance of the Pacific Coast; it even needed naval bases south of the Río Grande.

Mexico expressed its willingness in principle to negotiate all of these matters in exchange for a final agreement on the claims of the oil companies and other outstanding debts owed to the United States. In 1942 the Department of State overrode the objections of Standard Oil of New Jersey and reached an agreement with Mexico regarding both the value of the expropriated property and the terms of the deferred payment. Following this, the State Department informed the representatives of the companies involved that if they did not accept the terms of this agreement they could not count on any further assistance from the U.S. government. In November 1943, Standard Oil and the other companies involved signed a settlement agreement with Mexico, though not without great reluctance and loud complaints about having been abandoned by their government.[17]

In addition to these examples, we could mention others that show how at various times Mexico was able to use some interest groups in the U.S. to neutralize unfavorable policies emanating from Washington. At the time of the previously mentioned 1925 petroleum law and the resulting crisis, for example, then Secretary of Industry Morones, who was also the leader of an umbrella organization of the nation's principal labor unions—the *Confederación Regional Obrera Mexicana*—used his connections with organized labor in the U.S. to get the American Federation of Labor to oppose Washington's policy of aggressively defending U.S. oil interests in Mexico. It is difficult to say just how much influence AFL pressure had upon Coolidge's change in policy, but the effort was made.[18]

Another example can be cited. As a result of the 1938 State Department decision to support the boycott of Mexican oil exports engineered by the companies affected by the expropriation, it was not easy to get anyone to bypass the boycott and market the oil abroad. Nevertheless, once the appropriate price was met, two minor U.S. companies, Davies and Co. and Eastern States, were willing to face the wrath of the giant oil companies and of Secretary of State Cordell Hull to sell Mexico's oil in Europe. That was how up to the time that the Allies imposed a formal blockade upon Axis commerce, Mexico was able to partially frustrate the express attempts of the companies affected by the expropriation to "drown Mexico in its own oil."[19] The boycott was quite effective but in the early years of PEMEX, critical from a financial standpoint, Mexico was able to sell its oil in the world market in spite of Washington's opposition, precisely by using U.S. corporations.

Towards the end of the forties, PEMEX urgently needed funds to finance exploration and production. The giant companies which had been expropriated offered their resources in exchange for being admitted back into Mexico—even if in association with PEMEX. Mexico finally allowed several small, independent U.S. companies to explore for PEMEX for some years without having to admit their participation within the state-owned corporation.[20]

It should be stressed that in neither of the aforementioned instances did the U.S. government view the actions of the Mexican government, or of its allies, as a threat to its national interest. In each case, the incident was considered to be of marginal importance in the general context of U.S. foreign relations, and particularly minor in the context of U.S. domestic politics.

With respect to what has been discussed up to this point, it should be clear that if Mexico allies itself with certain agreeable interests in the United States, its actions may bear fruit. This is particularly true today, given that U.S. domestic politics are far more complex than they were in the past. On each side of any issue powerful interests are at stake; e.g., the big consumers against the big producers; gas and oil-exporting states, such as Texas, against energy-importing states, such as Illinois. For each case that may arise we should select our allies with caution, measure with care the degree of our commitment to them, and above all, consider how tenable Mexico's position may be in the context of the national priorities which the particular administration in Washington may have. It is difficult for an alliance with a domestic interest group—no matter how powerful—to yield a favorable outcome for a country like Mexico when it chooses to cross the U.S. government in a matter of high priority.

MEXICO'S OIL UNION—A DIFFICULT ALLY

The abundant literature on expropriation leaves no doubt that the cooperation of the oil workers with the government was important to the success of the nationalization process. As a rule this has been true, but the exceptions do not allow us to take for granted that as regards petroleum policy, workers' goals—as expressed by the union leadership—always coincide with the public interest.

The labor movement's militant stance was notable when the industry was in the hands of the foreign companies. From the very beginning of the Revolution, labor strikes in Tampico, Minatitlán and other oil producing and refining areas were frequent and sometimes violent. On some occasions, the cause of labor had the support of the authorities. One should also note that on others, this labor movement opposed some nationalist positions adopted by the government out of fear—founded on fact—that such measures would result in a paralysis of the industry and in widespread layoffs.[21] Thus, prior to the nationalization of the industry, workers and government did not always coincide in their struggle against the oil companies.

It was not until immediately after March 1938 that this conflict came to a head. To understand this one must first recall that Cárdenas did not expropriate the properties of the oil companies on the basis of the same arguments which his predecessors had employed against these powerful corporations. From the beginning of this struggle in 1916 to the Calles Administration, friction with the oil companies arose from conflicting interpretations of the appropriate paragraph of Article 27 of the Constitution. Cárdenas did not reopen this debate; indeed, he accepted the compromise embodied in the petroleum legislation such as it was enacted in 1928. Rather, he used an entirely different instrument of attack —the labor movement. The 1938 crisis, which had been developing since Madero, arose from the oil corporations' refusal to comply with a court order concerning a dispute with the newly created industry's labor union. As a new tactic, in 1937 and 1938 the government supported the union's demand for wage increases and improved fringe benefits for the oil workers.

However, by the time that the government assumed control over the oil expropriation, conditions in the industry had changed. It was immersed in crisis, and no longer had the resources to meet the demands that the workers had originally presented to the oil companies. Not all of the workers understood or accepted this situation, and their leaders insisted in having the original demands met. Indeed, they demanded the management and control of an industry which in principle, given its vital importance and wealth, was the property of the nation. Understandably, Cárdenas refused, and the reaction of some factions of the union was to call for a strike and even to commit sabotage.[22] Although this did not represent the general reaction of the workers, it cannot be denied that in some instances union interests opposed policies which can legitimately be considered to have favored the interest of the public as a whole.

At the present time, the wage scale and fringe benefits of the oil workers—around 100,000 permanent and temporary employees—are higher than the average of the Mexican labor force, and the union which represents them is not particularly distinguished for scrupulous labor practices. This union's corruption is partially explained by the favorable treatment it received from the government at the very beginning. For example, when the government negotiated the first union contract in May 1942, it granted concessions placing the oil workers in a relatively privileged position and chose not to be very strict in overseeing the union's labor practices. This treatment was accorded to the union to silence the protests that followed the initial confrontations and to exercise some control over a segment of labor recognized for its militancy. An immediate result of this policy was a substantial increase in the number of persons on the corporate payroll, even though production dropped. While in 1936 the ratio of wages and salaries to sales in the industry had been 20 percent, by 1939 this ratio had doubled to 42 percent.[23]

The oil boom we are now beginning to experience opens new worlds to conquer for a union which has established a record of forceful demands and to an industry characterized by a not very efficient use of resources. The latter problem was exacerbated by Echeverría's decision in 1976 to accept the reclassification of many management and non-union positions to others falling under a union contract. This increased unionization of the industry has diminished the flexibility of the corporation, since entry into intermediate technical positions is not made available on the basis of merit but on the basis of union connections.

Only time will tell if the government will succeed in keeping dysfunctional and corrupt union practices from spreading proportionately as the importance of PEMEX grows. To prevent the consequences of inertia taking their ultimate course, some difficult policy choices will have to be made.

THE FORMULATION OF PETROLEUM POLICY:
BETWEEN THE POLITICIANS AND THE TECHNOCRATS

Before an assembly of oil workers on March 29, 1978, President López Portillo disclosed that for some time PEMEX technicians had concealed information from the nation's political leadership thereby underestimating the nation's oil potential. This could have led to a series of policy choices whose consequences had transcended PEMEX and had affected the entire country.[24]

This is not new. From the very beginning, oil policy was formulated in the closed circles of political elites and in the offices of specialized departments. Without debate, Congress passed the law in 1884 which made hydrocarbon subsoil deposits the absolute right of the landowner. The only time the issue received much attention during the Porfiriato was in 1905, when Díaz himself requested an opinion of the Academia Mexicana de Jurisprudencia regarding a legislative proposal by two attorneys and an engineer that would have returned oil to the public domain. This amendment's objective was not to attack the newly established corporations, but to insure that private parties did not create obstacles for those who wanted to pump oil. The debate was conducted at an academic level and did not extend to the general public. The amendment did not pass.[25]

When the Constitutional Congress of Querétaro decided in 1916 to introduce reforms in Carranza's constitutional proposals, the debate centered around issues such as church-state relations, agrarian reform, and so forth. No debate took place when paragraph four of Article 27 of the Constitution, which altered the legal regime for oil production, was presented to the general assembly in January of 1917. Thus, one of the constitutional issues which was to shape Mexico's relations with the world powers of the time was accepted without further discussion by the highest legislative body of the nation.

This all-important constitutional provision was in reality the product of a small commission headed by Francisco J. Mújica and Pastor Rouaix, along with José N. Macías and Andrés Molina Enríquez. Rouaix, Macías and Molina always coordinated their position with that of Carranza.[26] It can be noted that in 1917 the country revolutionized its relations with foreign capital by changing its petroleum laws, without the nation's most politically conscious segments being completely aware of the fact.

In the end, the government's oil policy turned out to be one of the greatest achievements of the Revolution and the 1938 expropriation the high water mark of its nationalist enterprise. Let us not forget that on several occasions the original idea was almost lost as a result of the distance between the formulation of petroleum policy and the terms of public debate.

We might note, for example, that after 1918 Carranza decided not to propose any oil legislation to Congress and to manage the industry on the basis of the extraordinary powers conferred upon him. Substantive changes in the legal regime for oil production were introduced under the guise of technical and administrative regulation.[27] Until he died, Carranza had the last word on Mexican oil policy. Before and after the 1917 reforms, he formulated policy in consultation with the more important members of his cabinet and with the technical assistance and legal advice of a core group of specialists in the Department of Petroleum of the Ministry of Industry, Commerce and Labor.[28] Since then, the executive branch, surrounded by an influential technocratic group, has largely determined the course of petroleum policy.

Although the legislative and judicial branches were supposed to have a role in shaping oil policy, their input was actually minimal. To begin with, Congress only passed legislation on oil matters when the President requested it in 1925; and then it passed what the administration proposed. When it amended the law in 1928, it did so because Calles decided that such an amendment was necessary to defuse the tense relations with the United States. The terms of the legislative changes were the result of negotiations between then Secretary of Industry, Morones, and the U.S. Embassy—Congress simply passed the amendments as proposed.[29]

The judicial branch did not behave differently. The basic issue it confronted with respect to petroleum was how to interpret paragraph four of Article 27: Was it retroactive? In August of 1921, the Supreme Court decided, in connection with a suit brought forth by the Texas Oil Co., that it was not. This decision was communicated by the Secretary of Foreign Relations to the U.S. Embassy several days in advance of the Court decision itself.[30] When Calles decided to change the 1925 law, as noted earlier, all he had to do was to ask Morones to communicate this request to the High Court, with the indication that "the government is in danger."[31] Using the 1921 Texas decision as precedent, in November 1927 the Court declared the law unconstitutional and opened the way for the amendments to be introduced, and passed later by Congress.[32]

In summary, the oil issue has not been different from many others. Public discussion and access to pertinent information were lacking. By keeping many aspects of oil policy out of open debate, there can be no doubt that Mexico's authoritarian tradition is being reinforced, and the legitimacy of the government's oil policy is being eroded precisely when it most needs public support to deal with external pressures.[33] Policy choices which will affect present and future generations of Mexicans are made without most people being aware of their significance and without having an opportunity to influence the outcome.

WHO BENEFITS FROM THE PETROLEUM BONANZA?

One of the most significant future effects of the oil bonanza may be the achievement of a favorable balance of trade. By 1980, oil represented 68 percent of the value of all commodity exports— $10.3 billion. The importance of oil in earning foreign exchange is thus evident.

This poses a question of vital importance to the nation's destiny: what are we to do with the foreign exchange that we will earn by pumping a non-renewable resource out of the ground? The oil bonanza presents an opportunity which will not repeat itself; how the petroleum resources are used should be the object of considerable scrutiny. A number of possible alternatives exist, although there can only be one objective: to construct a long-term basis for generating other sources of wealth and energy to survive when the oil is gone. Unquestionably, history will judge this to be one of the major responsibilities faced by the López Portillo administration and its successor. National plans should be made with great care and realism. The National Development Plan (*Plan Global de Desarrollo*) is but the first step; it should be followed up as quickly as possible. There is no time to be lost.

Examples of extraordinary waste abound. There is no need to dwell on the irresponsibility of Arab potentates squandering their fortunes in Europe after having grabbed them from the oil multinationals. More instructive, perhaps, are the examples of Venezuela and Indonesia, whose societies are relatively more complex and developed. Neither of these countries can praise themselves for having made the wisest use of their oil income. But actually, we need not go outside of our borders to find pertinent examples. Between 1910 and the mid-1920s, Mexico saw an opportunity go up in smoke: the possibility of gaining something permanent from the oil income for the benefit of all.

What, indeed, was the social benefit derived from the oil boom of 1910-24? During that period, Mexico's oil fields produced around 1.2 billion barrels of crude, of which approximately 90 percent were exported. In principle, this oil wealth could have potentially made a substantial contribution to the national well-being; at one point (1921-22), the value of oil exports reached 6-7 percent of the gross domestic product. But the truth is that this did not happen.

There were many reasons for this. The most important was that this activity was conducted as an enclave, and most of the benefits went to foreign economies. One might add that, on the one hand, the petroleum industry never generated much employment—between 30,000 and 50,000 at its highest point. On the other hand, many of the industry's inputs—from machinery and technology to food for the labor force—had to be imported for the simple reason that these were not produced locally. This demand for products therefore was not translated into an important stimulus for the country's economic development.

This is why taxes levied upon the oil companies were the only vehicle for keeping some of the wealth in Mexico which would otherwise leave the country. These taxes, which the revolutionary regime had to struggle to impose, represented a substantial proportion of the federal treasury's income. In 1918 this proportion was 11 percent; by 1922 it had risen to 34 percent.[34] The state was not then in a position to use its budget for economic development. Its expenditures in this respect were minimal. Carranza barely spent an average of 6 percent of his budget in economic investment; Obregón spent 14 percent.[35] It would not be until 1925 that the Calles Administration would begin to spend federal monies in opening up irrigation districts, roads, etc. Thus, during the peak period of oil production, the state limited its spending to the bureaucracy and military. The benefits that Mexico received from its first oil boom were therefore few. At best, the income derived from oil exports made it easier for the revolutionary regimes and their successors to survive as constitutional governments.

In principle, the present situation is quite different. To begin with, the oil industry is no longer an enclave. PEMEX, the largest Mexican industrial firm, is an integral part of a government and a country with an infrastructure capable of channeling the resources earned from petroleum exports to other sectors of the economy. (In 1980, the firm paid $7 billion in federal taxes into the treasury.) The transfer of massive quantities of resources is indeed needed for agriculture, the capital goods industry and for the development of alternative energy sources. However, there is nothing automatic nor inevitable about this process. The future must be planned with a full sense of the gravity of our responsibility. The possibility of once again misusing our petroleum resource endowment is only too real. Corruption, irresponsibility, and the inertia of the present political system conspire to make this possibility loom large. Finally, we must avoid at all costs a danger which is already present—the risk of reaching a level of oil production more congenial to the interests of the central economies than to those of our own.[36] This, indeed, would be to repeat one of the most tragic mistakes of the previous boom.

By chance, Mexico today has in abundance a natural, nonrenewable resource which is urgently needed both by its economy and by the rest of the world. The type of economic growth that the country has experienced since the end of the nineteenth century has led, on more than one occasion, to a dead end. An unexpected turn has opened up new possibilities to correct some of the errors of the past, and in the process, to strengthen the role of the state as the director of the economy. If this opportunity is lost, it will be difficult to find another . . . and in any event our leaders will not be able to hide behind any of the excuses of the past—particularly that of being ignorant of the consequences of their decisions.

Notes

1. *Boletín del Petróleo* (January–June, 1917), p. 220.
2. Lorenzo Meyer, "La resistencia al capital privado extranjero, el caso del petróleo (1938-1950)," in Bernardo Sepúlveda et. al., *Las empreses transnacionales en México* (México: El Colegio de México, 1974), pp. 122-156.
3. The reader who would like to pursue the implications of these indicators further may consult, among others, the following works: Bernardo Sepúlveda and Antonio Chamucero, *La inversión extranjera en México* (México: Fondo de Cultura Económica, 1972); María del Rosario Green, *El endeudamiento público externo de México, 1940-1973* (México: El Colegio de México, 1976). René Villarreal, *El desequilibrio externo en la industrialización de México* (México: Fondo de Cultura Económica, 1977); José Luis Ceceña, *México en la orbita imperial; las empresas transnacionales* (México: Ediciones "El Caballito," 1970).
4. The nature of Mexican political dependence upon the United States has been the object of considerable attention by analysts. A general treatment of the present situation can be found in Mario Ojeda, *Alcances y límites de la política exterior de México* (México: El Colegio de México, 1977).
5. At the beginning of 1979, proven reserves were estimated to be 40.2 billion barrels, probable reserves 44.6 billion barrels, and potential reserves 200 billion barrels.
6. Harvey O'Conner, *World Crisis in Oil* (New York: Monthly Review Press, 1962), p. 69.
7. *Commerce Reports*, No. 235 (7 October 1918). In a letter from the Mexican Gulf Co. to A.L. Weil (20 August 1918), it was noted that in 1917 the U.S. had produced 350 million barrels of oil, but even so, it required an additional 42 million barrels from Mexico. See The Public Record Office, London, Foreign Office 371, file 139881, volume 3250, document 199881.
8. Edmund David Cronon, *The Cabinet Diaries of Josephus Daniels, 1913-1921* (Lincoln: University of Nebraska Press, 1963), p. 328.
9. As early as 1916 the English were aware that Mexico was willing and able to destroy the oil fields in the event of invasion. See *Report of the English Chargé d'Affaires in the Foreign Office*, 6 June 1916, Public Record Office, London, Foreign Office. 371, file 48, volume 2700, document 109289.
10. Lorenzo Meyer, *México y los Estados Unidos en el conflicto petrolero (1917-1942)*, 2nd. ed. (México: El Colegio de México, 1972) pp. 99-103.
11. Denis J. O'Brien, "Petróleo e intervención; relaciones entre los Estados Unidos y México, 1917-1918," in *Historia Mexicana* 27 (1977).
12. Ibid., pp. 124-126.
13. A good treatment of this problem can be found in Richard R. Fagen and Henry R. Nau, "Mexican Gas: The Northern Connection," in Richard R. Fagen (ed.), *United States Foreign Policy and Latin America* (Stanford: Stanford University Press, 1978); see also, *Comercio Exterior* 27 (November, 1977):1287-1296.
14. Lorenzo Meyer, *México y los Estados Unidos*, pp. 257-263.
15. See the discussion relating to oil in Stanley R. Ross, "Dwight Morrow and the Mexican Revolution," in *Hispanic American Historical Review* 38 (1958).
16. Standard Oil Company of New Jersey, "Confiscation or Expropriation? Mexican Seizure of the Foreign-owned Oil Industry," pamphlet published in New York, 1940.
17. Lorenzo Meyer, *México y los Estados Unidos*, pp. 433-457.

18. Harvey A. Levenstein, *Labor Organizations in the United States and Mexico: A History of Their Relations* (Westport, Conn.: Greenwood Publishing Co., 1971), pp. 128-131.
19. Lorenzo Meyer, *México y los Estados Unidos*, pp. 429-433.
20. Lorenzo Meyer, *"La resistencia,"* pp. 149-152.
21. See the opinions expressed by the U.S. chargé d'affaires in Mexico in 1927, where he explains why the oil unions did not support Calles's policy. National Archives, Washington, D.C., Schoenfeld to Department of State, 24 August 1927, 812.6363/2353.
22. Jesús Silva Herzog, *Petróleo mexicano* (México: Fondo de Cultura Económica, 1941), pp. 274-284.
23. J. Richard Powell, *The Mexican Petroleum Industry, 1938-1950* (Berkeley: University of California Press, 1956), pp. 131-132.
24. Some of the problems that PEMEX's first director during the López Portillo administration, Jorge Díaz Serrano, had to deal with in order to get reliable data on the petroleum reserves are discussed in a *New York Times* article which appeared on July 16, 1978.
25. Salvador Mendoza, *La controversia del petróleo* (México: Imprenta Politécnica, 1921).
26. Pastor Rouaix, *Génesis de los Artículos 27 y 123 de la Constitución Política de 1917* (México: Biblioteca del Instituto Nacional de Estudios Históricos de la Revolución, 1959), p. 161.
27. Lorenzo Meyer, *México y los Estados Unidos*, pp. 123-152.
28. *Ibid.*, pp. 118, 124, 128, 145-149.
29. *Ibid.*, pp. 229-230, 235, 269, 274.
30. *Ibid.*, pp. 173-175.
31. *Ibid.*, pp. 270-271.
32. *Boletín del Petróleo* 25 (January-June, 1928):256 ff.
33. The clearest example of this was the recent debate concerning the gas pipeline. The decisions were initially made without allowing for public debate. When Heberto Castillo, writing in *Proceso* in the fall of 1977, questioned the project just as the negotiations reached a crucial stage, he put PEMEX and the government in a corner. It became difficult for the Mexican negotiating team not to harden its position vis-à-vis Washington; that was the only way in which they could maintain some semblance of legitimacy after it had been eroded by Castillo, spokesman of the *Partido Mexicano de los Trabajadores*.
34. Lorenzo Meyer, *México y los Estados Unidos*, p. 35.
35. James Wilkie, *The Mexican Revolution: Federal Expenditure and Social Change Since 1910* (Berkeley: University of California Press, 1967), p. 36.
36. See Richard Fagen's article in this volume.

6
Mexican Oil at the Service of the Bourgeoisie

Jorge G. Castañeda

In Mexico, oil exists—and so does the Left. Denying one is as absurd as denying the other. If the Mexican Right wants to delude itself in taking wishful thinking for reality, so be it. But there is cause for concern in the position expressed by some sectors of the Left regarding the discovery of enormous petroleum reserves in our country. The following rather schematic set of hypotheses summarizes this position: 1) the increased extraction and export of hydrocarbons will not solve the country's present economic crisis; 2) the export of this nonrenewable resource will leave the country without an independent source of energy by the end of the century; 3) the bonds of dependence tying us to imperialism will only be multiplied and strengthened by the exploitation of our petroleum reserves. Just because these hypotheses have become conventional wisdom among some sectors of the Left does

---

Jorge Castañeda is a professor at the Facultad de Economía, UNAM, in Mexico City. He has degrees from Princeton University and the Université de Paris, and has published *El economismo dependentista* with Enrique Gett; *Nicaragua: Contradicciones en la revolución*, and *Los últimos capitalismos*. He is also a contributor to *Proceso*, *Uno Más Uno*, and *Le Monde Diplomatique*.

This chapter is a translation of "'El petróleo al servicio de la gran burgesía,'" first published in *Proceso* 110, December 11, 1978. Reprinted with permission. Not included here is a series of responses, written in a labor issue of *Proceso* and *Uno Más Uno*, nor the author's replies. The postscript was specifically written for this volume in October 1982.

Translated by Carlos Vásquez and Manuel García y Griego.
© 1983 by Jorge G. Castañeda.

not mean that they are automatically true. Let us examine each of them in turn.

To overcome the current economic crisis, or even to know when the country has emerged from it, one must first define it. If by "crisis" we mean the entire gamut of economic, social, and political problems which have characterized capitalist development in Mexico for the last fifty years, then neither God nor the devil can get us out. But if by crisis we refer to the more-or-less radical economic changes in the daily life of the nation, that is different. If we consider that the current economic crisis [1976–77] is a combination of conjunctural and national problems linked to long-existing international structures with their own set of difficulties, then one must cast the problem in different terms.

Among the economic effects of the crisis gripping the country since 1976 are the following: deficits in current accounts, a weakened currency, excessive price increases, a decline in domestic and foreign investment, economic growth rates lower than required by capital and levels of unemployment that have reached dangerous social and political proportions. Because of this, one could pose the question: can an increased export of hydrocarbons mitigate, minimize or even eliminate the effects of this crisis without effecting radical changes in either the political economy of the nation or in the very structure of the economy as presently constituted? The answer would be unequivocally yes—keeping in mind that this affirmation is limited exclusively to those effects which are conjunctural and national in scope. Obviously oil will not solve the international crisis, nor even its manifestations in Mexico, but this is not a discussion to be pursued here.

Based on the differences between projected and actual exports in the last two years and extrapolating this into 1982 and 1985, Mexico should export 2.5 million barrels daily in 1982 and 5 million barrels daily in 1985. These figures are based on calculations found in the specialized literature and from a recent colloquy of international experts. Using very conservative price estimates of $15 per barrel in 1982 and $18 per barrel in 1985, and a relatively high rate of inflation in the U.S. (7 percent annually), Mexico would earn an additional $9 billion more (at present rates of exchange) exclusively from the export of petroleum than it does today and approximately $20 billion more in 1985. In other words, assuming that everything remained the same and taking only oil exports into consideration, the country would have to multiply its current trade imbalance of $2.4 billion four times in order to have a deficit. This would be difficult to accomplish even for the most incompetent treasury secretary.

Yet this is only part of the problem, for we have only considered current accounts. To achieve a non-resolution to the problem of foreign finances, including that of a weakened currency, we would have to reach the virtually impossible trade deficit mentioned above and stop receiving the loans international banking institutions insist on making to good credit risks. Moreover, it would be necessary to export all of the capital earned from the export of petroleum which is unlikely, notwithstanding the proclivity of capital to invest abroad. To be sure, this does not mean the problem would disappear overnight nor that new contradictions will not arise.

The situation is similar with regard to domestic disinvestment, lack of foreign private capital, and insufficient economic growth. A rise in total national production as a result of an increase in the rate of investment would not necessarily translate into a growth in the labor force or an increase in real wages; rather it means a higher rate of growth in the gross national product.

Even without taking into consideration the enormous investments projected by PEMEX for the period 1978–1982, or the direct effects of the extraction of petroleum, the multiplier effect of the petroleum "boom" in other sectors of the economy should be considerable, particularly for domestic private investment. One need only consider the boom in steel production, in the construction of public works, and above all in the sector which has attracted the greatest investment in recent years—the petrochemical industry.

Furthermore, investment based on credits is gaining in importance. In a world in economic crisis, where international financial institutions must continue making loans (which is, after all, their livelihood) to an ever-increasing number of borrowers, a country which guarantees its debts with a sea of oil is a godsend. If in the last eight years Mexico, with its political, economic and social problems by now familiar to all, has been able to capture $25 to $30 billion of the world's savings, why, given new national and international conditions, should more not be accomplished? Why suppose this volume of investment will not generate economic growth rates similar to Japan's notwithstanding the graft, incompetence and corruption characteristic of the Mexican government?

If these predictions are correct, it should not be difficult to anticipate the growth in Mexico's GNP. We know that in 1978 the growth rate will be 5 percent to 6 percent. The recession in the U.S. in the first quarter of 1979 and perhaps into the second half of the year will probably limit Mexico's growth to the same level. But after 1980, and surely into 1985, the national economy should enjoy a 10 percent annual growth rate.

These figures are not without foundation; they represent the best estimates of prestigious international institutions, such as Citicorp Bank, one of the three largest banks in the world. Will petroleum then solve nothing? Perhaps, but disinvestments and slow growth, though they may be "nothing," will be affected radically even if no changes in the basic configurations of the economy take place. Considering that one can safely predict certain transformations, such as in the development and consolidation of the capital goods sector, the elimination of bottlenecks in transportation, etc., slow growth and disinvestment will be affected even though these transformations would themselves introduce a whole new set of problems and contradictions.

Still we have to deal with two crucial elements in our analysis —inflation and conjunctural unemployment. The latter is less complicated than would appear at first. It is one thing to create employment for previously employed Mexicans and another to generate employment for the entire Mexican population of working age. Although the jobs created directly by the oil production are relatively few, the secondary jobs created will help to reduce unemployment in certain sectors of the labor force. The construction of refineries, gas and oil pipelines, shipping ports, public highways, the services needed at refinery sites, the renovation of outdated equipment, all represent sources of employment which could absorb a good part of those who have lost their jobs in the last two years. And, of course, the growth in the secondary industries (e.g., steel mills, petrochemicals and capital goods) will also help create employment. In other words, oil will ameliorate the unemployment situation and make it less socially and politically explosive. After all, a worker who has lost a job is a very different sort of problem and a greater threat to capital than an unemployed youth who has never had a job. At least this has been the experience of the Mexican bourgeoisie, which unlike its Bourbon predecessors has both learned and never forgotten this lesson.

The problem of inflation is a more complicated matter. On the one hand, the above mentioned factors will help solve the problem cited earlier, and at the same time worsen inflationary pressures on the Mexican economy. On the other, inflation in some respects offers capital a way out of its dilemma. In any case, if the present and foreseeable rates of inflation of 15-29 percent are determined by an equilibrium between production and the money supply, then it is highly likely that in the near future the level of equilibrium will rise. Production will increase but so will the money supply. In monetary terms, the influx of dollars from oil sales and international credits will naturally be a factor in price increases regardless of the total increases in goods and services. Is inflation then an effect of the crisis that oil cannot manage?

Unfortunately this is not the case. A bourgeois government with minimal technical competence can, if it disposes of the necessary economic resources, distribute the effects of inflation in a socially and politically acceptable manner. Taxing, raising salaries, using privileged sectors of the labor force as examples of well-being, and a state controlled economy, all constitute mechanisms traditionally available to the Mexican state. Oil would seem to offer that state even more resources: incremental devaluations which would not undermine the "confidence" guaranteed to oil and capital; smaller medium-term budgetary deficits without deflationary results; greater negotiating room with private firms while at the same time enjoying a greater autonomy in negotiations with foreigners; the modernization of distribution networks, etc. Although the state cannot actually control the rate of inflation, it can at least utilize significant economic and social resources to administer the effects of that inflation. Moreover, it can also resort to something it did not invent, but will use if necessary—internal political reform and everything that it implies.

It is helpful to underline two conclusions in our analysis so far: First, oil can extricate the country from the conjunctural economic crisis but will do so in conformity with the interests of the country's dominant class—the Mexican bourgeoisie. In other words, government oil policy, however reactionary, will attempt to solve the main problems created by the current crisis, provided that this solution agrees with the interests of the most powerful sectors of capital in Mexico. To assume that oil can resolve the present crisis in favor of the popular classes would be both a theoretical and political error. To suppose that petroleum will resolve none of the problems but instead aggravate them all would also be an error.

The Left should not fear the solution oil offers to the bourgeoisie. Economic progress does not necessarily weaken it (as we have seen in the case of Iran), and economic crisis will not insure a rise in strength (as we have seen in the case of France). The political crisis to which the Left owes its recent entrance into mainstream politics will not be resolved because of oil. A number of problems will be solved; but neither oil nor capital will be able to solve *the problem* which will continue to provoke new contradictions under new conditions. That problem is *the exploitation of wage labor*, whose solution is capital's impossible dream and our greatest hope.

Some will argue that oil drilling at the projected rates will deplete the country of reserves by the year 2000 or even sooner. This objection is raised using a rather simplistic argument. If the extraction of oil is "X" million barrels daily and the rate of growth in that extraction is "Y" percent, and if the proven reserves are "Z," then with the use of these three factors one can project by what year we will deplete our reserves. Initially this argument seems irrefutable, but at least three factors not taken into account disprove it. First, if the ratio of increase in the production of oil is compounded to the rate of increase of proven reserves, an important fact becomes readily apparent. On December 1, 1976 our proven reserves were 6.4 billion barrels. By September 1, President López Portillo announced that our reserves were upwards of 20 billion barrels, an increase of 217 percent in less than two years! In December of 1976 PEMEX produced 800,000 barrels daily. By September 1978 there was an increase of 75 percent in production. In other words, the rate of increase of proven reserves was three times that of the rate of extraction. Therefore, to base any calculation of future proven reserves on *existing* levels without factoring in at least some increases—obviously less than at present rates of discovery—is entirely without justification and leads to miscalculations.

Secondly, how PEMEX calculates its proven and probable reserves is of significance since the national monopoly uses extremely restricted definitions of these two categories. For example, to determine proven reserves, PEMEX includes only primary recovery excluding what is recovered by injecting water or gas into fields presently in production and excludes fields not yet in production. At the same time, PEMEX includes only the known quantities for estimated reserves in the explored fields, but not fields which have not yet been put into production as is the practice in the United States. In other words, the calculations by PEMEX are conservative and tend to understate the proven and probable reserves. Projections made arithmetically without considering these two factors are not legitimate.

There is an empirical rule of thumb used by large oil companies for calculating proven reserves once the rate of production is known or for projecting the rate of production once the reserves are known. According to this rule, for every 10 billion barrels in proven reserves, 1.7 million barrels will be recovered when production reaches the rate of maximum efficiency. Thus, if one considers projections made by international specialists rather than those of PEMEX in 1982, daily production is estimated as 4.2 million barrels (2.5 million barrels external and 1.7 million barrels internal consumption). This would make the proven reserves in 1982 approximately 24 billion barrels. This figure squares with present government forecasts. By 1985, assuming a relatively moderate national consumption of 2 million barrels daily, production would be on the order of 7 million barrels with reserves totaling about 41 billion barrels. Assuming that production would not exceed 7 million barrels a day (even if the government gave in to imperialist pressures), and that if of the 200 billion barrels in potential reserves announced recently by President López Portillo only 41 billion barrels were confirmed as proven reserves, the production could last 18 years or until the year 2003. However, if only 41 billion barrels were confirmed as proven reserves, not only would this be contrary to international projections, but it would mean that the increase of proven reserves would decline 150 percent per year for the period 1976–1978, 14 percent a year for 1978–1985, and zero percent after that. Not only is this decline highly unlikely, but it seems to go against the basic principle that in large oil fields and not fully explored, production shows an increase rather than a decrease of proven reserves. It is safe to assume that even in the worst case, Mexican reserves would last until the year 2030, even at extremely high levels of export such as that of Saudi Arabia or at rates of extraction matched only by the U.S. or the Soviet Union.

The third factor in question relates to the objection that reserves would last 40–50 years and then dry up; the country would then be left without energy resources of its own and forced to import oil at high costs. This might be the case in the next 50 years were there no changes in the international and national energy situation. But there is already a visible move toward nuclear energy. France, England, Germany, Brazil, Pakistan, Iran, and South Korea, among others are developing medium and long range programs for the construction of nuclear plants to insure their energy future. In spite of technical, political, and social difficulties that still plague such programs, nuclear energy will play an important role in the supply of energy in these and other countries by the year 2000. If Mexico did not have significant reserves in uranium, if the geographic distribution of population represented an insurmountable obstacle to the installation of nuclear plants in the country, and above all, if Mexico really had to choose between nuclear energy and hydrocarbons, it might be legitimate to argue for conservation; when others had depleted theirs, we would still enjoy sizeable reserves.

None of these conditions limit us. According to the latest estimates of the *Instituto de Energía Nuclear*, Mexico has 11,000 tons of proven uranium reserves and 600,000 tons of probable reserves. While these figures are less reliable than those related to oil, the amount is nevertheless considerable. Moreover, there are many sparsely populated areas in the country where nuclear plants could be built with little danger or inconvenience to local residents. But the decision to resort to nuclear energy is really a moot point. The choice will be determined by the following: international competition; the relative cost-effectiveness of oil and atomic energy for the next twenty years; the development of industries that use either sources; new developments in nuclear technology, etc. It is not simply a matter of who has what resources and choosing between them based on their availability.

Were this the case, countries with ample coal reserves like England and France would consume that fuel and not oil which costs them so dearly to import. If the development of nuclear energy continues, and every indication is that it will, Mexico will have to resort to nuclear energy long before its oil reserves are depleted. It is safe to assume that when the predicted date for the depletion of our reserves arrives, they will be safely underground because of the low cost of the atom. Irony and history are strange bedfellows.

Important sectors of the Left in Mexico still maintain that even in the most favorable case—where oil makes it possible for the country to overcome its conjunctural crisis, reserves are not depleted in the near future, and nuclear energy is an alternative—our condition of dependence is such that things will be worse for us with nuclear energy than they were with oil. It would serve no purpose to engage in dependence-antidependence polemics, which are losing popularity anyway. Suffice it to say that although pressures from the United States in the area of oil grow daily, and although the Mexican government seems to do nothing to resist them, when it comes to oil the premises of dependency are paradoxical.

Who depends on whom? Japan, Germany and other countries which import all of their hydrocarbons, and the United States, whose president has declared that energy independence is the "moral equivalent of war," or the oil-exporting countries? If by 1985, Mexico provides half of all U.S. oil imports, as would appear to be the case, who will depend on whom? With a nationalized and well-integrated oil industry, strong international negotiating position, potential markets in an industrializing Third World just waiting to be tapped, could Mexico not dispose of its oil better than it does presently? It could sell to its northern neighbor because it represents a natural market, but also sell elsewhere should conditions become unfavorable or unacceptable. Should political pressures become so acute that military action is considered, U.S. intervention is not a foregone conclusion.

During the 1973 oil embargo of the Arab countries, when conditions lent themselves to such an option, almost no one opposed intervention. Yet the U.S. preferred negotiation to military confrontation because it understood the political costs of such a course. In the case of Mexico, such an intervention would seem even less likely. There is no greater mutual dependence than the buying and selling of a strategic product where both parties have a vested interest in the transaction. But it renders our threatened national sovereignty no service to defend it with the theory of dependence.

In conclusion, it seems only fair to offer an explanation for the position defended by elements of the Mexican Left. Although it might seem paradoxical, the hypotheses criticized here are the result of a maturing and strengthened Left. For the first time in many years, the organized Left can and should act not only by denouncing government politics but by proposing alternatives. It's doing just that; but like old soldiers, old habits never die, they just fade away. The habit of constantly denouncing has often burdened certain segments of the Left, and often alternatives proposed are based more on hackneyed slogans than on objective analysis. Denunciation becomes oppposition for its own sake or for the rationalizing of particular political strategies. Yet the same energy and maturity that has in part created this problem will ultimately solve it. We shall then move from a precarious strategy that attempts to justify itself, to one based on reality and objective analysis.

Any viable alternative must be the result of a thoroughgoing analysis. Denunciation becomes opposition for its own sake or for the rationalizing of particular political strategies. Yet the government policies regarding the utilization of revenues derived from the exports of hydrocarbons in a piecemeal fashion, the Left must provide an alternative to the national leadership of the bourgeoisie and its political representatives. In other words, we must provide an alternative to the economic, social and political regime which presently controls virtually all aspects of national life. This means that oil policies must be put in their proper perspective and their importance not overstated. To paraphrase Spinoza, "it does us no good to weep or lament; we must understand." This, indeed, is the challenge.

POSTSCRIPT: FOUR YEARS LATER

Publishing old articles (even if written only four years ago) can be risky. Arguments go out of fashion and lose their impact. Nonetheless, I agreed to have the above article reprinted here because I consider the basic argument—notwithstanding unavoidable statistical errors in forecasting—as correct now as it was then. In this postscript, written in 1982, I would like to explain why.

The argument made in 1978 rested on three hypotheses. First, oil would extricate Mexico's capitalism from its immediate crisis. Second, the export of hydrocarbons would not diminish significantly the country's future energy resources. Third, these exports would not in any way increase the country's external dependence. Let us consider briefly how this argument has survived the passage of time and the force of events.

When my article first appeared in late 1978, the crisis of 1976-77 had been left behind. An unprecedented economic boom followed, lasting for four years. Its most visible signs were economic growth rates of 8 percent per annum, investment growth rates in excess of 15 percent, investment-to-product ratios of nearly 25 percent, and fat profits for business. It must be noted that inflation levels were high, in the 25-30 percent per year range, but these were manageable, and they were managed. In particular for Mexico's finance capital, the hegemonic sector of the bourgoisie, this was a boom which would be long remembered. The stimulus for this extraordinary economic growth was oil—and the inflow of external capital (foreign investment, and above all, foreign credits) guaranteed by the export of oil.

The economic expansion was more intense and shorter-lived than I had expected in 1978; this was due largely to events external to the Mexican economy. This does not mean, of course, that these are of secondary importance, nor are they the only causes of the end of the boom witnessed in 1982. External factors explain the telescoping of events and the suddenness of the 1982 crisis; not its origins.

Between 1978 and 1982 the evolution of world demand and market prices for oil confounded expectations. First, the 1979 upheaval in Iran provoked an unexpected and sharp increase in the price of crude oil—a price hike that was probably untenable under any circumstances. Then, another set of unexpected events led to an unforeseen drop in the world's oil demand. It could not have surprised anyone that Mexico's external sector (finances and commodities) would depend upon world energy costs—this was the price to pay in order to get out of the 1976-77 crisis. What *was* surprising was the sharp fluctuation of oil prices: upwards during the first two-and-a-half years, downwards thereafter.

To have expected the government of the Mexican bourgoisie to adjust its plans accordingly would have been as utopian as demanding that it not use the magic wand of oil to get itself out of the earlier crisis. The acceptance of the long-term view, the assumption of immediate sacrifices in order to assure the future—such thinking is not to the liking of bourgoisies, however intelligent they may be, however modernizing their states may seem. López Portillo's government did what Mexico's capital asked it to do: get the economy out of the hole it had dug itself into.

The second hypothesis of our original article need only concern us briefly. In 1978, the ratio of oil production to proven reserves was 39 years (1.4 million barrels daily to 20 billion barrels in proven reserves). In 1982 the ratio is 65 years: 3 million barrels daily, 72 billion barrels in proven reserves. In 1978 this trend was foreseeable; in 1982 we can still expect it to continue for some time into the future. The problem of Mexican capitalism is not looming shortages of petroleum; the problem is not knowing what to do with it.

Finally, with respect to Mexico's supposed dependency, one can make a number of observations. It would be difficult to find a Third World capitalist country further removed from the stereotype of dependency than the Mexico of the last few years. As regards foreign policy, the centerpiece of dependence theorists' arguments, Mexico confounds expectations. Few bourgeois governments have been so confrontational in their relations with the United States as López Portillo's. And, with respect to the so-called economic terrain, the measures of September 1982—the nationalization of the banking system, general exchange controls, and the virtually unilateral suspension of payment on the foreign debt—are not precisely the kinds of responses characteristic of governments which have yielded to imperialism. The Mexican bourgoisie is neither dependent on imperialism nor anti-imperialist; it is not more of one or the other because of oil. The Mexican bourgoisie is what it has always been; sometimes with greater or lesser boldness, strength, and intelligence.

This does not answer a lingering question. Four years ago, I seemed to predict a lasting bonanza for Mexico's capitalism; by 1982 it was evident that it had entered one of its most serious crises in history. What happened is not the issue. Mexico's oil wealth made possible a four-year boom which ended in a crisis worse than the last one. The issue is whether oil can resolve this new crisis. The answer is necessarily tentative, but the available evidence suggests that it is in the affirmative. Indeed, within the framework of this system—which continues to be capitalist notwithstanding the nationalization of banks—it seems that oil is the *only* available instrument to get out of this predicament.

The problems that need to be resolved by the state, with or without López Portillo, are clear. The external debt is being renegotiated, but that does not mean it will not be paid; the payments will merely be spread out over time, given the diminished ability to meet payments. Since Mexico's non-petroleum exports, in the short run, do not have much elasticity of demand, where can such a solution come from, if not from selling more oil? In Mexico a budget deficit cannot be reduced merely by cutting public expenditures. It also requires a larger income to the government, and if this is to be in dollars, in the short term it can only come from the sale of oil. To get the economy on its feet will require additional imports and foreign exchange; the latter will have to be in the form of petrodollars. This will occur not because this is what is best for the country, but because it is the easiest, handiest, cheapest way out for the Mexican economy. These are the kinds of solutions dear to the bourgeoisie.

A problem remains, however. Given the present global recession, and the concomitant weakness of the world oil market, how does Mexico increase the export of crude oil? Actually, there are reasons to believe that there is room for such an increase. Part of this "solution" was already visible by late 1982: in August the Mexican government signed an agreement with the U.S. Department of Energy which will provide Mexico with advance payment for oil going to the U.S. strategic reserve. Moreover, even if world demand did not pick up quickly as a result of the expected economic recovery of the U.S. and Europe, there are still additional possibilities for export. Mexican efforts to substitute other sources of supply are one such possibility; one way to accomplish this may be the negotiation of agreements with European buyers, or Brazil, providing for the sale of Mexican oil in national currencies (and not in dollars). Petróleos Mexicanos does not face insurmountable obstacles to increase production and export—the production capacity is already there. The problem for the government will be to invent formulas which will make Mexican crude more attractive than that of other oil exporting countries. I have no doubt that we can rely on the imagination of the oil merchants of the Mexican government to find them.

In 1977-78 oil permitted Mexican capital a way out of its difficulties. Unfortunately for Mexico's workers, there are reasons to suspect that substantially the same will occur in 1982-83. When there is no opposition with force, crises simply transform capitalism, they do not topple it. With little opposition and with much oil, Mexican (transformed) capitalism will find its way out of this, and other crises. *Así será.*

7
Mexican Petroleum and U.S. Security

Richard Fagen

Now we have a choice. But if we wait, we will constantly live in fear of embargoes. We could endanger our freedom as a sovereign nation to act in foreign affairs. Within ten years we would not be able to import enough oil—from any country at any acceptable price.
—President Carter in a broadcast address on energy problems, April 18, 1977

Conservative reserve-to-production ratios used in the oil industry suggest that Mexico might be able to produce 10 million barrels a day by 1985 or 1990. Some Mexican government officials anticipate that production will indeed rise to these levels. If it does, Mexican petroleum could be an important factor in holding down world energy prices and in reducing the West's dependence on Saudi Arabia and other OPEC sources.
—Lead editorial, The New Republic, August 19, 1978

In the long run, Mexico is a "bigger threat to the U.S. than the Soviet Union." . . . *"One of the most serious problems we have to face"* is the doubling of the population of Mexico by the end of the

---

Richard R. Fagen is Professor of Political Science, Stanford University, Stanford, California. This is a revised version of an essay first published in *Foro Internacional* (México), No. 74, Vol. XIX, no. 2, October–December 1978. The English version first appeared in *International Security* 4 (Summer 1979):39–53. Reprinted with permission. This and related writings on the United States and Mexico have been supported by the Rockefeller Foundation.
© *International Security* and the MIT Press, 1979.

century, which, Colby said, would drive an additional 20 million illegal aliens across the border into the United States . . .
—Fragments from an interview with ex-CIA Director William Colby, *Los Angeles Times*, June 6, 1978

In the national security dialogue, the key word is *vulnerability*, followed closely by the related concepts of *stability* and *predictability*. No event in the past decade has made policy elites in the United States feel as vulnerable as the Arab oil embargo of 1973, the quadrupling of prices under the OPEC umbrella, and the subsequent management of both price and supply under cartel conditions. President Carter's oft-quoted statement that the energy issue in the United States is "the moral equivalent of war" has its roots in these events and clearly reflects the national security theme which runs through all discussions of petroleum and international and domestic politics.

ENERGY VULNERABILITY: PERCEPTIONS OF THE PROBLEM

At first glance, U.S. vulnerability in the energy area seems to be based on the fear of another oil embargo. While containing the seeds of an important truth, this greatly oversimplifies the situation. Actually, as noted in many contemporary analyses, a confluence of factors, trends, and predictions is involved. In brief, the major features of the landscape are the following:[1]

Over the past half decade:

- A continuing and even increasing U.S. dependence on imported oil as a percentage of all petroleum consumed in the United States. This derives from the fact that U.S. petroleum production has peaked while demand has increased—and will most probably continue to increase, albeit more slowly. (In 1977, the United States imported 8.7 million barrels per day [MBD] or 47 percent of its total oil consumption. In 1973, the respective figures were 6.3 MBD and 36 percent.)
- A steadily rising percentage of U.S. oil imports has been coming from OPEC countries, with the Arab OPEC nations becoming increasingly important both in absolute and percentage terms. (There is a widespread feeling that the United States is becoming a hostage to certain OPEC nations, particularly Saudi Arabia. The complexities introduced into U.S.-Middle East relations by this situation are legion, as are

the domestic consequences of the U.S.-Saudi and U.S.-Iranian linkages—and the disintegration of those linkages.)

Over the next half decade or more:
- A widely shared feeling that by the middle or late 1980s the current world oil surplus will turn into a shortage, thus placing new leverage in the hands of suppliers, particularly the Saudis, as the only OPEC country with substantial capacity to expand production—although this capacity is itself a matter of some controversy. (The most dramatic projection of this shortfall is contained in the CIA's *The International Energy Situation: Outlook to 1985*. The most controversial part of the CIA study is the prediction that Soviet and East European production could fall behind domestic needs by as much as 4.5 MBD by 1985, thus greatly increasing world demand for oil.)[2]
- Pessimistic projections concerning the possibility of developing alternative energy sources in the United States (and elsewhere in the First World) at a rate fast enough to substitute substantially for oil—thus lowering the demand for imported oil. (In the United States, the development of coal-related energy sources—and to a lesser extent nuclear and solar resources—is or at least was central to the Carter Energy Plan. For a wide variety of political, economic, and environmental reasons, however, most observers do not expect these energy alternatives to be developed nearly as rapidly as the Carter Plan envisaged. This is particularly the case given the massive legislative difficulties encountered by the Plan in 1978.)
- Serious doubts about the capacity of the United States as a society and economy to develop an effective program of energy conservation. U.S. per capita energy use is, with the possible exception of Canada, the highest in the world—double that of some European societies with comparable standards of living. This profligate use of energy is woven deeply into the fabric of U.S. society and is possibly not amenable to reduction at a rate fast enough to substantially affect U.S. oil imports. Compounding the problem of conservation is the particular nature of the political process in the United States, a process particularly open to the operation of special interests and "blocking coalitions:" Witness the success of the automotive industry, in alliance with sectors of the petroleum

industry and organized labor, in delaying and weakening legislation intended to mandate (or in some instances simply "encourage") the production of cars and trucks that achieve substantially higher fuel mileage. This political process is one of the most durable features of U.S. society.³

A situation in which world petroleum demand rises more rapidly than supply (and finally overtakes it), in which alternative energy sources come on line slowly in the United States, in which conservation makes only modest inroads into demand in the United States, and in which control over supply and price resides with OPEC—and particularly with the Saudis—is seen as a recipe for national and international disaster. One such scenario is sketched by Daniel Yergin:

> It need not happen. But, unless we bestir ourselves, it most likely will. By 1985 or 1986 or 1987, if present trends continue, we'll be staring at an energy crisis far worse than the one we went through in the early 70s. And then our present boredom with the energy problem, and with the Carter administration's efforts to cope with it, will seem like complacent sleep. In that event, the reality we wake up to is apt to be frightening. Prices will double or triple, in real terms, within a short time. The standard of living of every American will nose dive. The international monetary system will shudder and shake. Industrial nations will be pitted against each other in a bruising scramble for oil. The Western alliance could be shattered. In a number of countries, democracy itself might not be able to survive.⁴

In more measured, but no less foreboding language, a Rockefeller Foundation-sponsored study makes many of the same points:

> Consideration of the factors affecting prospective world oil supply must necessarily range broadly over political, economic, financial, and strategic or security issues . . . an eventual tightening of the balance between oil supply and demand may generate an unrestrained intergovernmental competition for supply.

It is entirely possible that despite the energy options open to industrial states, not enough will be done in time to avert, or even mitigate, that competition: the importing governments will not do enough to restrain consumption, to increase supply from their own undeveloped oil reserves, or to begin exploiting alternative energy sources. In that case, it is probable that the governments of oil-exporting countries will see no reason why they cannot link the availability of their oil even more closely to the securing of their own political and economic objectives; and it is quite possible they will enlist the support of a number of industrial nations which can see no alternative but to comply.

In all these circumstances, the consequent competition would not be only economic. The divisions within Western Europe between its own "North" and its energy-poor "South," the obtrusive role of the United States as a growing consumer and importer of energy, and the continuing total dependence of Japan on large volumes of imported oil: these and other factors would result also in an erosion of security and of the international economic and financial system.[5]

THE MEXICAN PETROLEUM BOOM

In this complex interplay of present and future, supply and price, domestic and international concerns, where does Mexico fit in? The answer is necessarily speculative—and increasingly the subject of acrimonious debate in the United States. Nevertheless, certain elements of the evolving situation are already coming into focus.

First, there is a rapidly growing realization that Mexico is moving toward the major leagues as an oil (and gas) producer and exporter. Symbolically, this coming-of-age of Mexico as a petroleum producer is best represented by the *Fortune* cover story of April 10, 1978, headlined "Mexico Becomes an Oil Power." That story ends with these sentences:

> Optimists on Mexican oil say that the total potential reserves come to perhaps 120 billion barrels, compared with a trillion in the entire Persian Gulf region. Whatever the true figure, there is certainly plenty to sustain production well into the twenty-first century at rates far higher than anything Pemex now plans. That is certainly good news for Mexico, for bankers holding Mexican debt, and for Mexico's oil-hungry neighbor to the north.[6]

The second half of 1978 and the first part of 1979 saw no lessening of U.S. enthusiasm about the prospects for Mexican petroleum. To the contrary, according to one (admittedly very optimistic) source, "Mexico is turning up oil fields so immense that they could overturn the conventional wisdom about world oil supplies and significantly alter the geopolitics of energy."[7]

True or not, even at present levels of proven reserves, it is generally felt that Mexican petroleum exports can and will have beneficial effects on world oil trade volumes, pricing and security of supply. Although it is a slight oversimplification, the general U.S. perspective is "the more world production and export capacity, the more diversity of sources, and the fewer local or international reasons to participate in an oil embargo (generally felt to be a problem that will originate in the Middle East, if at all), the better from the U.S. point of view." Mexican oil development is a plus on all three counts—as is, of course, oil development and export from other non-Arab OPEC sources. In fact, as estimates of Mexico's reserves skyrocket, a view of Mexico as a potential "OPEC-buster" has begun to appear in certain policy circles.[8]

Thus, the first perspective on the strategic importance of Mexican petroleum is essentially global. From that perspective it can be argued that Mexican oil will contribute to the postponement of the energy shortages and related problems currently forecast for the later 1980s or early 1990s. So viewed, it is in the interest of the United States for Mexico to produce as much oil as it can, as quickly as possible; since domestic use would not rise as rapidly as total production, maximum exports would result.

A second perspective, not incompatible with the first, emphasizes *security of supply* from a more narrowly national point of view. Even before the much-feared future scenario of ruthless competition, true shortages and rising prices begins, the United States clearly has a strong interest in diversifying and securing sources of imported oil. Recent events in Iran have only served to underscore the fragility of Middle Eastern supplies, and even optimists see no substantial chance of reducing the absolute amount of imported oil in the short or medium run. In this circumstance, the key role of Mexico as an increasingly important exporter— with special economic, political and geographical links to the United States—begins to come into focus.[9] *In other words, the strategic importance of Mexican oil at the present time—and particularly in the middle or late 1980s—is not a simple function of its percentage contribution to world exports, but rather a very complex function of Mexico's role as a rapidly expanding exporter geographically, politically, and economically intimately linked to the largest oil consumer in the world.*

From this perspective as well, the total production and export figures for Mexican oil are important. But even more important is the nature of the hydrocarbon relationship established with the United States and U.S. allies (or at least nations currently being treated in some favored fashion). To some extent, markets and marketing arrangements thus take precedence over supply—although the two are difficult to unbundle. Above all, the degree of security of Mexican supply would necessarily involve a whole range of subtle and complex "understandings," since for political reasons more formal agreements would be difficult to construct.

What is striking about both of these perspectives is the extent to which they elevate Mexico into the position of a key swing producer and exporter.[10] A barrel of Mexican crude oil is not just "another barrel on the world market." It is a barrel that softens upward price pressures; it is a barrel (if there are enough of them) that weakens OPEC; it is a barrel that might be available when other barrels are in short supply for either political or economic reasons. It is, in sum, a barrel with a very high "political value added." Note that this "political value added" of Mexican oil is not necessarily diminished even if the United States is highly successful in limiting energy use—and thus imports. Nor is it diminished even if Mexican oil comprises a relatively modest percentage of U.S. imports during the 1980s. Because the Mexican barrel is thought to be potentially more secure, it is correspondingly—and somewhat ironically—more crucial. When much else may be in doubt, so the logic goes, the United States can "surely count on Mexico."

MEXICAN DEVELOPMENT AND THE UNITED STATES

Because the United States is likely to care very deeply in the 1980s about the supply and markets of Mexican oil, it follows that U.S. policy makers will care even more deeply than they now do about both the internal and external implications of political and economic developments in Mexico. These concerns are manifold: the political cast of the government and its favorable or less favorable disposition to the United States; rates of petroleum development, exports, prices, uses of petroleum revenues and relationships with OPEC and other oil producers; and relationships with the Mexican-American and Chicano communities in the United States—communities which will assuredly have more weight and presence in U.S. politics in the 1980s than they do now.

Mobilized by these and similar concerns, in the fall of 1978 the National Security Council ordered an overview of U.S.-Mexican relations, known in policy circles as Presidential Review Memorandum (PRM) 41. Not surprisingly, the PRM identifies energy, trade, migration, and border-related problems as the main categories of issues that need to be addressed. A preliminary draft began with the statement that Mexico is emerging as "an economic power of strategic value to the United States," subsequently quoting CIA sources as suggesting that Mexican petroleum production might reach as much as ten MBD by 1990.[11] "For the United States," the draft continues, "Mexico represents a major new energy source, presently outside OPEC. Mexico could fill 30 percent of U.S. import needs by the mid-1980s, thus enhancing security of supply."

However tempting it may be, it is extremely shortsighted to frame U.S. security interests with regard to Mexico directly in supply and market terms. As the PRM itself seems to recognize, the U.S.-Mexico nexus is so complex, so historically and geographically conditioned and so affected by factors beyond the control of overt political decisions, that an "energy first" approach is almost certainly doomed to fail.[12] Although the bulk of this complexity cannot be dealt with here, it is important to sketch some of the non-energy elements and perspectives as they intersect with the national security dialogue.

At the core of this dialogue, although often tacit or masked by mystifying language, are U.S. fears of the Mexican "time bomb." The dominant and recurrent nightmare for U.S. policy elites involves the possibility of massive social unrest and the disintegration of political stability south of the border. In a limited but intense series of interviews, conducted in the fall of 1977 with U.S. government and business officials who were concerned with and involved in Mexico, the pivotal fear expressed was that the Mexican political situation would not "hold together." Precipitous changes in the politics and the economics of the Mexican nation were widely perceived as "unacceptable," although there was no consensus on what could or should be done in case "unacceptable" changes began to take place. But the vocabulary used was light years away from what might have been used had we been talking about a less economically and politically important country in the hemisphere (Paraguay, for example)—and the more important oil becomes, the broader the definition of "unacceptable" will tend to become.

The level of economic relationships between the two countries goes a long way toward explaining the sense of threat triggered by the possibility of a breakdown of politics-as-usual in Mexico. With almost 70 percent of Mexican exports going to the United States, with U.S. private banks holding more than 12 billion dollars in outstanding loans and credits, with almost four billion dollars in U.S. investments, with millions of American tourists visiting each year, and with several billion dollars sent back across the border by Mexicans working in the north, the interpenetration of the two economies is profound—and thus the interests in maintaining the system-in-being are very strong on both sides of the border.[13]

Threatening this system and the relations and benefits that flow from it, however, is the social justice and equity situation in Mexico—itself the dark underside of the "miracle" of aggregate growth. With one of the most unequal distributions of income in the world, with a population still growing at more than 3 percent a year (and thus doubling every twenty years), with perhaps one-third of the working age population under- or unemployed—and millions more working in the United States—Mexico is a country with severe development and equity problems. With growth slowed almost to a standstill in the mid-1970s, recovery still spotty in 1977-78, and debt and inflation still high, it is abundantly clear that no short-run solution to Mexico's developmental problems is imminent—even with oil.

This developmental situation is, of course, of direct relevance to the United States because of the profundity with which it is seen to threaten the possibility of continuing the system-in-being. Although the relationship between poverty, misery, exploitation, and inequity on the one hand, and social unrest and revolution on the other is complex and by no means mechanical, it is clear that "something has to be done" to change developmental patterns in Mexico if the longstanding political pact maintaining stability is not to come unraveled. The primary Mexican security threat for U.S. corporate and governmental decision-makers is thus a Mexico torn by civil and political strife, with real potential for moving toward an unchartered politics—a politics that is inestimably worse if it turns out to be of the socialist left, but by no means attractive if it turns out to be a politics of the militaristic right.[14]

The Mexican "time bomb" has a second set of implications for the U.S. security dialogue. Here the sense of threat does not turn directly on Mexican regime stability, but rather on what might be called the "spillover effects" of maldevelopment and rapid population growth. Spillover translates directly into the issue of immigration.

The complexity if not the full scope of Mexican immigration into the United States is by now coming into view and need not be reviewed here.[15] What does need to be stressed is that most of the U.S. public probably views Mexicans who are illegally in the United States as a serious problem. Segments of organized labor see the immigrants as "taking jobs from the American working man" (and woman). Bureaucrats, politicians, and anxious citizens perceive the migrants as users of services who pay less than their fair share of taxes. The Immigration and Naturalization Service is structured to view them as criminals. At the extreme, they are viewed as an actual or potential threat to the racial purity, social integrity, and political stability of the nation —and thus a national security problem. The interview with William Colby cited at the outset of this essay continues: the migration of Mexicans "is exactly what we did with black rural poor of the South in the 1920s . . . We sent them all to the central cities. It was a better life for them—but the social costs for our country have been fantastic. We've managed to ruin our public school system and created ghettos."[16] Racism and errors in social analysis included, Colby's statement crystalizes what is certainly a widespread feeling about the threat to the "American way of life" posed by a rapidly multiplying and northward-migrating Mexican nation.[17]

For at least some analysts, the proper approach to this floodtide of threatening Mexican immigration is clear: there must be a much-toughened stance by the U.S. authorities on the border. Others add to this notion that Mexico must use its oil revenues in ways that will sharply diminish "push" factors in Mexico; jobs must be created, working conditions and wages upgraded and patterns of land tenure restructured.[18] However correct these developmental suggestions may be for the long run—and we shall return to them in the final section—they are almost certain to prove ineffectual in the short run. Too many persons have already been pushed off the land in Mexico, the human and economic scale of the employment problem is too huge, the wage differentials and opportunities north and south of the border too large, the frontier too long, and the payoffs of (possibly) massive development projects too far in the future for push factors to be diminished rapidly. Meanwhile, politics in the United States dictate that the government must appear to be "doing something." That "something" can only lead in the direction of quasi-military measures along the border. Such are the consequences of framing the immigration issue in narrow national security terms.

"SOWING THE OIL:" LONG RUN PERSPECTIVES

If a national security perspective on the question of immigration leads almost inevitably to a rather nasty police approach to the problem (therein defined as too many immigrants), the developmental side of the equation is both more complex and far-ranging. Precisely because of the profound U.S. national interest in internal political and economic outcomes in Mexico, what Mexico does with its oil revenues is necessarily of deep concern to U.S. elites. Even if the oil revenue cannot be "sown" so as to achieve a relatively rapid and significant reduction in the northward flow of Mexicans, the Northern hope is that *petropesos* will be used in ways which ameliorate inequality and injustice sufficiently to keep the lid on the Mexican volcano. To sustain this hope, no highly developed sense of equity or concern for the downtrodden is necessary. It is quite sufficient to have a modestly acute sense of long-range U.S. interests coupled with a latent survival instinct. In this there is substantial congruence between U.S. and Mexican elites.

An optimistic scenario for the use of oil income envisages export revenues and new capital flows sufficient to enable the huge foreign debt to be repaid, capital goods for the further development of the hydrocarbons to be manufactured or imported, with enough left over to make massive investments in developmental projects that will—in time—reduce unemployment, arrest the flight from the countryside to the cities and help to reduce the glaring inequalities between those who live in comfort or opulence and the millions consigned to misery and poverty. While all of the above is taking place, populist measures (subsidies to basic foodstuffs and consumer goods, etc.) of the sort that have served the Mexican political system so well at critical moments in the past should aid in securing the time necessary to accomplish some needed structural changes. Roughly speaking, in this scenario the oil revenues are seen as the necessary and prior—if not by themselves sufficient—motor of reform.

A more pessimistic scenario emphasizes that the repayment of debt, increased foreign confidence and impressive liquidity have little to do with development—and even less with social justice. The critical issue of discovering (one might say *inventing*) ways of "sowing the oil" so as to benefit more than a small minority of the Mexican population remains. The experience of other oil-boom nations is sobering: Inflation, swollen import bills, luxury consumption, capital intensive industrialization, the continued neglect of agriculture, regional and other disequilibria, unsatisfied rising expectations, and in general an inability to break with many of the most unattractive patterns of the past are all common in the recent histories of nations otherwise as diverse as Venezuela and Iran. In this scenario significant structural reform tends to be seen as a necessary *precondition* to the effective use of the future flow of oil income, and such reform is not viewed as highly probable.

Official Mexican thinking as of early 1979 clearly suggested concern with some of the difficulties highlighted in the second, more pessimistic scenario. The relatively modest petroleum production goals for 1982, the serious warnings about inflation and the cautionary statements about the absorptive capacity of the economy all suggest that managing the boom in a relatively conservative fashion will be the basic policy for the second half of the López Portillo Administration. Immediately, these cues were picked up by important business publications in the United States, essentially seconding the notion that prudence in generating and investing oil revenues, rather than maximum production and exports, was the best policy for all concerned.[19] But whether the revenues are huge or simply large, and whether Mexico turns out to be a potential "OPEC-buster" or simply a substantial exporter, problems associated with "sowing the oil" so as to ameliorate inequality, unemployment, and misery remain.

From the point of view of the U.S. policy, the vexing aspect of these developmental issues is that in conventional diplomatic terms they are, in the main, considered to be Mexico's "domestic affairs." This inhibits both a clear articulation of U.S. security interests in how the oil is sown in Mexico as well as a frank admission that what the United States does in many areas is highly consequential for Mexican possibilities, decisions, and outcomes. There is a paradox here: Perhaps the most important long-run U.S. national security concerns relating to Mexican petroleum—issues involving the manner in which Mexican development is affected by the oil boom—are precisely those concerns that are most difficult to articulate both conceptually and politically. So complex and so historically fragile is the oil-reform social justice-political stability nexus, and so problematic and suspect is U.S. involvement in any attempt to affect that nexus in Mexico, that clear-headed discussion of the issues seems nearly impossible in governmental circles at this time.[20] Yet in the absence of such a discussion, more obvious and traditional security concerns will surely occupy center stage: Mexico as a future, more secure, petroleum supplier; Mexico as potentially another Cuba or Chile; and Mexico as an exporter of unwanted and threatening labor—unwanted and threatening at least in moments of substantial unemployment, welfare backlash, and recrudescent racism.

Some might argue that the recent elevation of Mexican-U.S. relations to the category of "high politics" contains within it the seeds of hope. Surely, the argument goes, with top-level public officials (instead of the third and fourth ranks) debating the issues, it will be possible to keep the "big picture" in focus, overcome bureaucratic infighting and fragmentation, and introduce coherence and rationality where little existed before.[21] But at least in the United States, the outcomes of the high politics of international oil do not present an altogether attractive picture—as recent events in Iran and elsewhere remind us. On the other hand, it is also true that the United States—despite its energy relationship to Canada—has never had to engage in the high politics of oil with a nation with which it has such a contiguous, asymmetrical and in many ways historically rich and conflictual relationship. This time, the international energy dialogue involves not only barrels of oil and cubic feet of gas, but also—and very directly—the lives, property, and futures of the citizens of two societies joined together along a 2,000 mile border. The dangers for Mexico and also for the United States of this situation are very substantial. But so are the as yet not understood and unforeseen opportunities.

Notes

1. Representative recent documents are *World Energy Outlook*, The Exxon Corporation, Exxon Background Series, 1977; *The International Energy Situation: Outlook to 1985*, Central Intelligence Agency, April, 1977; *U.S. Oil Supply and Demand to 1990*, New York: Petroleum Industry Research Foundation, Inc., October 1977; *International Energy Supply: A Perspective from the Industrial World*, International Policy Studies, the Rockefeller Foundation, May, 1978; John C. Sawhill, Keichi Oshima, and Hanns W. Maull, *Energy: Managing the Transition*, the Trilateral Commission, Triangle Paper No. 17, 1978; Daniel Yergin, "The Real Meaning of the Energy Crunch," *New York Times Magazine*, 4 June 1978. For a sketch of the main points of the Carter Energy Plan, see Congressional Research Service, "Excerpts from an Initial Analysis of the President's National Energy Plan," Library of Congress, 1 June 1977 (and subsequent analyses in the same series).

2. Estimates of when curves of supply and demand will cross vary widely. Among many variables (really unknowns) that enter into the equation are the willingness and capacity of present suppliers (Saudi Arabia in particular) to increase production, the rate and quantity of new oil discoveries, the economic and technological feasibility of extracting oil from shale and other unconventional sources, and the overall growth rates and levels of energy usage in both developed and less developed countries. For differing perspectives and much useful information, see "Energy in the Eighties: Can We Avoid Scarcity and Inflation?" *Hearings before the Subcommittee on Energy, Joint Economic Committee*, 95th Congress, 2nd Session, 8, 9, and 21 March 1978 (Washington: U.S. Government Printing Office, 1978). A composite estimate of the sources consulted suggests that serious shortages are likely to occur within about ten years.

3. Projections of the rate of substitution of non-oil energy sources, energy/economic growth relations in the United States, conservation possibilities and the level of domestic petroleum production combine—in the hands of different analysts—to produce quite different goals or predictions of the total oil import bill for the United States in the mid-1980s. At the extreme low end of the spectrum was the Carter Energy Plan's goal of six MBD in 1985. This was once regarded as the "centerpiece" of the plan, which if achieved would much reduce the oil import vulnerability of the United States. Not even the plan's most ardent supporters, however, now really believe that it can be achieved. The CIA, on the other hand, predicts as much as a 12-15 MBD import bill for the United States by 1985 (*The International Energy Situation*, p. 15). The Petroleum Industry Research Foundation, using what they call "optimistic" assumptions about conservation and alternative energy development, predicts a 9.6 MBD import level in 1985 (*U.S. Oil Supply and Demand to 1990*, p. 18).

4. Yergin, *op. cit.*, p. 32.

5. *International Energy Supply*, p. 32. In this study, the major focus of concern is on first world development and continued cooperation. Yergin is more narrowly focused on the United States and the absolute necessity of conservation given the

profligate use of petroleum in the U.S. He continues the passage quoted above by noting, "The United States dominates the world oil market. We use a third of all the oil used in the world every day. American cars and trucks alone use a seventh of all the oil used in the world . . ." For a much more extensive and well-documented presentation of this point of view, see Robert Stobaugh and Daniel Yergin, "After the Second Shock: Pragmatic Energy Strategies," *Foreign Affairs,* 57 (Spring 1979).

6. "Pemex Comes Out of its Shell," *Fortune,* vol.97, no.7, pp. 45-48. Quotation from page 48. If *Fortune* smiles can others be far behind? See, for example, the cover story in *Business Week,* "Mexico's Reluctant Oil Boom," 15 January 1979. Since the *Fortune* article was published, both official announcements of Mexican reserves and speculations about the "true" size of the fields have escalated. As of January, 1979, Mexico had announced "proven" petroleum reserves of 40 billion barrels, "probable" reserves of 44.6 billion barrels, and "potential" reserves of 200 billion barrels. Some of the wildest speculations published to date are found in William D. Metz, "Mexico: The Premier Oil Discovery in the Western Hemisphere," *Science* 202 (1978):1261-65. There a Mexican journalist is quoted as having told *Science* that Pemex *thinks it has* 700 billion barrels! (emphasis in original). In thinking about Mexican hydrocarbons, it should be remembered that the proven reserves to date are about 72 percent oil and 28 percent gas. For a detailed discussion on the gas issue in U.S.-Mexican relations, see Richard R. Fagen and Henry R. Nau, "Mexican Gas: The Northern Connection," in Richard R. Fagen (ed.), *Capitalism and the State in U.S.-Latin American Relations* (Stanford, Calif.: Stanford University Press, 1979). The most thorough, overall analysis to date (based on conservative, 1978 data) is *Mexico's Oil and Gas Policy: An Analysis,* Committee on Foreign Relations and the Joint Economic Committee, 95th Congress, 2nd Session, December, 1978 (Washington: Government Printing Office, 1979).

7. "Mexico: The Premier Oil Discovery . . .", p. 1261.

8. See, for example, the statement by Senator Edward Kennedy on 9 January 1979. Mexico is not currently a member of OPEC, although in general it follows OPEC pricing policies.

9. To the extent that Mexico is more likely than other suppliers to spend oil revenues in the United States, there are also balance of payments benefits to the United States from Mexican exports—whatever their destination.

10. At the beginning of 1979, Mexico was producing approximately 1.4 MBD of oil and exporting approximately one third of the total—mostly to the United States. Production targets for the end of 1980 were 2.25 MBD with approximately half of the total destined for export. Current Mexican plans are to hold production and exports roughly to 1980 levels until the end of the six-year presidential term in 1982. Outside estimates of Mexico's production capacity in 1985 range from a cautious low of about 3 MBD (the low end of the CIA estimates cited earlier) to the outlandish 10 MBD suggested in the *New Republic* editorial quoted at the outset. One clear limit to increased production is the problem of disposing of the associated natural gas that will be released by production levels above those currently planned for 1980—unless of course the gas is ultimately sold to the United States.

11. PRM-41 is, of course, classified. Preliminary versions, said to be very similar to the final version, leaked to the press. See, for example, "U.S. Study

Eyes Better Ties with Oil-Rich Mexico," *The Washington Post*, 15 December 1978, p. A-1.

12. For an elaboration of this point, see Richard R. Fagen, "Mexico and the United States: The Inescapable Relationship," *The Wilson Quarterly* 3 (Summer 1979).

13. For more background and detail, see, for example, Richard R. Fagen, "The Realities of U.S.-Mexican Relations," *Foreign Affairs* 55 (July 1977). See also, "Mexico: A Survey," *The Economist*, 22 April 1978.

14. It was a rightward, essentially military scenario for Mexico to which President López Portillo referred when he raised the specter of the "South Americanization of Mexico" in his February, 1977 visit to Washington. As suggested in an earlier essay, even a right wing "solution" to domestic unrest in Mexico would have very serious ramifications in the United States.

> . . . all scenarios would have in common the rupturing of the Mexican political consensus, the widespread use of force to suppress dissident groups, and a much larger presence of the military in public life. Viewed from the United States, such scenarios would have very serious ramifications. Border problems would escalate as political migration and pressures were added to the already substantial economic pressures . . . at some point U.S. territory would surely be used as a base for exile attacks back across the border. Private investment and bank lending would necessarily crumble. Sooner or later, U.S. citizens would almost certainly be killed if violence were at all widespread or long-lasting. The political dynamics unleashed in the United States as families, interests, and established relationships were broken would be unpredictable but surely grave. (Fagen, "The Realities of U.S.-Mexican Relations." p. 699.)

15. The most complete and judicious presentation of relevant knowns and unknowns is Wayne A. Cornelius, *Mexican Migration to the United States: Causes, Consequences, and U.S. Responses* (Massachusetts Institute of Technology, Center for International Studies, July, 1978). For an attempt to link the migration question to an analysis of U.S.-Mexican relations, see David F. Ronfeldt and Caesar D. Sereseres, "Treating the Alien(ation) in U.S.-Mexico Relations," (Santa Monica, Calif.: The RAND Corporation, August, 1978). For a relatively hardline Congressional view, concentrating on Mexico, see "Legal and Illegal Immigration to the Unites States," Select Committee on Population, U.S. House of Representatives, 95th Congress, 2nd Session, December, 1978.

16. *Los Angeles Times*, 6 June 1978. For a much more sophisticated and complex analysis, but one which is strikingly similar to Colby's in ideology if not in style, see Garret Hardin, "The Limits of Sharing," *World Issues* 3 (February-March, 1978) issue on immigration ethics (Santa Barbara, Calif.: Center for the Study of Democratic Institutions).

17. There are, of course, various economic interests that depend, in whole or in part, on the labor and purchasing power of the immigrants. From huge agricultural enterprises to motel chains to humble diners employing a single dishwasher, thousands of U.S. businesses depend on immigrant labor to do the work that many others seem not to want to do—at least not at the wages offered. From this

perspective, the immigrants are not a *problem* but rather the solution to a continuing need for a low cost, semi-skilled, non-unionized, and elastic labor supply. The owners, managers and foremen who hire, fire and often ruthlessly exploit the Mexican immigrants may share many of the negative and racist social and cultural perceptions of their fellow citizens, but they also know which side their bread is buttered on and thus continue to employ immigrant labor whenever possible.

18. In the hands of some, this argument is given a special twist. What is advocated is not just a tighter border policy on the part of the U.S., but an overt threat to "close down" the border to *force* Mexican elites to come to grips with their serious developmental problems. In other contexts this tactic is known as "deepening the contradictions" and it is, of course, widely resented in Mexico as well as fraught with difficulties and dangers for the United States. For an example of such reasoning and advocacy, see George W. Grayson, "Mexico's Opportunity: The Oil Boom," *Foreign Policy* no.29 (Winter, 1977–78), particularly p. 82.

19. See, for example, *Business Week*, "Mexico's Reluctant Oil Boom," *op. cit.*, and "Mexican Oil: The U.S. is most definitely *not* in the driver's seat," *Forbes* 22 January 1979. It should be noted that the business press shows only passing concern with the question of social justice. The major concerns are good relations with Mexico, prudent management and political stability south of the border. Issues of inequality and misery enter to the extent that they are seen as "destabilizing."

20. I am consciously avoiding an analysis of various interests and contradictions which make the discussion even more problematic. For example, given the capital intensive, income-concentrating aspects of most direct foreign investment, equity and employment-sensitive approaches to Mexican development would suggest that the U.S. government should actively *discourage* U.S. transnational corporations—particularly those engaged in manufacturing and certain sectors of agriculture—from locating in Mexico. The utopian nature of the suggestion is an index of the contradictions implied. For a more general discussion of this and related points, see Richard R. Fagen, "Equity in the South in the Context of North-South Relations," in Albert Fishlow *et. al.*, *Rich and Poor Nations in the World Economy* (New York: McGraw-Hill, 1978).

21. President Carter's 14–16 February 1979 visit to Mexico does not give much reason for optimism. The relatively cool and strongly nationalistic reception he received suggests that much hard bargaining between the two nations lies ahead. No matter how much "coherence and rationality" may be introduced into U.S. policy (and to date there does not seem to be very much), there is no necessary or easy convergence between U.S. and Mexican interests.

TRADE RELATIONS:
Escalating Conflict?

III

8
The Trade Issue in U.S.–Mexican Relations

G.C. Hufbauer, W.N. Harrell Smith IV, and F.G. Vukmanic

International trade policies do not arise in a vacuum; they reflect basic forces in national economic systems. The confluence of four such forces has awakened Mexican trade relations with the United States: first, Mexico's discovery of huge quantities of oil; second, Mexico's announcement of ambitious growth targets, coupled with unacknowledged inflationary consequences; third, the realization in both nations that large scale exports of manufactured goods from Mexico can substitute, in part, for large scale emigration of people; and, fourth, the vastly different approaches to international commercial policy in Mexico City and Washington, D.C. This short essay will outline these forces, sketch their trade consequences over the next five years, and speculate on the areas of policy harmony and policy tension between Mexico and the United States. Tables 1 and 2 portray the authors' rough estimates of the key dimensions of the Mexican and American economies for the years 1980 and 1985. Table 3 outlines the structure of bilateral merchandise trade.

G.C. Hufbauer and W.N. Harrell Smith IV are with the law firm of Chapman, Duff, and Paul, Washington, D.C. F.G. Vukmanic is Director, Office of International Investment, Department of the Treasury, Washington, D.C.

This paper was first published in *Mexico-United States Relations*, edited by Susan Kaufman Purcell, *Proceedings of The Academy of Political Science* 34 (1981): 136–145.

©1981, The Academy of Political Science.

Mexican oil reserves may amount to 250 billion barrels; proven reserves are now 60 billion barrels. But large reserves do not automatically translate into large exports. In the first place, the conservation ethic runs deep in Mexico. The Mexican people wish to husband their natural resources. No identifiable political constituency exists for the expansion of oil production beyond the levels necessary to support domestic requirements. Consequently, the Mexican government appears to have adopted an informal rule that daily oil production should not exceed 1 million barrels for each 10 billion barrels of proven reserves. Even this conservative ratio, however, would enable production of approximately 5 million barrels a day in 1985 and exports of 3 million barrels a day.

Moreover, the leading circles in Mexico are eager to avoid the "Venezuelan Syndrome," an economy dominated by oil, subject to rapid inflation, and marked by the sudden affluence of well-connected entrepreneurs. As Raúl Salinas Lozano, director of the Mexican Foreign Trade Institute, put it, "Mexico wants to be an economy with oil rather than an oil economy." If the price of oil increases over the next five years by an average rate of 4 percent annually in real terms and 14 percent annually in nominal terms, the price of oil in 1985 would reach approximately $60 a barrel. At that price, exports of 3 million barrels a day would yield foreign exchange earnings of some $65 billion annually—enough to threaten Mexico with the Venezuelan Syndrome. Accordingly, it is likely that exports will be held at lower levels, perhaps no more than 2.5 million barrels a day.

Press speculation notwithstanding, the level of Mexican oil exports is not likely to become a point of contention between the two nations. The United States realizes that Mexico wants to decrease the proportion of its oil exports sold to American markets. Thus the main United States interest in Mexican production is by way of its contribution to global oil supplies. In this context, the United States interest in Mexico's plans is as great as—but no greater than—the United States interest in the plans of Nigeria, Venezuela, Abu Dhabi, and other second-tier oil producing nations.

After tough bargaining, Mexico recently agreed to sell the United States up to 300 million cubic feet a day of natural gas at an initial price of about $4.38 per thousand cubic feet (with a price adjustment clause). This agreement not only provides Mexico with potential revenues of about $.5 billion annually; it also establishes the principle that Mexican gas will be priced to the American market at the world price of energy. This principle was reinforced in May 1980 when Mexico immediately followed Saudi Arabia in increasing the price of its crude oil by about $2 a barrel. The world price principle will undoubtedly extend to future sales of Mexican gas and oil.

MEXICAN DEVELOPMENT PLANS

Mexico is a land of economic planners. National officials have issued eight major sectoral plans, and each of the thirty-one states has issued its own plan. The government, in the third year of President López Portillo's administration, has superimposed on these sectoral and state plans a Plan of Plans—the *Plan Global de Desarrollo* (1980–82).

The Plan of Plans is built on the thesis of accelerated industrialization. It looks to an era of rapid economic growth, geographic decentralization, and the absorption of large numbers of unemployed workers. Not incidentally, this vision is consistent with a policy of spreading the oil wealth throughout Mexico.

Mexico's industrial sector, representing about 37 percent of its gross domestic product, grew at an annual rate of 9.5 percent in 1979. The plan seeks to accelerate development of Mexican industry through export-led growth, based on the well-founded supposition that many branches of Mexican industry cannot become economically efficient if their size is restricted to the domestic market. Under the plan, the industrial sector is targeted to grow at an annual rate of 11 percent, a figure considered necessary both to achieve an overall 8 percent annual growth in the economy and to provide a 4 percent annual growth in the level of employment. Eleven percent growth in industrial output may well require 15 to 20 percent in annual real growth of industrial exports.

A forbidding chain of logic, not fully spelled out in the plan, confronts this theme of rapid, export-led industrialization. First, the ambitious target for overall economic growth—some 8 percent a year in the face of major supply constraints—implies inflation at a rate exceeding 20 percent annually. Mexico's rate of inflation was comparable to the rates for the United States and other industrialized countries until 1973. Since then, Mexican inflation has exceeded the rate in industrialized countries by a margin of 7 to 9 percentage points. During the period 1974-79, overall growth has averaged less than 5 percent annually. It seems most unlikely that accelerating growth will be accompanied by decelerating inflation. High inflation might, in principle, be ameliorated by the application of strict monetary policies, including tight limits of credit extended to public sector enterprises. But Mexican officials have historically seen monetary tools as instruments to facilitate investment, not as weapons to fight inflation. Indeed, the monetary base has been expanded at rates exceeding 30 percent annually for several years.

Second, Mexican officials view the exchange rate as a target of policy, not as a tool of policy. To devalue is to admit economic failure. Mexican governments do, of course, devalue—but only in extremes. High domestic inflation, spurred by ambitious growth targets and ample credit, will be seen as an argument against, not for, exchange rate flexibility.

As a result, exports of Mexican industrial goods are likely to be squeezed between rapidly rising domestic costs and relatively fixed exchange rates. The scenario for 1985 presented in table 1 indicates some adjustment of the exchange rate—from the present level of 23 pesos to the dollar to perhaps 30 pesos to the dollar. But an adjustment of this magnitude would accommodate only about half the anticipated change in domestic cost levels between Mexico and the United States over the period 1980 to 1985. And it is likely that the López Portillo Administration will resist even a partial adjustment of the exchange rate since, from a balance-of-payments standpoint, none will be needed.

One way out of this dilemma is for the Mexican government to subsidize industrial development. Indeed, it is clear that the plan would provide significant incentives (for example, certificates of fiscal promotion, reduced prices for electricity and gas, and preferential rates on loans) to targeted industrial sectors, particularly those that have employment and export potential. Sectors given the highest priority are capital goods sectors, such as machine tools and electrical generators, and agribusiness, like food packing and fertilizer production. Other priority sectors are the steel, petrochemical, pharmaceutical, and textile industries. Under the plan, the government will use its oil resources directly and indirectly to persuade businessmen to enter these sectors. Petrochemical exporters, for example, might be sold gas feedstocks at prices up to 30 percent below the market level.

In addition, Mexico will impose export performance requirements and local-content requirements on foreign subsidiaries. Failure to meet these requirements will result in financial penalties, while compliance will yield financial benefits. As a harbinger of this approach, foreign automobile subsidiaries were required by the Mexican Auto Decree of 1977 to achieve a balance in their exchange earnings, with achievement rewarded by tax incentives. Local-content requirements under the Auto Decree are initially 50 percent for each model of an automobile but are "recommended" to rise to 75 and 80 percent for automobiles and trucks respectively by 1981. Failure to meet recommended levels will result in increased export requirements.

While the deployment of these export promotion tools may partly reconcile the tension between ambitious targets for the export of industrial products, a high inflation rate, and a relatively fixed exchange rate, many other countries have attempted this policy combination and few have succeeded. As shown in table 1, real industrial exports are not likely to grow faster than 10 percent annually over the next five years.

Equally important, the deployment of these tools will almost certainly create policy conflict. In the eyes of the United States, general devaluation is a perfectly acceptable means of stimulating industrial exports; but selective subsidies, export performance requirements, and similar sector-specific measures are viewed as unfair trade practices. Before exploring these tensions in greater detail, it is worth commenting on a closely related concern—migration.

The number of Mexican immigrants who have illegally entered the United States has been variously estimated between 2 million and 6 million persons, and the annual gross flow as high as 1 million persons. As tables 1 and 2 indicate, even with substantial growth, the Mexican gross domestic product per capita will probably not exceed one-fifth of the United States gross domestic product per capita in 1985, and unemployment rates may be substantially higher in Mexico. Thus the pressures to migrate will continue for the foreseeable future.

Responsible officials in both countries would welcome a reduction in the flow of labor from Mexico to the United States. It is widely agreed that Mexican industrial and agricultural prosperity, not repressive border restrictions, is the preferred method of reducing the rate of migration. And access to external markets—in the United States and elsewhere—is widely viewed as one ingredient of a successful industrial and agricultural strategy. An extra billion dollars of Mexican industrial and agribusiness exports probably would mean an extra 100,000 direct jobs in Mexico.

From the standpoint of labor policy, it follows that the United States should welcome rapid industrialization and agricultural growth, regardless of the commercial policy means used to achieve the end result. But general precepts drawn from labor policy must confront not only the precepts but also the statutory realities of commercial policy.

MEXICAN AND AMERICAN COMMERCIAL POLICY

If Mexico City is a haven for planners, Washington, D.C. is a haven for lawyers. Washington trade officials think in terms of *rules* of the game—"free trade but fair trade." Mexican trade officials think in terms of *targets*—sector-by-sector and even company-by-company. To achieve these targets, Mexican tariffs and strict quotas were the chosen instruments; today, subsidies, incentives, local-content, and export performance requirements are favored. But these tools conflict squarely with American notions of fair trade—codified in the General Agreement on Tariffs and Trade (GATT), the United States Trade Act of 1974, and the United States Trade Agreements Act of 1979.

This policy created a sheltered industrial base that concentrated on producing consumer goods rather than capital goods or intermediates. As a result, Mexico became more, rather than less, dependent on imported capital goods and intermediates, and its current account deficit increased over time.

Mexico's oil wealth both coincided with and abetted a change in development strategy. Import substitution was seen to have run into steep and unpromising terrain. Meanwhile, oil exports suddenly removed the balance-of-payment constraint on a more open development policy. The stage was set for a shift in Mexican trade policy from an inward-looking approach to a policy that advocated export promotion, selective import substitution concentrating on capital and intermediate goods, and a diversification of export markets and sources of supply away from Mexico's traditionally high dependence on the United States.

This shift in approach has led to a gradual relaxation of Mexican trade barriers. The government recognized the need to reduce barriers to selected imports that were essential to development and to subject domestic producers to increased import competition as a means of promoting efficiency and combating inflation. Since 1975, license requirements have been eliminated on about 5,000 items covering 35 percent of Mexican imports by value. However, most of the items affected were replaced by tariffs, which in some cases were extremely high. Quotas on a number of products have either been relaxed or eliminated, however, and tariff levels on many items have been reduced.

While Mexico has begun to liberalize its barriers to trade, it is unwilling to subject its producers to the multilateral discipline of the GATT or other multilateral agreements. Mexican critics of the GATT argued forcefully and thoughtfully that Mexican membership would hamstring the new export strategy by constraining the use of subsidies, export performance requirements, local-content requirements and other requirements that are at best questionable under the GATT rules. President López Portillo's announcement on March 18, 1980, that Mexico would not join the GATT signaled Mexico's belief that it can better achieve its goals by seeking bilateral arrangements and by solving trade disputes on a case-by-case basis. Indeed, the recent record contains much to encourage Mexican officials to believe that the United States will blink in particular cases. The natural gas price agreements, the tomato dumping case, and adjustments to the steel trigger price mechanism were all resolved in a manner favorable to Mexico.

In contrast with Mexico, the United States has a strong commitment to the principles of the GATT and other multilateral institutions, such as the International Monetary Fund. The hallmark of these institutions is that they promulgate rules that govern the conduct of countries and enterprises competing in world trade and financial markets. The rules are designed to ensure a "fair" commercial game, rather than to achieve specific commercial results.

TABLE 1.—PROJECTED MEXICAN PERFORMANCE

	1980	1985
Gross domestic product (billions of $ U.S. at 1980 prices; assuming 8 percent annual real growth)	$130	$190
Population (millions)	70	82
Gross domestic product per capita ($ U.S. at 1980 prices)	$1,840	$2,330
Unemployment rate	10%	12%
Price level index (1980 = 100; assuming 20 percent annual inflation rate)	100	250
Exchange rate (pesos per dollar)	23	30
Merchandise exports (billions of $ U.S. at current prices)	$16	$70
Of which: Quantity of oil exports (millions barrels/day)	0.9	2.5
Value of oil exports (assuming $30/barrel in 1980 and $60/barrel in 1985)	$10	$55
Merchandise imports (billions of $ U.S. at current prices)	($16)	($65)
Net services and transfers (billions of $ U.S. at current prices)	($2)	($5)
Current account deficit (billions of $ U.S. at current prices)	($2)	—

A SEARCH FOR ALTERNATIVES

The growth in trade among the United States, Canada, and Mexico has prompted at various times the thought of special trade agreements along bilateral or trilateral lines. The logic is simple. The European Economic Community and the European Free Trade Area, despite their internal problems, are successful and formidable trading blocs. Why not emulate these European arrangements? Yet the only agreement to date that even modestly approaches the European model is the automobile pact between the United States and Canada.

A currently popular, but by no means new, concept is the North American trade area, a sort of regional trilateralism embracing Mexico, the United States, and Canada. Congress, in fact, directed the administration in the Trade Agreement Act of 1979 to study the possibility of such arrangements and to produce a report by July 1981.

It seems most likely that Mexico and the United States could work out their part of the vision. The United States will remain firmly committed to a multilateral trading system so long as it remains the premier world economic power. Preferential bilateral arrangements will be pursued by the United States, if at all, not on center stage but in side arenas. Further, the United States is wedded to a system of economic rules, not economic targets; and apart from this ideological marriage, the United States is politically incapable of targeting selected industries for massive doses of import penetration or preferential access to export promotion.

By contrast, Mexican policy is geared toward the use of an array of policy instruments, designed to achieve target levels of output, imports, and exports, unfettered by international rules of commercial policy. And Mexico seeks, not to intensify its trading relations with the United States, but to diversify in favor of other nations. Mexico is favored in this endeavor by the fact that it is increasingly wooed by other industrial nations eager to sell capital goods on the basis of liberal export credits, sometimes with an admixture of aid terms that the United States finds difficult to match. Finally, Mexican nationalists see a North American trade area as a thinly veiled effort by the United States to gain preferential access to Mexican oil and gas; while American labor is suspicious of measures that would enlarge the scope of sections

TABLE 2.—PROJECTED UNITED STATES ECONOMIC PERFORMANCE

	1980	1985
Gross domestic product (billions of $ U.S. at 1980 prices, assuming 3 percent annual real growth)	2,410	$2,800
Population (millions)	222	233
Gross domestic product per capita ($ U.S. at 1980 prices)	$10,900	$12,000
Unemployment rate	7.5%	6.0%
Price level index (1980 = 100; assuming 10 percent annual inflation rate)	100	160
Merchandise exports (billions of $ U.S. at current prices)	$210	$420
Merchandise imports (billions of $ U.S. at current prices)	$260	$510
Net services and transfers (billions of $ U.S. at current prices)	$35	$90
Current account deficit (billions of $ U.S. at current prices)	($15)	—

806.30 and 807.00 of the United States Tariff Schedule (which impose duty only on foreign value added when components are supplied from the United States) and the Generalized System of Preferences, or expand textile, shoe, or steel imports. Faced with these practical obstacles, the North American trade area is not likely to find a prominent place in the negotiating agenda.

The possibility of Mexico-United States bilateral sectoral agreements has also surfaced. Special arrangements involving sectors where complementary Mexico-United States trade now exists, such as agriculture, automobiles, railcars, and petrochemical products, might have economic and political promise. However, a number of significant hurdles must be cleared before such arrangements can be seriously negotiated, not the least of which is serious opposition by United States interest groups that believe the United States-Canadian automobile pact has not benefited American labor.

In the future, the agenda is likely to be crowded with specific issues, with resolution sought on a case-by-case basis. As part of the Multilateral Trade Negotiations, the United States negotiated tariff cuts on a number of goods of which Mexico is the principal supplier. With Mexico's decision not to join the GATT, the United States must decide whether to retract those tariff concessions. Moreover, since Mexico decided not to join the GATT, there is the further question whether Mexico wishes to associate with particular GATT codes and whether other code signatories would in fact welcome a non-GATT member.

One area of immediate concern is the Subsidy/Countervailing Measures Agreement. If Mexico does not sign this agreement, or does not negotiate a substantially similar agreement with the United States, the United States will not invoke the injury test in applying its countervailing duty statute to imports from Mexico. As Mexico deploys an even wider range of subsidies to compensate for rapid domestic inflation and a relatively fixed exchange rate, a great many exports may be subject to countervailing duty proceedings, even though they do not cause material injury to United States industry. And even if Mexico associates directly or indirectly with the code, thereby acquiring the injury test, its drive to promote exports and its wide use of subsidies may well cause injury to import-sensitive industries, such as automobiles, steel textiles, and even petrochemicals.

TABLE 3.—BILATERAL MERCHANDISE TRADE
Billions of $ U.S. at current prices

	1980	1985
Mexican Exports to United States		
Total	$11.0	$40.0
Agricultural	1.8	4.0
Nonagricultural	9.2	36.0
Of which:		
Manufactures	2.1	5.0
Crude oil	6.5	30.0
United States Exports to Mexico		
Total	$11.0	$40.0
Agricultural	1.4	5.0
Nonagricultural	9.6	35.0
Of which:		
Manufactures	8.2	30.0

The United States Trade Agreements Act of 1979 did more than codify the fair trade rules agreed to in the Multilateral Trade Negotiations. In fact, it entrusted to the private sector the timing and control of trade remedies to a far greater degree than it had previously—a widely perceived political exchange for industrial and union acquiescence in the Multilateral Trade Negotiations. The net results of these various changes is that the United States executive branch retains very little policy discretion to modify the timing or outcome of unfair trade actions initiated by private litigants.

Exemplifying these changes, the Trade Agreements Act created mandatory fast track mechanisms for investigating the existence of foreign bounties or grants, sales in the United States at less than fair value, and the extent of injury caused by such practices. Under these fast track procedures, decisions are made under severe time constraints on the best evidence available—a particular problem for respondent importers and foreign producers. Further, the anti-dumping and countervailing duty administrative procedures were modified to allow new opportunities for judicial review of intermediate and final decisions made by the Commerce Department and the International Trade Commission. Finally, the Secretary of Commerce lost the authority that the Secretary of Treasury had to waive countervailing duties.

Another area of concern is the application of local-content and export performance requirements by the government of Mexico as a condition to foreign investments. The recently concluded Multilateral Trade Negotiations reduced tariffs and disciplined certain nontariff export measures, but performance requirements and local-content requirements were at best addressed indirectly. And while the Mexican government has decided not to join the GATT, the performance requirements of the Mexican Auto Decree of 1977 are frequently cited by United States officials as a troublesome type of practice that deserves further scrutiny. There is also a real concern that the government of Mexico may expand the application of such practices to other sectors, such as steel, textiles, and petrochemicals.

Despite the absence of agreement on a broad commercial policy framework or on individual conflicts, trade between the United States and Mexico is likely to expand significantly. The United States has historically been Mexico's largest trading partner, purchasing nearly 70 percent of Mexico's exports and supplying some 65 percent of Mexico's imports. With the prospective boom in Mexican imports, the Mexican market will become even more attractive to United States producers. While Mexico's policy of diversification will broaden its range of trading contacts, the United States will probably remain its major trading partner. This is due not only to geographical proximity but also to the size and relative openness of the United States market.

A good portion of Mexico's exports to the United States, approximately 25 percent, are shipped under the auspices of sections 806.30 and 807.00 of the United States Tariff Schedule. Exports to the United States are also promoted by intracompany sales of United States subsidiaries located in Mexico. Most of the trade between the United States and Mexico covered by sections 806.30 and 807.00 is the bulk of intracompany sales (categories that often overlap) are exports of manufactured goods, a sector of the economy that the Mexican government wants to expand.

Another important export, both in terms of contribution to total exports and to local-content, is agricultural produce. While some alternative markets are available for Mexican agricultural exports (Canada, for example), most countries maintain fairly steep barriers to agricultural imports. Further, fresh vegetables are a large portion of these exports, and the proximity of the large United States economy makes it very attractive.

Finally, on the export side, Mexico's sales of oil to the American market will be substantial, even if the share of total Mexican oil exports sold to the United States drops from the present figure of about 80 percent to the target figure of about 60 percent. On the opposite side of the trade ledger, the growth of the Mexican economy should offer a booming market for United States exporters. In particular, as Mexican development progresses, substantial opportunities should arise for the export of items such as oil drilling equipment, and computers and peripheral equipment.

In 1980, United States exports to the Mexican market will amount to about $11 billion. By 1985, if Mexico's efforts to diversify its imports are partly successful and the United States' share drops to a 60 percent level, United States exports to Mexico should still reach $40 billion (measured in 1985 prices).

In summary, a rapidly growing market—with an approximate bilateral balance between merchandise exports and imports—will do much to soothe the tensions that may arise on account of commercial policy differences. By the same token, despite the United States countervailing duty, antidumping duty, and omnibus unfair trade practice statutes, and despite the flareups that will occur from time to time on particular issues, many Mexican industrialists will continue to look to the United States as a destination for their exports.

9
The Mexican Economy: Recent Evolution and Future Projections

Centro de Investigación y Docencia Económicas

This article considers a series of alternative courses that the Mexican economy might take in the future, based on different assumptions about the type of domestic economic policy followed and the development of the international economic situation. This study of economic prospects is preceded by an analysis of recent economic developments.

In this first section, we study the phenomena which characterized the economic history of the 1970s: the increasing deterioration of the external sector, the resurgence of inflation and the trend towards stagnation in production and employment. This first section also suggests possible reasons for the crisis of 1976 and 1977. The second section considers the main effects of the "stabilization policy" that was implemented from the end of 1976, especially the effects of the devaluation of the peso on the price level, the distribution of income and the balance of payments. The section ends with a summary of the present situation which examines, in particular, the characteristics of the 1978 economic "recovery" and the appearance of new elements, such as the expected increase of oil production and exports.

Reprinted and edited from *Cambridge Journal of Economics* 4 (1980):177–197. This is a translation by Sian Phillips of an article which originally appeared in Spanish in *Economía Mexicana*, Centro de Investigación y Docencia Económicas (CIDE), 1979. For details of the econometric equations underlying the analysis presented here, the reader is referred to that publication. It is available from CIDE, Apartado Postal 10-883, México 10, D.F.
©1980 Academic Press Inc. (London) Limited.

TABLE 1.—SOURCES OF FINANCE FOR THE INDUSTRIAL TRADE DEFICIT, 1961–1975
As a percentage of the industrial deficit

	1961–65	1966–70	1971	1972	1973	1974	1975
Industrial deficit (as a percentage of manufacturing output)	12	11	10	10	11	11	13
Agricultural surplus*	49	38	29	29	19	3	2
Services surplus*	43	36	42	40	48	43	29
Oil surplus*	1	0	-3	-4	-9	-8	3
Foreign indebtedness	7	26	32	35	42	62	66

Source: Figures based on the Annals of Foreign Trade, Statistical Annals of PEMEX and Annual Reports of the Banco de México.
*The industrial deficit is made up of exports of manufacturing and minerals and imports of nonagricultural consumer goods, intermediate and capital goods. The agricultural surplus refers to the trade balance in agriculture, livestock, forestry and fisheries. The oil surplus comprises net exports of oil and petro-chemical products. The services balance comprises tourism, frontier transactions, value added by in-bond industries, transport and other services.

The final section presents the analytical framework used in the projections of the various courses that the Mexican economy could follow during the next decade in terms of output growth, the price level and the composition of final demand, under different assumptions about the use of oil surpluses and the future of the agricultural sector.

THE BACKGROUND TO DEVALUATION

The history of the Mexican economy during the 1970s was marked by a progressive deterioration in its capacity to finance imports required by previous growth rates of production and employment. The result has been a slowing down of economic growth coupled with an accelerated deterioration in the trade balance and current account.

The reason for the rapid deterioration in the balance of payments is to be found in a combination of factors, which could be summed up as the exhaustion of the internal sources of finance needed for the model of industrialization followed in the last decade. The story of this drying up of funds and its counterpart, growing dependence on foreign financial sources, is summarized in table 1. This shows the development of the industrial trade deficit as a proportion of manufacturing production and the contribution of the agricultural, oil and service sectors' balances to the financing of the industrial deficit. It also shows the residual deficit which has had to be financed by external sources. The model of industrialization followed was originally based on the premise that the industrial trade deficit, which would be incurred during the early stages of industrialization, would be financed by the foreign trade surpluses of the more traditional sectors—particularly agriculture. Then, through a combination of a declining import ratio and an increasing ability to export, the industrial sector itself would become increasingly able to finance its rapid growth. For a long period, import-substitution growth, encouraged by tariffs and import licences, did imply notably high annual rates of growth of industrial output (8% on average over the period 1950-70) without a rapid deterioration of the balance of payments. However, the form that industrialization took meant that the initial phase of rapid growth in the foreign trade deficit continued and showed no significant tendency to decrease as a proportion of manufacturing output.

TABLE 2.—RATIO OF IMPORTS TO TOTAL SUPPLY BY SECTOR (Percentage)

	1960	1965	1970	1975
Consumption goods	3.2	2.9	3.0	4.2
Intermediate goods	21.0	18.7	16.6	20.0
Capital goods	56.8	44.3	30.2	34.2

Source: Figures based on Annals of Foreign Trade and Domestic Product and Expenditure 1960–77 (Banco de México).

After a period of "genuine" import substitution of non-durable consumer goods and certain intermediate goods, industrial development proceeded on the basis of the growth of wholly new lines of production, mainly durable consumer goods. This was because of an extremely unequal distribution of income, which fostered rapid growth in these new sectors while inhibiting that of the "old" consumer and intermediate industries. The high import content and rapid development of the new production lines counterbalanced the effects on the industrial trade deficit of the import-substitution processes in the old and now stagnant consumer industries. Moreover, the new durable consumer goods industries developed by means of a strong participation of foreign capital, so that to the high import content was added a considerable expansion of payments abroad.

A second feature of the pattern of industrialization which is important for the understanding of the growing industrial trade deficit is the relative lack of development of capital goods industries. As shown in the ratios of imports to the total supply presented in table 2, import-substitution in the capital goods sectors lagged considerably behind those in consumer and intermediate goods industries. This was the result of the spontaneous tendencies of import-substitution industrialization (which implied a prior development of final stage industries), combined with the effects of policy: the structure of protection is much more favorable to consumer than to capital goods industries, while capital goods imports are in most cases subsidized. In the 1960s, due to their high import ratio and income elasticity, capital goods, in absolute terms, made a major contribution to the expansion of industrial imports and the trade deficit, despite a declining *ratio* of imports to total supply. During the 1970s when the earlier stages of easy-to-substitute imports became less important, even the decline of the import ratio could not be sustained.

This import-side view of the evolution of the industrial trade deficit, stressing the pattern of structural change, contrasts sharply with the usual argument that the main cause of the failure of Mexican manufacturing to reduce its trade deficit lies ultimately in the damage that protection, as the main policy instrument to promote industrialization, has done to competitiveness and export capacity. In this context, it is worth noting that the inward oriented nature of the industrialization process did not prevent the achievement, since the mid-1960s, of high rates of growth of industrial exports. During the period 1967–74, which witnessed an acute deterioration in the balance of payments, the rate of growth of manufactured exports was in fact 15 percent per annum.

The premises on which the development model was based were once again thwarted by a premature deterioration in the foreign trade surplus of the agricultural sector, and the consequent drying up of this source of finance for industrialization. During 1961–65, the agricultural foreign trade surplus financed almost half of the industrial trade deficit, but by 1974 it had ceased to be of any significance. Figure 1 relates the origin of the decline of the

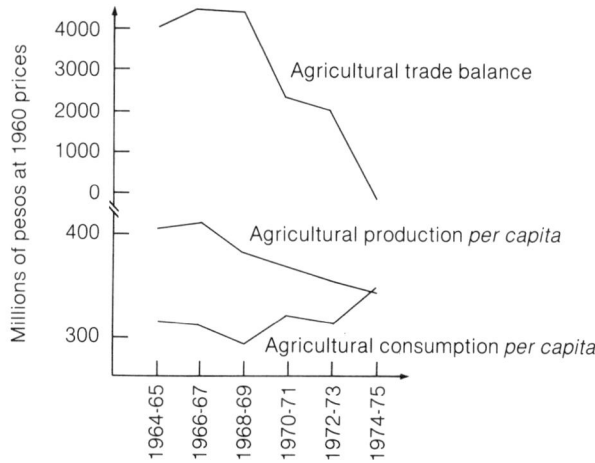

Figure 1. *Agricultural trade balance, agricultural production and consumption per capita, 1964–75*

Source: Data based on "Consumos Aparentes" from the Ministry of Agriculture. A selection of agricultural products was considered representing about 65% of total agricultural production between 1970 and 1975.

Note: In this figure two yearly averages are used to reduce the effect of the change in inventories on agricultural consumption, given that the latter is estimated as the difference between agricultural production and exports less imports. In spite of this procedure, the development of agricultural consumption *per capita* is probably exaggerated in the period 1974–75, because of the rapid accumulation of inventories in those years, balanced by a considerable reduction in 1976.

agricultural trade balance (the principal component of the trade surplus of agriculture, fisheries and forestry) to the shrinking gap between agricultural production and consumption per capita. This gap is, in turn, due mainly to the slow increase in agricultural output and to the resulting fall in the production *per capita*. While consumption of agricultural goods per head remained practically unchanged between 1964–65, production per head over the same period decreased by 15 percent.

The reduction in agricultural production *per capita* was no less important in the latter half of the 1970s. In percentage terms, it was actually greater in the first period (12 percent in 1965–70, 8 percent in 1970–75). The effect on the trade balance in agriculture at *constant* prices was also at least as important in the first period than in the second. However, during the 1970s the unfavorable evolution of the terms of trade between agricultural imports and exports brought about a more rapid deterioration of the trade balance measured at current prices.

Table 3 shows the effects of these developments on the agricultural trade balance: the effect of the reduction in the agricultural surplus between 1965 and 1972 was masked by the fact that international prices for exports grew faster than the prices paid for imports. Conversely, between 1972 and 1975 the terms of trade quickly returned to their 1965 level; this, combined with the continued deterioration in the trade balance at constant prices, almost eliminated the surplus in the trade balance measured at current prices.[1]

While the origins of the growing disequilibrium in the trade balance are to be found mainly in the expansion in the absolute terms of the industrial deficit, and in the behavior of agricultural production, we must note two further relevant elements. The first is the slowing down of oil production and the appearance of substantial deficits in the oil trade balance, which occurred just when the relative price of oil rose considerably on the international market. In the second place, the service sector, despite the incentives provided for its development, did not succeed in replacing the agricultural sector as the main source of finance for the industrial deficit. The services sector in fact lost its impetus at the end of this period.

The growing inability of internal sources to provide the funds necessary to finance the program of industrialization brought about an increase in the role played by foreign lenders. Hence,

TABLE 3.—AGRICULTURAL TRADE BALANCE AND TERMS OF TRADE, 1965–1975
Millions of pesos

	1965	1966	1967	1968	1969	1970	1971	1972	1973	1974	1975
Agricultural trade balance at 1960 prices	5186	6362	5781	5981	6595	4499	4552	4882	3446	-444	-808
ditto, deflated by the price of agricultural exports	6287	6537	6042	6938	6860	4925	4975	5528	3963	597	624
Agricultural trade balance at current prices	7029	7452	6809	7888	8163	6299	6652	7855	6690	1257	1367
International terms of trade between imports and exports	1.00	1.04	0.90	0.78	0.86	0.85	0.67	0.66	0.80	0.98	1.05

Source: Data based on the Annals of Foreign Trade.

while foreign loans financed only 7 percent of the industrial deficit in the period 1961–65, by 1975 this proportion had increased to 66 percent. This growing dependence on foreign loans had to face increasingly narrow limits. Thus, net income paid abroad rose from 29 percent of the deficit on current account in the period 1960–64 to more than 50 percent in the years 1974–77. (See table 4.) The foreign debt accumulated in order to cover the growing deficits in the balance on current account, which were originally caused by the deficits in the trade balance, ended up by creating an equivalent deficit in the balance of net income paid abroad. Thus the rate of foreign borrowing tended to be determined by the deficits, which were in turn caused by the very same accumulation of debts.

The limit encountered by the industrialization strategy is perhaps best illustrated by the fact that by 1975 the income arising from the export of manufactures and minerals was not enough even to cover the interest payments on the foreign debt created by that same strategy. Between 1960 and 1975 net property income paid abroad doubled as a percentage of manufacturing and mineral exports, amounting to 116 percent by the later date.

In sum, the 1960s industrialization program gave a long-term trend towards deterioration in the trade balance of payments on current account. This deterioration clearly implied the occurrence, sooner or later, of the 1976–77 crises. These events were, however, precipitated by three elements: the resurgence of inflation in Mexico, the international economic recession, and a remarkable flight of capital.

After the long period of reasonable price stability—the average annual rate of inflation between 1956 and 1970 being around 4 percent—the rate of increase of the price level started rising substantially in the early 1970s (see fig. 2). The successive fluctuations in the inflation rate during the 1970s appear, in the first instance, to be closely linked to the movement of international prices of both foodstuffs and raw materials (at the outset), and later of oil and its byproducts. Thus, the fall in the consumer price index between 1971 and 1972 could be attributed to a reduction in the international prices of foodstuffs and raw materials. Similarly, the rise in the rate of inflation in 1973 and 1974 seems to be linked to the rapid growth in the price of raw materials and imports of intermediate goods during that period, and to the big rise in public sector prices and tariffs, particularly of oil and its byproducts.

TABLE 4.—TRADE DEFICIT AND NET INCOME PAID ABROAD, 1960-64 TO 1974-77
Percentage of the deficit on current account

	1960-64	1965-69	1970-73	1974-77
Trade deficit	71	59	56	48
Net income paid abroad	29	41	44	52

Source: Domestic Product and Expenditure 1960-77 (Banco de México).

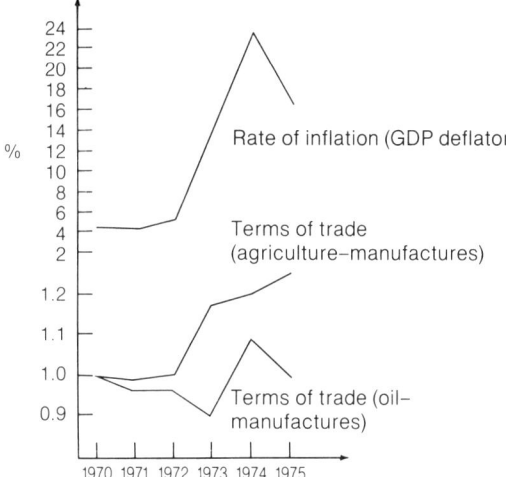

Figure 2. The main inflationary pressures, 1970-75
Source: Domestic Product and Expenditure 1960-77 (Banco de México).

The movements of international prices combined with internal conditions were to lead to an acceleration in the rate of inflation which was greater than the rate abroad (especially in the U.S.). The element most relevant for an explanation of this phenomenon would appear to be the internal situation, characterized by the crisis in agriculture and the slowing down in oil production, which amplified the effect of the rise in the respective international prices. For example, in basic foodstuffs the rapid rise in import prices in 1973-74 was combined with a fall in domestic production, which increased the import content of agricultural consumption and hence reduced the effectiveness of the government's agricultural prices policy designed to neutralize the effects of the imported inflation. Externally, the Middle East oil crisis in 1973-74, and the quadrupling of oil prices which accompanied it, coincided with a period when, for the first time in many years, the Mexican economy experienced large deficits in its trade balance in oil.

As a result of this conjunction of a movement of international prices and the internal disequilibrium between the various sectors, a sharp change occurred in the internal terms of trade between the manufacturing sector, on the one hand, and agriculture and oil on the other (see fig. 2). The result was a noticeable reduction of real manufacturing income (compared with what would have happened had the change in terms of trade not taken place). This, in turn, led to an incompatibility between the demands of labor and capital for the reduced real value added. Under these conditions, inflation in the manufacturing sector was bound to rise rapidly, re-shaping income distribution and/or gradually re-establishing the original inter-sectoral terms of trade.

The increase in the rate of inflation was certainly detrimental to the foreign competitiveness of the manufacturing and service sectors. The latter's diminished contribution to the trade balance, referred to earlier, seems in fact to be partly linked to the rising inflation rate. As is shown in table 5, it is precisely in the part of the service sector balance (tourism, cross-border transactions), which is sensitive to the behavior of relative prices, that the main cause of the relative decline in its surplus is to be found. One should add two further points to this explanation of the behavior of the service sector's balance: first, a boycott of tourism in Mexico during the later years of the period; second, and more important, the trend increase in Mexican tourism abroad.

The erosion of the manufacturing and the service sectors' competitiveness, both at home and abroad, plus the slow growth in world demand, aggravated the long-term trend deterioration in the external sector. These two factors meant that, in order to maintain the previous rate of economic growth, the trade and current account deficits would have to be substantially increased. However, what occurred was a marked fall in the rate of growth, in order to avoid further deterioration in the balance-of-payments disequilibrium.

As seen in fig. 3, through the 1960s and in the early 1970s there was a long-term worsening of the trade deficit as a proportion of GDP; but the short-term fluctuations in this ratio were related in a fairly systematic way to the variations in output around its long-run trend. This behavior highlighted the growing restriction imposed by the external sector on the achievement of an increase in the rate of growth, as well as the lack of any policy measures which might have relieved this conflict between the evolution of the external sector and that of total production. By 1974, this conflict reached a point at which the behavior of the trade balance and that of output became diametrically opposed: the 1974–75 recession was accompanied by a rapid increase in the trade deficit as a proportion of GDP.

TABLE 5.—COMPONENTS OF THE SERVICES TRADE BALANCE, 1971-1975
As percentage of the overall trade services balance

	1971	1972	1973	1974	1975
Surplus in transport	-1	-1	-1	-1	-3
Surplus in value added by in-bond industries	13	17	21	27	30
Surplus in tourism	37	36	36	31	26
Surplus in frontier transactions	45	43	39	34	38
Surplus in other services	6	5	5	9	9

Source: Annual Reports, Banco de México.

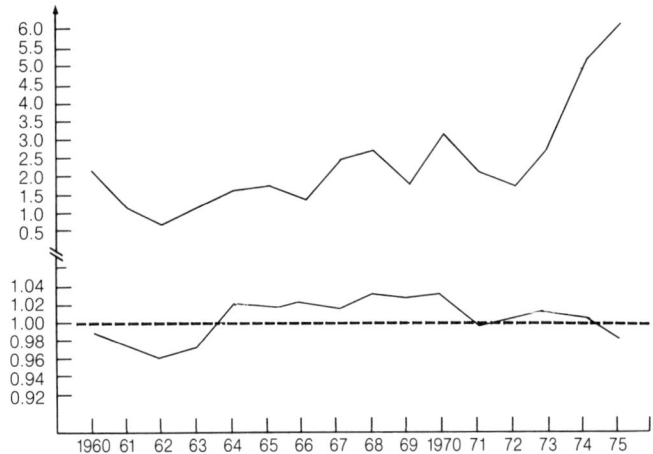

Figure 3. *Trade deficit as a percentage of GDP and deviations of output from trend, 1960-75*

Source: Domestic Product and Expenditure 1960-77 (Banco de México).

Why did the external sector not respond as it had always done in the past to the growing shortfall of GDP from its historical trend level? The agricultural crisis is an important element in the answer to this question; so, to some extent, is the slowdown in oil production. Both of these create a negative association between the growth of production and the deficit in the trade balance. In this sense, the crisis in the external sector did not turn out to be an automatic side effect of previous growth in demand. The traditional policy of deliberately depressing the economy was bound to fail, given the long established structural problem of deterioration in the trade balance. This deterioration continued rapidly in 1974 and 1975.

The second relevant phenomenon is the exhaustion, to which we have referred above, of the easy phase of this process of import substitution of capital goods, which brought about a remarkable acceleration in the growth of capital goods imports, despite the deceleration in the rate of growth of total, especially private, investment. This line of argument helps to explain the apparently paradoxical inverse relationship between the behavior of the current account balance and that of output and investment.

Finally, one must also take into account the fact that inflation did not respond significantly to the policy measures adopted to deal with it. The main methods tried during the period were the control of aggregate demand and a prices policy. Given the nature of the inflation, these policies were bound to fail. On the one hand, the pressure of internal demand does not appear to have had any significant effect on the rate of inflation, at least not as far as most products are concerned, *viz.* agricultural products, whose prices follow international prices, industrial products, and public goods and services. On the other, the prices policy introduced at the end of 1974 was based on the system of price fixing by cost variation, hence accomplishing no more than the institutionalization of a method normally followed by firms in the industrial sector. This occurred at a time when, in order to avoid acceleration of price rises in that sector, either profit margins or labor's share of manufacturing income would have had to be reduced. The safeguarding of profit margins via such an official prices policy only resulted in later reliance on a wages policy as the main anti-inflationary instrument.

THE EFFECTS OF THE 1976 DEVALUATION

The thrust of the economic policy package introduced during 1974 and 1975, in order to combat inflation and redress the external imbalance, was intensified towards the end of 1976, when policy measures agreed upon with the IMF were adopted as part of a stabilization program. This was designed to deal with the foreign currency crisis precipitated by speculation against the peso and a substantial flight of capital. The diagnosis of the economic situation used to justify the adoption of these measures can be summarized as follows: the disequilibrium in the balance of payments was generated by a general excess of aggregate demand—created, in turn, by an excessive expansion of the fiscal deficit—as well as by the marked degree of protectionism that accompanied industrial development. These two phenomena would have led to the peso becoming increasingly overvalued; hence the decision to devalue the peso—from 12.5 pesos to the dollar to a final parity of around 22.8 pesos to the dollar—and the introduction of measures designed to cut public expenditure in real terms, to restrict domestic credit expansion and to liberalize foreign trade. Finally, after the 22 percent emergency increase in minimum wages decreed in October 1976, and a relative extension of official price policies, a substantial shift in prices and wages policies was undertaken, leading to increases of only 10 percent and 12 percent in the annual minimum wage revisions of 1977 and 1978 respectively (compared with rates of inflation on the order of 30 percent in 1977 and 17 percent in 1978). On the other hand, price controls were substantially liberalized in February 1978.

A superficial evaluation of the effects of these measures might lead one to believe that these policies were relatively successful in achieving their planned objectives. The inflation rate, once the general level of prices had risen, as expected following devaluation, quickly fell from 30 percent in 1977 to 17 percent in 1978. The deficit on current account was reduced by approximately $1.3 billion in 1977. Finally, economic growth recovered and reached a rate of 6.6 percent in 1978.

A detailed analysis of the effects of devaluation, however, suggests a very different picture. In the first place, an analysis of the effects of devaluation on prices and the distribution of income suggests that the rate of inflation would have fallen rapidly anyway, even without the above-mentioned policies, until it reached a level similar to that of international inflation by 1978. Moreover, this could have been achieved with a higher level of economic activity and a rise in real wages. The first reason for these conclusions is that in the first eight months of 1976 inflation was clearly slowing down, to such an extent that the anticipated overall rise in consumer prices in 1976 was around 10-11 percent; secondly, the period 1977-78 was characterized by a considerable reduction in the main international agricultural prices (on the order of 17 percent in 1977, measured in foreign currency). This phenomenon offered the possibility of a gradual deceleration in the rate of inflation, along with a sustained rate of increase in real wages.

The points we have mentioned suggest the following observations. First, the recent deceleration in the rate of inflation, whose speed was determined by the movement of international agricultural prices and by wage settlements, seems to have been unrelated to the fiscal and monetary policies implemented by the government. Second, the *net* effects of devaluation on the level of prices and on the distribution of income, exacerbated by the increase in profit margins arising from the doubling of the peso value of the foreign debt, could have reinforced rather than compensated for the negative effects on the level of economic activity

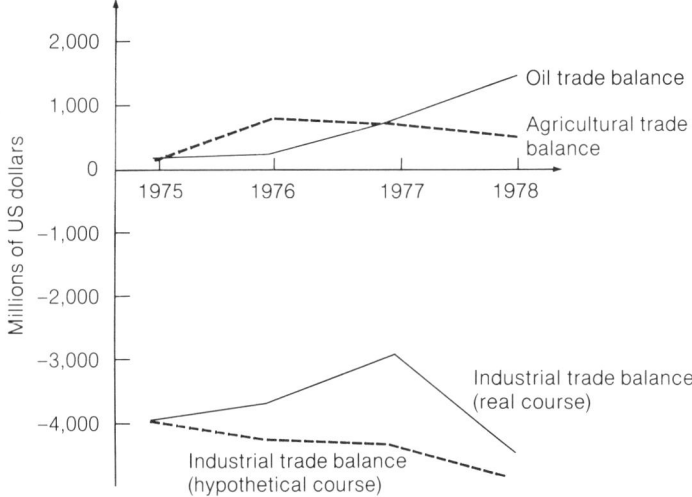

Figure 4. Behavior of the trade balance by sectors, 1975–78
Source: Economic Indicators (Banco de México), and estimates described in the text.

of the government's fiscal and monetary policies. This could also help to explain the failure to reduce the balance of payments disequilibrium, as we shall see later.

Figure 4 shows the movement of the sectoral balances in the years 1975–78. After increasing in 1976, largely as a consequence of a favorable movement in the external terms of trade,[2] the agricultural trade surplus regained its downward trend because the growth in production was lower than that of population. Given the nature of this important element in the balance-of-payments disequilibrium, and the low elasticity of demand for agricultural products with respect to relative prices and real aggregate income, it is not surprising that devaluation does not seem to have succeeded in correcting the disequilibrium.

The effects of the devaluation on the trade balance were concentrated mainly in the trade in industrial goods. The reduction in the industrial trade deficit in 1977, arising from the substitution effects of devaluation and from the economic recession, is an important element in explaining the reduction in the global trade deficit for that year.

However, a comparison of the actual industrial trade balance with that estimated for a hypothetical path, generated by the

268   C.I.D.E.

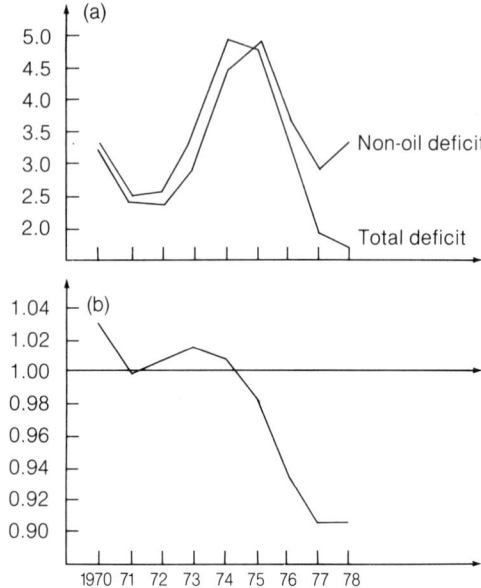

Figure 5. (a) Non-oil deficit and total deficit in the balance of trade, 1970–78 (as percentage of GDP)
(b) Deviations of GDP from trend, 1970–78

Source: Economic Indicators; Domestic Product and Expenditure (Banco de México).

assumption of a fixed exchange rate and based on structural behavioral relationships determining imports and exports, suggests that the effects of devaluation were of a temporary nature.[3] By 1978, as a result of the inflationary effects of devaluation, the industrial trade deficit had rapidly reached the level at which it would have stood without devaluation. Thus, if in 1978 the deficits in the trade balance and the current account were smaller than one would have predicted, by extrapolating the rapid deterioration experienced in the first half of the 1970s, this fact appears to be mainly linked to the performance of the trade balance in oil, which in turn was determined by the recent exploitation of considerable reserves and by the decision to export massive amounts of oil.

The importance of this new element in the recent development of the external sector, and the temporary nature of the effects of devaluation, can be seen more clearly in figure 5. It is evident that the non-oil deficit in the trade balance (as a proportion of GDP), in contrast to the overall deficit, resumed its upward trend in 1978 despite the enormous gap created by the economic crisis between total production and its historical trend level. It is worth noting that in 1978 the non-oil trade deficit as a proportion of GDP was far greater than in 1971, even though the later recession was much deeper than the earlier one. Figure 5 also shows the limited nature of the 1978 economic "recovery," which failed to raise the level of output to what would be expected on the basis of its historical trend rate of growth.

ALTERNATIVE PROSPECTS FOR THE MEXICAN ECONOMY

The main characteristics of economic development in the 1970s— a growing imbalance in the current account of the balance of payments, slow growth of output, and high rates of unemployment and inflation—influenced one another and initiated a process of economic decline which could not be reversed by the policies which were adopted, including devaluation of the peso. However, the prospect of oil production and exports undoubtedly offers a chance to break an essential link in this chain of cumulative deterioration. This link is the financial constraint imposed on economic growth by the previous behavior of the external sector.

The possibility of reversing these trends by means of a considerable trade surplus in oil depends to a large extent on the strategy adopted for the use of oil revenues. The direct contribution of the oil industry towards increasing production and employment is relatively small. More important are its direct effects, which will depend on the type of economic policy adopted in the immediate future.

In principle, the net oil surplus (excluding all the payments abroad associated with oil development, and also the deficit in the agricultural trade balance) could be used in various ways. Here we consider three alternatives: (1) its use for expenditure on additional imports, without significant changes in economic policy; (2) the repayment of the external public debt over the next ten years; and (3) its use for additional investment within the framework of an industrial policy whose medium-term objective would be to reduce the deficit in the trade balance in manufactures. The implications of the three strategies for the Mexican economy are examined up to 1990, on the basis of a large macroeconometric model. Comparisons of alternative strategies are made in terms of a common set of assumptions and of targets to be achieved. The analytical framework of the model used in the projections, as well as a precise definition of the assumptions, targets and the alternative scenarios, are given in the appendix.

In considering the results of the analyses presented below, the reader should note that the exercise which was carried out was to simulate the effects of different economic policy strategies. The alternative projections make no claim to predict the future development of the Mexican economy. This is because, first, since the overall effects of each strategy can only be evaluated over a long period, we have chosen a period of analysis of ten years, a period in which there is inevitably a considerable degree of uncertainty about evolution of the exogenous variables as well as the maintenance of structural behavioral relationships. Thus, the different strategies must be considered in relation to each other, rather than individually. Second, each of the strategies (except, as we shall see, the second) appears in pure, and possibly extreme, form. Finally, the assumption, introduced in the first and third alternatives, of equilibrium in the current account over the entire period can be seen as unrealistic, given the capacity for increased external indebtedness within both the public and the private sectors, and the traditional welcome for foreign investment. In this sense, the exercise should be seen as an attempt to answer the following question—in what way can the generation of a considerable oil surplus contribute to a reversal of recent economic trends without increasing the country's dependence on foreign finance?

Figures 6 and 7 present the rate of growth of GDP for each of the three alternative strategies, under each of the two variants: (A) that agricultural production grows at its recent (low) trend rate and the sector's trade balance continues to deteriorate (agricultural crisis); and (B) that there is a trend increase in agricultural growth permitting long-term sectoral trade balance (agricultural recovery).

THE LIMITATIONS OF OIL

The behavior of total production based on alternative 1A shows the limitations of a policy of massive oil exports, if the recessive

Figure 6. Alternative growth rates of GDP, 1979–88, under three alternative strategies. Variant A (agricultural crisis). For the definitions of the three strategies, see text and appendix.

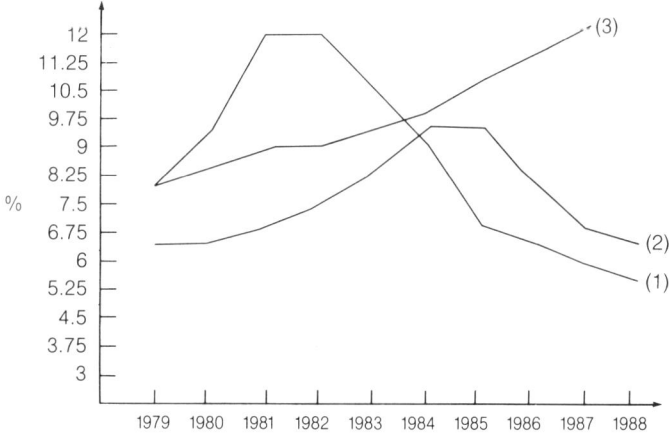

Figure 7. Alternative growth rates of GDP, 1979–88, under three alternative strategies. Variant B (agricultural recovery). For the definitions of the three strategies, see text and appendix.

trend in Mexican agriculture continues and the oil surpluses are absorbed by the economy, in the absence of policy measures capable of altering the structural relationships of economic performance.

Oil's direct contribution to the balance of payments is undoubtedly substantial. It allows an annual rate of growth of 6.6 percent on average for the whole of the next decade, with the current account of the balance of payments in equilibrium. This compares very favorably with the average rate of growth of 4.7 percent for the period 1970-77, when one considers that this was only achieved with a current deficit, equivalent, on the average, to 3.0 percent of GDP. Put another way, oil production and exports permit a reduction in the current account deficit from 3 percent of GDP in 1970-77 to approximately zero for the next ten years, while at the same time raising the rate of economic growth.

However, the results indicate that strategy A is subject to violent fluctuations in the rate of growth. In fact, during the first phase of 1979-82, rising oil production and exports would lead to a general economic boom, with rates of growth of around 10-11 percent in 1981-82. Once the growth of oil exports had reached a peak in 1982, the economy would be confronted with the dilemma of either continuing to increase its external indebtedness or experiencing a rapid slowing down of economic growth. In either case, from 1985 onwards the economy would return to its recent trends of relatively low rates of growth combined with growing foreign indebtedness. The re-emergence of these trends is illustrated by the fact that, towards the end of the 1980s, rates of growth of more than 3 percent cannot be sustained with equilibrium on the current account.

The reason for this rapid slowing-down in economic growth is to be found in the swift increase in the non-oil deficit on current account, brought about principally by the manufacturing and agricultural deficits. By 1982, the agricultural and manufacturing deficits make up practically the whole (94 percent) of the surplus in oil trade (see table 6). By 1988, this percentage has risen to 115 percent, despite the slow rate of growth during the period 1983-88. After a short-lived economic boom, the lack of any significant change in economic policy would lead to the reappearance of recent trends towards a stagnation of production. The trade balance in oil would thus suffer a fate similar to that of agricultural surplus in the model of economic development of the 1960s and

TABLE 6.—MANUFACTURING AND AGRICULTURAL
DEFICITS AS A PERCENTAGE OF THE OIL SURPLUS,
1982 AND 1988

	1982	1988
Manufacturing deficit	86.0	85.0
Agricultural deficit	8.3	30.0

1970s. From being the main source of finance for the deficit in industrial trade (and now for an increasing agricultural trade deficit) in a rapidly growing economy, it would gradually become inadequate for sustaining a high rate of economic growth.

THE ECONOMIC IMPLICATIONS OF REPAYING THE FOREIGN DEBT

A comparison of two different strategies, 1A and 2A, allows us to evaluate the economic implications arising from the repayment of the foreign debt over the next ten years, if the only alternative is the continued absorption of the oil surplus by the economy, with no change in economic policy.

It is interesting to note, in the first instance, that in spite of the much stricter target imposed on the current account in strategy 2, and the high rates of growth that can be achieved in strategy 1 during the oil boom of 1980–83, the difference between the average rates of growth for the whole decade is surprisingly small: 6.6 percent for the first and 5.8 percent for the second. This result can be explained by the fact that the settlement of the foreign debt during the next decade would gradually free the economy from the financial burden of paying interest on the debt. This, in turn, would allow an increase in production and real national income, compatible with a given target on the current account. The effect of the gradual lifting of the burden of debt repayment can be seen more clearly when one compares the evolution of total exports minus interest paid on the foreign debt (deflated by the price of manufacturing exports) under the two strategies (see fig. 8). By 1983, the increase in the value of this variable in strategy 2 (above that which is obtained in the first strategy), combined with the

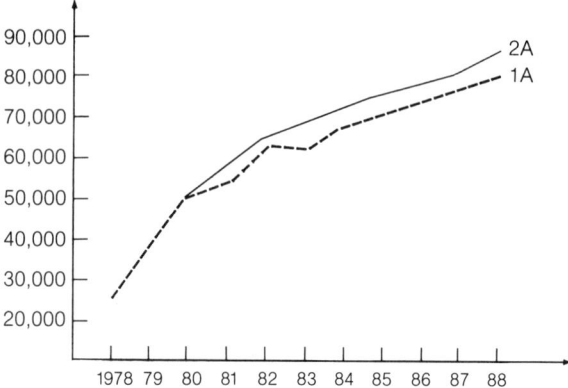

Figure 8. Total exports minus interest paid on the public foreign debt in strategies 1A and 2A, 1978-88 (deflated by the price of manufacturing exports) (millions of pesos at 1960 prices)

gradual reduction of the target in the current account of the balance of payments, enables us to explain the form that the path of output growth will take. It will explain, in particular, the increase in economic growth around 1982, which follows an initial phase of very slow growth, and the maintenance of higher rates of growth towards the end of the period than those presented by the first strategy.

The repayment of the foreign debt does encounter limitations, however, which restrict the effects of the benefits mentioned above. In the first instance, economic growth is very slow, and, despite the increase which occurs in the period 1982-84, GDP does not in this strategy achieve the level arrived at by extrapolating earlier trend rates of growth into the period 1979-88 (see fig. 9).

Secondly, the repayment of the debt does not prevent a slowing down in economic growth around 1985. As in the first alternative, this is the consequence of a rapid growth in the deficits on agricultural and industrial trade.

These results seem even more limited if one remembers that, in this strategy, repayments of foreign debt end in 1988. If the total net oil surplus in each year were to be used for the repayment of the debt, economic growth in the first years of the next decade would be negative. This is because the corresponding target in the balance of payments would be equivalent to having

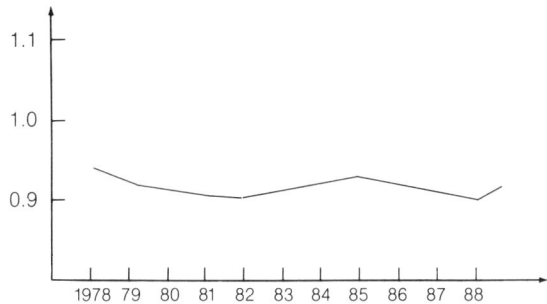

Figure 9. *Deviation of GDP from trend (1960-78) projected strategy 2A, 1978-88*

an equilibrium on current account, excluding the trade surplus in oil and agriculture, and corresponds approximately to what would happen to the Mexican economy if it exhausted foreign sources of finance and could not count on the appearance of oil surpluses.

THE EFFECTS OF AN INDUSTRIAL POLICY

The strategies already analyzed have in common a trend towards a slowing down in economic growth, which is more or less rapid in each case. This is caused by the continuing deterioration of the trade balances in agricultures and manufactures. We shall now examine the contribution which an industrial policy, with the objective of slowing down or eliminating the continuous increase in the industrial deficit, would make towards fostering economic growth.

The effects of the industrial policy on the manufacturing trade balance can be fully appreciated by comparing the behavior of exports and imports in the industrial policy strategy with a hypothetical strategy which has the same rate of economic growth but no industrial policy.[4] Table 7 shows what would happen to exports of manufactures and minerals and imports of capital and intermediate goods as a result of these two different strategies.

As can be seen from the table, the industrial policy (in variant A) has the effect of increasing the annual growth rate of exports of manufactures by 3.6 points and reducing the growth of imports of capital and intermediate goods by 1.3 points for the whole of the period, compared with the no industrial policy alternative. The

TABLE 7.—INDUSTRIAL EXPORTS AND IMPORTS WITH AND WITHOUT AN INDUSTRIAL POLICY (1 AND 2 RESPECTIVELY)

In annual rates of growth

		1979–83	1984–88	1979–88
Variant A				
Rate of growth of GDP		7.80%	8.45%	8.12%
Exports of manufacturing and minerals	(1)	10.64%	13.61%	12.12%
	(2)	7.70%	9.41%	8.55%
Imports of intermediate and capital goods	(1)	13.29%	4.31%	8.71%
	(2)	11.11%	8.96%	10.03%
Variant B				
Rate of growth of GPD		8.80%	11.50%	10.14%
Exports of manufacturing and minerals	(1)	11.07%	14.22%	12.63%
	(2)	7.70%	9.41%	8.55%
Imports of intermediate and capital goods	(1)	14.58%	7.41%	10.94%
	(2)	12.18%	12.28%	12.23%

greater effect on exports is due, partly, to the fact that exports are lower than imports initially. It is also due to the additional imports of capital goods generated by the additional investment, which do not occur in the strategy without an industrial policy.

The differences between the first and second five-year periods are worth noting. These should be attributed to the way in which industrial policy operates. Thus, for example, while in the first five-year period the industrial policy results in a higher growth of imports (owing to additional imports of capital goods and to the time lag before the effects of the policy are felt), the second five-year period sees a rapid decrease in imports as the full effects of the policy come into force.[5]

The most important element to note is that, as a consequence of the above-mentioned effects, at the estimated rate of growth, the growth in exports is greater than that of imports of capital and intermediate goods. This is the opposite of what happens in the strategy which does not include an industrial policy. If this continued in the long term it would allow the trend towards the persistent growth of the industrial deficit to be reversed and, eventually, completely eliminated. It is what happens to the industrial deficit which enables us to explain the substantial rise in the average rate of economic growth compared with those in earlier strategies and which, above all, helps explain the possibility of maintaining high rates of growth once the oil boom has started to decline.

THE ROLE OF AGRICULTURE

A comparison of variants A and B enables us to examine the effects of economic recovery in the agricultural sector. The increase in the rate of growth of agricultural production from approximately 2 percent to 4.7 percent has important effects on all three strategies, although its contribution to economic growth is considerably greater when its effects are combined with those of an industrial policy. In fact, in this case, agricultural recovery allows a rise of two points in the growth rate, more than in the other strategies.

The explanation for this, which may seem surprising at first sight, is to be found in the double effect of output growth in agriculture. On one hand, the elimination of the agricultural trade deficit allows resources to be freed which could be used to provide the additional investment referred to in the industrial policy strategy, thus reinforcing the strategy's effects on the trade balance in manufacturing and on economic growth. On the other, the direct effects of agriculture on total production and on the balance of payments make it possible to increase the rate of economic growth given a target for the balance on current account.

To the above effect one has to add the possible effects of agricultural production on the future rate of inflation. These will now be considered.

INFLATION, THE AGRICULTURAL CRISIS AND CONSUMPTION: THE VIABILITY OF THE VARIOUS STRATEGIES

The assumptions about the exchange rate, agricultural prices policy and wages policy, common to the three strategies and their variants, lead in all cases to a gradual slowing down in the rate of inflation, so that by 1983 it falls to a level equal to the rate of increase of international prices for manufactures and subsequently remains at that level. This slowing down of internal price rises is partly the result of an international rate of inflation which is approximately constant and initially lower than the domestic rate. It is also due to the neutralization, by means of the agricultural prices policy, of the internal effects of the change in the international terms of trade between manufactures and agricultural products markets and between Mexico's agricultural imports and exports. Finally, it is the result of the development of wage settlements which, in spite of the recent decrease in labor's share of national income, do not lead to (ex-ante) increases in real wages greater than the growth in industrial productivity.

The last two assumptions are not equally realistic in all three strategies. The future development of the relative prices of imported agricultural products constitutes a major potential source of inflation.[6] A rise in the relative price of agricultural imports would imply considerably higher prices for agricultural products than those based on estimated international rates of inflation. In the absence of countervailing policy measures, this rise would be imported into the Mexican economy. The history of the first half of the 1970s could then easily be repeated if the premise that a prices policy and agricultural subsidies would cancel out the effects of this inflationary pressure is not fulfilled. The continuation of the agricultural crisis would aggravate the task of the prices policy, to such an extent that some form of agricultural recovery would appear to be a necessary condition for preventing an increase in the rate of inflation. This is reinforced by the fact that inflationary pressure from outside would combine with the domestic inflationary pressure arising from the continuous *per capita* fall in agricultural production. For this reason the variants which consider a continuation of the agricultural crisis may be accompanied by a rate of inflation so much higher than those resulting from our assumptions, that the characteristics of these variants have to be seriously questioned. Indeed the latter would be faced with the alternatives of a reduction in estimated economic growth to maintain the assumed current account balance, a policy of successive devaluations, or finally the abandonment of the assumed current account balance.

The possibility that wage settlement might lead to a gradual reduction in the rate of growth of nominal wages depends fundamentally, leaving aside the question of future agricultural development, on whether ex-ante rises in real wages coincide with ex-post rises in *per capita* workers' consumption. While wage negotiations are based on an increase in real wages equal to that of labor productivity from 1981 onwards, an indication of the connection between ex-ante wage increase and ex-post increases in disposable income is shown by the growth of private consumption and its share of GDP. In four of the projections analyzed there is a trend towards slow growth in consumption and/or a reduction in its share, which suggests a growth in workers' consumption *per capita* lower than the ex-ante growth in real wages. This result can be seen most clearly in the debt-repayment strategy (especially in the variant which includes an agricultural crisis), but it is also present, in the long term, in the first strategy. Given the ex-ante increases in wages and the assumed development of public expenditure, this outcome may be interpreted as a situation in which the attempt to raise internal savings and the slow-down in economic growth necessary to achieve the corresponding target in the current account in the balance of payments, lead to the implementation of a deflationary fiscal policy. This would reduce the ex-post growth in worker's disposable income, by means of increases in public sector tariffs, direct and indirect taxes, or a reduction in transfers, below the ex-ante increase in real wages.

This situation, where the increase in disposable real incomes is lower than the increase negotiated ex-ante, would lead to a conflict about the distribution of disposable income in the private sector; this in turn would lead to much greater rises in prices and nominal wages than those originally envisaged and would also bring into question the viability of the above-mentioned strategies.

In fact, the economic policy strategy with the greatest chance of being implemented, in order to prevent an increase in inflation arising from the behavior of private consumption, would be the abandonment of the assumed targets in the current account, which would make a contractionary policy unnecessary. This would mean, in the debt-repayment strategy, the lengthening of the period of repayment or, realistically, the abandonment of its objectives, leading to a course similar to the first alternative. However, since the same result occurs in this strategy, albeit later, this would imply in the final instance going back to the model of economic development followed to date and the reappearance of the more recent trends in the Mexican economy.

Notes

1. Given the general rise in international prices for agricultural products in the 1970s, the effect of the terms of trade can be seen more clearly by considering the performance of the agricultural trade balance deflated by the price of agricultural exports.

2. Terms of trade increased by approximately 20 percent in 1976. This trend, favorable to export products, was maintained in 1977 and 1978.

3. The hypothetical path of no devaluation was obtained by means of a model of the trade balance and price behavior which is summarized below, in "Alternative Prospects for the Mexican Economy."

4. In this part we shall concentrate on the variant which includes the continuation of the agricultural crisis, and in the next section we shall consider the alternative variant.

5. The slowing down of the growth of imports can also be attributed partly to the differences, in the two five-year periods, in the domestic rate of inflation. This factor, together with the different development of world demand, should also be considered in relation to the difference in behavior of exports during the two periods.

6. The terms of trade between agricultural exports and imports have, in the recent past, followed a relatively regular cycle. The considerable deterioration in the relative price of imports from 1975 onwards, which leads to the lowest terms of trade for many years, leads one to expect some recovery in the future.

APPENDIX: ANALYTICAL FRAMEWORK OF THE
MACROECONOMIC MODEL AND DEFINITIONS OF THE
ALTERNATIVE STRATEGIES

The analytical framework for the strategies described in the section "Alternative Prospects for the Mexican Economy" consists of a system of identities and behavioral equations estimated over the period 1960-76, which may be briefly described as follows.

Output is disaggregated into four sectors: agriculture (including livestock, forestry and fishing); oil, gas and petrochemicals; industry and services (excluding oil and public services); and public services. The main characteristics on the output side of the model are the treatment of total, agricultural and public services output as exogenous variables, oil production being determined by the domestic oil requirements (dependent on GDP), given exogenous values for oil exports and imports, and industry and services output being determined residually.

Domestic expenditure is disaggregated in a conventional manner. Private fixed investment and stockbuilding are determined through an accelerator mechanism. Given behavioral equations for exports and imports, and the treatment of GDP and public expenditure as exogenous variables, private consumption is then determined as the residual claim in a resource balance equation.[1]

Exports and imports are disaggregated into agriculture, oil industry and services, with a further disaggregation of industrial imports into consumption, intermediate and capital goods. Agricultural exports are dependent on world demand and domestic agricultural output, while imports are determined by domestic agricultural output and consumption. Oil exports and imports are treated as exogenous. Industrial exports depend on world demand and the ratio of export to U.S. prices, while industrial imports are a function of domestic expenditure variables and the ratio of import to domestic prices. Service exports and imports are extrapolated on the basis of historical trends. Export and import prices are considered to be determined by world prices, with the exception of industrial and services export prices, which are influenced by domestic costs.

Net income paid abroad is disaggregated into various components, which are either extrapolated at constant prices on the basis of historical trends (as in the case of transfers from abroad) or determined by behavioral equations (as for interest payments on external public debt).

The price level is determined mainly by international prices and domestic costs. The former are the main determinant, together with official price policies, of agricultural prices. Domestic normal costs (including imports, domestically produced raw materials and labor costs) determine industrial and services prices. Finally, wage changes are considered to be determined by past price changes and ex-ante real wage increases, which are treated as exogenous and assumed to be influenced by wages policies.

Each alternative scenario is defined by a different set of values for exogenous variables, targets and instruments. More precisely, given a set of common assumptions on exogenous variables (excluding GDP and agricultural output), each projection consists in finding values for the endogenous variables, as well as for GDP and agricultural output, given target values for the current account balance and the agricultural trade balance. GDP and agricultural output may then be seen as instruments in achieving the given target values for the current account and the agricultural trade balance. Leaving aside the question of agricultural output and trade balance, the three alternative scenarios are defined as follows:

(1) The first alternative, of no changes in economic policy, refers to a situation of equilibrium in the current account in the ten years beginning in 1979, the external public debt remaining on average roughly at its 1978 level. The net oil surplus is therefore spent on additional imports, the composition of which would be determined by the structural relationship inherent in the economy in the recent past, without these relationships being affected by significant changes in economic policy.

(2) Repayment of external public debt refers to a cumulative current account surplus over the same ten years approximately equal to the total external public debt in 1978, a surplus which could decline as total indebtedness were to be reduced.

(3) Finally, industrial policy refers to a strategy where the current account remains in equilibrium and the accumulated net oil surplus for the period 1979–82/3 (approximately

equal to the total resources used to repay the external public debt under the second alternative) would be used for additional investment between 1979 and 1986, with the medium-term objective of reducing the trade deficit in the trade manufactures. In this respect, the industrial policy considered is similar to that proposed in the Industrial Plan elaborated by the Ministry of Industry and Public Enterprise.[2] Additional annual investment would rise gradually to 10 billion pesos at 1960 prices in the variant which reckons on the continuation of the agricultural crisis, and to 11.5 billion pesos in the alternative variant of agricultural recovery, and would remain at that level until 1986. The import content of this additional investment would be about 50 percent higher than the average of total investment. Finally, for every 100 units of this investment, 50 units of additional productive capacity would be generated, with an average gestation period of two years. In addition, for every 100 units of additional productive capacity, 25 units of additional manufacturing exports would be generated, with an average lag of 1.5 years, and 25 units of capital and intermediate goods, by way of import substitution.[3]

One of the main uncertainties concerning the future development of the Mexican economy is the performance of the agricultural sector. For this reason, in all three alternatives, we shall consider two variants. In the first, we assume a continuation of recent trends in agricultural production (including forestry and fisheries), and a growing deterioration in this sector's trade balance. The second variant considers a recovery in the rate of growth production to a level that would permit the long-term maintenance of equilibrium in the agricultural sector's trade balance. In the ensuing discussion, the first variant will be labelled A and the second B.[4]

The three alternative scenarios mentioned all embody the following common assumptions about the development of the international economy and about domestic economic policy:

(a) World demand, which is assumed to be determined by the growth of the U.S.'s GDP, enters into recession in 1979–80 (an average annual growth rate of 2.5 percent in that period), and grows from 1981 onwards at an average rate of 3.5

percent per year. This growth rate is lower than for the decade 1960-70, and presupposes the continuation of the recessive trend of the present decade.

(b) Prices of manufactured goods on the world market increase at an annual rate of 7 percent from 1979 onwards. The terms of trade between oil and manufactured goods rise by 3 percent in 1979 (given the forecasted average annual increase of 10 percent in the price of crude oil in 1979) and remain constant from 1980 onwards. The international prices for Mexican agricultural exports rise at the same rate as do world prices for manufactured goods, while international prices of imported agricultural goods rise more rapidly, so that by 1982-83 the terms of trade of 1976 are re-established.[5]

(c) Assumptions about exports and imports of oil and its by-products are based on the plans of PEMEX (the Mexican state oil enterprise) for production and exports up to 1982, excluding those exports of natural gas originally envisaged. This implies, together with the assumption on oil prices, an oil surplus gradually rising to approximately 11 billion dollars in 1982, and its maintenance at constant prices from then onwards.

(d) Public expenditure (except in the case of the third alternative) increases on average at a rate which, in real terms, is equal to the trend growth rate of the last two six-year presidential periods (and of the present one).

(e) Prices policy and subsidies for agriculture neutralize the inflationary pressure caused by the rapid increase in prices of agricultural imports, so that the terms of trade between agriculture and industry are maintained at their present level.

(f) Wage settlements are accompanied by a progressive easing of wage restrictions. The ex-ante increases (based on an extrapolation of the previous year's inflation rate) in real industrial wages progress from -2.6 percent in 1979 to 2 percent in 1980, and thereafter equal the trend growth in industrial productivity (approximately 4 percent from 1981 onwards).

(g) The exchange rate remains fixed at its present level of 22.8 pesos to the dollar.

It must be noted that the last three assumptions do not possess the same degree of realism under each of the alternative strategies. Their credibility and the consequences of their non-fulfillment are considered in the text, in the discussion of the feasibility of the various strategies.

Notes to Appendix

1. This procedure is similar to that followed in the earlier versions of the Cambridge Economic Policy Group model. See K.J. Coutts, Postmortem on five years of CEPG forecasting (CEPG, 1977).

2. Cf. *Plan Nacional de Desarrollo Industrial 1972-82* México: Secretaría de Patrimonio y Fomento Industrial, 1979. The Industrial Plan presents a number of specific measures which would enable a massive investment effort to take place and which are directed to several policy objectives, including in particular, regional decentralization.

3. The discussion of the specific measures which would enable this massive investment effort to take place with the above-mentioned characteristics goes much further than this first approximation of the problems. In particular, it must tackle such problems as: What would be the nature of the incentives provided and of state intervention (subsidies for private investment, the development of mixed enterprises, public investment)? Which areas of industry should be developed; how should investment be shared among the regions; what emphasis should be put on import substitution or on export promotion? All these are problems of both a political and economic nature, which need a wider ranging discussion than the present one. This exercise enables us, however, to gain some idea of what could be achieved under certain specified conditions.

4. For a discussion of the problems of the agricultural sector, see the paper by Gonzalo Rodríguez (and the references contained therein) CIDE (1979, pp. 89-120).

5. This last assumption is justified and discussed in the text.

References

Cambridge Economic Policy Group. *Economic Policy Review*, no.3, Cambridge, Eng.: Department of Applied Economics, 1977.

Centro de Investigación y Docencia Económicas. *Economía Mexicana*, no. 1. México: CIDE, 1979.

10
The Case Against GATT, 1980

Colegio Nacional de Economistas

The Mexican government has requested that all interested segments of our society express their opinions about Mexico's potential entry into the General Agreement on Tariffs and Trade (GATT). The Colegio Nacional de Economistas believes that such consultations can shape governmental policy with respect to fundamental issues affecting the country's future, and therefore strengthen the spirit and democratic practices of the nation.

As a contribution to this consultation, the Colegio organized several events in which public officials, businessmen, economists, jurists, and journalists participated. They analyzed and debated the implications of Mexico's eventual entry into the General Agreement on Tariffs and Trade.

The present document was prepared by members of the Colegio and draws from arguments and information presented at those meetings. With intellectual integrity and professionalism, it expresses the Colegio's views regarding the implications of Mexico's adherence to the General Agreement.

PRECONDITIONS FOR JOINING GATT

The official message sent by the Secretary of Commerce to the General Director of the General Agreement on Tariffs and Trade

---

This paper is a translation of the original which was presented to José López Portillo, Constitutional President of Mexico, Mexico, D.F., March 9, 1980. Translated by Margarita E. Ayala-Addelson.
© 1983 by El Colegio de México.

stated clearly and categorically that Mexico's eventual entry into the Agreement would be determined by two factors:
a) "The final results of the Multilateral Trade Negotiations (MTN), particularly with regard to the proposed special and differential treatment in favor of developed countries."
b) "The terms of these negotiations."

Because Mexico has stated that these two considerations will be crucial in making the final decision, we analyze both of these below.

RESULTS OF PAST MULTILATERAL TRADE NEGOTIATIONS

The Group of 77[1] [of which Mexico is a member] repeatedly and openly expressed its dissatisfaction with the results of the Multilateral Trade Negotiations. This occurred in Arusha (February 1979), in Manila on the occasion of the Fifth UNCTAD,[2] in New York at the Meeting of Foreign Ministers (September 1979), and in Havana at the Preparatory Meeting for the Third General Conference of the non-aligned [Third World] countries. All of the above mentioned meetings ended with declarations concluding that notwithstanding the years of work since the Tokyo Meeting, concrete actions demonstrating preferential treatment for developing countries in trade matters have not resulted. On the contrary, the agreements adopted have been designed to strengthen the economic expansion of industrialized nations, to force a major trade liberalization on the part of the developing countries and, paradoxically, to promote a more protectionist stance on the part of the industrialized nations.

PROTOCOL OF ADHERENCE TO THE AGREEMENT

In the opinion of our members, which is supported by consultations made with jurists specialized on the subject, the commitments that Mexico would assume by adhering to the General Agreement go beyond the guidelines actually set forth in the Draft of Protocol. We consider it extremely important to draw attention to the fact that *joining GATT does not mean that Mexico would assume only those commitments explicitly outlined in the Draft of Protocol.* The Draft only mentions in its resolutions that "Mexico's government can adhere to the cited

Agreement under the conditions set forth in the mentioned Draft." It also means that Mexico would agree to join a market system which is governed by general norms that are obligatory for all its members. This is a legal reality from which political commitments arise. The consequences of the obligations that Mexico would undertake, so obviously avoided in the Draft of Protocol, merely constitute the tip of an iceberg.

In effect, by joining, Mexico would commit itself to changing the instruments of its development policy so that they are consistent with the economic philosophy, practices, and trade norms contained in the General Agreement. Consequently, the basic mechanisms utilized by the Federal Government to promote production, to protect productive activities, and to stimulate exports will have to be discarded because they are not compatible with the economic philosophy, norms, and practices of the GATT. The following norms and practices which presently constitute Mexican policy instruments for stimulating exports are incompatible with the General Agreement:
- use of certificates of fiscal promotion [tax rebates] for certain industries (CEDIs) in their present version;
- extra CEDIs for stimulating the formation of foreign trade consortia;
- direct subsidies to energy sources foreseen in the *Plan Nacional de Desarrollo Industrial* (National Industrial Development Plan);
- implicit subsidies derived from differences between the internal prices of hydrocarbons and petrochemical raw materials, and the prevailing ones in the international market;
- compensated exchange, industrial development programs, norms for integration of national components of industry;
- the foreign currency budget policy, the imports quota policy, and the use of the public sector's purchasing power as an instrument for industrial development.

INCOMPATIBILITY OF THE GATT WITH NATIONAL DEVELOPMENT POLICIES

The incompatibility of these policy instruments with the GATT can be seen when the text of the General Agreement is examined. Several opinions submitted by the contracting parties[3] themselves are transcribed below. These appear in the Working Group's report, and clearly show the incompatibility of the General Agreement with a number of Mexican economic policies.

With respect to the policy on observing local content in industrial production and foreign exchange compensation, paragraphs 36, 38, 39 and 40 state:

> A member made a reference to the *Decreto para el Fomento de la Industria Automotriz* of June 20, 1977, that specifies in Article VII the minimum percentages of local content in automotive vehicles. . . . The member added that in his opinion, these provisions seemed to be incompatible with the General Agreement, particularly with paragraph 5 of Article III; unless they could be justified by the said Agreement's provisions concerning incipient industries . . . With regard to a question as to whether or not the Mexican authorities planned to extend to other sectors the type of system which existed in the automotive industry, Mexico's representative responded that local-content and export performance requirements were concepts applicable to other sectors . . . The Working Group accepted this response with the understanding that the policies discussed not harm the rights and benefits of the other members of the General Agreement . . . Some members of the working group declared that, after *joining, if Mexico wished to extend such measures to industries other than the automotive, it would have to follow the provisions and procedures of the General Agreement.*

On the subject of export stimulation, paragraph 49 states:

> Mexico's representative declared that his government considered the application of incentives to be a key element of its development policy, especially as regards the promotion of exports and the decentralization of industry . . . Some members of the Working Group stated that in this respect *they reserved their rights arising from Article VI of the GATT.*

In some cases, the Working Group report includes before-the-fact pronouncements which assume that Mexico will renounce the use of certain economic policy instruments which are incompatible with GATT. For example, in the area of public sector commerce, paragraph 46 states:

> The Working Group made note of the *assurances given by Mexico's representative* that the public sector's activities would be carried out on a market basis that conforms with the provisions of the General Agreement, particularly with respect to nondiscrimination.

It is obvious that in the first place, such assurances by Mexico would imply the denial of any preference whatsoever to national over foreign suppliers, except for the occasional 15 percent surcharge applied by international financial institutions to insure that foreign loans are applied to purchases from foreign companies. In the second place, they lessen the public sector's flexibility to select suppliers and to choose technologies.

Similar statements of tacit acceptance are expressed in paragraph 43:

> In answer to requests for further information about the [Mexican] system of compensated exchange, Mexico's representative declared that it originated with a development plan that was no longer in effect.

During a meeting on the Subsidies Code, held in Geneva, Switzerland on March 29, 1979, United States representatives pointed out that the Mexican government's Executive Order of December 29, 1978, which sets a higher price schedule for energy sources and basic petrochemical products destined for export, violates the code and should be gradually eliminated. Moreover, the Order of January 24, 1980, which provides incentives for the production of capital goods, presents a similar problem. Likewise, the FOMEX loans that provide credit at preferential rates for export activities are considered to be violations of the Code. Similarly, if Mexico accepts this code, the country must give up new export incentive schemes. Finally, some government subsidies presently under consideration, e.g., those which seek to encourage the research of new technologies, will also be incompatible with the Subsidies Code of the GATT.

According to the norms of the GATT, the sale price of export products must be proportional to their production costs. Thus, these prices should not be affected by direct or indirect subsidies, and the GATT considers as valid only the reimbursement of indirect duties affecting production and marketing costs. The implications of this should be underscored. If Mexico accepts these conditions, it will not be able to provide export incentives in those areas of production where it wants to become competitive. Since it will be impossible to establish a selective export stimulation policy, the country will be forced to devalue the peso progressively to keep the national exporter price differential sufficiently attractive to participate in the international market. In this manner, to insure the profitability of certain types of exports, repeated currency exchange adjustments will have to be carried out. These will have significant social, economic, and political costs, since such a policy would affect the entire economy.

INCOMPATIBILITY OF THE GATT WITH POLICIES FOR PROTECTION OF NATIONAL INDUSTRY

Extensive discussions on protectionism have frequently suggested that Mexico should remove trade restrictions. On repeated occasions, the Colegio has drawn attention to the distortions in national production caused by irrational policies that excessively protect Mexico's industry. Nevertheless, it has also maintained that a greater productive efficiency and capacity to export will never be achieved in the free market nor the "fair" competition that foreign trade liberalization would ostensibly provide. The experience of those developing countries that followed this course made it abundantly clear that incipient industries have been annihilated through competition with large international enterprises. The Colegio recognizes that in the present world it is impossible to develop strong industry without protection. Every industrialized nation presently has an extensive and varied set of protectionist measures, though primarily of a non-tariff nature, which will continue to be utilized in spite of the Codes of Conduct derived from the Tokyo Round Negotiations. Thus, by liberalizing its foreign trade, Mexico would be committing economic suicide. The issue is not protectionism for its own sake, but its use as an instrument for industrial rationality and employment generation.

Even the General Agreement recognizes the need of developing nations for protecting those economic activities fundamental for assuring their development. Nonetheless, the only formula permitted by the GATT is tariff protection. For this reason, according to the Draft for Protocol of Adherence (Article III), Mexico commits itself to continue "to eliminate quantitative restrictions and prior licenses for most imports." Similarly, it commits itself to present a report every two years outlining the steps it is undertaking to eliminate non-tariff barriers.

As a complement to this decision, Mexico is obligated to eliminate the official price system and to adopt a customs valuation system in order to meet GATT norms, because some "members of the Working Group stated that Mexico's application of official prices was incompatible with Article VII of the General Agreement. They also declared that the Mexican authorities should take measures so that the valuation system employed by Mexican customs houses be consistent with the provisions of the General Agreement."

Mexico's acceptance of these norms entails serious risks. A trade policy which seeks protection by relying exclusively on tariffs is vulnerable for several reasons. First, a growing proportion of foreign trade operations corresponds to transactions within firms (between parent companies, branches, subsidiaries, and agencies). This allows trade to be valued on the basis of "virtual" prices according to prevalent practices of over- or under-invoicing which provides tax and commercial advantages to the multinational corporations. In other words, an *ad-valorem* tariff would be applied to monetary values manipulated at the convenience of the seller.

Second, the effect of a tariff can be nullified by the differential in the inflation rates of Mexico or other countries. To correct this, it would be necessary to establish within each country a continuous exchange adjustment system. Because of this, the majority of developing countries presently utilize exchange controls and frequent devaluations as instruments of trade protection, as well as to promote export competitiveness.

Third, in an international market demand strongly influenced by a high concentration of income, a trade protection system based entirely on tariffs deforms the composition of imports. This situation is becoming more evident ever since Mexico instituted a policy of relative trade liberalization. A study of the elimination of previous import license requirements should demonstrate the import of goods that do not satisfy basic social needs and which, on the contrary, are destined to serve—indeed, to create—sophisticated consumer tastes within high-income segments of the population. The polarization of consumption patterns fostered by trade liberalization is politically and morally inadmissible. Finally, it is necessary to point out that the industrialized countries themselves, particularly Japan and the European Economic Community, became aware of the limited effectiveness of tariffs as an instrument of protection and introduced a variety of non-tariff restrictions. Theoretically, these restrictions are to be eliminated with the new Codes of Conduct negotiated since the Tokyo Round.

INCOMPATIBILITY OF THE GATT WITH NATIONAL CONTROL OF EXPORTS

Industrialized nations are bent on insuring the supply of non-renewable raw materials by eliminating export restrictions. To be sure, the Mexican Delegation stated ambiguously that the control of exports by means of prior license "is neither permanent nor is it temporary in the sense it be of a fixed and limited duration, but each case is constantly reviewed to determine whether the circumstances which originally led to export controls still apply." Nevertheless, a member of the Working Group, "after pointing out that Article XX stipulated that certain conditions had to be observed, declared that his Delegation maintained its position that Mexico's measures relating to export controls should comply with Article XX of the General Agreement" (Paragraph 48 of the report).

In view of the ambiguity of the Mexican Delegation's declaration, we consider it a matter of the utmost importance to underscore the danger of permitting the country to run the risk of losing its autonomy to decide at what level certain natural resources will be exported (see Article XX, paragraphs g and h, of the Agreement). According to our Constitution, those resources constitute the patrimony of the nation.

By the same token, Mexico would be giving up, at the outset, the use of the export of raw materials, primarily hydrocarbons, as an instrument of negotiation. Such a concession would also nullify the proposal made by the President before the General Assembly of the United Nations concerning the use of petroleum as an instrument for structuring the world economy. We will treat this subject in greater detail below.

DOES THE GATT HAVE FLEXIBILITY WHEN VIOLATIONS OCCUR?

In short, Mexico's entry into the GATT translates into at least a moral obligation to abandon all of those practices, norms, and instruments of economic policy which have been used, some recently, to stimulate economic development, protect economic activities, promote exports and conserve non-renewable natural resources. Mexico's development policy would in effect have to be adapted—indeed subordinated—to the principles and rules stipulated by the GATT.

In some instances, the nation's administrators have openly recognized such incompatibilities. Nevertheless, they have read some flexibility into the GATT, and argued that GATT violations are frequent and subject to negotiation. We argue that Mexico should not adhere to an agreement that it will not observe at the outset. Otherwise, the implication would be that Mexico plans to redesign its development policy and instruments to suit the guidelines of the General Agreement. If that is the intent, we must recognize that the country would be abandoning the enforcement of certain legal provisions based on constitutional precepts. An example of the latter would be the provisions of paragraph two of Article 131 of the Constitution, especially those concerning the foreign currency budget.

These effects have been played down by arguing that Mexico's economic development policies are safeguarded in the Protocol's preamble. Nevertheless, in the opinion of legal experts, the preamble basically consists of unilateral declarations made by Mexico. In paragraph 56 concerning the Working Group's conclusions, as well as Article V of the Draft of Protocol, the contracting parties clearly express some doubt about the thrust of Mexico's economic development policies, and particularly the practices contemplated in the *Plan Nacional de Desarrollo Industrial*.[4]

In the normative section of the Draft of Protocol, Article I, paragraph *b* states that Part II of the General Agreement will be applied by Mexico in a manner compatible with its current legislation at the time the Protocol is signed. In this respect, it is necessary to mention that according to the tradition of GATT, when domestic standards are of a mandatory legislative nature, their adaptation to the General Agreement is not required. However, when such standards are of an administrative and discretionary nature, they should be applied according to the norms of the General Agreement. In Mexico, most of the legal provisions relating to economic development are not legislative but administrative regulations issued by the Executive. Even such legislative provisions as do exist provide considerable discretion to the administrative authorities for their application. If Mexico adheres to the GATT in the future, its legislation and regulation in the area of economic development will also have to submit to the standards established by the General Agreement.[5]

At one extreme, it has been argued that all violations of the General Agreement by any of the contracting parties are subject to negotiation. With respect to this point, it is necessary to underline a fundamental fact: Every violation consented to implies a right to demand additional concessions. It is naive to assume that negotiation amounts to the simple process of persuading the contracting parties. Acceptance of any violation by GATT members entails the obligation of the violating member to a concession in return, directly or indirectly, tariff or non-tariff, but always political. This political reality cannot be ignored.

At the other extreme, it has been argued that Mexico should participate in the forum provided by GATT in order to influence the outcome of commercial negotiations. The possibility has even been suggested that Mexico lead the underdeveloped nations in pressing their claims for redress. However, these claims lack political realism. The chances of developing countries to improve the outcome of commercial negotiations depend to a great extent on the political goodwill of the industrialized nations. In recent years, the absence of political goodwill on the part of the industrialized countries has been evident in the UNCTAD and the North-South dialogue. If these forums have not demonstrated much cooperation, it is illusory to believe that economic advancement can be achieved in a forum such as GATT.

INFLEXIBILITY AND UNCERTAINTIES IN THE NEW GATT

From Mexico's point of view, the GATT is a forum where tangible benefits will not be easily gained for its economy, and where the country will find itself obligated to assume new commitments on a daily basis.

It must be kept in mind that the Tokyo Round of negotiations took place because it had become necessary to "update" the GATT to avoid a collapse caused by its evident inefficiency in regulating competition—indeed, conflict—between industrialized nations. The renewal of GATT through the Codes of Conduct seeks to establish stricter rules of behavior in the international market. If these tend to prevent unfair trade practices among developed countries, they also severely constrict the possibilities of developing nations for trade expansion.

Some Mexican officials have admitted that the Codes of Conduct are too rigid in restricting certain types of trade practices. But they assert that Mexico will not sign unacceptable Codes.

Even the GATT members, while agreeing that the Codes in some way constitute regulatory provisions of the General Agreement, have not been able to define the juridical links. Some interpret them as obligatory for the contracting parties when the Codes have been signed by two-thirds of the members. Other naively suppose them as obligatory only for the signatory nations. Since the Codes were established to put in force the norms and practices of the General Agreement, the industrialized countries will find in some way or another practical formulas for persuading the underdeveloped nations to adapt their internal policies to the norms of the Codes.[6]

Regardless of what one assumes, the relationship of the Codes of Conduct to the General Agreement is perhaps one of the least known, least certain, and most relevant aspects of the new GATT. This in itself is sufficient reason for Mexico to postpone joining the General Agreement until events permit a clearer perspective of the consequences of the obligations that Mexico will assume.

Two extremely important questions need resolution. The Code of Safeguards, whose approval met firm opposition from the most important industrialized countries, will continue to be discussed during the course of 1980. From the contents of this Code, it will be possible to infer the circumstances in which countries can introduce exceptions to the established norms for promoting economic development. The members of the GATT will also debate the Code on Supplies during 1980. As a consequence of OPEC's oil embargo in 1973, the industrialized countries, the primary consumers of petroleum, have stressed two major concerns: (1) the leverage of the petroleum-producing countries, and (2) the vital importance of crude oil to the economic process. Petroleum-consuming countries seek to introduce this issue in the GATT by establishing norms such as Article XX prohibiting export restrictions. Nevertheless, these provisions do not fully resolve the problem of the security of the supply of strategic raw materials. Therefore, a decision has been made to modify these provisions based on the negotiations that will take place in the GATT, which will culminate with the Code on Supplies.

The majority of OPEC members do not participate in the GATT, and those countries that do only recently severed the ties that bound them to colonial powers. The outcome of any negotiation in this forum is expected to be favorable to industrialized nations. Moreover, developing countries that import petroleum could always join the industrialized nations in demanding supply guarantees and price moderation in petroleum. It is a risky business for petroleum-producing countries to negotiate trade matters in a forum where the interests of petroleum consumers predominate.

Recognizing these political realities, the developing world has been using the leverage afforded by the supply of petroleum and other strategic raw materials since 1974 to insist on the establishment of a New International Economic Order (NIEO). This has been accomplished not within the GATT, but in the United Nations General Assembly.

In response to these concerns, a new series of global negotiations will begin in August 1980 between all members of the United Nations to formulate the New International Economic Order. Petroleum will provide the developing world a leverage for negotiating a greater availability of technology, some reform in the international financial and monetary system, greater access to international markets for their products, the price indexing of their raw materials, the restructuring of world-wide industry, the establishment of more secure agriculture and food productive systems and so on.

The central feature of the President's proposal for a World Energy Plan, presented before the United Nations General Assembly, is precisely this idea of linking energy to the matters of international economic cooperation as enunciated above.[7] In other words, the Plan is conceived with the New International Economic Order in mind. For all of these reasons, an isolated discussion of secure supplies within the GATT would undermine the broader negotiations that begin in August of 1980. It would also undercut various proposals of the Group of the 77, including that of establishing a World Plan on Energy Sources.

From another perspective, the Trilateral Commission itself views the power of food in the following terms: "The developing nations depend just as much on the developed countries for the supply of food and manufactured goods as the developed countries depend on the former for their supply of energy and raw materials." Based on this argument, some Mexican government officials have publicly taken the position that Mexico should sign the future Code on Supplies. Aside from the fact that such a declaration implies accepting the perpetuation of the country's food dependency, it constitutes an admission that Mexico should exchange secure markets for its energy for secure access to food supplies. Without trying to downplay the serious implications of this position, it is pertinent to discuss the other side of the coin. During the talks on agricultural trade of the Tokyo Round, there was considerable interest in arriving at a consensus in the areas of cereals. The failure to successfully conclude these talks, and the failure to arrive at a wheat agreement in the UNCTAD, lays bare the position of some industrialized nations to not willingly give up their power as food exporters.

In summary, it is our opinion that the only viable option for negotiating global energy and food matters is in the World Energy Plan, which will be discussed within the United Nations starting in August of 1980.

POLICY OPTIONS

In light of the far-reaching implications that would flow from a Mexican decision to join the General Agreement, and keeping in mind our responsibility as a professional body, we, the members of the *Colegio Nacional de Economistas*, consider it an obligation not only to express our opinion on this subject but, in keeping with our experience in this area, to recommend alternative courses of action to the Mexican government.

PROSPECTS OF THE INTERNATIONAL ECONOMY

In recent years a number of factors, such as increased protectionism, global inflation, and the instability of foreign currencies have depressed the volume of world trade. From 1965 to 1973, the average annual growth in the volume of exports was about 9 percent in real terms; between 1973 and 1977, growth slowed down to an average of 4 percent. Export price trends are difficult to predict but one can assert that they will be unfavorable for the developing countries.

In this environment of shrinking global economic activity, the World Bank has recognized that the industrialized nations have become increasingly protectionist, and that strong pressures persist to adopt even more protectionist measures. In part, these pressures arise from the slow growth experienced by their economies and the resulting high levels of unemployment. The urge in industrialized countries to erect trade barriers is also a result of the narrow range of manufactured products stimulating the growth of exports from developing countries. To restrain these imports, industrialized nations have resorted to a number of hidden protectionist measures, such as orderly marketing agreements, new import quotas, minimum price levels for imported goods, as with steel and agricultural products, new voluntary export restrictions and countervailing duties, administrative obstacles to imports and subsidies to some domestic industries to keep production levels in excess of that justified by market demand. Recent experience suggests that these new trade barriers—discussed at the Tokyo Round—will prevail, and that the new codes to be established by the GATT with respect to these issues will not foster trade liberalization for a select group of developing nations which they consider to be *newly-industrialized* countries. The results of the Tokyo Round confirm this. The new rules provide for a differential treatment for developing nations according to their level of development. Mexico, Brazil, Argentina, Taiwan, and South Korea, fall in the newly-industrialized category. The view of the industrialized countries is that the nations of intermediate development should bear the cost of readjustment for the world economy. This position by the industrialized countries was made clear at the Third General Conference of ONIDU held in New Delhi, India, in a document which states in unequivocal terms:

> Furthermore, it will become necessary that a larger number of developing nations contribute to the adjustment process and reinforce their resistance to protectionist policies adopted abroad by opening their own markets, not only to developed nations but also to other developing countries. As they continue to develop, they should gradually assume greater obligations to uphold the trade system.

THE STRATEGY OF THE UNITED STATES

The drafting and enactment of the United States Trade Agreements Act of 1979 ends a long process in which the United States tried to resolve its domestic economic problems by redesigning the international trade system. At the end of the sixties, the United States began to have serious problems in its foreign trade, evinced by a growing trade deficit. The persistence and severity of this problem affected the stability of the dollar, intensified inflationary pressures, and destabilized the world economy. For this reason, in December of 1971 the U.S. sought to modify the functioning of the international trade system. To achieve this, the international commerce of an increasing number of countries had to be brought under control, and failing that, fundamental changes in the GATT had to be made. The Tokyo Round no doubt represented the beginning of a new world trade system. The essence of the new guidelines was established by the Codes of Conduct and the institutional changes made in the GATT, as well as by the introduction of new concepts such as the *graduation principle*, relative reciprocity, selectivity, access to supplies, voluntary export restrictions, and order agreements. All of the preconditions of international adjustments were incorporated to the U.S. Trade Agreements Act of 1979.

To take advantage of the benefits made available by the Tokyo Round, President Carter proposed on September 26, 1978, an Exports Program which was approved the following year and which included:
- A more active role for the EximBank, increasing its financial endowment to provide a greater flexibility in setting international rates, determining maturity periods, and establishing the proportion of transactions which it finances. (According to Congressional Representative McDonald's calculations, the Purchase Code alone could open a potential market of $20 billion for producers.)
- Increased government loans to small companies. Loan guarantees in the amount of $100 million will be made available.
- Incentive programs for exporters. The budget of the Departments of State and Commerce will increase $20 million.
- A strengthening of agricultural exports, with a budget increase of $1 billion for short-term loans to U.S. farmers, and the opening of agricultural offices in the most important importing countries. Other elements of this program are a 20 percent increase in funds destined for marketing programs with agricultural cooperatives and legal assistance to facilitate the granting of immediate export credits for certain agricultural products.

- The establishment of negotiations for reducing tariff barriers and commercial subsidies abroad to facilitate the penetration of U.S. goods in the international market.
- The presentation of demands for reciprocity from industrialized countries and from countries of intermediate development (Brazil, Korea, Mexico, Argentina, Taiwan).
- The creation of a National Export Council which will coordinate the activities of all federal departments and agencies related to foreign trade.
- The restructuring of the Department of Commerce, giving it broad powers to encourage U.S. investments abroad.

No doubt, trade with Mexico is an important element in the United States Exports Program. According to former Ambassador Patrick Lucey, within the next few years, Mexico will rise from the fifth to the second most important trading partner of the United States.

DOMESTIC STRATEGY FOR TREATING FOREIGN ISSUES

Given the complexity of the present global context, which can be characterized as in a transitional phase of redefining economic frontiers and areas of commercial influence, it is imperative that Mexico fix upon a domestic strategy that will enable it to deal successfully with international pressures and to exercise its muscle, for its own benefits, as a petroleum exporter. The elements of such a strategy might constitute:
- A foreign trade policy effectively connecting the administrative and support activities of the government with the goal of defending against unfair imports, and incorporating the objectives of the *Plan Nacional de Desarrollo Industrial* (National Industrial Development Plan) and a rational and vertical strategy from the standpoint of exportable products.
- A foreign policy framework making the most of petroleum as a negotiating instrument, at the bilateral, regional, and multilateral levels.
- The design of a domestic policy reconciling the goals of food and agricultural self-sufficiency with the above.
- The definition of what role the rate of exchange should play for the Mexican peso, taking into account the present domestic and international economic situation.

Once Mexico's decision to enter into the GATT is postponed, it will be possible to explore several avenues of negotiation based on the use of petroleum as an instrument of political and trade bargaining.

BILATERAL NEGOTIATIONS

Irrespective of what order of priority is ultimately established for bilateral discussions on this matter, the case of the United States must be considered at once. Of particular concern are the possible implications and effects U.S. trade legislation and the Subsidies and Countervailing Duties Code of the GATT may have on Mexico's exports given the subsidy of its industries.

If Mexico were not a member of the GATT nor conducted its commerce according to the provisions contained in the Trade Agreements Act of 1979, the United States could apply countervailing duties against those Mexican goods whose production were subsidized as provided for in the Tariff Law of 1930. In such a case, U.S. government officials would have the *discretionary* power to impose countervailing duties without substantiating that the injury had actually occurred and the foreign country involved would lack any means of defense other than diplomatic negotiations on a case-by-case basis.

Assuming that Mexico were a member of the GATT and had signed the Code on Countervailing Duties, the U.S. International Trade Commission could apply these duties if it were to determine, as a result of *careful* investigation, that an industry of the United States had suffered material damages, or had been threatened with material damages; or if the establishment of an industry in the United States had been materially delayed due to the inflow of subsidized imports. Though the law provides the offending exporters with some defense against trade restrictions, the concepts employed are ambiguous, and their application is subject to administrative interpretation. The law does not clearly define the scope of "material damages," nor does it explain what is meant by "an industry threatened," nor does it spell out when the establishment of an industry has been "materially delayed." Furthermore, the new law states that when a preliminary decision has been made—an event that occurs almost as a matter of course—customs authorities will store imported goods and require that a bond be posted to guarantee the payment of duties. This procedure makes even more ambiguous the application of the concept of substantiating injuries since the importations have been preempted by the "preliminary decision." Moreover, the time limit for reaching a final decision on whether to apply countervailing duties has been shortened considerably.

As it can be observed in the case where a country has not joined the GATT, the application of countervailing duties by U.S. authorities is unilateral. When a country has joined, damages must first be proven before duties are levied. However, the criteria applied to establish damages are ambiguous, and U.S. government officials have considerable discretionary authority to interpret them. One can infer from this that in the future, for both cases, the U.S. will administer its trade laws as instruments of geopolitical relations.[8]

These trade practices are sure to spread to other developed countries which, one way or another, are likely to incorporate similar provisions to their trade legislation. In view of this, we should explore the possibility of using bilateral agreements as a vehicle for negotiating the application of these norms. It would be appropriate to begin discussions with those industrialized nations that do not as yet have domestic standards as regards this, and which have demonstrated the political will to find alternatives. In this manner, precedents would be established so that appropriate bargaining could be conducted with other countries.

REGIONAL NEGOTIATIONS

It is absolutely essential that Mexico's relations with the rest of Latin America extend beyond political issues. The upcoming debate on the reorganization of the Latin American Free Trade Association, LAFTA, makes possible the most practical and realistic decisions. Petroleum could play a central role in this negotiation and, as the case may be, in future ones deriving from it.

The new emphasis on reaching partial agreements among Latin American nations, which may set the tone for their economic integration, will undoubtedly encourage agreements among the different countries of the region. As in the case of bilateral and multilateral negotiations, a Mexican entry into the GATT would restrict all possibilities for taking advantage of its petroleum resources in the Latin American region starting July of 1980.

MULTILATERAL NEGOTIATIONS

As stated previously, any decision to isolate supply security at the time of Mexico's entry into the GATT would significantly undermine the bargaining power of the Group of 77 in the Global Negotiations beginning August of 1980. Serious political consequences, such as a diminished support of the World Energy Plan by OPEC Nations and a tarnished image in the world community, would undermine the viability of the Plan. It would also undermine the very concept of a World Energy Plan which is based on the idea that energy sources are an integral part of a negotiating package to establish a New International Economic Order. Thus, Mexico should not compromise its bargaining power in the GATT, at least not until the alternatives are spelled out in an appropriate forum of the United Nations.

In summary, taking into account the arguments discussed in this document, the *Colegio Nacional de Economistas* would recommend that the Mexican government postpone any decision to join the GATT. It should not take action until uncertainties are dispelled with respect to the application, character and consequences of the existing Codes of Conduct and of those Codes that will be considered in the future, especially those regarding Supply and Protections. By the same token, this postponement will afford time to know the results of the July 1980 negotiations in the LAFTA and of the August 1980 negotiations in the United Nations when the President's proposal on energy sources will be considered. By then Mexico will have formulated its policy on foreign trade and have linked it to its economic policies on production and employment.

In preparing this document, the authors tried to conduct a careful and open-minded analysis. The intent is to contribute, as far as their collective knowledge and competence permits, to the formulation of decisions which will serve the national interest.

NOTES

1. The Group of 77, originally 77 countries, now more than a hundred, refers to an informal coalition of underdeveloped nations within the UNCTAD who have pressed for more favorable terms of trade from developed nations. This group constitutes the "Southern" end of the North-South dialogue [eds.].

2. This refers to the fifth meeting of the United Nations Conference on Trade and Development, a forum to discuss the economic needs of developing countries [eds].

3. These refer to the nations represented at the meeting in which the Mexican delegation discussed the conditions for entering GATT.

4. Two issues in the preamble of the Draft of Protocol contradict positions that Mexico has traditionally adopted in international forums. First, Mexico is not recognized as a developing country. This implies accepting the "graduation principle." Second, it is recognized that the results of the Multilateral Trade Negotiations were favorable to the developing nations. This contradicts the position expressed by the Group of 77.

5. According to the information gathered by the Colegio, no legal research has been conducted to determine the compatibility of Mexican legislation and their regulatory provisions with the provisions of the General Agreement.

6. Until now, all underdeveloped countries have rejected the Codes, with the exception of Brazil and Argentina.

7. The reference is to the World Energy Plan submitted by President López Portillo to the United Nations General Assembly [eds].

8. This is evident in the case of Mexican vegetable exports. In 1979 the U.S. Department of Treasury ruled that according to the criteria of the 1930 Law, "dumping" had not occurred. However, in the last month [February 1980] the case has been unexpectedly reopened under stricter guidelines which threaten Mexican exports. The turnaround has been justified with the argument that the Trade Agreement Act of 1979 now assigns the responsibility of ruling on such matters to the Department of Commerce.

MIGRANT WORKERS:
A Problem for Whom?

IV

11
Unequal Exchange in the Binational Relationship: The Case of Immigrant Labor

Jorge A. Bustamante and James D. Cockcroft

The flow of Mexican migrant labor to the United States is a century-old phenomenon caused by Mexico's uneven economic development and vulnerability to domination by U.S. capital.[1] In spite of recent changes, the underlying pattern persists: strong demand for temporary immigrant labor by certain U.S. employers and an abundant supply of such labor in specific regions of Mexico.

Growing investments by U.S.-based transnational corporations (TNCs), which in Mexico are concentrated in the most dynamic sectors of industrial production, have increased the capital required for the creation of new jobs and drained Mexico of exorbitant amounts of money. New U.S. direct investment in Mexico has doubled every 5 years since 1970, while Mexico's outflow of

---

Jorge A. Bustamante is the author of *Espaldas mojadas, materia prima para la expansión del capital norteamericano* (El Colegio de México, 1975); *La inmigración mexicana en los debates del Congreso de Estados Unidos* (CENIET, 1978); with Francisco Malagamba, *México-Estados Unidos, Bibliografía extensiva sobre estudios fronterizos* (El Colegio de México, 1981). He is the Director of the Centro de Estudios Fronterizos del Norte de México, Tijuana (CEFNOMEX).

James D. Cockcroft is the author of *Mexico: Class Formation, Capital Accumulation and the State* (New York: Monthly Review Press, 1982); *El imperialismo, la lucha de clases y el estado en México* (Nuestro Tiempo, 1979); *Intellectual Precursors of the Mexican Revolution* (Austin: University of Texas Press, 1968, paperback ed., 1976). A sociology professor at Rutgers University, he is presently directing a research project on "Migration and Border Problems" based at the Universidad Autónoma Metropolitana de Azcapotzalco in Mexico City.

The authors would like to thank the editors of this volume, Carlos Vásquez and Manuel García y Griego, for their critical suggestions and attentive editing.

© 1983 by Jorge A. Bustamante and James D. Cockcroft.

dividends, interest, and other payments to foreign investors has been twice as large as the inflow of new foreign investments.[2] This "suction-pump" effect of foreign investors receiving more from Mexico than what they put into its economy—together with Mexico's increased foreign loans, declining terms of trade, and periodic flights of domestic capital—has generated in Mexico a process of relative decapitalization and a growing indebtedness.

Mexico continues to send two-thirds of its exports to the same neighboring country from which it receives two-thirds of its imports. Because of the overwhelming influence of U.S. economic interests upon economic activity in Mexico, such activity responds only partially to Mexican interests. This defines a situation of economic dependence. An important conclusion to be derived from this is that neither the conditions of economic underdevelopment nor one of its specific manifestations, the migration of Mexican workers to the United States, are attributable entirely to internal factors. U.S. private interests acting in Mexico have created a Mexican domestic economic situation which is instrumental to the migration of workers to the United States. U.S. governmental promotion of TNC activities in Mexico, which contribute to Mexico's unemployment and underemployment problems, is glossed over when the U.S. government blames Mexico for its surplus population problem as the cause for Mexican labor migration to the United States.

Mexico's growing dependence on the United States compounds its inability to absorb its labor force. Mexico's productivity disadvantages vis-à-vis the more advanced industrialized countries are historically rooted in colonialism, foreign domination of the economy after independence, and preference by Mexican investors to utilize low-wage labor to the detriment of a more complete mechanization of production. This condition is further aggravated by its relative decapitalization and growing indebtedness. Given Mexico's relative sub-capitalization, or lack of adequate capital to generate sufficient employment, the size of the relative surplus population has continued to increase. Increased investments by TNCs contribute to the abundance of surplus population by elevating the level of capital needed for the creation of each new job.

As Marx noted, a relative surplus population, "a population of greater extent than suffices for the average needs of the self-expansion of capital" is a "condition of existence of the capitalist mode of production." Industrial capitalism, Marx pointed out, "depends on the constant formation, the greater or lesser absorption, and the re-formation of the industrial reserve army of surplus population." Attracted and driven back from the points of production, this reserve army allows for rapid expansion of production when desired by employers and reduces the likelihood of long strikes or rapidly rising wages which might make production unprofitable.[3] But Marx did not live long enough to witness the incredible size of the surplus population that results from industrial capitalism's expansion into less developed regions of the world. In Mexico, the steady increase in relative surplus population contributes to combined unemployment and underemployment rates of 40 percent and up. The persistence and growth of a mass of unemployed and underemployed beyond a minimum labor reserve necessary for any capitalist system of production is itself a manifestation of economic underdevelopment.

At the same time that the level of capitalization in Mexico has not been sufficient to create enough jobs for the labor force, many companies in U.S. agriculture and industry, particularly in certain regions, have maintained a longstanding demand for temporary Mexican labor. Through the use of transient low-wage labor in some sectors of the U.S. economy, employers have been able to hold back the rise in wage levels of the stable work force, hike profit rates and increase capital accumulation. The presence of an immense pool of job-hungry laborers in Mexico facilitates capital accumulation not only for those U.S. employers hiring immigrant workers but for all capitalists in the United States and Mexico. For example, Mexican monied interests like the North's "Monterrey group" are collaborating more and more with U.S. investors in Mexico by taking advantage of the low price of Mexican labor. Also, the traditional role of a reserve army of labor (serving as a check on all labor's demands for better wages, unions, etc.) is accentuated as Mexican surplus population and migration increase.

Traditional employers of migrant labor like agribusiness and the garment industry are not the only ones dependent on cheap labor. As a result of the widespread economic crisis generated by the 1973-1975 recession affecting major U.S. industries like automotive and steel, and Mexican and U.S. capital in general, most capitalist employers perceive intensified use of cheap unskilled and semi-skilled labor as a principal, though not the only, way out of the structural crisis in the accumulation of capital. If for garment, electronics, and restaurant industries, immigrant labor has become fundamental at the point of production for their survival or growth, for industries in general, the presence of an expanded and internationalized reserve army of labor facilitates economic recovery and subsequent expansion. Thus, in recent years the demand for immigrant labor in the United States has not only persisted but expanded even though U.S. official unemployment rates have reached politically intolerable levels of nine percent and up.

This demand is rooted in history and expanded by the increased internationalization of the labor market. One end of the market may be located in an impoverished "ranchería" (cluster of tiny farm plots) in a state like Michoacán (west of Mexico City), whose local economy has reproduced four generations of labor power which migrates to the other end of the same labor market, located perhaps 2,000 miles away (a restaurant or automotive chassis factory in Chicago, an agribusiness field in south Texas or California's Imperial Valley, a garment or electronics factory in Los Angeles, or a middle class household employing a domestic in any of the border states). It encompasses a system of relations for production of two countries where the main actors, employers and workers play out their roles with little doubt as to the scope of their own rights.

When the migrant worker comes into the U.S. labor market, he enters into a labor relation in which the U.S. employer has the unique power, granted by present U.S. immigration law, of deciding unilaterally whether the immigrant is to be treated as a worker or as a criminal. The current law (U.S. Congress, 8 U.S.C., Section 1324), instead of explicitly prohibiting, permits an employer to hire undocumented workers, at the same time that undocumented aliens are made deportable. Thus, sanctioned by what in fact is a labor law disguised as an immigration law, the Mexican migrant laborer is in a defenseless position. His or her relationship to the employer personifies the historical relationship between Mexico and the United States: slave-boss. The labor relation undocumented-migrant/boss is conducive to super-exploitation, that is, payment of labor power below its value—what it takes for a laborer to sustain himself. The migrant's illegal status and the corresponding threat of deportation assure the system of his or her sub-standard wage payments. This privileged condition with which the boss confronts the Mexican migrant worker, a condition reinforced by law, helps maintain the migratory flow not only for industrial plants that might otherwise "run away" to other countries where cheap labor is available, but also for agribusiness and ever more varied sectors of industrial and services production in the United States seeking to combat the tendency of the rate of profit to fall by saving on wages.[4]

This system implies the reproduction of Mexican labor power at minimal costs to capital. U.S. capital does not have to bear the costs of educating and nurturing these human beings until they migrate in early adulthood. The costs of subsistence—and therefore the reproduction of labor power—are maintained at a minimal level through a system which encourages a migrant to come alone and to remit (by U.S. standards) small amounts home for the subsistence of the migrant's Mexican family.[5] Because of the intensity of their exploitation, the migrants themselves have their productive capacities used up relatively early in life and are then discarded to the margins of society to be replaced by new waves of younger migrants. An undetermined number of migrants are killed or disabled in the course of their travels and labors.

The migration of Mexican labor power represents an unequal exchange in which Mexico—through the export of human capital—subsidizes the U.S. economy. Data obtained from interviews by Mexican researchers on tens of thousands of migrants in the late 1970s show that the migrant workers are not the poorest, the most likely to be unemployed, nor the least educated. In other words, they are not at the bottom of the social pyramid. From this it may be inferred that the migration out of Mexico represents the transfer of a significant investment by Mexico mainly by Mexican workers in the form of human capital to the United States. For the latter, employment of Mexican migrant workers represents a savings in the costs of producing and reproducing this human capital, since it normally remains in the United States only temporarily.

The costs of producing and reproducing this Mexican labor power are minimal for the U.S. economy. Undocumented Mexican labor is economically functional not only for certain U.S. capitalists, but for the U.S. system as a whole. Mexican migration constitutes an unequal exchange because the country of origin and its working class subsidize the country of destination through the transfer of human capital. Even though the total amount of this subsidy may not be very large by U.S. standards, it is significant to Mexico, a country where resources for the development of human capital are limited. This unequal exchange undermines U.S. government claims that Mexican migration represents a cost for the U.S. economy and a benefit for Mexico (on the grounds that migration allows Mexico to export its unemployment problem).

Recent studies have confirmed modern capital's growing preference to "dequalify" (lower the demand for skills) and rotate labor.[6] Migration of Mexican workers to the United States is not unrelated to these trends. Certain jobs that used to require skilled labor now require more capital and unskilled (or semi-skilled) labor. Automation, the use of computers, and similar changes in the forces of production mean higher costs in constant (fixed) capital as compared to variable capital (labor power). In turn, capital has "dequalified" labor making it easier to hire and fire workers, i.e., to rotate labor. Rotation of labor serves capital's interests because seniority privileges are undermined, wages revert to the starting level for newly hired employees, and workers in general become interchangeable, making them think twice before striking or demanding a higher wage.

In the international context of the U.S. and Mexican economies, "dequalification" and rotation of labor adds to the size of the reserve army of labor. While U.S. capital migrates to Mexico, cheap Mexican labor migrates to the United States. This unequal exchange is compounded by the drain on Mexican resources by U.S. investors and by the subsidy provided to the U.S. economy in the form of transferred human capital. U.S. minorities, including women in the work force, feel the effects of rotation of labor particularly hard. "Dequalification" and rotation of labor, like migration, help capital to recover from the structural crisis of accumulation.

Every day more is scientifically known about this international system of capital and labor flows. For example, in the case of Mexican migratory labor, sufficient data now exists to develop a social profile of the undocumented Mexican labor force. Nine men for every one woman migrate to the United States (though more women are beginning to migrate). Most migrants are between 18 and 25 years of age. More than 50 percent are bachelors who, over 80 percent of the time, come from eight states in Mexico and usually go to California or Texas. About 85 percent of all undocumented entries by Mexicans to the United States end in a departure from that country within one year's length of stay. These, then, are temporary migrants. The proportion of migrants from urban over rural areas is increasing. The demand for their labor is growing in different areas with an accelerated expansion in services and industry more than compensating for a tapering off of demand in agriculture. Furthermore, U.S. demographic data indicate a growing scarcity in those sectors most demanding of semi-skilled or unskilled labor, which translates into an expansion in the demand for unskilled labor in the 1980s.

Historically, this phenomenon has been basically one of temporary migration to specific regions in the United States, even though the industries employing them have changed over time. For regional blocs of U.S. capitalists, particularly in the Southwest, the lower costs of reproduction of labor power made possible by the migratory flow have become either essential or taken for granted. The implications of recent changes in the U.S. economy and population are that this historical demand for cheap labor will not disappear within the next few decades—some industries require it for their survival. Thus, temporary Mexican migration is likely to increase further (even if unemployment rates decline in Mexico), reinforcing the migration phenomenon as a persistent and structural one. Economist Clark Reynolds refers to this process in the broader context of the "silent integration" of the two economies.

In spite of repeated and vigorous rejections of the "North American Common Market" idea by President José López Portillo and Premier Pierre Trudeau, President Ronald Reagan remains an advocate of a common market with Mexico and Canada. Whether publicly stated or not, part of President Reagan's strategy with regard to the issue of Mexican immigration may be to link a supposed resolution of the issue with a gradual advancement toward a common market. The already existing "silent integration" of the U.S. and Mexican economies has created a de facto common market, one operating in the border zones for many years and now reaching central Mexico, in sectors like the Mexican automotive industry (dominated by foreign capital) or the U.S.-owned *maquiladora* assembly plants. Official U.S. acceptance of a specified number of Mexican migrant workers could readily be converted into a beachhead or justification for making this silent integration an official common market. Establishing a formal common market which builds on the existing economic integration is one of the most ambitious business projects in recent times among powerful sectors of monopoly capital in both nations, particularly in the north of Mexico and the southwest United States —a project long backed by Reagan and other U.S. politicians (e.g., California's Governor Jerry Brown).

Scientific research has exposed many myths about the so-called "undocumented," but it has yet to have an impact on U.S. public opinion where emotional political definitions still rule over reason. Certainly the figures on the volume of the migratory flow of Mexican workers are much lower than what the U.S. mass media have disseminated. All empirical studies on the size of the Mexican undocumented population in the United States at various points between 1975 and 1977 concur that the total must be at least 235,000 and no more than 2.9 million.[7]

In general, these workers do not displace U.S. workers, as they have been accused of doing, because the undocumented respond to a labor market with different rules. These rules are unacceptable to U.S. workers. When an employer in the United States lays off undocumented workers, he makes room not just for any workers but for those who are in highly vulnerable and exploitable conditions specific to that sub-class of workers.

Whoever is familiar with the historical and social context of the economic crises (periods of depression or recession) of 1907, 1921, 1929-34, 1947, 1954, 1974 and 1980-82 in the United States knows that during each crisis the presence of Mexican migrant workers was blamed for many of its symptoms—especially high unemployment. During these crises, the organized working class, particularly the American Federation of Labor (AFL) and later the AFL-CIO, firmly believed that Mexican immigration was an important cause of unemployment and demanded mass deportations and/or sealing of the border with Mexico. Such demands make a number of erroneous assumptions: (1) that Mexican immigration causes unemployment in the United States; (2) that with existing resources the border can be made impenetrable to undocumented migrants; and (3) that if the flow were to be seriously reduced, no dislocations in the U.S. economy, particularly in certain regions and industries, would result. The spurious causal linkage has proven politically effective when Mexican immigration has been ideologically identified as a cause outside of the system that need only be removed for the system to correct itself. In this way, undocumented immigrants have served as scapegoats for a U.S. capitalist system which has remained innocent of the charge of creating unemployment.

The alleged employment effect of undocumented migrants in the U.S. labor force were not the only factor contributing to massive deportations of Mexicans during these crises. Xenophobia and racist views also played an important role. As a consequence, Mexicans have been rejected as legitimate members of U.S. society. Such views were expressed by upstanding citizens like AFL president Samuel Gompers, who in the 1920s alleged that Mexicans had an inferior capacity to produce. These views were made socially acceptable by arguments such as those of Theodore Lothrop Stoddard, who in 1920 asserted that Mexicans were culturally inferior and undesirable immigrants because they were "born communist."[8] These nativist views, popular in the 1920s, are becoming fashionable again.[9]

Common to these economic crises is the contradiction between the ideological proposition that deportation drives should be undertaken or the border closed, and the economic interests of employers who benefit from the availability of Mexican migrant labor. During the administration of Jimmy Carter, this ideological position had currency in Washington. Secretary of Labor Ray Marshall proposed closing the border on the premise (typical of how some "liberals" reason) that by adopting repressive actions against undocumented Mexicans residing in the same communities as other persons of Mexican origin in the United States, they would be benefiting the disadvantaged Chicano workers presumably most seriously affected by the labor market competition of the undocumented worker. The dominant ideology once again shifted toward traditional anti-immigrant positions taken up by the AFL-CIO. The recently-arrived and more conservative administration in Washington has stated a variation of the same theme: deportations and anti-immigrant measures are justified on the basis that stopping the migration flow is what is best for the migrant and his or her family.[10]

In the Reagan Administration, policy debate on immigration has taken place mainly within the constituent groups of the

Republican Party. Employers seeking an open border for a regular provisioning of Mexican labor power oppose nativists who wish to close it. The former lobby for a guest-worker program which would increase the controlled flow of immigrant labor into specific U.S. industries and occupations. The latter use arguments that range from the paranoia expressed by ex-CIA director William Colby when he said in 1978 that Mexican immigration would represent in future years a greater threat to the United States than the Soviet Union, to the belief that Mexican immigration may result in a separatist movement within the Southwest of the type Canada has experienced with Quebec.[11]

Once again in the long history of Mexican migration to the United States, ideological interests enter into contradictions with specific economic interests. But this contradiction is ameliorated by all of capital's need for low-wage labor to extricate itself from crisis—and a convenient scapegoat for unemployment. Hence, the Simpson–Mazzoli bill, passed by the Senate and sent to the House in August, 1982, had a fair chance of becoming law. If implemented, it would have let in temporary Mexican workers in unprecedented numbers, while claiming to restrict illegal immigration.[12]

Mexico, as of 1981, did not have an articulated policy with respect to emigration to the United States. Some U.S. supporters of employer-backed proposals for an open border seek signs of Mexican backing in order to use it in the internal U.S. debate under the deliberately inflated guise of furthering bilateral relations, noting the high cost of ignoring a country so important as Mexico. These voices play up the notion of helping Mexico establish an escape valve for its surplus population.

U.S. policy formulation on undocumented migration issues involves a medley of factors, domestic and international. As already observed, Mexican migrant labor has proven highly functional for the U.S. system both economically and politically—migrants as an economic subsidy and a political scapegoat. In the international sphere, bilateral relations have frequently been affected by the issue. For example, the 1942–64 bracero program directly involved both governments. In the 1980s, a number of bilateral issues will impact on U.S. decisions about immigration: oil, trade, common market, North–South dialogue, etc. There is widespread speculation that the issue of the "undocumented" will enter (or has already entered behind the scenes) into the negotiations on these matters. For example, legal admission of more Mexican immigrants may, publicly or behind the scenes, end up as a factor linked to U.S. endeavors to obtain Mexican energy resources on more advantageous terms or to Mexican efforts to improve the terms of bilateral trade.

In mid-1981, Reagan announced his intention to resolve the question of Mexican migration by proposing legislation which would authorize the admission of Mexican workers with guest-worker cards. The proposed program, which with slight modification became represented by the Simpson-Mazzoli bill, offered no assurances of workers' rights for the migrants. Under the Reagan program, a migrant worker would be required to pay taxes and contribute to the social security system like any other worker but would not be permitted to receive social security benefits or obtain those services paid for by workers' taxes. In direct contradiction to one of the objectives of immigration law, which provides for the reunification of families where one or more members are outside the United States, the Mexican immigrant worker would not be allowed to bring his or her family until years after he became a permanent resident alien.

The legislation contemplated by Reagan would give amnesty for those undocumented workers who can show that they entered before January, 1980, are not otherwise excludable, and who would become temporary residents, with visas renewable every 3 years. Only after 10 years of continuous residence would he or she be allowed to apply for permanent residence. Few Mexican migrants would eventually qualify for permanent residence since they rarely stay for more than a year or so continuously. ("Amnesty" is a process by which criminals or political prisoners are pardoned by the state; it is inapplicable to workers—since when, under capitalism, is it a crime to sell one's labor power cheaply to an employer?) The Reagan proposal also called for an increased budget for the Border Patrol and fines on employers hiring "undocumented" workers.

There is considerable opposition to the Reagan proposals. The AFL-CIO perceives them as favorable to employers and contrary to the interests of U.S. workers. Every major Chicano rights group has come out against the Reagan plan for the so-called undocumented. Herman Baca, director of the Committee for Chicano Rights headquartered in San Diego, called it another bracero program equivalent to slavery which will "only lead to an increase in violence and to the creation of an apartheid-type system for Chicanos."[13] Reflecting on the proposal which has been cloaked as one promoting a good-neighbor relationship, some in Mexico have referred to it as one in which "we are the good and they are the neighbor."

To appreciate the strength of dissatisfaction of Chicano groups with the proposed program, one must recall that their existence is historically rooted in struggles quite similar to those of the migrant workers from whom many Chicanos are descended. While Chicanos no longer have as much in common with the migrants as they once did, they nonetheless are subject to INS stop-and-search raids at their workplaces, in their cars, on buses, or on the sidewalks of U.S. cities. For the authorities, the Ku Klux Klan, and many racists, all Mexicans are alike. What happens to Mexican migrants affects Chicanos as well as all U.S. citizens of Latin American descent, a fact which partially explains why such groups oppose employer sanctions and increased deportations. Under President Carter's human rights rhetoric and immigration proposals (e.g., deportation drives, employer sanctions, and the tortilla curtain of spiked steel wire fencing many feet high partially completed along the U.S.-Mexican border) as well as President Reagan's quite similar get-tough policy masked by talk of amnesty, millions of the Spanish-speaking have faced the prospect of mass arrest or deportation and the daily terror of uncertain status (confusion or lack of information about necessary documents, etc.). Paramilitary units of the Ku Klux Klan periodically roam the border, and the INS in early 1981, and again in 1982, stepped up the pace of factory round-ups.

A little publicized cause of both Carter's and Reagan's policies is the growing organizing activity, including incipient unionization and strikes, among the undocumented workers themselves. In response to the Reagan plan, many of their organizations decided to unite into the National Coordinating Council of Mexican Workers in the United States. In Maricopa County, Arizona, Mexican farmworkers recently established a militant labor union which, for the moment at least, broke more than a century of super-exploitation of thousands of fieldhands who previously had no recourse. In urban areas like Los Angeles–San Diego, undocumented Mexican workers have begun forming unions in the garment and electronics industries and held successful strikes. The garment workers' union (ILGWU), faced with falling national membership, has begun to welcome the undocumented into its ranks. Parts of the AFL-CIO, also facing declining membership, have also shown support for the undocumented even though the organization as a whole favors restricting Mexican immigration.

In recent years, rank-and-file union members in both countries have carried on a struggle to democratize their unions and resist social welfare cutbacks, decline in real wages, and other hardships imposed because of economic crisis. This, together with growing signs of support for the undocumented appearing among Mexican and some U.S. unions, caused some capitalists of both nations to be concerned about what the future may hold. Potential international workers' unity is a threat which capitalists seek to avoid at all costs.

Among its many goals, the Reagan guest-worker proposal aims to nip in the bud this nascent unionization and militancy among Mexican migrant workers. It further aims to regulate and control the flow of cheap labor for the benefit of employers. The unpredictability of the migratory flow, its relatively unorganized character, and its potential for social unrest in the U.S. society cause the state, as arbiter of capitalist interests, to seek a regularization and disciplining of immigration to make migrant labor more manageable and reliable. Finally, the Reagan proposal serves to further divide the multinational U.S. working class along lines of racism, jingoism, and ethnocentrism at the expense of all Latinos and all workers residing in the United States. It does this by singling out Mexican workers as scapegoats and by stimulating controversy among various organized groups.

If implemented, the Reagan "guest-worker" program will attract to U.S. consulates in Mexico, or wherever contracts are offered, tens of thousands of job-seekers, each of them demanding an increase in guest-worker quotas. Those who do not find a place within the quota will go anyway (without legal entry permits) and end up competing for the same jobs for which the guest workers have been contracted. Employers of all workers in states like California and Texas will likely use the legal presence of cheap

Mexican labor as an excuse (and scapegoat) for holding all workers' wages down. Chicanos will protest the Mexican government's tolerating the program, creating a strong division between Chicanos and Mexicans. The pan-Mexican working-class unity for better treatment of all workers on both sides of the border, an idea with a century-long history, will thereby suffer another setback. Specific capitalist interests in agribusiness, industry, and services will rejoice. But the final form of the program's various components and its eventual implementation will continue to be a focus of political struggle and controversy, suggesting that once again, the undocumented—and racism—will not go away as a major issue in U.S.-Mexican relations and U.S. politics for years to come.

Notes

1. This is a revised and expanded version of an article titled "México-EU: La frontera invisible," which appeared in *Nexos*, no. 42 (June, 1981), pp. 3-7. Much of the theoretical elaboration is drawn from James D. Cockcroft, *Mexico: Class Formation, Capital Accumulation and the State* (New York: Monthly Review Press, 1982) and "Mexican Migration, Crisis and the Internationalization of Labor Struggle," *Contemporary Marxism*, no. 5 (August, 1982).

2. Since 1978, the pace of U.S. new direct investments in Mexico has doubled every year. See Banco de México, annual reports.

3. Karl Marx, *Capital* (New York: International Publishers, 1967), vol. I, chapter 25, pp. 630-645.

4. In the short run, heightened use of inexpensive labor power combats the tendency of the rate of profit to fall. This tendency, inherent to the capitalist mode of production, derives from the growth in the organic composition of capital, or the ratio of constant capital—instruments and raw materials of production—to variable capital (labor power, the only source of surplus value). Although modified by monopolies' ability to control prices, the tendency of the rate of profit to fall is one component of the occurrence of periodic crises in capitalist accumulation. For elaboration on this tendency and the character of capitalist crisis, consult Manuel Castells, *The Economic Crisis and American Society* (Princeton, N.J.: Princeton University Press, 1980), along with various issues of *Monthly Review*.

5. The theoretical formulation for this has been developed by a number of authors, including Claude Meillassoux, who notes that capitalists prefer migrant workers, especially temporary migrants, since their subsistence cost is lower and they can be paid less. The lower the cost of subsistence, the lower the wage rate and the higher the capitalist profit. Under these conditions the capitalist appropriates not only a surplus value but a labor rent, resulting in super-exploitation of the workers. See Claude Meillassoux, *Mujeres, graneros y capitales* (México: Siglo Veintiuno, 1977), pp. 160-161.

6. See, for example, Harry Braverman, *Labor and Monopoly Capital* (New York: Monthly Review Press, 1974).

7. Cf., Manual García y Griego and Leobardo F. Estrada, "Research on the Magnitude of Mexican Undocumented Immigration to the U.S.: A Summary," in Antonio Ríos-Bustamante (ed.), *Mexican Immigrant Workers in the U.S.* (Los Angeles: UCLA Chicano Studies Research Center, 1981), pp. 51-70.

8. Theodore Lothrop Stoddard, *The Rising Tide of Labor Against White World-Supremacy* (New York: C. Scribner's Sons, 1920), pp. 107-108. Fashionable in the 1920s and 1930s, these racist arguments were backed by many books and articles, such as "Immigration from Mexico," by C. M. Goethe, in Madison Grant and Charles S. Davidson (eds.), *The Alien in Our Midst; or, "Selling Our Birthright for a Mess of Pottage"* (New York: The Galton Publishing Co., Inc., 1930). Championing white supremacy, the article claims to demonstrate "scientifically" that Mexicans are racially inferior.

9. See the chapter by Wayne Cornelius included in this volume.

10. For example, a fact sheet on immigration and refugee policy issued by the Department of Justice and released by the White House, 30 July 1981, p. 2, cites the President's statement: "Immigrants who enter the United States illegally are creating problems for themselves, as well as for the country."

11. The chairman of the U.S. Senate Subcommittee on Immigration, Alan K. Simpson, has publicly proclaimed himself to be a restrictionist.

12. See James Cockcroft, "Immigration Bill Threatens All Workers," *Guardian* 13 October 1982.

13. Herman Baca, various press conferences, and interview reprinted in Committee on Chicano Rights, *A Chicano Perspective on the President's Immigration Proposals* (San Diego, 1981).

12
Labor Market Projections for the United States and Mexico and Their Relevance to Current Migration Controversies

Clark W. Reynolds

The purpose of this essay is to reassess the relations between the United States and Mexico by demonstrating current and future economic interdependence, particularly in the exchange of labor. The supply of labor in the United States is projected on the basis of current demographic data, and the demand for labor necessary to meet planned or projected levels of output in selected years is then calculated. The results of comparing the supply and demand for labor in the two countries are of course sensitive to the particular parameters used, especially considering the wide range of current predictions concerning sustainable rates of growth of output and productivity in both countries. In general, it appears that employment generation in post-petroleum Mexico may be just able to keep pace with its rapidly rising labor force. But only a sustained rate of growth of output in excess of 7 percent per annum will permit Mexico to soak up its large pool of unemployed and underemployed workers.

The author is a professor at the Food Research Institute, Stanford University. He is the author of *The Mexican Economy: Twentieth Century Structure and Growth*, and (with Carlos Tello) *Las relaciones de México-Estados Unidos*. The author wishes to acknowledge the valuable assistance of Robert K. McCleery in the preparation of this monograph and underlying research material. Assistance was also received from Don H. Bovee, especially in the international trade projections appendices, and Nguyuru H. Lipumba. This article first appeared in *Food Research Institute Studies*, vol. XVII, no. 2, 1979.
©1979 by the Board of the Leland Stanford Junior University.

The United States is faced with the opposite problem. Regardless of the short run effect of the 1979–80 recession, an eventual shortfall of labor of some five million workers is likely by the year 2000, even given current levels of immigration and the maintenance of a substantial pool of undocumented aliens in this country. A curtailment of immigration combined with the Bureau of Labor Statistics low projection could result in aggregate shortfalls of 18 to 33 million workers within the period of this study. In short, even ignoring Mexico's oil reserves and the United States hunger for energy, it seems that the two countries share more than a border and are destined to move toward closer ties which may be mutually advantageous.

BACKGROUND

The major North American states—Mexico, Canada, and the United States—are drawing closer together through the exchange of labor, commodity trade, capital flows, and technology transfers even as their governments attempt to strengthen national autonomy and security in an increasingly multipolar world. The relative growth of Mexico and Canada in output and production has outstripped that of the United States in recent years. In 1960 Mexico and Canada had a combined gross national product one-tenth that of the United States. In 1976 their joint output was 14 percent of United States production, and by 2000 it is expected to total one-fourth. The combined population of Canada and Mexico amounted to 29 percent of the United States population in 1960 and 40 percent in 1976; by the year 2000 it will be 50 percent. These figures suggest that the North American region is likely to show an increasingly balanced distribution of output and population among its three major partners in the years to come.

However, it is by no means clear that the internal distribution of income will be more nearly equal in labor-abundant Mexico in the face of her burgeoning population and work force without a major effort at job creation and the export of a significant fraction of the labor force. In the United States the demographic imbalance caused by the baby boom is inspiring dire predictions of social upheavals, failure of the social security system, and other major structural changes early in the next century. Without substantial immigration, there will simply not be enough productive labor, given the declining rates of investment and productivity growth, to sustain the living levels of those outside the work force, not to mention those with redundant skills who remain "structurally unemployed." Hence, growth and distribution in the two countries will depend on mutual interaction in all major economic dimensions. Notwithstanding the desire of each of the North American economies for maximum self-determination, they are destined to be bound together even more by strong connections in resource endowments, product mix, and demographic structure.

Trade in goods and services between the two countries is still highly asymmetrical, with about 67 percent of Mexico's exports directed to the United States markets, while only 4 percent of United States exports go to Mexico. However, the discovery of substantial new petroleum reserves will permit continued rapid growth of oil exports. Energy exports are already affecting the level and balance of trade with the United States. The traditional current account surplus in favor of the United States is falling sharply and will almost certainly shift to a deficit during the next two decades, unless Mexican import restrictions are substantially liberalized. The current account balance will also be affected by trends in exogenous international capital flows. Mexico is already the second largest borrower of financial capital in the Third World (after Brazil). By the mid-1980s Mexico will have the option of using its expanded petroleum rents either to reduce debt exposure or to spur imports for domestic growth. Foreign direct investment could also increase significantly in the years ahead. Whatever the trend in net capital flows and implications for the trade balance, Mexico's share of the United States imports is certain to rise, while the share of United States exports should increase as well in response to the rapid expansion of Mexican purchasing power.

The Mexican contribution to the United States work force comprises two major flows made up of those who migrate permanently (legal and undocumented) and those who migrate temporarily. Mexican migrants form a rotating pool of labor only part of which adds to the annual stock of workers as measured in decennial population censuses. In table 1 estimates of these components are presented in terms of their evolution from 1940 to 1975. While the undocumented component is highly conjectural, the

TABLE 1.—MEXICAN CONTRIBUTIONS TO THE U.S. LABOR POOL FOR SELECTED YEARS*
(Thousand workers)

	1940	1950	1960	1970	1975
(1) Mexican labor force	5,858	8,345	10,213	12,955	15,400 est.
(2) Legal and undocumented temporary migrant workers (per year)	300	500	500	600	900
(3) Cumulative stock of permanent undocumented workers (beginning in 1940)	—	500	1,000	1,550	1,925
(4) Cumulative stock of legal immigrant workers (beginning in 1940)	—	30	210	470	650
(5) Total Mexican workers in U.S. labor pool[a]	300	1,030	1,710	2,620	3,475
(6) Mexicans working in U.S.: as share of Mexican work force (5) + (1) = (6)	5.1	12.3	16.7	20.2	22.6

*Mexican labor force totals for 1940, 1950, and 1970 are from the census data on economically active population age 12 and over (including unemployed). The 1960 census figure was adjusted to correct for overcounting of rural workers (for details see Clark W. Reynolds, 1979, "A Shift-Share Analysis of Regional and Sectoral Productivity Growth in Contemporary Mexico," working paper, International Institute for Applied Systems Analysis, Laxenburg, Austria). A detailed discussion of Mexican labor force and employment data is in Donald Keesing (1977), "Employment in Mexico, 1900–70," in J. W. Wilke and K. Ruddle, *Quantitative Latin American Studies*, UCLA Latin American Center, Los Angeles; his adjusted labor force total for 1950 is 8,272 and for 1960 is 9,691. For 1940 and 1970 they are the same as the census figures. The estimates in Row (2) are based on the number of legal temporary workers (including braceros from 1942 to 1964) plus an estimate of undocumented workers during the previous five-year period (double the number of illegals deported reduced by one-fourth for non-participants in the work force). The figure is reduced by 20 percent more in 1975 to provide the most conservative possible estimate, in view of the speculative nature of the methodology used. Row (3) is based on the assumption that 10 percent of the seasonal migrants in Row (2) elect to remain in the United States each year. Row (4) represents the net cumulative legal migration of workers assuming that legal migrants from Mexico have a .65 labor force participation rate and a 5 percent attrition rate.

Figures on legal and undocumented migration and labor participation rates are from F. Ray Marshall (1978), "Mexican Migration of Workers," in S.R. Ross, ed., *Views Across the Border: The United States and Mexico* (University of New Mexico Press, Albuquerque); Domestic Council Committee on Illegal Aliens (1976), Preliminary Report, Washington D.C.; and Wayne Cornelius (1978), "Mexican Migration to the United States (with Comparative Reference to Caribbean-Basin Migration): The State of Current Knowledge and Recommendations for Future Research," Working Paper No. 2, Center for U.S.-Mexican Studies, University of California, San Diego. The figures in the table represent estimated numbers of workers who will participate in the U.S. labor market at some time during the year cited, either as temporary or permanent additions to the stock of manpower and do not represent man-years of labor. Hence Row (2) includes workers who might have been employed in Mexico as well as in the U.S. during that year, since the average period of employment of temporary Mexican workers in the U.S. is from three to six months. Jorge Bustamante (1978), "National Survey on Outmigration in Mexico: Description and Preliminary Findings," paper presented at the Symposium on Structural Factors Contributing to Current Patterns of Migration in Mexico and the Caribbean Basin, El Colegio de México, Mexico City; Jorge Bustamante and Roberto Chande (1979), "Análisis estadístico de las expulsiones de indocumentados mexicanos," El Colegio de México, Mexico City; and Wayne A. Cornelius (1978).

a"Mexicans" in the United States refers to all legal and illegal immigrants from Mexico who entered this country between 1940 and the present and their progeny, regardless of place of birth. This is clearly not the same as "people of Mexican origin" as detailed in a recent *Current Population Survey*. The magnitude of the difference (about one and one-half million people) can be explained as being all legal and illegal immigrants and their descendants who came before 1940. It is assumed, unrealistically perhaps, that most of the illegals are counted in this survey. Otherwise the gap would be greater.

TABLE 2.—TRENDS AND PROJECTIONS OF UNITED STATES AND MEXICAN OUTPUT AND POPULATION, 1950 TO 2000*

Year	Gross national product (million 1977 dollars)		Population (millions)		GNP per capita (1977 dollars)		Ratio of GNP per capita
	U.S.	Mexico	U.S.	Mexico	U.S.	Mexico	
1950	756	15	152	26	4,984	586	8.5
1960	1,043	27	181	35	5,776	780	7.4
1970	1,522	54	205	49	7,430	1,095	6.8
1977	1,887	74	217	63	8,701	1,180	7.4
1985	2,399	120	235	79	10,209	1,519	6.7
1990	2,787	161	247	89	11,283	1,809	6.2
2000	3,762	294	273	109	13,780	2,697	5.1

*U.S. compound output growth rate for 1977 to 2000 at 3 percent per annum, Mexican output growth rate of 6 percent p.a.; U.S. population growth projected at 1 percent p.a. including migration 1977–2000 (see below); Mexican population growth assumed to decelerate, reflecting the second phase of the demographic transition from 2.8 percent p.a. 1977–85; to 2.5 percent p.a. 1985–90; and 2.0 percent p.a. 1990–2000. Note that the U.S. population projections above assume that there will be sufficient net immigration to permit a sustained 1 percent compound annual rate of growth. With no net immigration, the U.S. Bureau of the Census projects the following levels of U.S. population: (in thousands) 1985, 228,912; 1990, 237,028; 2000, 248,372 (this series reaches zero growth around the middle of the twenty-first century), U.S. Bureau of Census, *Current Population Reports*, series P-25, cited in U.S. Department of Commerce (1978), *Statistical Abstract of the U.S.*, Washington, D.C., pp. 8f. The U.S. population projections in the table imply a cumulative net immigration from 1978–85 of 6 million; from 1975 to 1990 of 10 million; and from 1978 to 2000 of 25 million, or 1.5 million people per year in the last decade of the century (more than twice the current flow).

figures reflect the best available estimates of the permanent and rotating components of the labor pool, reconciled with the census data from each country.

The two countries have the greatest interdependence in the area of employment. Since 1940 an estimated two and a half million Mexicans joined the United States work force as permanent residents, while it may be conservatively estimated that at least one million more are in the labor pool each year as temporary migrants (table 1). By 1975 at least three and a half million workers from Mexico had joined the United States job market, not counting those born of Mexican parents. The pool is growing by about 170,000 per year, while the annual growth of the total United States work force is 1.7 million. Hence at least 10 percent of the growth in supply of American labor is represented by Mexican migrants. This number equaled 30 percent of net growth in the Mexican labor force by the mid-1970s, while the pool of Mexicans in the United States (accumulated since 1940) amounted to one-fifth of the economically active population of Mexico in 1975 (table 1). Temporary migrant workers alone represented 5.8 percent of the Mexican labor force in that year. It is evident that Mexican workers play a far greater role in the United States economy than does United States–Mexican trade, direct investment, or financial transactions.

TRENDS IN OUTPUT AND POPULATION GROWTH IN MEXICO AND THE UNITED STATES

Since 1950 the rate of growth of Mexican gross national product (GNP) has been almost double that of the United States. From 1950 to 1970 this was enough to more than compensate for Mexico's accelerating rate of population growth, so that even though United States per capita income grew, the gap between the two countries fell from 8.5 to 1 in 1950 to 6.8 to 1 in 1970 (table 2). In the 1970s the picture began to change. Mexico's demographic explosion had begun to eat up most of the output growth, and by 1977 the income gap widened 7.4 to 1. Slower growth and widening per capita income gaps between the United States and Mexico might well elicit a migratory response northward. Table 1 shows that the Mexican migration substantially increased in the 1970s to make the present pool of Mexican labor in the United States by far the largest in history. However, Mexico's recent petroleum discoveries could generate the savings needed to accelerate the growth of production, while family planning measures introduced by the government in the early 1970s should slow population growth. Government sources suggest a lowering of annual rates of population growth from 35 per thousand in the 1960s to 29 in the mid-1970s with the downtrend expected to continue.[1]

Table 2 assumes that these factors of output growth and fertility decline must combine to reverse the disequilibrating trends of the early 1970s and permit Mexico again to outstrip the United States in rates of growth of per capita output. Mexico is hoping that its GNP will grow at 7 to 7.5 percent annually between now and the end of the century. Assuming a 6 percent compound rate of GNP growth and 2.8 percent population growth rate, one may project that the Mexico-United States per capita income gap would recover its 1970 ratio by 1985. That is partly because the United States output is projected to grow at only 3 percent annually, though its population growth will remain at no more than one percent. Later in the essay it will be shown that short of a totally implausible productivity miracle the United States will not be able to sustain even a modest 3 percent rate of output growth assumed in table 2 without a substantial immigration of labor. Even the most optimistic growth of Mexico's GNP at rates well beyond the 6 percent annually shown in table 2 will be unable to absorb the tidal wave of demographic growth of earlier years between now and 2000. If there is no outlet for Mexico's impoverished workers, attempts to support them by make-work projects or income transfers will eat up the scarce savings needed for investment. Associated social and political pressures will tend to discourage private investment. If the gap between rich and poor across the border and over the fences of the *barrios* of Mexico are allowed to magnify, they could lead to domestic and international security problems that no rate of growth would resolve.

PROJECTIONS OF THE SUPPLY OF LABOR IN MEXICO

The labor supply in Mexico during the next 20 years depends upon three main factors: past demographic trends, desired participation rates of men and women of working age, and the expectations of gainful employment. Other factors which bring about changes in desired labor force participation are future fertility rate declines and the changing role of women in Mexico. Summarized here are some of the most important findings of research on determinants of Mexican labor. They are pieced together into a framework consistent with the projections of output, population, and exchange between the United States and Mexico.

The growth of the Mexican labor force between 1970 and 2000, based on two sets of estimates for those of working age (A and C) and alternative assumptions about labor force participation, are given in table 3. These projections are assumptions about future demographic trends, since most of those who will be in the age group 15 to 64 between now and the end of the century have already been born. The economically active population is expected to double between 1980 and 2000. The number of job seekers will increase by 20 million, with a relatively rapid growth of women and with an overall 3.5 percent compound annual rate of growth of labor supply. Depending upon the overall demographic projection used, the gross labor participation rate will rise from 26 percent in 1970 to 30 percent (high population estimate) or 38 percent (low population estimate).

Even if education improves markedly in Mexico during the coming decades, the majority of workers will have little more than a basic primary school education, and any improvement in educational skills or training will have to be through adult classes, on-the-job training, and home study (Urquidi, 1974). The labor supply will be heavily weighted by those qualified only for "unskilled" occupations at least into the 1990s. This will exacerbate whatever excess supply conditions are suggested by the aggregate projections, as structural employment problems will almost certainly worsen.

Lower demographic growth rates mean a possible increase in labor force participation by women, so that the slowdown population growth will have the paradoxical effect of increasing labor supply between 1980 and 2000. As a consequence the need to find means of absorbing that labor will increase rather than decrease as the demographic transition moves into its decelerating phase.

PROJECTIONS OF THE DEMAND FOR LABOR IN MEXICO

Will a doubling of the supply of labor in the next 20 years be matched by new jobs? In the past Mexico has had one of the

TABLE 3.—PROJECTIONS OF MEXICAN LABOR SUPPLY, 1970–2000*

Year	Total population estimate (millions)			Population, ages 15–64 (millions)			Economically active population (millions)			Labor participation rate (percent)					
										Active pop. ÷ pop. ages 15–64			Active pop. ÷ total population		
	A	B	C	A	B	C	A	B	C	A	B	C	A	B	C
1970		50			25.5			13.0			51.0			25.8	
1980[a]	70	70	72	36.3		36.3	20.4		20.4	56.2		56.2	29.1		27.8
1985	79	81		42		42.6	24			57					
1990	89		100	50		52.2	29		28–30	58		54–58			28–30
2000	109	123	135	68	70.3	74.0	41		40	60		54	38		30

*Estimate A is based on the assumption of a rapidly declining population growth rate reaching 2.0 by 1990–2000 (see notes to table 2). For the economically active population, Estimate A assumes a rising participation rate for the age group 15 to 64, based primarily on growing female participation and anticipating that Mexico will become more comparable to other developing countries. Its female labor force participation ratio is relatively low by international standards (Peter Gregory, 1976, "Employment and Unemployment in Developing Countries," World Bank, Washington, D.C.).

Estimate B is the low fertility projection III of Francisco Alba (1977), *La población de México: evolución y dilemas*, El Colegio de México, Mexico City, which reduces fertility more gradually achieving a population growth rate of 2.03 for 1995–2000.

Estimate C is based on the projection of Victor Urquidi (1974), "Empleo y explosión demográfica," *Demografía y Economía*, vol. VII, no. 20, which is slightly higher than Alba's moderate fertility decline based on a population growth rate of 2.4 percent in 1995–2000 leading to a population of 135 million by the year 2000.

[a] Estimated.

lowest sustained rates of open unemployment in the developing world (Gregory, 1976; Keesing, 1977), despite very wide fluctuations in the level of economic activity and in demand for labor in the more productive high-wage occupations. Rather than becoming involuntarily unemployed in slack periods, Mexican workers have tended to voluntarily withdraw from the labor market, to find low-income self-employment in the informal sector, or to remain idle for large portions of the year. For example, between 1940 and 1950 female labor participation rates doubled as jobs became more plentiful, but then fell again between 1960 and 1970 as the labor market weakened (Keesing, 1977). In the 1960s the growth of self-employment in urban services was substantial, as modern sectors failed to provide enough jobs for migrants from agriculture (McFarland, 1973, as cited by Gregory, 1976). By the mid-1970s labor migration appears to have accelerated in the face of a severe domestic recession.

Since the labor supply in Mexico tends to shift with subsistence level demand, the labor slack shows itself less in terms of open unemployment than in other indicators:

1. lagging or declining earnings of unskilled labor;
2. falling female participation rates;
3. increased seasonal unemployment and underemployment;
4. increased self-employment (especially in the urban informal sector);
5. slowed emigration from the rural to urban areas within Mexico; and
6. increased pressures for migration to the United States.

By the late 1960s the Mexican economy began to face serious obstacles to continued rapid growth in output, productivity, and employment. The "Mexican miracle" heralded during the postwar period was running out of time. Its much vaunted agricultural productivity growth plummeted in the face of land and water constraints, even though demand for agricultural products continued to grow. The postwar "import-substituting" industries, which achieved important gains during previous decades, began to show the effects of serving a limited domestic market behind quantitative and tariff barriers that permitted high prices and low quality relative to more vigorous export-oriented manufacturing industries abroad. By the early 1970s output growth and employment had decelerated sharply even though capital formation continued

TABLE 4.—OUTPUT AND EMPLOYMENT GROWTH IN MEXICO, 1978–83, AND NET INVESTMENT REQUIREMENTS*

	1977	1978	1979	1980	1981	1982	1983	Compounded annual rate of growth (percent) 1977–83
Gross domestic product (billion 1977 dollars)	74	79	84	91	98	105	110	6.61
Net investment (billion 1977 dollars)		8.7	10.4	11.9	13.4	15.1	15.5	
Employment (thousand employees)	17,057	17,687	18,316	19,012	19,730	20,522	21,241	3.66
Increase in employment (thousand employees)		630	629	696	718	792	719	
Incremental capital/labor ratio (net investment per additional job in 1977 dollars)		13,800	16,500	17,000	18,700	19,100	21,500	
Capital/labor ratio (capital per job in 1977 dollars)		6,900	7,090	7,370	7,670	8,030	8,770	
Incremental capital/output ratio (net investment ÷ change in GDP) (percent)		1.84	1.80	1.99	1.84	2.05	3.16	

*Data are from the DIEMEX/Wharton Mexican econometric model, Wharton Econometric Forecasting Associates (1979), "DIEMEX/Wharton: Mexican Econometric Model Pre-Meeting Solutions," Philadelphia, Pennsylvania, with values in billion 1960 pesos converted to 1977 U.S. dollars at a rate of one 1960 peso = $.181 U.S. dollar of 1977 purchasing power.

to expand. Productivity growth had fallen to a fraction of its earlier levels. Hence by mid-decade the Mexican economy appeared to be in serious trouble and was no longer able to absorb more than a fraction of its rapidly increasing work force (Reynolds, 1979).

Some of the causes of the malaise were policy-induced, including an overvalued exchange rate that hurt exports and favored unproductive imports, increasing conflict between government and the private sector during the period from 1970 to 1976, the expectation of agrarian reform, new laws restricting foreign direct investment, and foreign borrowing by the Mexican government. A jolting peso devaluation in 1976 created a major squeeze on corporate working capital and triggered a flight of short-term funds that drained foreign exchange reserves and stopped the economy cold (Reynolds, 1978; Tello, 1979; Villar, 1979). But harmful as these policy measures were, there were more important underlying problems associated with an increasingly inward-looking character of the economy that neglected the foreign market, serious inequalities in the distribution of income and wealth, increasing urbanizaton, and the spread of slums. The latter conditions created social unrest and political uncertainty that dampened expectations of potential domestic and foreign investors. The failure of potential leaders in the private sector to respond with courage and imagination to the immense problems of poverty and underemployment worsened the condition.

Given this background, Mexico's announcement of the discovery of major petroleum and natural gas reserves during the early days of the López Portillo administration was greeted with understandable skepticism. As these announcements were gradually confirmed, expectations shifted from doubt to euphoria, and the predictions of Mexico's petroleum-led growth potential skyrocketed. A team from the World Bank provided a set of output forecasts assuming a sustained GNP rate of growth of 7 percent for Mexico through the year 2000 (World Bank, 1978, table 40, p. 106). The Wharton moderate projection model suggests a more modest 6.6 percent rate of output growth for the period 1977 to 1983 (table 4), and most of the projections in this paper assume a 6 percent rate of growth of gross domestic product through 2000 (table 2). Sustained growth at 6 percent per annum implies a doubling of output every 12 years, and will require an enormous expansion in the capital stock, infrastructure, skilled labor, and managerial pool. This will in turn require a major expansion in imports of goods and skilled labor services creating strong pressures for an opening of the Mexican economy to increased foreign trade and investment. While it will be difficult to turn outward the inward-looking orientation of Mexican planners, policy makers, and private entrepreneurs, the growth projections carry with them a relentless logic to do so.

Assuming that a 6 percent sustained growth rate may be achievable through the year 2000, what will be the consequences for Mexico's absorption of its work force and for wages of the lowest income groups? There are far more serious problems, and failure to find adequate answers will generate social pressures and political conflict that could prevent realization of Mexico's new development dream.

A major difficulty in assessing the impact on employment of alternative growth and investment strategies is the lack of hard information about the current structure of labor supply and demand, and its change under alternative development strategies. The most recent input-output study of Mexico for the year 1970 (Mexico, SPP, 1979), an excellent tool of sectoral planning, will require a complementary matrix of labor inputs by skill and occupational category if it is used to project labor demand. Nor is there any manpower-planning framework which would permit linking Mexico's ambitious new industrial production plan (Mexico, SPFI, 1979) with projections of labor supply in order to determine the outlook for workers at all skill levels. This is needed to project additional education and training requirements in order to determine the immigration of skilled workers and managers that will be needed in the coming years. Not only are the employment implications of the industrial development plan unclear; the present administration has no agricultural development plan capable of providing rural employment projections nor does one appear to be forthcoming.

Given the shortage of reliable information relating output to employment and productivity in even the basic sectors of the Mexican economy, and in view of the shaky nature of production forecasts, one cannot expect to generate very robust labor demand projections. As a second best approach, a relatively crude employment forecast has been devised based on past trends in labor output ratios and expected rates of productivity growth.

In table 4 the DIEMEX/Wharton projections of output and employment through 1983 are used as reasonable indicators of growth. They rest on the following moderate assumptions about border openings for productive imports starting in 1980: achievement of readily realizable crude oil export targets rising from 375,000 barrels per day in 1977 to 1,105,000 in 1983, and expected gas exports of 1 billion cubic feet per day beginning in 1980 rising to 2 billion in 1983. The model's projections of petroleum export revenues need to be revised upward, however, given the recently announced price of $22.60 per barrel for Mexican crude, as the model projects the price to reach only $18.45 by 1983. The projected natural gas price in the model, $2.81 per thousand cubic feet in 1980, rises to $3.41 in 1983, and that figure is also subject to upward revision assuming that an export agreement will be reached with the United States. The model's exchange rate is semi-fixed, rather optimistically projecting the rate of inflation to decline from 32 percent in 1977 to 11 percent in 1983. This is unlikely given the liquidity-increasing effect of increased petroleum export revenues, government deficits, sustained foreign borrowing, and imported inflation.

The model projects output to grow at 6.6 percent annually through 1983, somewhat above the more conservative estimate of 6 percent for the period 1977-85 used in this paper (table 2), and below World Bank projections of 8 percent per annum for the period 1980-82 (World Bank, 1978). The United States State Department shows even more optimism projecting a real rate of growth in Mexican GNP of 8 percent or more throughout the 1980s (U.S. Foreign Service, 1979). Hence there may be some reason to expect Mexican employment growth to exceed the rate of 3.66 percent per annum projected in table 4. The investment requirements for growth would rise accordingly, in terms of Mexico's present strategy which is to favor the creation of the third stage of import-substituting industry for the production of capital goods, even as it intends to reduce the effective protection of consumer and intermediate goods imports.

Table 4 indicates that additional jobs could be created with net investments of $7,000 per job, based on past trends in factor utilization and a gradual rise in the capital-output ratio. The substantial difference between this figure and the marginal capital output ratio of $16,500 stems from the nature of Mexico's development plans. Most new investment takes place in industries like petroleum and heavy manufacturing with high capital-labor ratios. The ratio of output to worker is higher in these industries, causing per capita output of the *employed* labor force to rise relative to other development strategy results, although alternative effects on per capita income are ambiguous.

It is conceivable that a majority shift in the pattern of production and technology toward more labor-using and capital-saving activities would substantially raise the demand for labor per unit of output. This is by no means clear in fact. The government's present development plans focus on capital formation for growth of heavy industry, producer gods manufacturing, and the creation of infrastructure for the regional decentralization of industry, all of which are likely to increase rather than decrease capital-labor ratios.

There is evidence that a moderate growth in the petroleum and gas-based expansion of the economy will permit the demand for labor to just about keep up with growth in its supply. On the basis of estimates in table 4, if output were to grow by 6.6 percent annually until 2000, employment would rise by the same amount as labor supply, or 20 million jobs (table 3). However, all segments of the market would not be expected to grow proportionately, and it is almost certain that simply equating overall supply and demand would not correct structural imbalances, as low-skilled workers would remain underemployed. Pay differentials would continue to widen between workers with different educational levels and access to high productivity employment. To raise real wages of the poorest workers given the current 20 to 30 percent rate of underutilization of Mexican manpower in 1975, another 4 to 6 million jobs would have to be created by the year 2000. With an employment elasticity of output of .55, this would require a sustained real rate of growth of GNP of 7 percent, between now and the year 2000, and the present pool of one to three million Mexicans working abroad would have to be maintained.

TIGHTNESS IN THE LABOR MARKET, RELATIVE WAGES, AND PRICES AND INCOME SHARES

General tightness or slackness in labor markets have the most dramatic effect on the earnings of low-skilled workers like those in agriculture and personal services. When markets are tight, workers in those sectors are attracted into higher wage industrial employment and into modern commerce and service activities. The employers of lower wage labor (for example, barbers, restaurant owners and farmers) are forced to offer higher wages as well. This may induce them to invest in productivity-increasing machinery, mechanized food operations, and mechanical harvesters. The price of the goods or services produced in these sectors will also rise giving the illusion of productivity growth. Thus in economies with tight labor markets, like that of the United States in 1979, the benefits from productivity growth in leading economic sectors spread to the mass of workers. But in economies with slack labor markets, workers in low-wage occupations are unable to participate significantly in rapid productivity growth because of the large number of potential competitors for their jobs. Where there are barriers to entry, such as unionization, the jobs themselves may be seen as "capital goods" with access to them bought and sold. In Mexico this is common for jobs that pay more than a pittance, and even union officials are involved in their sale. When industries raise wages beyond the going rate, long queues of workers form outside the gates waiting for a chance at the lottery.

It is necessary to distinguish between the fact of low wages in Mexico and the alleged "low productivity" of its labor. In fact, Mexican workers may perform precisely the same task as their North American counterparts, with equal or greater skill, yet receive one-eighth to one-tenth of the U.S. wage for the same job (Reynolds, 1979; Keesing, 1977). Barbers in Mexico earn 50 cents for a haircut that would cost $5.00 north of the border. Cooks, waiters, and maids may receive $60 a month for their services in Mexico, while they could earn $600 in the United States. The price of their final product tends to be lower as well, so that such labor-intensive goods and services in Mexico cost a fraction of their United States price, *relative* to the cost of manufactured goods whose prices are set by international market conditions (plus import protection). It is not surprising that the labor share of national income in Mexico is a fraction of that of the United States share (50–60 percent rather than 80 percent), while the return to land, capital, and other assets is more than double the United States figure (40–50 percent rather than 20 percent). Moreover, skilled workers, managers, and university-educated people

TABLE 5.—LONG TERM PROJECTIONS OF DEMAND FOR LABOR IN MEXICO, 1980 TO 2000*
(Million workers employed)

	1980	1985	1990	2000 (1)	Projected labor force 2000 (2)	Projected employment gap 2000 (3) = (2) − (1)
GNP growth rate of 4 percent compounded annually	19.0	21.2	23.7	29.5	40–41	10.5–11.5
GNP growth rate of 6 percent	19.0	22.4	26.4	36.7	40–41	3.3–4.3
GNP growth rate of 6.6 percent	19.0	22.9	27.5	39.8	40–41	0.2–1.2
GNP growth rate of 7 percent	19.0	23.1	28.1	41.5	40–41	−1.5 – −0.5

*Million workers employed is calculated based on an estimated output elasticity of labor demand of .554 (table 4) from DIEMEX/Wharton model applied to projected rates of output growth (Wharton Econometric Forecasting Associates, 1979, "DIEMEX/Wharton Mexican Econometric Model Pre-Meeting Solutions," Philadelphia, Pennsylvania). Such an elasticity is consistent with historical trends and with a projected pattern of petroleum-led growth, in which heavy industry and producer goods manufacturing figure prominently in development strategies. The projected labor force (supply of labor) for the year 2000 does not take into consideration present underutilization of employed labor (19.0 million active population in 1980) which amounts to 20 to 30 percent of the work force working only part of the year (approximately 2 to 3 million man-years of labor slack not including 1.3 million working in family enterprises without pay and 6 million self-employed, the majority of which are at the subsistence level) (Donald Keesing, 1977, "Employment and Lack of Employment in Mexico, 1900–70" in J.W. Wilkie and K. Ruddle, *Quantitative Latin American Studies*, UCLA Latin American Center, Los Angeles). An additional 3 to 4 million workers are employed at least part of the year in the United States. Moreover, there is a downward bias in the reported labor participation rate owing to slack in the labor market (see Peter Gregory, 1976, "Employment and Unemployment in Developing Countries," World Bank, Washington, D.C.; Donald Keesing, 1977; and this paper).

in Mexico earn wages that are a multiple of 10–20 times the wages of unskilled labor, while in the United States the multiple is much lower.

Where major gaps in real wages for the same skills and occupations exist across a relatively open frontier, and where the products are not easily tradable (most services and construction must be consumed on the spot), market forces induce migration. Migrant labor flows tend to raise the relative wages of unskilled workers in the slack labor market (Mexico) and lower them in the tight labor market (United States), if they cause changes in the total labor supply. The *relative* price of goods and services affected by changing wage costs would also tend to rise in Mexico and fall in the United States. Figures on recent patterns of migration (table 1) indicate that Mexican migration to the United States has had a far more than marginal impact on the market for unskilled labor in both countries. Hence, *relative* wage and price effects must have almost certainly resulted from these migratory flows, though in the United States they may have merely slowed the growth of real wages in low-skilled occupations. The word "relative" is underscored here because if both output and productivity are growing rapidly in the receiving country, it is possible for the wages of unskilled labor to rise, though they would rise more rapidly in a protected job market. In fact, real wages in the United States have stagnated or declined in recent years for most workers except those in industries whose unions are particularly strong, like auto manufacturing, teamsters, construction workers; doctors; and employees, like corporate executives, with more direct access to the profit pool. After-tax earnings of working class households have declined in real terms during the past decade. This is associated with a decline in the rate of growth of output and productivity of labor, low rates of investment, and lagging research and development. Labor tightness (insufficient migration in low-skill areas) may have adversely affected wages and productivity growth by constraining the ability of American industry to hold its own in increasingly competitive international markets. However, in the absence of growth, migration has probably held down relative wages of unskilled labor.

The findings of an earlier section indicate that if Mexico's output growth can be maintained at 6.6 percent annually until the year 2000, the demand for labor will just keep pace with supply. A

TABLE 6.—EFFECTIVE UNITED STATES LABOR SUPPLY BASED ON
LABOR FORCE PARTICIPATION IN 1990, EXTENDED USING THREE ASSUMPTIONS*[a,b]
(Millions of workers)

				Participation ratios[c]			Participation ratios (16–64 age group)		
	1985	1990	2000	1985	1990	2000	1985	1990	2000
Labor supply I (high)	113.8	122.0	134.8	67.7	69.7	72.1	75.7	78.6	81.1
Labor supply II (medium)	110.0	116.1	126.8	65.3	66.2	67.2	73.2	74.8	75.7
Labor supply III (low)	106.1	110.5	119.5	63.0	63.0	63.3	70.6	71.2	71.3

*Data for 1990 are from U.S. Department of Labor (1978), Bureau of Labor Statistics, *Monthly Labor Review*, Washington, D.C.

[a] Assumes immigration of 400,000 per year, military of 2.1 million (constant).

[b] It is customary to speak of excess demand for labor apart from a normal level of employment. Even the most ardent Humphrey-Harkins Act supporters recognize that frictional unemployment exists due to search time involved in changing jobs. It is not optimal on the individual or economy-wide level for people to remain at one job for their entire economically active life. Invariably a certain percentage of the work force is between jobs. Structural unemployment is another unhappy fact of life. The skills required for a particular job may not match those of the individual looking for work. It may be prohibitively costly to relocate oneself to where the job is available, and transmission of information concerning job openings is neither perfect nor costless. Although a constant 4.5 percent rate of frictional unemployment is assumed, there is evidence that this rate is growing over time and may already be too low. Current estimates run from 4 percent (Humphrey-Harkins Act), to Democratic Secretary of Labor Ray Marshall's 4.75 percent estimate as expressed in the Employment and Training Report of the President, to Milton Friedman's 6 to 7 percent estimate. Clearly an underestimate of this "normal rate" would lead to an underestimate of the total labor force necessary to provide any given level of employment and thus understate the potential labor shortages.

[c] Follows Bureau of Labor Statistics convention of ratio of civilian non-institutional labor force over civilian non-institutional population 16 and over.

7 percent sustained growth rate for the same 20-year period would begin to absorb Mexico's severe underemployed and would almost certainly raise real incomes of the majority of Mexico's poor. The relative price of agriculture products, domestic services and labor-intensive commodities would rise accordingly, forcing a change in the lifestyle of Mexico's elite. Still, growth rates of 6 to 7 percent imply a tripling or quadrupling of output between now and the year 2000 and an even more rapid growth of imports of capital and intermediate goods, managerial know-how, and skilled labor. Rapid growth is essential to relieve dependence on migration, but will require increased dependence on foreign markets for trade, investment and skilled labor. Since more effective labor absorption with rising wages is a *sine qua non* for social and political stability, and stability is needed to elicit investments for further growth, improved links with the United States commodity, labor and capital markets are essential to whatever priority is chosen—growth, employment or distribution.

PROJECTIONS OF THE SUPPLY AND DEMAND FOR LABOR IN THE U.S. ECONOMY, 1985-2000

Several rough projections of aggregate labor supply and demand through the year 2000 are presented in table 6. Estimates of the rate of growth of the labor supply are adapted from Bureau of Labor Statistics projections published in the *Monthly Labor Review* (U.S. Department of Labor, 1978). Since almost the entire labor force of the year 2000 has already been born, the primary variables in predicting the labor force are the participation ratio, the unemployment rate and the amount of net immigration over this period.

Participation ratios have been rising at increasing rates over the past few years, primarily due to rapidly increasing labor-market participation among women. The decrease of the "push effect" of falling birth rates and a lessening of the "pull effect" of a tight labor market will most likely combine to cause participation rates to increase at decreasing rates until 2000. The participation rates implicit in the labor-supply projections are also given in table 6.

Immigration is assumed constant at 400,000 per year, which is slightly above current figures. Unemployment is assumed to fall to 4.5 percent in 1990 and remain there. Tables 7 and 8 present estimates of the labor supply net of this "structural and frictional unemployment."

On the labor-demand side two theoretical constructs were employed to arrive at total employment demand projections. For the first run, output-labor ratios were used in combination with a 3 percent annual rate of growth of aggregate output and a modest rate of growth of labor productivity based on an annual increase in the output-labor ratio of 1 percent. This productivity estimate is slightly below the historical trend figure of 1.3 percent growth from all sources. Using the formula $L^d(t) = Y^d(t)/OL(t)$, where $Y^d(t)$ is desired output (3 percent growth) in year t, OL is output-labor ratio in year t, and $L^d(t)$ is the labor necessary to produce the desired level of output. (See table 7.)

Although the exact magnitude of the impending labor shortages implied by table 6 should not be relied upon, it is clear that shortfalls will occur if the United States pursues a goal of 3 percent per annum growth of GNP or greater without major increases in migration.

For the second run, a Cobb-Douglas production function is used: $Y^d_t = A_t \times L_t^{0.7} \times K_t^{0.3}$ where Y^d_t is desired output; $A(t)$ is a constant in any given year, but is a function of technological change (labor augmenting, capital augmenting, and jointly augmenting) over time; L_t is the labor force at time t; and K_t is the contemporaneous capital stock. A simple algebraic transformation gives

TABLE 7.—UNITED STATES LABOR DEMAND AND SUPPLY PROJECTIONS TO THE YEAR 2000

Year	OL (Output-worker) (1977 dollars)	Y (GNP) (billions of 1977 dollars)	Labor demand (A) (millions of workers)	Labor supply I (from table 6)
1970	18,606	1,522	81.80	81.8
1977	20,380	1,887	92.60	92.6
1985	22,070	2,399	108.70	113.8
1990	23,190	2,787	120.16	122.0
2000	25,621	3,762	146.83	134.8

TABLE 8.—U.S. LABOR DEMAND AND SUPPLY PROJECTIONS TO THE YEAR 2000

Year	Labor demand (B) L_t	Labor supply I	Labor supply II	Labor supply III	Desired GNP (Y_t^d)	Capital stock (K_t)
		(millions of workers)			(billions of 1977 dollars)	
1970	81.80	81.8	81.8	81.8	1,522	5,069.35
1977	92.60	92.6	92.6	92.6	1,887	6,091.78
1985	103.97	113.8	110.0	106.1	2,399	7,268.84
1990	112.14	122.0	116.1	110.5	2,787	7,992.47
2000	131.81	134.8	126.8	119.5	3,862	9,441.14

TABLE 9.—ALTERNATE ASSUMPTIONS CONCERNING THE
SUPPLY OF AND DEMAND FOR LABOR*[a]
(Millions of workers)

Labor force projection, model and year	Labor force I	Labor force II	Labor force III
Output labor model: demand (A)[b]			
1985	+ 5.10	+ 1.30	- 2.60
1990	+ 1.84	- 4.06	- 9.66
2000	- 11.03	- 20.03	- 27.33
Cobb-Douglas model: demand (B)[c]			
1985	+ 9.83	+ 6.03	+ 2.13
1990	+ 9.86	+ 3.96	- 1.64
2000	+ 3.99	- 5.01	- 12.31

*(−) indicates shortfall (excess demand for workers) and (+) indicates labor surplus.

[a] By the year 2000, population figures include 8.5 million immigrants, 6 million in the labor force at year 2000 participation rates, thus the maximum anticipated shortfalls are 33.3 to 18.3 million, with zero net immigration over this period. If the existing pool of approximately 2 million illegal aliens in the work force is also deported, the shortfall could be as high as 35.3 million by the year 2000.

[b] Assuming 1 percent annual rate of growth of labor productivity (output per worker).

[c] Assuming 1.38 percent annual rate of growth of factor productivity.

labor demand as a residual: $L_t = \left[Y_t^d / (A_t \times K_t^{0.3}) \right]^{1.428}$ and the results are compared to labor supply projections in table 6. (See table 8.)

A_t, the measure of productivity gains from all sources, is assumed to continue the 1.38 percent growth rate it displayed in the period 1960–77. If the period 1970–77 is used as the base period to compute productivity growth, the resulting 1.04 percent estimate would substantially increase labor demand (L_t) in all periods.

The labor demand figures generated in this fashion run slightly below the Bureau of Labor Statistics (BLS) high projected labor force, but we are well above either of the other predictions. As a sidelight, it is interesting to note that even the BLS predicts a shortage of labor, as they offset their unrealistically high predictions of labor force growth with even more optimistic output growth goals (3.65 percent).

As a summary, table 9 shows the extent of shortfalls or surpluses, given alternate assumptions concerning the supply of and demand for labor. Only by combining the most optimistic estimates concerning the rates of growth of the labor force and productivity with lower GNP growth estimates than those made by government agencies can a sufficient supply of labor be predicted through the end of this century without increasing immigration.

In addition to the aggregate shortfall detailed above, there is a clear indication that the unskilled and semiskilled job categories will bear the brunt of the shortages. The United States labor force is becoming better educated and more experienced. Blacks and older immigrants who were previously counted on to do distasteful but necessary work in our modern economy are moving up the socioeconomic scale, leaving new immigrants (legal and illegal), students, and some women at the low end of the occupational scale (Piore, 1978). For students this is likely to be their first experience in the job market, perhaps on a part-time or temporary basis, and as the percentage of the population in this category declines in the next few years, so should their share in low-skill employment. Tomorrow's women will have increased access to education and training opportunities and accordingly will be better able to compete for jobs in the higher skill occupations.

It seems that without a substantial increase in immigration, traditional domestic sources of supply will not provide the necessary volume of unskilled labor to meet even a moderate target

TABLE 10.—ACTUAL AND PROJECTED EMPLOYMENT FOR 1975 BY LECHT*

	Lecht	Actual	Difference (percent)
Total labor force (million)	93.6	94.8	-1.30
Employed labor force (million)	89.8	87.0	3.22
GNP (billion dollars)	1,967	1,687	16.60

*Data are from Leonard Lecht, *Manpower Requirements for National Objectives in the 1970s*. U.S. Department of Labor, Washington, D.C. 1968 rate of growth for United States GNP. Employers faced with this shortage may react in various ways. Industries may move abroad at an increasing rate in search of a steady supply of labor, a response which has already begun to take place. Mechanization of jobs previously done by hand, such as the picking of certain crops, is a second alternative, as is upgrading pay and working conditions to draw higher skilled workers into lower skilled jobs.

Harold Wool projects the supply of labor for "lower level" jobs through the 1980s under assumed conditions of full employment (1976).[2] He demonstrates that while the civilian labor force is projected to grow at a yearly rate of 1.75 percent in the period 1970-85, the supply of labor for lower level jobs will increase by only 0.64 percent per year, with almost all of this increase concentrated in the 1970-80 period. "Comparisons of these labor supply projections with recent Bureau of Labor Statistics projections of employment or labor demand by occupation under a full employment model in turn result in potential surpluses of workers for high-level occupations and potential shortages for lower level occupations" (Wool, 1976). Unfortunately, Wool does not make clear the extent to which immigration, both legal and illegal, enters into his calculations.

Leonard Lecht made projections of a similar nature (1968). Analysis of his work in retrospect illustrates some of the problems in projecting current trends any significant distance into the future. He assumed 4.5 percent per annum growth of GNP, 3.5 percent yearly growth of labor productivity, and a constant unemployment rate of 3.9 percent. As a result he overestimated 1975 GNP by about one-sixth. Yet his estimate of the 1975 labor supply is surprisingly close to the actual number, since the overestimate of GNP growth is offset for the most part by the overestimate of the growth of productivity. Table 10 compares his projections to the actual numbers.

Nevertheless, there is compelling evidence that the aging demographic structure of the United States will lead to an increasing shortfall of labor to fill low-skilled jobs. The demand for migrants to fill the gap may be as high as 15 to 30 million workers by the year 2000, if United States GNP is to continue to grow at past rates of 3 percent or better, unless one of two circumstances occur: either there will have to be a massive increase in participation rates, or a much accelerated growth of investment and productivity coupled with a much higher rate of savings than in recent decades. In short the United States has an almost certain need for migrant labor in the decades ahead if it is to maintain its position in the international economy. The migrants need not come from the south, but given the likelihood of a sustained surplus of unskilled labor in Mexico despite its highest growth projections, most of the migrants will be Mexican.

SUMMARY AND CONCLUSIONS

Despite limited information about current labor market structure and rather speculative projections about government policy and private expectations affecting future investment and growth in Mexico and the United States, the following propositions seem reasonably secure:

1) Mexico's supply of labor will grow at 3.6 percent annually and reach a total of 40 million workers by the end of the century. (Underemployment is now 4 to 6 million.)
2) Mexico's GNP is likely to grow at about 6 percent annually over the same 20-year period, provided that the economy has access to substantial inputs of skilled labor, technology, capital, intermediate and consumer goods.
3) A 6 percent rate of GNP growth will suffice to keep pace with a rise in the labor force including a modest increase in participation rates and will not begin to absorb the 4 to 6 million workers plus more than 3 million Mexican workers presently employed full or part-time in the United States.
4) For Mexico to begin to mop up its underemployment, enabling it to raise real wages of less skilled workers significantly, GNP would have to grow at a sustained rate of over 7 percent annually until the year 2000, a goal almost unprecedented among developing nations. Such an achievement would place an even greater dependence on foreign trade, capital, technology, entrepreneurship and skilled labor, much of which would have to come from direct foreign investment. While such investment might well be in close association with Mexican capital and entrepreneurship, its role in the economy would be critical. The United States would almost certainly have to figure prominently in the process.

5) Even if total labor demand should grow at the same pace as supply, structural problems are certain to become serious, leading to shortages in more skilled occupations and surpluses in less skilled ones. The faster the rate of output growth, the greater the structural imbalances, and hence the greater the need to link labor markets between the United States and Mexico to balance supply and demand for skills.
6) The level of income of the mass of Mexican workers, and their income shares, are likely to be influenced most by the tightness or slackness of the labor market. There are presently about 4.0 million Mexicans working in the United States during some part of the year, and the number is growing at about 170,000 per year. (See table 1.) Such a flow will have to be sustained if Mexico is to achieve a significant tightening of its labor market, even at the most optimistic GNP growth projections, in view of the current high level of underemployment. If Mexico is successful in raising real wages toward United States levels, there are likely to be increased entrants from Central America into the Mexican work force especially in the southern regions.

It would be incorrect to give the impression that there is a labor pool in Mexico which can supply 20 million workers to the United States in the next 20 years, or that such a massive influx of people of another cultural heritage would not give rise to social problems and conflicts. The traditional pool from which migrants flow both to America and metropolitan areas within Mexico is a declining fraction of the total population, and as the marginal product of labor in this sector rises as a result of outmigration, the relative incentive to leave declines. In short, there is no endless queue of Mexicans clamoring to enter the United States, as it seems some policy makers fear. Although on the basis of the imprecise figures it would not be unheard of to have a million Mexican immigrants entering the United States in one year, this pace has historically never lasted for five years, much less 20, and problems of assimilating so many newcomers are too numerous and complex to be covered here.
7) The demand for labor in the United States, based on rather modest growth projections for GNP of 3 percent per annum,

will almost certainly outstrip supply in the next 20 years, placing enormous pressures on the labor market to encourage increasing levels of immigration. The political-economic conditions associated with the proximity of the two countries, plus the likelihood of surplus unskilled labor in Mexico in the years ahead, will make continued and growing migration from that country a sine qua non of mutual growth with social and political stability.

8) United States direct investment in Mexico may have a significant impact on employment of low-skilled labor. While its traditional direct investments have been relatively capital intensive and may not be expected to produce more than 25,000 to 50,000 jobs per year assuming an investment rate of 500 million to 1 billion dollars per year (appendix 2), the establishment of a much larger number of in-bond assembly plants (*maquiladoras*) throughout Mexico could generate up to one million additional jobs by 1985. With a rapid growth of output of 6 to 7 percent annually, the combined total of as much as 1.25 million new jobs between 1980 and 1985 would represent 28 percent of the estimated 4.4 million growth in the labor force during the same period. Such investment plus immigration of Mexican labor into the United States labor market at just above current rates could go far to reverse the trend in surplus labor in Mexico and begin to increase the real incomes of Mexico's poor.

9) Perhaps more important, if Mexico's economy were permitted to develop on a broad front—including light, medium, and heavy industry—and if its agriculture were stimulated as well in labor-using directions, it could provide new growth centers in North America to serve a continent-wide market. Such a balanced transformation of Mexico, linked with access to United States markets, technology, and financial capital, could also help the United States to achieve its own growth objectives. Labor, capital, and technology would be permitted to follow lines of dynamic comparative advantage on a region-wide basis. Of course this implies a rather significant restructuring of United States industry away from more traditional lines of production in which certain economic and social costs will be incurred. In appendix 1 Mexican trade with the United States is projected

through the year 2000 if current trends continue even without a major shift in trade policy by either country.

10) The framework of this analysis has stressed the interdependence of output, employment, and income distribution both in the Mexican and United States economies and between them. A consistency framework for trade and balance-of-payments projections appears in appendices 2 and 3. The magnitude of Mexico's prospective economic and population growth underscores the fact that changes south of the border will have far more than incremental consequences for the United States. Stresses and strains within Mexico, if they occur, would shake the continent, but success in Mexican development would be likely to carry with it major benefits for her continental neighbors. To maximize the mutual benefits from Mexico's economic and demographic growth, it may well be necessary for the United States to engage in a fundamental reassessment of its own national economic goals. Such a reassessment is long overdue, in the face of chronic inflation, balance-of-trade deficits, slowed output and productivity growth, and one of the lowest rates of savings and investment in the world. It may well be that in the future the United States will need Mexico as much or more than Mexico will need the United States, even without considering important complementarities in the energy area.

REFERENCES

Banco de México. *Indicadores Económicos.* Mexico City. Various issues, 1973–79.

Bolin, Richard. "Reasons for Success of the Mexican Border Industrial Free Zones." United Nations Industrial Development Organization. New York, 28 January 1977.

Gregory, Peter. "Employment and Unemployment in Developing Countries." *Preliminary Report to the World Bank.* Washington, D.C., 1976.

International Monetary Fund. "International Financial Statistics." Various issues, 1961–79.

Keesing, Donald B. "Employment and Lack of Employment in Mexico, 1900–70." In James W. Wilkie and Kenneth Ruddle, *Quantitative*

Latin American Studies. Los Angeles: UCLA Latin American Center, 1977.

Lecht, Leonard. *Manpower Requirements for National Objectives in the 1970s.* Washington, D.C.: U.S. Department of Labor, 1968.

McFarland, E.L., Jr. "Employment Growth in Services: Mexico 1950–69." Ph.D. dissertation, Williams College, Williamstown, Massachusetts, 1973.

México, Secretaría de Patrimonio y Fomento Industrial. *Plan Nacional de Desarrollo Industrial.* Vol. 1, México, 1979–82.

———, Secretaría de Programación y Presupuesto. Banco de México. United Nations Industrial Development Organization. *Matriz de insumo-producto de México año 1970.* Vols. I to IV, México, 1979.

Piore, Michael J. *Birds of Passage: Migrant Labor and Industrial Societies.* Cambridge, Mass.: Cambridge University Press, 1979.

Reynolds, Clark W. "A Shift-Share Analysis of Regional and Sectoral Productivity Growth in Contemporary Mexico." Laxenburg, Austria: International Institute for Applied Systems Analysis, 1979.

Tello, Carlos. *La política económica en México 1970–76.* México: Siglo Veintiuno, 1979.

Urquidi, Victor, "Empleo y explosión demográfica." *Demografía y Economía.* Vol. VIII, no. 20, México, 1974.

United States Department of Commerce, Industry and Trade Administration. "Overseas Business Reports." Washington, D.C. Various issues, 1978–79.

———, Bureau of Labor Statistics. *Monthly Labor Review.* Washington, D.C. 1978.

United States Department of Labor, Bureau of Labor Statistics. *Occupational Outlook Handbook.* 1978–79 Edition, Washington, D.C.

United States Foreign Service, Department of State. *Foreign Economic Trends and Their Implications for the United States.* Washington, D.C., 1979.

Villar, Samuel I. del. "El manejo y la recuperación de la economía mexicana en crisis (1976–1978)." México: El Colegio de México. 1979.

Wharton Econometric Forecasting Associates. "DIEMEX/Wharton: Mexican Econometric Model Pre-Meeting Solutions." Philadelphia, Pennsylvania, 1979.

World Bank. *Special Study of the Mexican Economy: Major Policy Issues and Prospects 1977–82.* Vols I and II, Washington, D.C., 1978.

Wool, Harold. "Future Labor Supply for Lower-Level Occupations." *Monthly Labor Review* 99 (March 1976).

PREFACE TO APPENDICES 1 TO 3

Recent developments in Mexico have put United States–Mexican economic relations at a crossroad. The discovery of huge petroleum reserves may profoundly change trade relations between the two countries. Removal of Mexico's foreign exchange constraint through sales of petroleum will allow Mexico to take a more independent stance in regard to its northern neighbor. At the same time the United States will find it difficult to reduce its share of imports from Mexico because of its need for petroleum and natural gas as well as American industry's use of Mexican labor in production sharing, not only in the in-bond industries but, as shown above, throughout the United States economy. If the United States does not actively seek to improve relations with Mexico now, especially in regard to her vast labor surplus, Mexico may choose to reduce its dependence on imports from the United States over the next two decades. The trade balance could then turn decidedly in Mexico's favor, aggravating the United States balance of payments problem. The United States will now have to adjust to becoming more dependent upon Mexican imports. In appendix 1 possible trends in United States–Mexican trade are discussed on the basis of alternative assumptions about the degree of interconnection.

The United States share of total direct foreign investment in Mexico has also been slipping in recent years. Although the direct impact of such investment in terms of jobs or additions to total GNP is not very large, foreign investment tends to occur in the most dynamic sectors and fosters domestic imitation which can be potentially important to the pattern of economic change in Mexico. Trade discussions are likely to be linked with measures to expand United States direct investment in ways suitable to Mexico's desire for maximum control over its process of economic growth, yet which will elicit important responses from United States firms. The United States might well consider offering Mexico a new set of trade and investment policies which would at least maintain the present share of United States involvement in the Mexican economy. (This is an underlying assumption in appendix 2.) Failure to do so would result in the erosion of the United States market position in Mexico's rapidly evolving economy. The United States must recognize, in the light of the facts and figures presented in this paper, that good trade and investment relations with Mexico will be far more important to the United States economy through the year 2000 than will its interaction with the Chinese. The political and security implications of economic relations between the two countries will also far exceed the importance of those with China. Appendices 2 and 3 discuss direct foreign investment and the Mexican balance of payments in this perspective.

APPENDIX 1
SOME MEXICAN TRADE PROJECTIONS WITH IMPLICATIONS
FOR UNITED STATES EXPORTS AND IMPORTS

The United States' share of Mexican imports in 1977 was 63.6 percent. It was higher in the 1950s and 1960s, but during the 1970s, it remained close to 63 percent. Canada is the major trading partner of the United States, but Mexico is the most important trading partner among the developing countries and ranks fifth overall. In manufactures alone, Mexico is the third largest importer of United States production, even ahead of Japan. Given the growth potential described elsewhere in this paper, Mexico will soon become the fourth largest trading partner and second largest importer of United States manufactures as its trade with the United States surpasses that of the United Kingdom.

Presently, Mexico has a low trade ratio (exports and imports divided by gross domestic product). In 1977 it was .21, lower than all South American countries and Canada with the exception of Brazil (.15) and Argentina (.17). Among the major oil-exporting nations the lowest trade ratio is Indonesia's which was .4 in 1977. (Trade data are from International Monetary Fund, 1979.) The World Bank projects an increase in the Mexican trade ratio to .265 by 1982, associated with an 8 percent rate of growth of gross national product (GNP) in the early 1980s. Whether or not the ratio moves that fast, there will have to be an increase if Mexico intends to shift from import substitution to export promotion. This shift will be essential for rapid growth in output and productivity. The petroleum industry will provide another major push. Before long, if Mexico wishes to gain increased access to the major industrial markets, it will probably elect to join the General Agreement on Trades and Tariffs (GATT) and to continue to lower many import barriers.

If Mexican GNP grows at about 6 percent per year until the year 2000, and its trade ratio increases to .35, Mexican imports will grow at 10 percent per year, from 6 billion current dollars in 1977 to more than 52 billion 1977 dollars in the year 2000.

Exports will grow at a slightly lower rate under the 6 percent growth assumption which is consistent with the World Bank forecast that its current account will remain in deficit. The United States share of Mexican exports is likely to increase, assuming eventual agreement on natural gas sales, increased sales of petroleum products, and further establishment of in-bond* industries throughout Mexico. The balance of trade between Mexico and the United States on current account, traditionally in favor of the United States, has been steadily decreasing and may soon shift to a Mexican trade surplus.

Because of the political realities of petroleum and natural gas consumption in the United States, Mexico will find itself with substantial bargaining power in future trade negotiations and may well choose to link sales of natural gas and petroleum to the establishment of additional in-bond industry and improved access to the United States market for cash crop exports on a much broader basis than simply winter vegetables and fruits. Mexico's major exports in 1977 by order of importance were crude petroleum, coffee, cotton, tomatoes, assorted machinery and shrimp. Mexico will be attempting to enter the international market in producer goods and consumer durables in the next 20 years. This will depend on foreign markets and on United States direct investment to provide managerial ability, technical information, and specific links to the United States domestic market. For these reasons, although the United States bargaining position with Mexico has eroded, it has not disappeared. It will become apparent to both sides that continued and improved access to the United States domestic market may help to accelerate and diversify Mexican trade so as to minimize dependence on petroleum. Failure by the United States to capitalize on its location and historical advantage in trade with Mexico will almost certainly result in a negative balance of trade with Mexico and slow growth of its own economy.

*In-bond industries are assembly plants for foreign businesses exempt from tariffs on their imported intermediate goods which produce solely for export.

In 1976 and 1977 Mexico was able to reduce its total imports in spite of poor harvests and increased government imports of grains. This reduction in imports was largely borne by the private sector and was associated with a slowdown of the rate of growth of gross domestic product (GDP) to 1.7 percent in 1976 and 3.2 percent in 1977. Bottlenecks in production caused by austerity measures essential during the difficult transition from high to more moderate rates of inflation were a major cause of the slowdown, but these bottlenecks were removed in 1978 as the current account was allowed to return to its petroleum-deficit position (Villar, 1979). In 1978 President López Portillo called for 16.5 billion dollars worth of new investment in the state-owned petroleum corporation, PEMEX, by 1982 and 1 billion dollars worth of new investment per year in electrical power generation to permit a 10 percent annual growth in electricity output. Most of the capital goods needed for expansion of electrical power and about half of those for petroleum investment must be supplied from abroad (United States Department of Commerce, 1978–79).

Mexico still imports few consumer goods. According to the United States Department of Commerce, in the near future Mexico will need heavy industry equipment, construction machinery, tractors and other heavy agricultural equipment, locomotives, railroad rolling stock, iron and steel items (automotive and machine parts, pipe, sheet metal, etc.) and scrap, chemicals and a wide variety of raw and semi-processed materials. The current account deficit is likely to remain high at least until 1982 as the current presidential term comes to an end, partly to speed growth and partly because Mexican public sector deficits have historically risen as a share of GNP (World Bank, 1978).

The growth of trade largely depends on the willingness of the Mexican government to accelerate its petroleum production. In the past, realized investment in the petroleum sector has tended to lag behind government forecasts. Estimates of an 8–9 percent annual growth of GDP starting in 1980 depend on petroleum production growing much more rapidly than is consistent with current Mexican government plans though there is already evidence that output will be stepped up over targets announced in 1979. Real growth of Mexican economy is more likely to hold at around 6 to 7 percent per year even under the most favorable conditions. Attempts at faster growth will run up against a shortage of skilled labor and managerial capacity and will produce severe inflationary pressures. A slower growth of petroleum exports implies a slower growth of the trade ratio which will probably not exceed .25 by 1985.

Table A 1.1 provides estimates of Mexican trade with the United States to the year 2000, assuming growth of the Mexican economy at both 6 and 7 percent per year.

APPENDIX 2
UNITED STATES DIRECT INVESTMENT IN MEXICO

At the end of 1976 total United States direct foreign investment was about 3 billion. Of this amount 2.2 billion was in manufacturing, mostly chemicals, transportation equipment, primary and fabricated metals, food processing, non-electrical machinery, electrical and electronic machinery. Most investment was in import-substituting industries with high capital requirements so that except for in-bond clothing and electronic industries, employment generation per unit of capital was lower than for the Mexican manufacturing sector as a whole.

The United States has traditionally accounted for more than 70 percent of total direct foreign investment in Mexico. The following tabulation lists the total United States direct foreign investment in Mexico valued at the end of the year in millions of dollars:

1963	1965	1967	1969	1970	1971	1972	1973	1974	1975	1976	1977
907	1,177	1,343	1,631	1,786	1,838	2,025	2,379	2,854	3.177	2,984	3,175

In 1973 under the Echeverría Administration, laws were passed which were intended to limit foreign participation in Mexican industry. But even before the new laws were enacted, foreign participation in total private fixed investment had declined from 5 pecent in the 1960s to 4 percent in the early 1970s. The downward trend continued and foreign participation in private fixed investment fell to 3 percent by 1977.

The Law for the Promotion of Mexican Investment and the Regulation of Foreign Investment limited foreign ownership in equity in new business to 49 percent. In some industries foreign ownership was limited to 40 percent or forbidden altogether.

Two laws having to do with patents, trademarks, and inventions shortened the period of patent protection to 10 years. Trade-

TABLE A1.1—UNITED STATES SHARE OF MEXICAN TRADE: TWO ALTERNATIVE PROJECTIONS*
(Millions of 1977 dollars)

Year	Total exports	Exports to the U.S.	Assumed U.S. share (percent)	Total imports	Imports from the U.S.	Assumed U.S. share (percent)
Projection 1: U.S.–Mexican trade-linked projection[a]						
1980	8,400	5,900	70	11,400/11,800	7,500/7,800	66
1985	14,600	10,800	74	15,400/16,800	10,800/11,800	70
1990	22,000/23,000[b]	16,500/17,200	75	23,000/26,000	16,800/19,000	73
2000	50,500/57,200	37,900/42,900	75	52,400/63,200	39,300/47,400	75
Projection 2: independent Mexican trade policy projection[c]						
1980	8,400	5,900	70	11,400/11,800	7,300/7,600	64
1985	14,600	10,100	69	15,400/16,800	9,200/10,100	60
1990	22,000/23,000	14,300/15,000	65	23,000/26,000	13,100/14,800	57
2000	50,500/57,200	32,800/37,200	65	52,400/63,200	26,200/31,600	50

*The trade ratio is assumed to rise to .225 in 1980, .25 in 1985, .28 in 1990, and .35 in the year 2000. Imports are projected to exceed exports by the average of the two estimates for the current account deficit taken from either the 6 percent or 7 percent growth projections in the Mexican balance of payments tabulation in appendix 2.

[a] Projection 1 assumes a rising share of U.S.–Mexican trade in total Mexican exports and imports.

[b] The figure on the left side of the slash assumes a growth rate of the Mexican economy of 6 percent per year. The one on the right assumes a growth rate of 7 percent per year.

[c] Projection 2 assumes a declining share of U.S.–Mexican trade in total Mexican exports and imports.

marks had to be Mexicanized and under certain conditions could be expropriated by the government. For some products, including some chemicals and pharmaceuticals, patent protection is not available. In 1977 a decree was issued which allowed the Mexican government to set a foreign currency budget for any foreign business in order to improve Mexico's balance of payments.

These laws, together with recession and devaluation of the peso, resulted in a decline in new direct foreign investment (DFI) from a high of 678 million (U.S. dollars) in 1974 to an estimated low of 530 million in 1978. Recent estimates by the Banco de México indicate that 1979 investment may be considerably above values in recent years.

World Bank projections of new DFI are .95 percent of GDP, a much higher share than historical rates. In the 1960s new DFI was as high as .65 percent of GDP. In the 1970s values have ranged from .44 percent to .60 percent of GDP.

Increased foreign investment will be welcomed by Mexico if it serves to generate substantial increases in employment and if investors are willing to locate away from the major urban centers. Under López Portillo many import-licensing restrictions have been removed and new foreign industry, with 51 percent of the equity owned by a Mexican silent partner, may qualify for low-cost loans or grants if the establishment of the business meets the needs of the surrounding community. By and large foreign business receives the same treatment as domestic business. Expectations of lowered inflation and reduced government borrowing (external debt limit of 3 billion dollars in 1978) over the next five years should encourage foreign investment. Because of past investment patterns and the location advantage of sharing a common border, the United States should continue to dominate foreign investment in Mexico.

Especially important to Mexico are the in-bond industries. In 1974 almost 25 percent of Mexican exports to the United States was value added generated through production sharing. Mexico allows complete foreign ownership of in-bond industries and frees them from patent limitations. No duty is charged by either the United States or Mexico on the components that move to Mexico and back across the border. Customs duties are charged only on the value-added component.

In 1971 Mexico was fifth among all countries in terms of value added as a processing platform to the United States. In 1977 Mexico was third, after West Germany and Japan, in spite of having temporarily priced itself out of the processing market at the end of 1974 due to an overvalued peso and a rise in the minimum wage in the in-bond industries which drove labor costs above those in Japan for comparable work. Richard Bolin estimated that 250,000 jobs may have been created directly and indirectly with an investment per job ratio of only $700 (1977).

Bolin believes, on the basis of past growth of the in-bond industry, that as many as 300,000 jobs may exist in this sector by 1983 with another 600,000 jobs generated indirectly.* In-bond industry requires little Mexican investment besides needed infrastructure, creates more employment than a comparable level of investment in other industries, and provides foreign exchange earnings. For these reasons, trade discussions with Mexico should definitely be linked with further United States investment in Mexican production-sharing industry.

Each of the 300,000 direct jobs is estimated to produce $5,000 value added per year. The 600,000 indirect jobs are estimated to produce half as much. Total addition to GNP due to the in-bond industry in 1983 is estimated at 3 billion dollars (Bolin, 1977). The figures on increased jobs per dollar of investment, both direct and indirect, cited above seem to be somewhat exaggerated. However, the amount of additional in-bond investment may well exceed the Bolin projections (through 1983) by the mid-1980s if the United States and Mexico can agree to additional incentives for such industries and given the likelihood that United States firms will elect to shift some Asian production toward Mexican markets. For this reason a total increase of direct and indirect employment in such industries may be projected of one million jobs by the mid-1980s, plus up to 50,000 jobs per year in other United States direct investment in Mexico, totaling 1.25 million new jobs by 1985 if a major new effort can be established between the United States and Mexico in these areas.

*Private communications, 1979.

APPENDIX 3
PAST VALUE AND PROJECTIONS
OF THE MEXICAN BALANCE OF PAYMENTS
THROUGH THE YEAR 2000: DISCUSSION AND TABLE

The first projection in the tabulation of appendix 2 assumes a growth rate of GDP of 6 percent per year until 2000, generated without external borrowing and with moderate levels of DFI. Present goals of 16.5 billion dollars worth of new investment in the government-owned Pemex will probably result in a continued current account (trade balance of goods and services) deficit and continued external borrowing until 1985. From 1985 on it is assumed that the government will keep the balance of payments in equilibrium and allow the current account deficit to roughly equal the inflow of new DFI.

New DFI in the 1960s ranged from about .60 percent to .65 percent of GDP. In the 1970s through 1977 values fluctuated more widely from a high of .60 percent in 1970 to a low of .45 in 1975 and 1977 (preliminary estimates, Banco de México, 1979). In the 6 percent growth projection new DFI is assumed to be as low as .55 percent of GDP or as high as .70 percent of GDP. The latter figure is higher than has been seen in the last two decades, but is lower than recent figures for Venezuela (.76 percent of GDP in 1977) and Brazil (1 percent of GDP in 1977, International Monetary Fund, 1979).

World Bank projections assume that the balance on current account will remain in deficit in the foreseeable future. It is imperative that Mexico avoid allowing the peso to become over-valued relative to the dollar in terms of rates of inflation in the two countries and the relative cost of tradables. In 1974 due to overvaluation of the peso and a rise in the Mexican minimum wage along the United States border, Mexican wages in terms of dollars rose higher than comparable wages in Japan (Bolin, 1977). The inflated wage bill diverted investment toward Asia and cost Mexico thousands of jobs. Now that Mexico has a major source of export earnings in petroleum there should be no reason to attempt to lower the cost of producer goods imports through currency overvaluation. Allowing the current account deficit to offset long-term capital flows will help to maintain the peso and Mexican wages and exports at a competitive level.

TABLE A3.1.—MEXICAN BALANCE OF PAYMENTS: SELECTED YEARS FROM 1962–78 AND ALTERNATIVE PROJECTIONS TO THE YEAR 2000 FOR THE CURRENT AND LONG-TERM CAPITAL ACCOUNTS*

(Millions of dollars)

Year	Balance of goods and services	Long-term capital	External credit	Direct foreign investment	Other	Errors and omissions	Short-term capital	Variation in Bank of Mexico reserves
1962	-120.2	224.7	147.5	90.3	-13.1	-87.6		16.9
1968	-632.2	379.0	136.6	116.8	125.6	302.2	—[a]	49.0
1970	-924.0	503.9	324.2	200.7	-21.0	523.2[b]	—[a]	102.1
1972	-789.4	790.4	557.8	214.9	17.7	263.7[b]	—[a]	264.7
1973	-1,175.4	1,676.1	1,370.7	286.9	18.5	-378.4	—[a]	122.3
1974	-2,558.1	2,730.8	1,999.2	362.2	369.4	-135.8	—[a]	36.9
1975	-3,768.9	4,339.9	3,477.5	362.3	500.1	-406.0	—[a]	165.1
1976	-3,068.6	4,650.9	4,464.4	299.1	-112.6	-2,454.2	551.0	-320.9
1977[c]	-1,550.3	4,380.3	4,149.9	327.3	-96.9	-458.7	-1,867.1	504.2
1978[c]	-2,462.5	4,330.6	4,076.8	293.6	-39.8	81.6	-1,727.1	222.5

Projection[d]				
1980	-3,000	3,000	2,400	600
1985	-660/-840[e]	660/840	—	660/840
1990	-890/-1,130	890/1,130	—	890/1,130
2000	-1,620/-2,060	1,620/2,060		1,620/2,060
Alternative Projection[d]				
1980	-3,600	3,600	3,000	600
1985	-2,260/-2,440[e]	2,260/2,440	1,450/1,320	810/1,120
1990	-2,890/-3,130	2,890/3,130	1,750/1,550	1,140/1,580
2000	-5,720/-6,160	5,720/6,160	3,480/3,060	2,240/3,100

* Sources: Banco de México (1973–79), *Indicadores Económicos*, various issues.

[a] Until 1976 short-term capital was included in errors and omissions.

[b] Errors and omissions in 1970 and 1972 include the values for special drawing rights.

[c] The figures for 1977 and 1978 are preliminary estimates.

[d] Both projections are in 1977 dollars.

[e] The left side of the slash represents an estimate of direct foreign investment of .55 percent of gross domestic product and the right side represents an estimate of direct foreign investment of .8 percent of GDP.

The second projection is based on a growth rate of GDP of 65 percent until 1980 and of 7 percent from 1980 to 2000. The World Bank's long-range projection was also 7 percent (1978). Growth of the labor force as projected by Wharton at 3.6 percent per year through 1983 would require a growth rate of about 6.6 percent simply to maintain present employment levels (1979). Long term growth above 7 percent is probably not possible given the present skill levels and managerial capacity in the Mexican economy. The capital requirement for increasing the growth rate by a percentage point from the earlier projection will mostly be generated by internal savings which were 22 percent of new GDP from 1970-1977 and are estimated to continue at that level, and by external borrowing. Capital is related to GDP through an assumed capital/output ratio of 2.1 which corresponds with Wharton's figures for 1978-83 (Wharton, 1979).

New DFI will contribute somewhat less in bringing about the increased growth rate. In this projection new DFI is estimated to be .65 percent of GDP at a minimum and .90 percent of GDP at a maximum. The latter value is an ambitious projection, almost as high as present levels in Brazil where there are fewer barriers to DFI. Brazil presently has the highest rate of new DFI as a percent of GDP (1 percent) of any major country in the western hemisphere and one of the highest in the world. A leap of new DFI in Mexico to .90 percent of GDP implies that there will be a new attitude toward DFI in Mexico on the part of the Mexican government and foreign investors.

External borrowing in the 7 percent growth projection model is quite small. It is predicted on the premise that private and public investment are complementary in Mexico, and that the Mexican government will not resort to foreign borrowing to meet public consumption goals. This was not always so in the past, but may be possible by 1985 with increased installed capacity in the petroleum sector generating additional government revenues.

Total external debt is estimated to be about 35 billion dollars in 1985 in the 6 percent growth projection model and about 40 billion dollars in 1985 in the 7 percent growth projection model. The former figure, given an expected increase of exports as a percent of GDP to about 11 percent by 1985, implies a debt service ratio (debt service/exports) of less than .40; the latter figure of less than .42. The debt service ratio for 1977 was .48. The

World Bank has estimated a fall in the debt-service ratio to .39 by 1982 based on projections of a substantial increase in the export to GDP ratio and rapid growth of the economy in the early 1980s (1978). In any case the falling debt service ratio from a peak of .48 in 1977 is likely to improve Mexico's profile in the eyes of the international financial community.

13
America in the Era of Limits: Migrants, Nativists, and the Future of U.S.–Mexican Relations

Wayne A. Cornelius

> *Once upon a time . . . our people, proud of their institutions . . . entertained the thought that their country was destined to serve as the world's refuge. . . . They have come to realize that such a flood cannot fail to affect the institutions which have made and preserved American liberties.*
> —Albert Johnson, Chairman, House Committee on Immigration and Naturalization, U.S. Congress, 1927[1]

> *As children and grandchildren of immigrants, we have made immigration such a part of our mythology and folklore that it is immensely difficult to come to grips with the new realities that face us. . . . Frontier America is gone, replaced by an America of 7.6 percent unemployment. . . . Our increasingly scarce resources, our own severe economic problems, and our own social fabric demand a rational [more restrictive] immigration policy.*
> —Richard D. Lamm, Governor of Colorado, 1981[2]

The post-1970 wave of immigration—most of it illegal, most of it from Mexico and other Spanish-speaking countries—has aroused some deep-seated anxieties among large segments of the

---

Wayne A. Cornelius is Professor of Political Science and Director of the Center for United States–Mexican Studies at the University of California, San Diego. A slightly different version of this essay appeared as "America in the Era of Limits: Nativist Reactions to the 'New' Immigration," Working Papers in U.S. Mexican Studies 3, Program in United States–Mexican Studies (La Jolla, Calif.: University of California, San Diego, 1982).
©1982 by Wayne A. Cornelius

U.S. population. There is some debate among academics regarding the durability of today's anti-immigrant, often specifically anti-Mexican, sentiments. Some observers, noting the spasmodic character of nativist movements in the United States and the average citizen's lack of accurate information about the "new immigrants," view the present level of anti-alien hostility as an ephemeral current of public opinion that will respond to the passage of time and to public education efforts. Others—including this author—believe that these attitudes and perceptions are likely to persist and even harden over the next two decades, if only because the broad economic and social problems at home and the international economic and political forces that threaten American hegemony in the world are also likely to endure and to intensify. In other words, the domestic and international problems which will confront the United States in the remainder of this century are highly conducive to a long-term revival of anti-immigrant sentiment.

While there is some question about whether public officials in the U.S. are following or leading general public opinion on the immigration issue, I will argue in this essay that at best, the present configuration of public attitudes and perceptions sets important limits on the range of policy choices available to U.S. officials. They reduce the leeway which public officials feel they have in dealing with immigration policy. At worst, this anti-immigrant climate of opinion may force the choice of a punitive, discriminatory policy, at all levels of the U.S. political system.

This paper is an attempt to describe the main features of the public opinion climate in the United States in which the current debate over immigration—especially illegal (undocumented) immigration from Mexico—is occurring. It sketches the public's specific perceptions and attitudes toward immigration, as well as some of the broader social, economic, and political forces operating in the U.S. today which condition mass attitudes toward immigrants. How, for example, are shifts in public opinion regarding ethnic minority groups, government spending, crime, and resource scarcity affecting public preferences for a U.S. immigration policy?

The following analysis is based on data from various public opinion surveys conducted nationally and in certain cities during the past 35 years, letters from individual citizens concerned about Mexican immigration which were sent to the editors of major newspapers and to this author since 1977, and telephoned comments received from 116 viewers of a "public feedback" program on Mexican immigration broadcast by San Diego's public television station in March, 1981. While the consistency of the themes that emerge from these diverse sources of information is quite high, we lack the kinds of data—particularly from in-depth interviews with persons holding nativist views—which would enable us to choose among competing explanations for the findings. This is, therefore, an exploratory and incomplete analysis.

AMERICAN NATIVISM IN HISTORICAL PERSPECTIVE

When we put our anti-immigrant, nativist movements in historical perspective, dating back to the movement in the 1830s which advocated immigration restriction to prevent further arrivals of Catholic immigrants from Europe, it becomes clear that nativist sentiment has bubbled just beneath the surface in the U.S. during most of the last 150 years.[3] The most vehement nativist agitation (thus far in our history) occurred during the period from 1830 to 1860, when the main targets were not Mexicans but the Irish and Germans.[4]

The level of public tolerance for Mexican immigrants has fluctuated markedly during the present century, usually in response to changing levels of economic stress and manpower shortages caused by foreign wars. Three times during the last 60 years (in 1920-21, 1930-35, and 1953-54), anti-immigrant sentiment among the U.S. public emboldened officials to carry out mass round-up and deportation campaigns aimed specifically at Mexicans.[5] If these surges of anti-Mexican nativism are viewed as a cyclical phenomenon—something that seems to happen at least once in a generation—it could be argued that the U.S. is now overdue for another such nativist spasm.

The point is that the attitudes, perceptions, fears and prejudices that underlie such movements do not go away once the immediate stimulus of an economic recession or international reverse of some kind passes. They remain latent in the body politic, waiting to be tapped and manipulated by politicians and special interest groups that have no reservations about appealing to the baser instincts of their constituents. Indeed, we may be

TABLE 1.—SHOULD LEGAL IMMIGRATION BE KEPT AT ITS PRESENT LEVEL, INCREASED, OR DECREASED?*

Survey and date of interviewing	Percentage of respondents favoring:		
	Present level	Increase	Decrease
American Institute of Public Opinion (Gallup Poll) December, 1945 (asked about persons from Europe)	32	5	37
American Institute of Public Opinion June, 1965	39	8	33
American Institute of Public Opinion March, 1977	37	7	42
Associated Press–NBC News Poll August, 1981	27	5	65

*Missing data ("don't know" or unascertained responses) are not reported here. However, it is significant that the proportion of respondents not expressing any opinion declined from 20 percent in the Gallup, 1965, survey to only 3 percent in the most recent Associated Press–NBC Poll. Thus, rising levels of public information (or misinformation) about immigration have been translated into a more restrictionist climate of public opinion.

Sources of data: Gallup, 1945: *The Gallup Poll: Public Opinion, 1935–1971*, vol. 1 (1935–1948) (New York: Random House, 1972), p. 555. Gallup, 1965: *Gallup Political Index*, August, 1965, p. 15. Gallup, 1977: *The Gallup Poll: Public Opinion 1972–1977* (Wilmington, Del.: Scholarly Resources, Inc., 1978), vol. 2 (1976–1977), p. 1050. AP–NBC Poll, 1981: *The San Diego Union*, August 17, 1981, p. A-9. All of these surveys are based on national samples of at least 1,500 adults, with an error factor of (plus or minus) three percentage points, 95 percent of the time. Sampling error is higher when results are compared across different surveys.

entering a period in which such appeals to nativism are increasingly respectable, because they can be cloaked in an aura of protecting our basic values as a society, the hard-won living standards of the middle class, or even the national security.[6]

What explains the cyclical or spasmodic nature of American nativist agitation? Certainly, fluctuations in the unemployment rate and the level of general economic insecurity among the U.S. population are highly correlated with the rise and fall of anti-immigrant sentiment, particularly as directed against Mexican immigrants in the present century.[7] Yet, additional factors were probably involved, such as the reverses suffered by the United States in the international political and the economic arenas. Writing in the early 1950s, to explain the rise of McCarthyism and other public responses to the international communist threat, Elmer Davis speculated that, beset with feelings of fear and frustration, those Americans who could not face these problems in a more rational way "take it out on their less influential neighbors, in the mood of a man who, being afraid to stand up to his wife in a domestic argument, relieves his feelings by kicking the cat."[8] Such feelings, as well as the "kicking-the-cat" response, were certainly present during the anti-Mexican outbursts of the early 1920s, 1930–35, and 1953–54.

Also relevant is the fact that witch-hunting and scapegoating are "typically American" pursuits, going back to our earliest days as a nation. The anti-freemasonry and Temperance movements of the 19th Century, the 19th and 20th century anti-Catholic movements, the "Red scares" of the 1920s and 1950s, are all manifestations of what Richard Hofstadter has called "the paranoid style in American politics":

> The recurrence of the paranoid style over a long span of time ... suggests that a mentality disposed to see the world in the paranoid's way may always be present in some considerable minority of the population. But the fact that movements employing the paranoid style are not constant but come in successive episodic waves suggests that the paranoid disposition is mobilized into action chiefly by social conflicts that involve ultimate schemes of values and that bring fundamental fears and hatreds, rather than negotiable interests, into political action. ... The paranoid tendency is aroused by a confrontation of opposed interests which are (or are *felt* to be) totally irreconcilable, and thus by nature not susceptible to the normal political processes of bargain and compromise.[9]

TABLE 2.—DO YOU FAVOR OR OPPOSE ALLOWING ADDITIONAL SOUTHEAST ASIAN REFUGEES TO COME TO LIVE IN THE UNITED STATES?

Survey and date of interviewing	Percentage of respondents who:		
	Favor	Oppose	Don't know
The Harris Survey, June, 1975............	37	49	14
The Harris Survey, July, 1977............	31	57	12
The Roper Poll, September, 1979.........	19	72	10

Sources of data: Harris, 1975: "Viet Refugees Given Cold Reception by Public," The Harris Survey, news release dated June 26, 1975. Harris, 1977: "Close the Door to Refugees," The Harris Survey, news release dated August 25, 1977. Roper, 1979: Walter Huddleston, "Seventy-two Percent Believe Refugee Program Excessive," statement in *The Congressional Record*—Senate, September 17, 1979, p. S12815 (the tabular survey data are reprinted as an appendix). These results are from national samples of 1,400–1,500 adults, with an error factor of (plus or minus) three percentage points, 95 percent of the time. Sampling error is higher when results are compared across different surveys.

This, according to Michael Teitelbaum, is precisely the kind of confrontation of interest which is generating pressure for immigration restriction in the United States today:

> The many critics of current U.S. immigration policy cannot be simply dismissed as xenophobic restrictionists. Even unthreatened and non-xenophobic people with progressive and humanitarian instincts differ greatly, sometimes vituperatively, in their perceptions of and prescriptions for American immigration policy. In large part this is because the debate is a contest of 'right' versus 'right.' Excluding the kooks on the fringes, all sides advocate human rights and justice; none supports persecution and injustice. The disagreement is about which basic rights have precedence over which other basic rights; consensus in such a setting is, unsurprisingly, elusive.[10]

Whatever the present situation, it is true that in the past, such collisions of fundamental concerns about status mobility, morality, religion, and culture have given rise to political movements which have had an explicitly anti-immigrant dimension.[11] In all these movements, the alien was seen as a threat to the American middle-class way of life. Today, U.S. politicians speak not of threats to middle-class lifestyles but of the danger posed by the private cultures of recent immigrants, which (allegedly) threaten to overwhelm or seriously dilute the public culture that mainstream (middle-class) Americans seek to perpetuate.[12]

Viewing such movements in an even broader, socio-biological perspective, Orrin Klapp theorizes that "every society, indeed every living thing, needs a balance between openness and closedness which varies according to the system. If it opens too far, it will feel a strain to come back to more . . . closing." Klapp contends that "modern society has wandered into a crisis of social noise," inducing many people to want to close boundaries, to strike back at real or imagined enemies, to insist on zero growth policies, and other kinds of defensive "closing" responses. Klapp also notes that such defensive reactions are intimately related to a felt need to preserve a sense of individual and collective identity:

> When an alien group or strange information invades a community, it should be no surprise to find that closing centers on sharpening collective identity and preserving it from the noise of conflicting styles. . . . Ways of life, life-style, collective identity, seem to be one of the important things protected by closing to immigration.

TABLE 3.—SHOULD IT BE AGAINST THE LAW TO EMPLOY ILLEGAL ALIENS?*

Survey and date of interviewing	Percentage of respondents who think it:		
	Should	Should not	Don't know
American Institute of Public Opinion (Gallup Poll), March, 1977	82	14	4
American Institute of Public Opinion (Gallup Poll), September–October, 1977	72	23	5
American Institute of Public Opinion (Gallup Poll), November, 1980	76	18	6

*The exact question asked was, "Do you think it should or should not be against the law to employ a person who has come into the U.S. without proper papers?" Under current (1981) U.S. law, it is not a crime for a U.S. employer to knowingly hire an illegal immigrant. Legislation which has been proposed to close this loophole ("the Texas proviso") in the existing Immigration and Nationality Act is commonly referred to as "employer sanctions" legislation.

Sources of data: Gallup, March and September–October, 1977: *Gallup Opinion Index*, Report no. 151 (February, 1978), p. 3. Gallup, 1980: "Most U.S. Citizens Favor a Hard Line Toward Illegal Aliens," by George Gallup, *The San Diego Union*, November 30, 1980, p. A-22. National samples of 1,500–1,600 respondents, with sampling error of (plus or minus) 3 percentage points, 95 percent of the time. Sampling error increases when comparing results across surveys.

Such concerns may easily underlie closing rationalized on other grounds, such as property protection or even fear of 'lawlessness.'[13]

As discussed below, much of the current furor over illegal immigration is justified publicly by a concern about rising crime rates and the contagion of lawlessness in U.S. society, which is blamed partly upon official tolerance of high levels of illegal immigration.

THE NEW AMERICAN NATIVISM: SOME EMPIRICAL INDICATORS

Since 1945, when George Gallup asked his respondents in a national survey whether more European immigrants should be allowed into the U.S., the American public has consistently favored *lower* levels of immigration than those permitted under U.S. laws. As shown in table 1, the proportion of the U.S. public favoring a decrease in *legal* immigration rose sharply from 1965 to 1981, even allowing for problems of comparability from one national survey to another. The data also show low levels of public tolerance for admission of political refugees from Southeast Asia, Cuba, and Haiti (table 2), and steadily rising support for employer penalties legislation, a national counterfeit-resistant worker identification card, and other measures advocated by many public officials and special interest groups as tools for reducing illegal immigration (tables 3 and 4).

A survey of the San Diego County population conducted in the fall of 1979 found that nearly half of the respondents felt that legal immigration should be reduced; only 15 percent believed it should be increased. But the most interesting finding of this survey was the specific *anti-Mexican* bias that it detected, even in a local area whose economic livelihood depends heavily upon continued access to low-cost Mexican labor and consumer spending by Mexican immigrants and tourists. Respondents were asked to evaluate whether immigrants coming from seven different countries or regions of the world had positive or negative effects on life in San Diego. The results were striking: Canadian and West European immigrants were perceived as having the least negative effects on San Diego, while Mexican immigrants were seen as having the most negative impact—even more so than immigrants from other Latin American countries (see table 5). Clearly, it is not just immigration, or even illegal immigration, that concerned

TABLE 4.—SHOULD EVERYONE IN THE U.S. BE REQUIRED TO CARRY
AN IDENTIFICATION CARD, SUCH AS A SOCIAL SECURITY CARD, OR NOT?

Survey and date of interviewing	Percentage of respondents who think everyone:		
	Should be	Should not be	Don't know
American Institute of Public Opinion (Gallup Poll), March, 1977	45	50	5
American Institute of Public Opinion September–October, 1977	65	30	5
American Institute of Public Opinion November, 1980	62	33	5

Sources of data: March, 1977: *The Gallup Poll, Public Opinion 1972–1977* (Wilmington, Del.: Scholarly Resources, Inc., 1978), vol. 2, p. 1051. September–October, 1977. *Gallup Opinion Index,* Report no. 151 (February, 1978), p. 5, November, 1980: George Gallup, "Most U.S. Citizens Favor a Hard Line Toward Illegal Aliens," *The San Diego Union,* November 30, 1980, p. A-22. National sample sizes range from 1,500–1,600, with an error factor of (plus or minus) three percentage points, 95 percent of the time. Sampling error increases when comparing results across surveys.

the average citizen in San Diego: The *country of origin* for most of the immigrants—Mexico—was also an important consideration. While we lack comparable data from other parts of the country, it is highly unlikely that the results from San Diego represent only a local aberration, especially in the U.S. Southwest.

What kinds of people are most likely to hold anti-immigrant or anti-Mexican attitudes and beliefs? The available evidence, from opinion surveys, letters, and other reactions to media reports on immigration, suggests that the new American nativists are drawn disproportionately from the following segments of the U.S. population:

- Older people—those over 50 years of age, especially retirees.
- People who hold higher-status jobs (white collar workers and skilled, blue-collar workers).
- College-educated people, or at least people with a complete high school education.
- White people.
- Males.
- Residents of the Midwest and the South (followed by the East and the West).
- Members of labor unions (or members of "labor union families").
- People who classify themselves as "moderate" to "conservative" in political philosophy.
- People who are "isolationist" rather than "internationalist" in their world view (oppose foreign aid, and participation in international organizations; are chauvinistic, ethnocentric, etc.).
- People who are economic conservatives.
- People who are paranoid and hostile (toward other people in general).

One quantitative analysis of survey data collected from national samples in the middle and late 1950s demonstrated that these last four attitudinal orientations correlate positively with a restrictionist position on immigration.[14] While we lack comparable analyses of more recent survey data, the qualitative evidence from letters and unstructured interviews strongly suggests the existence of a coherent attitudinal syndrome among a significant minority of the U.S. population which includes anti-immigrant sentiments.

It is striking that so much of the hard core of the new American nativists seems to consist of white, reasonably well-educated, middle-to-upper-class, middle-aged males. Ironically, these people are the least likely to be threatened in the labor market by poorly educated, monolingual (Spanish-speaking), unskilled Mexicans and most other recent illegal immigrants entering the United States. Clearly, they are motivated to take a hard line by other kinds of concerns, unrelated to labor market impacts. What are these concerns?

IMMIGRATION IN THE "ERA OF LIMITS"

The politics of immigration in the U.S. today is, increasingly, the politics of inflation, resource scarcity, high taxes and government deficits. As the mass media tell us incessantly, we now live in "the era of limits." Instead of boundless horizons, the average American now sees real or imagined limits popping up everywhere.[15] There is a pervasive sense of constraints on our natural resources (both at home and abroad); on the ability of the U.S. economy to provide enough well-paying jobs for all who seek them; and on the capacity of our society to integrate poorly educated, low-skilled, culturally "different" people into productive roles.

Intentionally or unintentionally, many of the country's opinion leaders now foster the image of the U.S. as a closed ecological-economic system, whose absorptive capacity has already been exceeded, and which is increasingly overburdened by the poor of *other* countries which cynically choose to export their poverty, unemployment, and overpopulation. According to ecologist Garrett Hardin, the new wave of immigrants threatens to exceed the "carrying capacity" of our geographic area. We have reached the "limit of altruism."[16] Or, in the words of Senator Alan Simpson of Wyoming, the American people now suffer from "compassion fatigue."[17] And if there is still any compassion left, it should be visited upon our own poor, not foreigners. As a letter-writer from Des Plaines, Illinois, put it,

> "NO COUNTRY IN THE WORLD, NO SOCIETY, NO ECONOMY, can POSSIBLY keep up with the burgeoning population of Mexico. ... Even with our wealth, growth (industry) and general expertise, we are having a vast unemployment problem, slums, urban decay,

unemployment of our 'over 65' forced into a virtual pauper's fixed income. Why not correct *these* things?"[18]

Since the late 1970s, many Americans have also seen their real incomes being eroded by the country's high rate of inflation. Paychecks that don't go nearly as far as they once did are blamed increasingly on excessive government spending, which in turn is blamed on costly cash-assistance programs benefiting mostly minorities (blacks, Chicanos, Puerto Ricans, illegal aliens). Even foreign aid programs are viewed as a form of welfare for the poor (and wealthy elites) of foreign countries. The anti-immigrant sentiment of the 1970s and 1980s forms part of the public backlash against the expansion of the social welfare economy in the United States.[19] The presence of illegal immigrants and refugees is generally perceived as an important factor contributing to government spending for social welfare programs, since these immigrants are popularly believed to be heavy consumers of all kinds of tax-supported social services. While the more sophisticated members of the public don't believe that once Mexican illegals enter the U.S., they head straight for the welfare lines, many citizens *do* believe it. When confronted with the overwhelming social science evidence that contradicts their belief, they take a don't-confuse-me-with-the-facts stance:

> *I'd* like to live a little, *too*, but with the excessive taxes, I can only EXIST, and when I am forced to ultimately retire, must I face the future with a fixed income in an inflation world? . . . I don't enjoy the thought of eating dog food, just because my taxes are so high, MUCH OF IT because we are forced to care for these illegal aliens.[20]
>
> I cannot feel sorry for the aliens who have FICA [Social Security taxes] taken from their pay checks. I'm delighted to hear that we do get something from these aliens that have no right to be in the United States. And what do they receive in return? . . . Better living conditions, free clinics, unemployment [compensation], and even welfare. From other articles I have read I do not believe your 0.5% figures on aliens who receive welfare payments.[21]

A poll of Los Angeles residents taken in March, 1981, found that 62 percent felt that illegal immigrants "take more from the U.S. economy through social services and unemployment benefits than they contribute to the U.S. economy through taxes and productivity." Only 18 percent of the respondents believed that

TABLE 5.—SAN DIEGO RESIDENTS' EVALUATION OF THE EFFECTS OF IMMIGRATION FROM VARIOUS SOURCE COUNTRIES/REGIONS ON LIFE IN SAN DIEGO

Immigrants originating in:	Percentage of respondents who perceive negative or slightly negative impact on San Diego
Canada	11.8
Western Europe	16.6
Africa	21.6
Asia	35.8
Middle East	32.2
Latin America [entire region]	30.6
Mexico	40.0

Source of data: Residential telephone survey of 500 randomly-selected adults living in the San Diego, Calif., area in late summer and early fall, 1979, as reported in C. Richard Hofstetter and Brian Loveman, "Communication Media and Perceptions of Undocumented Immigrants: The Case of San Diego," paper presented at the Annual Meeting of the International Communication Association, Division VI, Political Communication, Acapulco, Mexico, May, 1980, p. 8.

the illegals contribute more than they take, and only 4 percent thought that they pulled their own weight in the society.[22] In the San Diego County survey cited above, over 70 percent of the respondents believed that undocumented workers make extensive use of tax-supported social services, especially welfare (44 percent), health services (47 percent), and schools (22 percent). However, only 26 percent of the respondents claimed to *personally know* of a case in which an illegal immigrant utilized public services.[23] It is noteworthy that both of these surveys were conducted in cities where social science research findings about the substantial tax contributions and low rates of social service utilization among illegal immigrants had been widely publicized through local newspapers during the previous three years.

Such findings seem to indicate a hardened public perception that immigrants—regardless of their legal status here—are a burden on the U.S. economy and society; that these workers contribute little of value—certainly nothing that is *necessary* to the country. Rather, they are superfluous, free-loading and potentially disruptive.[24]

Many of the people who are angry about the "give-away programs for illegal aliens" are also angry about the treatment which they themselves receive from the governmental system. These are people who have some kind of beef with the federal government bureaucracy, which they feel has been unresponsive to their needs or has abused or cheated them out of some benefit to which they were supposedly entitled. They resent illegal immigrants because the mere presence of these people in the U.S. is believed to give them automatic access to valuable public benefits to which the illegals have no right, while the average U.S. citizen who *is* entitled to receive such benefits often finds it difficult to obtain them. Thus, in an important though roundabout way, citizens' perceptions that the system isn't working any more, at least to their personal benefit, are fueling anti-immigrant hostility. As a financially-pressed 26-year-old Anglo secretary complained to the San Diego public television station, "Why are there so many special programs for immigrants while U.S. citizens can't get on welfare?"[25] Senior citizens who have problems with their Social Security payments are also more likely to respond in this way.

There is, of course, no empirical basis for the popular belief that illegal immigrants—or even legal immigrants—receive preferential treatment by government agencies providing social services. Illegal immigrants are barred by federal law from receiving cash-assistance benefits of any kind, and most agencies dispensing such benefits have instituted effective screening procedures. Still, numerous public officials and even major newspapers still reinforce the mythology, with reports like the one under a headline, "Illegal Aliens Receiving U.S. Housing Aid," "Preliminary inquiries by congressional investigators suggest that substantial numbers of illegal aliens receive federal housing subsidies while hundreds of thousands of citizens wait months or years for similar assistance." Six paragraphs later in the same story, we learn the empirical basis for this inflammatory assertion: Auditors from the Congressional General Accounting Office believe that there are "substantial numbers" of illegal aliens living in federally assisted housing projects, but "federal housing officials said they could not estimate the total number of illegal aliens receiving subsidies because applicants were not asked about their citizenship or immigration status."[26]

For other Americans, immigration from Mexico is a problem primarily because of its alleged contribution to crime and to disregard for the law in the United States. People living in areas near the southern border often blame Mexican migrants for increased crime rates in their communities, especially for petty theft and burglary. In the 1979 San Diego County survey, for example, 57 percent of the respondents believed that illegal immigration increased the level of criminal activity in San Diego.[27] In fact, undocumented migrants from Mexico are far more likely to be the *victims* of crime during their stay in the U.S. than perpetrators of it.[28] It is too risky for them to expose themselves to detection by local law officers, who often collaborate closely with the U.S. Immigration Service.[29] Nevertheless, Mexican illegals are commonly believed to be a major source of crime and higher law-enforcement costs in many southwestern cities.

Others criticize the immigrant for making a mockery of our legal system, through the mere act of illegal entry into the United States. This "illegality-breeds-illegality" theme is prominent in the Final Report of the U.S. Select Commission on Immigration and Refugee Policy. One of the principal justifications for a stepped-up border enforcement effort provided by the Commission's Chairman was that "widespread illegality erodes confidence in the law generally,"[30] which contributes to rising crime rates among the *non*-immigrant portion of the population.

Illegal immigrants—as well as refugees and other legal immigrants—are also thought to contribute to higher tax bills for law enforcement and various cash-assistance programs by taking jobs away from disadvantaged U.S. citizens, who are then driven onto the welfare rolls or into lives of crime in order to support themselves. Restrictionist lobbying organizations have hammered away at this theme, with both hard-pressed white middle-class taxpayers and racial minorities (blacks, Chicanos) as target groups.[31] While there is not a single scientific study of "structural unemployment" among U.S. minority group members which identifies immigration (legal or illegal) as a significant contributing factor to the employment problems of these groups,[32] many members of the general public seem convinced that there is a strong causal relationship. Such feelings are even stronger among the black segment of the population. For example, 55 percent of the blacks interviewed in a January, 1979, national *New York Times–CBS*

News survey thought that most illegal immigrants take jobs away from American citizens, as compared with 34 percent of the whites interviewed.[33] There is a long history of hostility between the U.S. black community and new immigrants, dating to the turn of the century, which provides fertile ground for such fears, even among blacks who have had no personal experience of competition with immigrants in the labor market.[34]

The existence of these public concerns—and the often vast discrepancies between public perceptions and the empirical realities as we understand them to date—suggest something more basic at work here than simple ignorance, or even public ignorance skillfully manipulated by opportunistic politicians and sensation-seeking journalists. Rather, many Americans seem to have a *need to believe* that immigrants are to blame for their problems. If the illegal alien did not exist, he would have to be invented. Perhaps there are just too many Americans looking for someone to beat up on because of double-digit inflation, high taxes, high crime rates, unemployment, and a host of other domestic economic and social problems. During the past 150 years, immigrants have often served as the most convenient, most visible scapegoats for such problems, and there is no evidence that their usefulness in this regard has diminished.[35]

This way of viewing the new immigration, and the restrictive policy prescriptions which flow from it, are undoubtedly related to a more generalized sense of loss of control observed among the U.S. population in recent years. Many Americans seem to fear that they are losing control over their own affairs, that the country itself has lost control of its destiny, both at home and abroad, and is hurtling toward some unknown destination with no one in the driver's seat. Inflation and government spending are out of control. Social morality is changing rapidly. There are seemingly limitless invasions of privacy, at the hands of both government and large corporations. As public opinion analyst Daniel Yankelovich recently observed,

> Increasingly during the late 1970s and early 80s, domestic economic problems were tied to international developments—the eroded position of U.S. industries due to foreign competition, serious trade imbalances, slippage in the value of the dollar, and so forth. . . . In the public eye, American travails in the world arena are part of a pervasive concern about 'loss of control.'[36]

One of the many forms of loss of control which bothers the American public is loss of control over the country's borders: the sense that, due to incompetence and lack of will on the part of our elected officials, we are now at the mercy of Caribbean dictators who inundate us with unwanted refugees (the Cuban push-out of the spring, 1980; the exodus of Haitian boat people). We are equally at the mercy of irresponsible, self-interested Mexican politicians and business elites who are allegedly content to use the U.S. as a dumping ground for their overly numerous, unemployed people.

> Mexico is talking poor, but if other oil experts can be believed, the recent oil discoveries in Mexico may equal or SURPASS those in some countries in the Mid-East. . . . It's time we woke up and stopped being patsies—Uncle Stupid.[37]

> Why help Mexico solve its overpopulation and unemployment problems by admitting illegals into the U.S., especially when Mexico has for decades blamed the U.S. for all its ills and problems? Why encourage Mexico to go on damning our economic and social systems and then plaguing us with their unemployables and incompetents?[38]

> America does not owe Mexico *anything*.[39]

Many people who clamor for more restrictive immigration and refugee policies seem to be responding to the message communicated in a 1981 advertising campaign for a U.S. auto maker whose product was seriously threatened by foreign competition: "America is not going to be pushed around any more," especially by "third-rate" countries like Cuba, Haiti, Mexico, Iran, Libya, etc.

To many Americans, this seems to be an entirely rational and appropriate response to a world turned upside down. Sociologist Richard Sennett, describing supporters of the Moral Majority movement, sees them as people who "feel dislocated in America now; who fear the society they were brought up to believe in is disappearing, or has disappeared."[40] It is plausible that a large segment of the new American nativists are similarly motivated. This helps to explain the highly emotional quality of their response to public policies such as bilingual education; even to bilingual services provided by the private sector (e.g., telephone companies).

Bilingualism and the whole notion of cultural pluralism are under fire in the United States today. Again, the furor over bilingualism and biculturalism stems directly from public concerns about immigration, and especially immigration from Mexico and other Spanish-speaking countries, because *that kind* of immigration is more likely to accelerate the emergence of a truly bilingual, bicultural society. Such a development is viewed as fundamentally threatening by most English-speaking people in the United States. These concerns have been legitimated by many of the country's opinion leaders. For example, according to a former Ford-Foundation officer writing in the influential journal *Foreign Affairs*:

> American immigration flows have come to be dominated to an unprecedented degree by immigrants speaking a single foreign language—Spanish—contrary to the intention of recent immigration reforms to encourage all forms of diversity and pluralism. . . . Over the past decade perhaps 50 percent or more of all legal and illegal immigrants to the United States have been from [that] single foreign-language group. Such linguistic concentration is quite unprecedented in the long history of U.S. immigration. While there were substantial concentrations of a particular language group in past decades. . . . those concentrations that did occur proved to be short-lived.[41]

Why such concern about the predominance of a particular language group in the current wave of immigration which is not, incidentally, unprecedented in the history of U.S. immigration? Because Mexicans and most other Spanish-speaking nationalities are believed to be incapable of assimilating rapidly and completely into American society. They allegedly preserve, far more tenaciously than previous immigrant groups, the language and other elements of the home-country culture. Moreover, because of the home country's proximity to the U.S., the "fragment culture" of emigrés living in the U.S. is constantly being replenished and reinforced by newly arriving migrants and by those who shuttle back-and-forth between Mexico and the United States.

All this, in the view of many Americans, sets the stage for cultural separatism and, inevitably, political separatism, whipped up by allegedly opportunistic Chicano politicians seeking to expand their power base.[42] In short, failure to adopt a much more restrictive immigration policy—particularly one that emphasizes enforcement along our southern border with Mexico—will lead according to this view inevitably to widespread social and political turmoil.

The spectre of a "Spanish-speaking Quebec in the U.S. Southwest" was raised and elevated by such people as former CIA

Director William Colby to the status of a major national security threat.[43] Even some of the more temperate commentators on national immigration policy have begun to characterize the new wave of immigration from Mexico and other Spanish-speaking Western Hemisphere countries as a threat to U.S. security, defined broadly as the capacity to protect the individual and collective welfare and identity of U.S. citizens. In his supplementary statement for the Final Report of the U.S. Select Commission on Immigration and Refugee Policy, Senator Alan Simpson, of Wyoming, summed up the problem as he saw it:

> The impact of immigration on the national interest depends on the number and characteristics of immigrants and on how well they assimilate the values and way of life of the American people. . . . The present immigration flow differs from past flows in one . . . significant way. Immigration to the United States is now dominated to a high degree by persons speaking a single foreign language, Spanish, when illegal immigration is considered [in the estimate of total numbers]. *The assimilation of the English language and other aspects of American culture by Spanish-speaking immigrants appears to be less rapid and complete than for other groups.* . . . If immigration is continued at a high level and yet a substantial portion of the newcomers *and their descendants* do not assimilate, they may create in America some of the same social, political and economic problems which existed in the country which they have chosen to depart. . . . Finally, if linguistic and cultural separatism rise above a certain level, the unity and political stability of the nation will in time be seriously eroded.[44]

This definition of "the problem" was directly and forcefully contradicted by the Select Commission's own professional staff, which wrote, in *its* final report:

> Despite the apprehensions of Americans with regard to these questions [of faulty assimilation and cultural/political separatism], it became apparent in the course of our investigations—through site visits and testimony at public hearings as well as research—that the new immigrants are making considerable progress in becoming Americans. . . . In the course of its site visits, the Select Commission visited a great many schools, where the evidence is overwhelming that refugee and immigrant children are adapting well. If American history is any guide, the generation of children born in the United States will perhaps be *too* eager to cast away their cultural inheritances. . . . There is no reason to believe that Mexican Americans will not continue to be loyal to the United States.

... Among naturalized [Mexican-born] citizens, according to one study, electoral participation is 71.1 percent, far above the national average. Such activity does not change the fact that Mexican immigrants have low rates of naturalization. Nor should it obscure the fact that Mexican immigrants along with French-Canadian immigrants report the most difficulty in speaking English, according to a Select Commission study. But these facts have not and do not interfere with the demonstrated, overriding loyalty of Mexican Americans who have served this country well in so many capacities. ... A sound immigration policy will promote many U.S. national interest goals but *will not by itself promote national unity or purpose*.[45]

This benign, optimistic view of the future role of today's new immigrants in U.S. society and politics is not shared by most members of the general public, nor with few exceptions by their elected representatives. Many view immigrants from Mexico as enlarging what is considered to be a problematic, "dysfunctional," potentially disruptive minority group—the Chicanos. The traditional stereotype of the Mexican worker as a quiet, docile, undemanding beast-of-burden[46] is giving way to a much more threatening image emphasizing the militant disposition among unionized Mexican farmworkers: "You are quite wrong that Mexican workers do not pose a threat. . . . Your ideas are somewhat dated generalizations about Mexicans happy to do the dirty, hard work. Here in California they have recently shown more proclivity for striking, demonstrating, etc. etc. than [for] picking up a hoe and whistling 'Cielito Lindo.'"[47]

CONCLUSION

Though the vast majority of U.S. citizens have never had direct, sustained contact with a Mexican immigrant—legal or illegal—most members of the general public seem to have accepted at face value the claim of public officials and special interest representatives that Mexican illegals are to blame for many of the country's social and economic ills. While the real merits of such claims range from arguable (depending on how much significance one attributes to anecdotal evidence vs. social-scientific evidence), to misleading (half-truths), to demonstrably false (e.g., that illegal immigrants are major contributors to rising welfare costs), it cannot be denied that the residue which they have left in the public mind is politically potent.

The set of attitudes, beliefs, and perceptions described in this essay constitutes an important constraint on the range of immigration policy options which are likely to be considered seriously by the U.S. president and Congress, regardless of the political party in power. For example, they make employer sanctions legislation a much more likely choice, and virtually rule out a broad amnesty for long-term illegal immigrants who wish to remain permanently in the United States. The immigration policy options that *do* have broad public support in the U.S. (more aggressive border enforcement, employer sanctions, even mass round-up and deportation campaigns) are precisely the measures which would affect Mexican interests most adversely, and which, if implemented, are likely to cause greatest strain in U.S.-Mexican political relations.

The trend in national survey responses over the past three decades has been toward a harder line on immigration generally, and on undocumented immigration in particular. This trend is likely to persist and intensify, as debates over bilingual education and other domestic policy issues (e.g., health care for indigent patients at public hospitals) focus public attention upon the size of the Spanish-speaking population in the U.S. and its rapid growth. Moreover, the problems of the U.S. economy—stagflation, declining productivity—are deep-seated and of a long-term character. Even if today's generation of political leaders makes the tough, politically risky choices which economists say will be needed to correct these basic structural problems,[48] there will be considerable economic insecurity—if not continued decline in living standards—for a substantial portion of the U.S. population for many years to come. Scapegoats will still be needed, and Mexican immigrants will almost certainly be available in large numbers to play the role—given the projected high demand for their labor by U.S. employers, and the projected surplus of unskilled labor in Mexico's rural areas and small cities for at least the next 15 years.

The stage has been set for another sharp anti-immigrant, anti-Mexican backlash, and when it comes, U.S.-Mexican relations will deteriorate swiftly, regardless of other interests which may be at stake in the bilateral relationship. Mutual interests in economic areas such as trade, energy, and tourism may not be sufficiently strong to offset the inflammatory effects of a punitive

U.S. immigration policy targeted mainly at Mexicans. In other words, if any single issue is likely to provoke a major confrontation between the U.S. and Mexico during the remainder of this century, it is immigration.

Notes

1. "Foreword," in Roy L. Garis, *Immigration Restriction* (New York: Macmillan, 1927), pp. vii–viii.
2. "Halt! U.S. Can't Absorb All Its Immigrants," *Rocky Mountain News*, Denver, Colorado, 19 July 1981.
3. For a general survey of American nativist movements, see John Higham, *Strangers in the Land: Patterns of American Nativism, 1860–1925* (New Brunswick, N.J.: Rutgers University Press, 1955).
4. The most detailed studies of this early phase of American nativism are Ray Allen Billington, *The Origins of Nativism in the United States, 1800–1844* (New York: Arno Press, 1974); L. Dinnerstein, R.L. Nichols, and D.M. Reimers, *Natives and Strangers: Ethnic Groups and the Building of America* (New York: Oxford University Press, 1979), pp. 85–143; and Ira M. Leonard and Robert D. Parmet, *American Nativism, 1830–1860* (New York: Van Nostrand Reinhold Co., 1971).
5. On the 1920–21 repatriation, see Lawrence A. Cardoso, *Mexican Emigration to the United States, 1897–1931* (Tucson, Arizona: University of Arizona Press, 1980). On the repatriation campaign of 1930–35, see Abraham Hoffman, *Unwanted Mexican Americans in the Great Depression: Repatriation Pressures, 1929–1939* (Tucson, Arizona: University of Arizona Press, 1974). On the 1953–54 campaign, see Juan Ramón García, *Operation Wetback: The Mass Deportation of Mexican Undocumented Workers in 1954* (Westport, Connecticut: Greenwood Press, 1980).
6. Suitably impressed with such arguments, 45,000 citizens of San Diego County could bring themselves to vote in November, 1980, for the Grand Dragon of the Ku Klux Klan of California, who was running as the Democratic Party's candidate for Congress in the nation's most populous congressional district. He lost, but some observers speculated that he probably could have won had he been slightly more respectable, avoiding anti-semitic rhetoric and participation in vigilante patrols against Mexicans at the border.
7. Jorge A. Bustamante places heavy emphasis on these economic indicators as determinants of public tolerance for the presence of Mexicans in the U.S. labor market. See, for example, his "La migración indocumentada México-Estados Unidos: relación entre dinámica política y estructuras económicas," paper presented at the Primer Encuentro sobre Impactos Regionales de las Relaciones Económicas México-Estados Unidos, Guanajuato, México, July, 1981.
8. Elmer Davis, *But We Were Born Free* (New York, 1954), pp. 35–36.
9. Richard Hofstadter, *The Paranoid Style in American Politics and Other Essays* (New York: Knopf, 1965).
10. Michael S. Teitelbaum, "Right versus Right: Immigration and Refugee Policy in the United States," *Foreign Affairs* 59 (Fall, 1980):22. This view of the immigration policy-making process, as a confrontation of "irreconcilable" basic

rights (those of immigrants, on the one hand, and those of U.S. natives, on the other), also seems to have been shared by most members of the U.S. Select Commission on Immigration and Refugee Policy. See especially the introduction by Commission Chairman (Rev.) Theodore M. Hesburgh and the "Supplementary Statements by Commissioners" (Appendix B, pp. 331-420) in *U.S. Immigration Policy and the National Interest, Final Report and Recommendations of the Select Commission on Immigration and Refugee Policy with Supplemental Views by Commissioners, March 1, 1981* (Washington, D.C.: U.S. Government Printing Office, 1981).

11. See, for example, Joseph R. Gusfield, *Symbolic Crusade: Status Politics and the American Temperance Movement* (Urbana, Ill.: University of Illinois Press, 1966), pp. 55-57, 155-157; Donald L. Kinzer, *An Episode in Anti-Catholicism: The American Protective Association* (Seattle, Washington: University of Washington Press, 1964), pp. 90, 204; Robert K. Murray, *Red Scare: A Study in National Hysteria, 1919-1920* (Minneapolis, Minn.: University of Minnesota Press, 1955), pp. 265-266; William Preston, Jr., *Aliens and Dissenters: Federal Suppression of Radicals, 1903-1933* (Cambridge, Mass.: Harvard University Press, 1963), pp. 11-33. I am indebted to Ina R. Dinerman of Wheaton College (Mass.) for encouraging me to pursue this line of inquiry.

12. See, for example, the statements of Senator Alan K. Simpson presented at a conference, "Immigration: A Time for Decision," organized by the San Diego City Club, Rancho Bernardo, Calif., 22 June 1981. Simpson is Chairman of the Subcommittee on Immigration and Refugees, Committee on the Judiciary, United States Senate. He was also an influential member of the U.S. Select Commission on Immigration and Refugee Policy.

13. Orrin E. Klapp, *Opening and Closing: Strategies of Information Adaptation in Society*, American Sociological Association Rose Monograph Series (Cambridge and New York: Cambridge University Press, 1978), pp. ix, 135, 140.

14. Herbert McClosky, "Personality and Attitude Correlates of Foreign Policy Orientation," in James N. Rosenau, ed., *Domestic Sources of Foreign Policy* (New York: Free Press, 1967), pp. 93-97, especially table 16.

15. See Richard J. Barnet, *The Lean Years: Politics in the Age of Scarcity* (New York: Simon and Schuster, 1980), chapter I, for an analysis of the origins of these perceptions.

16. Garrett Hardin, *The Limits of Altruism: An Ecologist's View of Survival* (Bloomington, Ind.: Indiana University Press, 1977).

17. Quoted in Ricardo Chavira, "Star Players in Immigration Policy Drama Have a New Look," *The San Diego Union*, 3 May 1981, p. A-10.

18. Personal letter to the author, 1977. Emphasis in original.

19. See Steven P. Erie and Michael K. Brown, "Blacks and the Legacy of the Great Society: The Economic and Policital Impact of Federal Social Policy," *Public Policy*, forthcoming, 1981.

20. Personal letter to the author from a resident of Des Plaines, Illinois, 1977. Emphasis in original.

21. Personal letter to the author from a female senior citizen living in Cincinnati, Ohio, 1978.

22. Harry Bernstein, "Seventy-five Percent of Jobless Would Accept Menial Work," *Los Angeles Times*, 6 April 1981, Part I, page 10. The poll cited was a

telephone survey of 1,681 adults with a sampling error of (plus or minus) four percentage points.

23. Hofstetter and Loveman, "Communication Media and Perceptions of Undocumented Immigrants," op. cit. [table 5], pp. 10-11.

24. For a more detailed explication of the view that immigrant labor is superfluous to the "real" needs of the U.S. economy (i.e., it is simply a *preferred* source of cheap, pliant labor for some employers who could do without it), and a discussion of the empirical evidence which contradicts that view, see Wayne A. Cornelius, "Mexican Migration to the United States," in Susan Kaufman Purcell, ed., *Mexico-United States Relations* (New York: Academy of Political Science, 1981), pp. 67-77; and Clark W. Reynolds, "Labor Market Projections for the United States and Mexico and Their Relevance to Current Migration Controversies," in this volume.

25. Call received in response to a live "public feedback" program on Mexican immigration, 25 March 1981, KPBS-TV, San Diego.

26. A *New York Times News Service* story published in scores of newspapers throughout the U.S. on or about 16 March 1981.

27. Hofstetter and Loveman, "Communication Media and Perceptions of Undocumented Immigrants," op. cit., p. 11.

28. Marshall Carter, "The Political Economy of Crime in the U.S.-Mexico Borderlands: A Preliminary Essay and Investigation from El Paso-Ciudad Juárez," revised version of a paper presented at the Meeting of the North American Economics Association, Washington, D.C., November, 1978; Thomas D. Cordi, "The Impact of Undocumented Immigration on the Administration of Justice in San Diego County," Ph.D. dissertation in progress, Dept. of Political Science, University of California, Berkeley, 1981.

29. U.S. Commission on Civil Rights, *The Tarnished Golden Door: Civil Rights in Immigration* (Washington, D.C.: U.S. Government Printing Office, September, 1980), pp. 91-93; and Cordi, "The Impact of Undocumented Immigration," op. cit.

30. Rev. Theodore Hesburgh, "Introduction," *U.S. Immigration Policy and the National Interest,* op. cit., p. 11.

31. See, for example, a solicitation letter distributed nationally in 1980 by the Federation for American Immigration Reform (FAIR), a Washington, D.C.-based restrictionist organization, which began,"Disadvantaged Americans pay a particularly heavy price for illegal immigration. Millions of illegal workers compete with minorities, youth, and women for scarce jobs. . . . Allowing uncontrolled immigration to deprive our own disadvantaged of desperately needed economic opportunities is not only unreasonable and unjust, but it has also aggravated ethnic and racial tensions to the point of violence in parts of the country."

32. See, for example, the comprehensive review of these studies provided in Garth L. Mangum and Stephen F. Seninger, *Coming of Age in the Ghetto; A Dilemma of Youth Unemployment: Report to the Ford Foundation* (Baltimore, Md.: Johns Hopkins University Press, 1978).

33. Data supplied to the author by the Director of Special Projects, *The New York Times*, February, 1979. Other data from the same survey were reported in William K. Stevens, "Millions of Mexicans View Illegal Entry to U.S. as Door to Opportunity," *The New York Times*, 12 February 1979, pp. 1A and B10.

34. See Stephen Steinberg, *The Ethnic Myth: Race, Ethnicity, and Class in America* (New York: Atheneum, 1981), pp. 201-202, 221.

35. The use of immigrants as scapegoats for domestic economic and social problems is, of course, not limited to the United States. For case studies of the same phenomenon in other countries, see Gary P. Freeman, *Immigrant Labor and Racial Conflict in Industrial Societies: The French and British Experience, 1945-1975* (Princeton, New Jersey: Princeton University Press, 1979); Myron Weiner, *Sons of the Soil: Migration and Ethnic Conflict in India* (Princeton, N.J.: Princeton University Press, 1978); and Alejandro Portes and John Walton, *Labor Class and the International System* (New York: Academic Press, 1981).

36. *Foreign Affairs* 59 (Winter, 1981). See also D. Yankelovich, *New Rules: Searching for Self-Fulfillment in a World Turned Upside Down* (New York: Random House, 1981).

37. Personal letter to the author from a resident of Des Plaines, Illinois, 1977. Emphasis in original.

38. Personal letter to the author from a retiree living in San Diego, Calif., 1978.

39. Letter to the Editor from Steve Teitelbaum, *The New York Times*, 25 February 1979, p. 16E.

40. Quoted in Yankelovich, *Foreign Affairs* (Winter, 1981):702.

41. Teitelbaum, "Right versus Right," *op. cit.*, pp. 26-27.

42. See, for example, Arthur F. Corwin, "A Note on Acculturation," in Corwin (ed.) *Immigrants—and Immigrants: Perspectives on Mexican Labor Migration to the United States* (Westport, Conn.: Greenwood Press, 1978), pp. 353-354.

43. Such was the message communicated by Colby in two widely quoted interviews granted to *Playboy Magazine* and *The Los Angeles Times* in June, 1978. Colby described population growth in Mexico over the next 20 years and the spillover effects of this growth into the U.S. (via illegal immigration) as the single greatest threat to U.S. national security in the years ahead—greater even than the threat posed by the Soviet Union.

44. "Statement of Commissioner Alan K. Simpson," Appendix B, *U.S. Immigration Policy and the National Interest, op. cit.*, pp. 408, 412-413.

45. Lawrence H. Fuchs, "Chapter IV: First Principles of Immigration Reform—E Pluribus Unum—More Than a Motto," in *Staff Report of the Select Commission on Immigration and Refugee Policy*, 30 April 1981 (Washington, D.C.: U.S. Government Printing Office, 1981), pp. 145, 149, 156-157.

46. See, for example, Cletus E. Daniel, *Bitter Harvest: A History of California Farmworkers, 1870-1941* (Ithaca, N.Y.: Cornell University Press, 1981), pp. 67, 105-106.

47. Personal letter to the author from a man living in Sacramento, California, 1979.

48. See, for example, Lester C. Thurow, *The Zero-Sum Society: Distribution and the Possibilities for Economic Change* (New York: Basic Books, 1980).

CHICANOS AND THE BINATIONAL RELATIONSHIP:
Actors or Subjects?

V

14
Chicanos and U.S. Foreign Policy: The Future of Chicano–Mexican Relations

Rodolfo O. de la Garza

During President Luis Echeverría's administration (1970–1976), the Mexican government initiated a series of activities that suggested a new and positive interest in Chicano affairs.[1] This change was influenced in part by Dr. Jorge Bustamante, Mexico's internationally recognized authority on undocumented workers who, as a result of his extensive educational and personal experiences with Chicano academics and community, became convinced that it would be mutually beneficial to Chicanos and Mexicans to forge a close alliance.[2] The general pattern of increased interest and cooperation initiated under President Echeverría continues today and seems irreversible, that is, Chicanos and Mexicans will surely interact with increasing frequency. What is not clear is the areas in which contacts will expand, who will benefit most from them, or how quickly they will be established. The objective of this study is to suggest answers to these and other questions regarding this nascent relationship.

There are several reasons why this developing relationship merits serious attention at this time. Although the Chicano movement began in the 1960s, it is only very recently that the

---

Rodolfo O. de la Garza is Director, Center for Mexican American Studies and Associate Professor of Government, University of Texas, Austin. He is co-author, with F. Chris García, of *The Chicano Political Experience: Three Perspectives*. This article originally appeared in *Southwest Political Quarterly* 33 (December 1980):571.
©1980, The University of Utah.

political potential of Chicanos and of the Hispanic community in general is gaining recognition. At the same time Mexico has risen in international stature because of its recent oil finds. This improved status and the undocumented worker issue combine to increase the importance attached by the United States to good relations with Mexico.[3] These simultaneous developments have led to speculation that conditions are now propitious for creating a close relationship between Chicanos and the Mexican government, and about the effects such an alliance might have on U.S. domestic and foreign policy.[4]

It is important to exercise caution in predicting how this relationship will develop because its impact on Chicanos and Mexico is unclear. It could enhance the internal political stature of Chicanos and enable them to deal more effectively with U.S. political leaders and institutions. Through such a relationship Chicanos might embarrass the United States and gain public recognition that is otherwise unavailable to them. Such a relationship might benefit Chicanos directly and ultimately assist them in developing the political and economic resources needed to challenge more effectively the dominant political structures. Conversely, because the U.S. government may consider such a relationship as potentially threatening to national interests, Chicanos may risk, if they identify too closely with Mexico, their future as well as their tentative and recently won political legitimacy. The possibility of these conflicting consequences has not prevented various segments of the Chicano community from advocating their respective viewpoints. Thus, because such a relationship might affect the political future of the Chicano community, and because it might also have significant implications for United States–Mexican relations, the basis on which a Chicano–Mexican relationship might develop and what its consequences might be must be examined. Finally, it is necessary to reiterate that this study is intended as a clarification of some of the factors that will affect the evolution of this relationship and should not be considered as a defense or attack on closer ties between Mexicans and Chicanos. If it achieves its purpose, this study should also enhance our understanding of Chicano, Mexican and U.S. politics.

This paper will consider first why Mexico might attempt to establish closer contacts, and what it might gain or offer the Chicano community. It will then examine the foundation on which such a relationship might be built, what Chicanos might gain or lose from it and, if it were established, what impact Chicanos might have as a lobby for the Mexican government.

THE MEXICAN PERSPECTIVE

Its unique relationship and vulnerability vis-à-vis the United States suggest that Mexico might profit greatly from having a Chicano lobby. The Mexican economy has been so tied to the American economy that the distinction between U.S. domestic and foreign policy affecting Mexico is blurred because almost any important decisions affecting the American economy has significant impact on the Mexican economy. Furthermore, Mexico's resistance to any policy that will reduce the flow of undocumented workers to the United States (the most troublesome aspect of U.S.-Mexican relations)[5] is opposed by almost every interest group involved, and some Chicano organizations seem to be the only groups publicly supporting Mexico's position.[6] Mexico would seem to profit from having its concerns continuously raised and defended in the American policy-making arena, and Chicanos seem to be the only group that is likely to perform this function.

Even though Chicanos are the principal group openly defending the Mexican position on the issue of undocumented workers, this may not be sufficient reason for Mexico to seek closer ties with them. Although there is an increasing number of Mexican officials evaluating the potential of this relationship, relatively few officials are still concerned or well informed about Chicano issues. In the view of one Mexican academic specifically involved in designing educational programs for Chicanos, "Mexican officials never thought Chicanos could be important and interesting to Mexico, and there may only be five who think so today."[7] Furthermore, at least two of Mexico's recent secretaries of foreign relations were known to be openly hostile to Chicanos.[8] Some Mexican analysts, moreover, see no basis on which to build stronger bonds. "There may be a few connections on some specific interests such as the issue of undocumented workers. Except for that, I don't see what groups in Mexico are tied to Chicano interests. I think there may be clashes even over illegal immigration. The Mexican government may accept conditions which Chicanos wouldn't accept."[9] Mexico's need for Chicano lobbyists may also be obviated by its ability to negotiate a favorable border policy and other concessions in exchange for an oil agreement beneficial to the United States.

Should Mexican officials conclude that Mexico would benefit from such a relationship, it becomes important to consider on what foundations it might be built. From an economic perspective, Mexican officials and businessmen might begin to utilize Chicano businessmen and professionals as their representatives in the United States. Given the paucity of Chicano businessmen and professionals, however, the advantage to Mexico of such efforts would be extremely limited. Few Chicanos, after all, are partners in major law firms, agricultural firms or large import-export companies, and it is precisely in these areas where Mexican commercial interests would best be served.[10]

A greater possibility of strengthening linkages and ties exists in educational and cultural areas. Currently, for example, the *Secretaría de Educación* (Department of Education) is developing materials for bilingual programs in the United States,[11] and the San Antonio, Texas branch of the *Universidad Nacional Autónoma de México* offers a continuing series of classes and lectures designed to promote increased awareness of Mexico and to foster closer relations with Chicanos as well as with Texans in general. Furthermore, the Mexican government, publishers and Mexican universities are showing an ever-increasing interest in Chicano affairs as is shown by the sharp rise in conferences and publications focusing on various aspects of the Chicano experience.[12] The most significant development in this area is the *Becas de Aztlán* program, begun under the Echeverría Administration. This program offers $10 million in scholarships over the next five years for Chicanos to study in Mexico.[13]

This type of assistance is significant because it addresses one of the principal goals of the Chicano movement. Since the 1960s, Chicanos have demanded bilingual programs and increased scholarships for professional training. While not explicitly political, these programs do respond to real Chicano needs and may contribute substantially to tying Chicanos more securely to Mexico.

Beyond these, it is unclear what inducements Mexico could use to draw Chicanos into a closer relationship. Chicanos would no doubt expect Mexico to assist them with their internal political struggle, but there are at least three reasons why this is unlikely.

First, a fundamental plank in Mexican foreign policy is nonintervention in the internal affairs of another nation.[14] Commenting on the issue of Chicano civil rights would violate this principle, and thus Mexican officials may be expected to abstain from such activity. During a recent meeting with Chicano leaders in Mexico City, for example, President López Portillo "was very careful not to say anything that could be considered interfering in the internal affairs of the United States."[15] Second, given the Mexican regime's authoritarian tendencies and frequent use of violence to suppress dissidents,[16] Mexican officials would make themselves extremely vulnerable to similar criticisms should they begin to criticize domestic policies in the United States. Finally Mexico's economic health is so dependent on good relations with the United States that Mexico is unlikely to risk that relationship in behalf of Chicanos. This reasoning would seem to explain why President López Portillo did not participate in a meeting in Mexico City of the National Council de la Raza, a major Chicano umbrella organization, after initially committing himself to attend. Between his initial commitment and the actual meeting, U.S. State Department officials seem to have communicated their displeasure about the prospect of closer Chicano–Mexican relations, and this seems to have kept both President López Portillo and U.S. Ambassador Patrick Lucey away from this meeting.[17]

It would, furthermore, be presumptuous to conclude that Chicanos will automatically respond to Mexican overtures out of a sense of cultural unity as some writers have argued. This view characterizes the Chicano movement as having "a clear ideological thrust in the direction of greater political identification with Latin America," rather than as an effort aimed at enhancing the internal social, political and economic status of Chicanos.[18] Such a view also ignores the historical antipathy between Chicanos and Mexicans and mistakenly equates Chicano identification with Mexican cultural symbols with Chicano support for the Mexican polity. A substantial percentage of Chicanos articulate a commitment to the maintenance of Spanish and other cultural traditions, but there is no evidence of their knowledge about or support for the Mexican social and political systems.[19]

Moreover, while recognizing a cultural bond, Chicanos and Mexicans also acknowledge differences. As several Chicano writers have pointed out, Chicanos often go to Mexico expecting to find themselves but come away instead understanding that being Chicano is not being Mexicano.

> I am revolted by the feelings welling up inside of me. Why do I feel this mania for order and sterility? Why am I so ashamed of the mordidas, poverty and prostitution? Why do the sneers of the gabacho soldier boys swaggering into cantinas offend me?
> Finalmente viene la realización de lo que verdaderamente somos, una mezcla. Hay que aceptar parte de nuestra "americanidad" tanto como nuestra "mexicanidad." We must find the happy medium entre los dos, y ser orgullosos de nuestro mestizaje cultural as we are of our racial mixture.[20]

Mexicans also are unsure about how to view Chicanos. Octavio Paz's essay on the Pachuco, for example, is brilliant but misguided because he saw the Pachuco as a Mexican. The Pachuco was a Chicano and can only be understood as such, and today many Chicano academics strongly disagree with his views and resent how others have used that essay to stereotype and condemn Chicanos.[21] Furthermore, Mexicans have long criticized Chicanos for not being culturally pure, for speaking a "bastardized Spanish" and betraying their traditions.[22] Mexican and Chicano academics agree that such views are held by Mexican elites, but the Mexican working class also seems to share them as the following words by an undocumented worker indicate:

> (I) started to learn a little bit about the United States, especially about the pochos, the Mexican-Americans who lived around there. To me a pocho was kind of dumb, because they didn't try to advance themselves. . . . Once in a while I would hear some pocho ask, "In Mexico do they have radios?" or they would ask if we knew about houses or cars? . . .
> If a person is born in Mexico the Mexican-American laughs at you and calls you a dumb person because you come from a dumb country. There is a lot of discord, you see. We don't look like brothers. We are not united. We don't feel the brotherhood.[23]

These attitudes, in combination with Mexico's unique relationship with the United States, may explain why, except for a brief period immediately following the U.S.–Mexican War, Mexico has been so unconcerned with the well-being of Chicanos. Following that war, Mexican officials did their best to ensure that the interests and rights of Mexicans living in the lands that would henceforth be part of the United States would be protected, and the Mexican government also offered land and supplies to any Mexican citizen living in these areas if they would return to the motherland. In addition to these efforts, Mexican representatives were soon protesting the U.S. government's unwillingness to respect and enforce the guarantees of the Treaty of Guadalupe Hidalgo.[24] It must be emphasized that at this time the distinction between Chicanos and Mexicans was only beginning to develop, and therefore Mexico's actions may be interpreted as being primarily in behalf of Mexicans rather than in support of Chicanos.[25]

From the 1850s until the 1970s, Mexican regimes have continued the pattern of strongly defending the interests of their citizens in the United States and ignoring, being hostile to or manipulating Chicanos. Under President Porfirio Díaz's regime (1876-1910), Chicanos frequently asked Mexican consuls in the Southwest to assist them, but their requests were often ignored. When Reies López Tijerina, the leader of the New Mexico land grant movement, initially went to Mexico in 1956 to request support, he was jailed and expelled. In the 1960s, when Chicano officials in Washington D.C. went to the Mexican embassy to join in the celebration of Mexican Independence, they were unceremoniously "kicked out."[26] What best illustrates this pattern, however, is Mexico's behavior during the Bracero Program and towards Chicano land claimants in Texas.

Mexico agreed to participate in the Bracero Program in 1942 only after receiving guarantees that Mexican workers would be well treated. Within one year after the program's initiation, however, braceros in Texas were so abused that the Mexican Secretary of Labor announced that no more braceros would be sent to that state. From then until the end of World War II, Mexico protested the treatment received by Mexicans in the United States, and Mexico even went so far as to use international meetings to voice its grievances. With the end of the war, Mexico's protests declined. This might be explained by the fact that the United States was now less concerned about maintaining a close relationship with Mexico and therefore Mexico was no longer in a position to pressure the United States on racial policies. It might also be explained by the fact that Mexico benefitted greatly from the Bracero Program, and therefore to continue pressing on this issue might jeopardize the program's extension.[27]

Although Mexico protested the maltreatment suffered by Mexican workers and anti-Mexican discrimination in general, there is little evidence of Mexico having systematically concerned itself with Chicano interests.[28] Nonetheless, Mexico's activities in behalf of braceros may also have temporarily improved Chicano working conditions. Abuse of and discrimination against Chicanos did not abate after the war, however, and Mexico showed no concern for their situation.

The manner in which Mexican regimes have responded to Chicano land claimants raises additional questions about the depth of Mexico's concern for Chicano well-being.[29] In 1923 the Mexican government through its consul in San Antonio, Texas included in its claims against the United States those of Chicanos for losses they incurred in Texas since the U.S.–Mexican war. These claims became part of the total claims which the Mexican government presented to U.S. officials to counter U.S. claims against Mexico for losses suffered by U.S. citizens during the Mexican Revolution of 1910. The specific arrangements for dealing with these and other issues are known as the Bucareli Agreements of 1923.

From 1923 to 1941 few of the claims of either country were processed. In 1941 each nation agreed to study and act on the claims each had presented, and Mexico also agreed to compensate the United States $40 million for the difference in total claims each country had filed. Since American claims totaled $99 million more than the Mexican claims, the agreement was clearly beneficial to Mexico. The United States entered into this and other arrangements very favorable to Mexico because of the desire to have close, friendly relations with its southern neighbor in anticipation of the outbreak of World War II.[30]

Although the Mexican government agreed to act on the claims it had presented, it has refused to do so. President Ávila Camacho did submit an executive order in 1941 asking the Mexican Secretary of the Treasury to study the issue and draft a bill to approve, adjust and pay these claims, but the bill was never submitted to the Chamber of Deputies.[31] In 1955, a group of these Chicano land claimants travelled to Mexico City to inquire about their claims, and they demonstrated at the executive residence after the President refused to meet with them. The claims issue was again raised during the Echeverría regime, and Reies López Tijerina, who met with President Echeverría on several occasions, alleges that President Echeverría told him that Mexico was finally willing to settle this issue.³² Once President López Portillo assumed office, however, he was reluctant to proceed with this commitment, and negotiations between representatives of the Mexican Foreign Relations Office and lawyers for the claimants continued for two years. Finally, after a series of private meetings during which the Chicano attorneys became convinced that Mexico would agree to a settlement, President López Portillo, in February, 1978, publicly announced: "We don't have the money to pay for the lands of those American citizens who have these problems. Nor should we. Imagine such a thing."³³ The Chicano attorneys then requested the legal basis for this decision, and they were once again invited to meet with representatives of the Foreign Relations Office in July. Once in Mexico, however, their meeting was cancelled, and they were told that they would be given no further explanations. They returned to the United States and cabled another request for an explanation from President López Portillo. In August, 1978, Chicano land grant claimants demonstrated at the Mexican consulate in San Antonio, Texas, and the California Chapter of La Raza National Lawyers Association issued a resolution asking for Mexico "to issue a principled response" to these claims.³⁴ In October, the Chicano attorneys received a telegram from President López Portillo's office stating that the issue had once more been sent to the Secretary of Foreign Relations for further study.

Overall, then, it is unclear what kind of relationship Mexico might be interested in establishing. Mexico is clearly promoting cultural and educational exchanges which offer substantial benefits to Chicanos. It seems unlikely that Mexico will be equally supportive of Chicano political activities, particularly if doing so arouses the ire of the U.S. government. Given its new-found oil bonanza, Mexico may no longer need any assistance in achieving its objectives in Washington. Finally, in view of the historical absence of a coherent policy vis-à-vis Chicanos and the nature of the Mexican political system, one Mexican official suggests that it is unlikely that Mexico would initiate a policy responsive to Chicano needs because of cultural bonds or altruistic commitments. According to this official, President Echeverría "used" Chicanos but had "no genuine interest in them. President López Portillo does not want to develop relations with them until it is clear how each can help the other."³⁵ Another official cautioned

Chicanos against expecting any genuine support. "It would be naive to expect that Chicanos would be treated differently than lower class Mexicans. They will treat you as they treat their own people—in purely symbolic ways."[36]

THE CHICANO PERSPECTIVE

The Chicano response to closer ties with Mexico is mixed. Some, such as Vilma Martínez, head of the Mexican American Legal Defense and Education Fund, see closer ties with Mexico as the means for improving the Chicano internal political situation. "We all understand that Washington will finally have to listen to us because of Mexico."[37] The premise of this view is that if Chicanos associate themselves more closely with Mexico, as Mexico's importance to the United States increases, so will Chicano political stature. Furthermore, supporting the Mexican position on immigration policy also enhances Chicano political fortunes since each additional immigrant, legal or not, is seen as a future supporter of Chicano interests.[38] A close relationship with Mexico, according to this perspective, will provide Chicanos with an international forum for voicing grievances, and many Chicano scholars see this as particularly valuable since the American press and other public forums have been inaccessible.[39]

Others are cautious about proceeding in this direction because it may jeopardize recent and still tenuous Chicano political gains. To the degree that Chicanos are excluded from the political process in this country, it may be to their advantage to strengthen their relationship with Mexico. As their internal political situation improves, however, Chicanos may have less need for such ties. While acknowledging the tentative status of recent gains, it may be said that the political fortunes of Chicanos have improved measurably. The 1975 Extension of the Voting Rights Act substantially altered state and local political processes allowing the election at these levels of an increasing number of Chicanos,[40] and there are now more high level Chicano and Hispanic federal political appointees than ever before. Another indicator of this improved status is the effort by State Department officials to inform and consult with Chicanos and the Hispanic community generally regarding American foreign policy. In January, 1978, the

State Department invited selected Hispanic leaders to Washington to meet Department officials and discuss the Panama Canal treaty and other issues.[41] The League of United Latin American Citizens (LULAC), the nation's largest Chicano voluntary association, has since established an Hispanic lobby on Inter-American affairs to institutionalize these contacts.[42] The State Department invitation suggests that some Department officials recognize that the Hispanic community may be particularly responsive to Latin American criticisms of American policy toward Latin America, as well as have special insight regarding those policies, a view shared by LULAC leaders. The invitation may also be indicative of the U.S. government's efforts to develop closer relations with Hispanics and thus prevent closer ties from developing between Hispanics and Latin America.

These gains might indicate that Chicano demands for recognition as Americans eligible to exercise the rights and privileges inherent in U.S. citizenship are beginning to be realized. Groups such as the American G.I. Forum and LULAC, the two largest Chicano voluntary associations, emphasize their *Americanness*, and even La Raza Unida, the radical Chicano political party, justifies its activities by appeals to the traditions of American politics and political freedoms.[43] By openly seeking Mexico's support or lobbying for pro-Mexican policies, Chicanos might raise the specter of disloyalty, and the legitimacy of their newfound status would be questioned. Thus, Hispanic officials at the State Department advised members of the National Council de la Raza to exercise caution in their dealings with Mexican officials. "They said we couldn't let ourselves be viewed as agents of a foreign power...."[44] Nonetheless, the above-cited examples suggest that the mere possibility of closer ties to Mexico and Latin America enhances the Chicano's political stature, and carefully developing this relationship might contribute positively to Chicano political fortunes.

Indicative of the risks inherent in a close association with Mexico is the fact that those Chicano leaders who have most actively pursued this relationship are José Angel Gutiérrez and Reies López Tijerina. While there is a great difference in their apparent motivations and their accomplishments differ considerably, today they have two things in common: they have both contributed to the gains achieved by the Chicano movement, and neither is associated with what may be considered mainstream American politics. Thus, since neither stands to gain much by dealing with U.S. policy makers, they have little to lose and everything to gain from working with Mexico.

Other Chicano groups may be more reluctant to support closer links with Mexico because this would imply supporting the continued influx of undocumented workers. Some Chicano legislators in Texas point out that undocumented workers in their districts displace many of their constituents in the labor market, and they therefore favor limiting immigration.[44] The United Farm Workers have also opposed continued immigration, but currently their position is ambiguous since they are now attempting to unionize undocumented workers.[46] Historically, many Chicano organizations opposed the Bracero Program because of its perceived impact on the labor market, among them the American G.I. Forum, the Colorado Federation of Latin American Groups, the Bishop's Committee for the Spanish Speaking, the Illinois Federation of Mexican American Organizations and the Mexican American Educational Conference Committee.[47]

Chicano businessmen and professionals might actively support closer ties if Mexico would work closely with them. Mexican businessmen, for example, could do business primarily with Chicano firms or with Chicano employees in Anglo banks and corporations. To date, Mexican businessmen and government officials have shown little inclination to support Chicanos in this way, but Chicano businessmen and officials are hopeful that Mexico might soon adopt such a policy and are actively seeking to develop such linkages.

Still other sectors of the Chicano community may endorse policies supporting Mexican interests without necessarily endorsing closer ties to Mexico. Chicanos in border cities, for example, recognize that the well-being of their communities is intimately tied to keeping the border open and maintaining close relationships with their Mexican counterparts. They are likely to lobby for liberal trade and immigration policies out of immediate self-interest rather than because of any concern for Mexico's well-being.[48] Many Chicanos will also oppose stricter immigration controls for fear of the increased discrimination and harassment of Chicanos resulting from such measures, and because restricting immigration may prevent immediate relatives from coming to this country.[49] Chicanos may in fact find themselves opposing Mexican immigration in principle and supporting the legal or illegal entry of their friends and relatives.[50]

Finally, most Chicanos are unlikely to be concerned about relations with Mexico. Most Americans place a rather low priority on foreign policy matters,[51] and there is no reason to believe that Chicanos will differ substantially from this norm. To the extent that Chicanos are politically active, they direct their energies toward local issues such as police brutality, housing, employment and education.[52] Thus, relations between Chicanos and Mexicans may well be limited to contacts and programs developed by small groups of Mexican and Chicano elites, and neither of these will be able to claim that they are acting in response to any kind of popular mandate.

Overall, then, the future of Chicano–Mexican relations is nebulous. From an economic perspective, Chicanos could benefit substantially if Mexican firms would work closely with them, but there is no indication that such a pattern is developing. Furthermore, Chicanos are not well represented in the types of firms with which Mexicans work most closely. Moreover, many Chicanos fear that undocumented workers will displace them in the labor market if immigration continues at its present pace. Economically, the impact of closer ties with Mexico seems mixed.

Politically, a similar dilemma exists. Such a relationship could enhance the status of Chicanos but might jeopardize their recently won gains. Pursuing closer ties might also cause serious divisions within the Chicano community for the reasons described above, and this would surely reduce the Chicano's political potential. A major gain for Chicanos from this relationship will be the ready access offered to public forums. This is an important asset; one that Chicanos will surely attempt to develop whatever the overall nature of Chicano–Mexican relations.

Even if this relationship develops, it is doubtful that in the foreseeable future Chicanos will be in a position to influence U.S. policy toward Mexico. Studies on the impact of ethnic groups on U.S. foreign policy indicate that a group's success depends on five factors: Its importance as a pivotal voting bloc, its ability to contribute financially to campaigns, its ability to dominate or influence an important sector such as labor or the media, its ability to demonstrate group solidarity, and its advocacy of policies that are not discordant with American interests.[53] Few ethnic groups meet these criteria, and thus it is not surprising that Greek Americans, Americans of Eastern European descent, and Afro-Americans have had so little impact on policy decisions. Chicanos also fail to meet these criteria; it may even be argued that they meet none of them at the present time. Furthermore, the task of a Chicano lobby is more complicated than that of similar lobbies because it might require Chicanos to align themselves with Mexico against the United States. Other lobbies would seldom encounter such a problem. Chicanos, for example, could find themselves supporting Mexico's position on the price of natural gas to be sold to the United States, while the Greek lobby is concerned with influencing U.S. attitudes toward the resolution of disputes between Greece and Turkey, or the Jewish lobby is concerned with U.S. involvement in Israeli-Egyptian affairs. Under such conditions, it is unlikely that a Chicano lobby would be very successful.

CONCLUSION

While the type and frequency of contacts between Chicanos and Mexicans will surely increase in the coming years, there is no reason to conclude that this relationship will become comparable to that of American Jews and Israel, as one Chicano leader suggests.[54] Although committed to expanding its educational and cultural ties, Mexico seems unlikely to support Chicano political activities because of possible negative U.S. government reactions, and because it is uncertain that a Chicano lobby could achieve the desired results. Mexico's oil reserves may obviate any need Mexico might have had for such a lobby. Moreover, should Mexico decide to develop this relationship, it would have to modify further its historically rooted anti-Chicano biases, and such a change in official attitudes and general public opinion will not be quickly or easily achieved.

Chicanos would profit more from this relationship than would Mexico. Although they run some political risks in identifying too closely with Mexican interests, they might increase their political currency by using Mexico's attention to win otherwise unavailable concessions from U.S. policy-makers. Chicanos will also profit from access to the Mexican media. Economically, Chicano businessmen would benefit from improved relations if Mexico chose to assist them. Such gains might be offset, at least in the minds of many Chicanos, by the loss of jobs resulting from continued Mexican immigration.

To pursue this relationship might be in the interest of Chicanos, but it is unclear why Mexico would be enthusiastic about it. Ironically, Chicanos seem to be in a position vis-à-vis Mexico similar to the one they are with regard to the American political process. In both instances, they seek to improve their status but lack the resources to make U.S. or Mexican officials responsive to them. Furthermore, in view of the way the Mexican government has responded to Chicanos and its own citizens historically, Chicanos would be naive to expect Mexican policy-makers to be more sensitive to their needs than U.S. policy-makers have been. Neither government has a history of being concerned with Chicanos, and there is no reason to expect that either will change its policies for altruistic reasons. If a strong Chicano-Mexican relationship is to develop, Chicano leaders must pursue it with a clear understanding of the gains and risks involved. It would be presumptuous to assume that such a relationship will necessarily serve Chicanos better than a greater involvement in the American political process, or that it will be built easily and automatically on cultural foundations.

Notes

1. In the interests of clarity and brevity, "Chicanos" will be used as a general term identifying all U.S. citizens of Mexican descent, "Hispanics" will refer to all other U.S. citizens of Hispanic origin, and "Mexicans" will refer to citizens of Mexico in Mexico.

2. Interview with Dr. Gilbert Cárdenas, University of Texas at Austin, Spring, 1979. According to Dr. Cárdenas, he, Dr. Juan Gómez-Quiñones, and other Chicano scholars had extended conversations with Dr. Bustamante when the latter was doing his graduate work at Notre Dame University. The idea of close Chicano-Mexican relations first developed during this period.

3. Matthew Nimetz, Counselor of the Department, Department of State, *Current Policy* 46 (November 1978), (Bureau of Public Affairs, Office of Public Information).

4. See, for example, Ron Dorfman, "Black Gold, Brown Power," *Dallas Magazine* (December 1978):117-126; Richard Reeves, "Mexican America," *Esquire*, 2 January 1979, pp. 8-10.

5. Nimetz, *Current Policy*, pp. 2-3.

6. The 1978 legislative priorities of the National Council of La Raza, the principal Chicano umbrella organization, rank immigration as the issue of greatest concern. See "Public Policy and Legislative Priorities," 4 April 1978.

7. Interview, Mexico City, Fall, 1978. Numerous other Mexican officials and scholars interviewed during the fall and spring of 1978-79 made almost identical comments.

8. In 1971, while a member of the Chamber of Deputies, Lic. Santiago Roel, Secretary of Foreign Relations under President López Portillo until May, 1979, responded to requests for an interview with an accusation that I was a traitor to Mexico and other harsh criticisms about the fact that I was not really a Mexican. I pointed out that I was born in the United States and thus could not be a traitor to Mexico, but this made no difference. He made similar anti-Chicano remarks to Professor Caesar Sereseres, Department of Political Science, University of California, Irvine.

9. Interview, Fall, 1978, Mexico City.

10. Chicano commercial activities are described in Jake Fuller, "The Top Ten Mexican-American Business Execs in Texas," in *Texas Business* (June 1979): 25-37. See Ron Dorfman, "Black Gold . . ." for a related but differing view of this subject.

11. Interview, Directora General de la Unidad de Programas Culturales Especiales, Secretaría de Educación, Mexico City, fall, 1978.

12. During the past year conferences have been held at the Universidad Nacional Autónoma de México, the Universidad de Guadalajara, and the UNAM campus in San Antonio. Among the publications are *América ocupada* (translation of *Occupied America* by Rodolfo Acuña) (Ediciones ERA 1976), Gilberto López y Rivas, *Los Chicanos: una minoría nacional explotada* (México: Nuestro Tiempo, 1971), and Reies Tijerina, *Mi lucha por la tierra* (México: Fondo de Cultura Económica, 1978).

13. Dorfman, "Black Gold . . . ," p. 121.

14. Frank Brandenburg, *The Making of Modern Mexico* (Englewood Cliffs: Prentice Hall, 1964), pp. 320-321.

15. As quoted in Dorfman, "Black Gold . . . ," p. 121.

16. Rodger D. Hansen, *The Politics of Mexican Development* (Baltimore: Johns Hopkins Press, 1971).

17. Dorfman, "Black Gold . . . ," p. 123. Mexico's unwillingness to offend American authorities on such issues is also described in Juan Gómez-Quiñones, "Piedras contra la Luna, México en Aztlán y Aztlán en México: Chicano-Mexican Relations and the Mexican Consulates, 1900-1920," in James W. Wilkie, Michael C. Meyer and Edna Monzón de Wilkie, eds., *Contemporary Mexico: Papers of the IV International Congress of Mexican History* (Berkeley: University of California Press, 1976) pp. 494-528.

18. These contrasting views may be found in Irene Fraser Rothenberg, "Mexican American Views of U.S. Relations with Latin America," *Journal of Ethnic Studies*, 6 (Spring 1978):63; F. Chris García and Rodolfo O. de la Garza, *The Chicano Political Experience: Three Perspectives* (Duxbury, Mass.: Duxbury Press, 1977).

19. Leo Grebler et al, *The Mexican American People* (New York: Free Press, 1970), pp. 381-384.

20. Carlos Morton, "Mexican Diary, 1954-1977," in *Nuestro* (April 1978): 34-35. See also Enrique Hank López, "Back to Bachimba," in Ed Ludwig and James Santibañez, ed., *The Chicano: Mexican-American Voices* (Baltimore: Penguin Books, 1971), pp. 261-270; Rodolfo O. de la Garza, "A Chicano Perspective

of Mexico," paper presented at the Border Studies Conference sponsored by the Southwest Cross-Cultural Institute, University of Texas at El Paso, Fall, 1975.

21. Octavio Paz, *El laberinto de la soledad* (México, D.F.: Fondo de Cultura Económica, 1959); Miguel Montiel, "The Social Science Myth of the Mexican American Family," *El Grito*, 3 (Summer 1970):56-63; Octavio Romano V., "The Historical and Intellectual Presence of the Mexican American," *El Grito*, 2 (Winter 1969):32-46.

22. Oscar J. Martínez, *Border Boom Town: Ciudad Juárez Since 1848* (Austin: University of Texas Press, 1978), pp. 106-108.

23. As quoted in Eugene Nelson, compiler, *Pablo Cruz and the American Dream: The Experience of an Undocumented Immigrant From Mexico* (Salt Lake City: Peregrine Smith, 1975).

24. David Weber, *Foreigners in their Native Land* (Albuquerque: University of New Mexico Press, 1973), pp. 163-168, 151. Fidelia Miller Prickett, "Ramón Ortiz: Priest and Patriot," *New Mexico Historical Review* 25 (October 1950):386-87; Leonard Pitt, *The Decline of the Californios* (Berkeley: University of California Press, 1966), pp. 210-213.

25. Gómez-Quiñones, "Piedras contra . . . ," does not distinguish between Chicanos and Mexicans and thus offers a different perspective of Mexican policy. This distinction is also blurred in Arthur F. Corwin, "Mexican Policy and Ambivalence Toward Labor Emigration to the United States," in Arthur F. Corwin, ed., *Immigrants-and Immigrants* (Westport, Conn.: Greenwood Press, 1978), pp. 187-190.

26. Gómez-Quiñones, "Piedras contra . . . ," p. 505; Peter Nabokov, *Tijerina and the Court House Raid* (Albuquerque: University of New Mexico Press, 1969), pp. 216-217: Dorfman, "Black Gold . . . ," p. 127.

27. Carey McWilliams, *North From Mexico* (New York: Greenwood Press, 1968), pp. 264, 270; for a thorough discussion of the Bracero Program, see Richard B. Craig, *The Bracero Program: Interest Groups and Foreign Policy* (Austin: University of Texas Press, 1971), and Vernon M. Briggs, Jr., Walter Fogel and Fred H. Schmidt, *The Chicano Worker* (Austin: University of Texas Press, 1977).

28. Corwin, "Mexican Policy . . . ," p. 188.

29. The material describing the Chicano land claimants issue is taken from extensive interviews with Robert Salazar, principal attorney for this group. See also, Robert Salazar, "Texas Land Grant Heirs Seek Compensation," in *Agenda: A Journal of Hispanic Issues* 9 (Mar/Apr., 1979):14-16.

30. U.S.-Mexican relations during this period are described in Karl M. Schmitt, *Mexico and the United States, 1821-1973* (New York: John Wiley and Sons, 1974) and Cole Blasier, *The Hovering Giant: U.S. Responses to Revolutionary Change in Latin America* (Pittsburg: University of Pittsburg Press, 1976).

31. *Diario Oficial*, Tomo XXIX, Diciembre 31, 1941, Sección Quinta, pp. 1-2.

32. Interview with Robert Salazar, fall, 1978.

33. *Los Angeles Times*, February 18, 1978.

34. *La Raza National Lawyers Association Resolution*, mimeographed, 1978.

35. Interview, spring, 1979, San Antonio, Texas.

36. Interview, fall 1978, Mexico City.

37. As quoted in Reeves, "Mexican America," p. 8.

38. Reeves, "Mexican America," p. 10.

39. Those holding this view include Dr. Gilbert Cárdenas, Dr. Oscar Martínez, University of Texas at El Paso, and Dr. Caesar Sereseres.

40. Charles Cotrell and Jerry Polinard, "The Impact of the 1975 Voting Rights Act on the Texas Electoral System," a paper presented at the Western Political Science Association Meeting, April, 1977; John García, "The Extension of the Voting Rights Act: The Case of Arizona," paper presented at the Western Political Science Association Meeting, April, 1977.

41. Interview with Peter Johnson, Foreign Service Officer, August 10, 1978.

42. *Rocky Mountain News*, 14 May 1979.

43. García and de la Garza, *The Chicano Political Experience*.

44. As quoted in Dorfman, "Black Gold . . . ," p. 123. See also Astri Suhrke and Lela Garner Noble, *Ethnic Conflict in International Relations* (New York: Praeger, 1977), pp. 3-12.

45. Interviews conducted with Chicano Texas state legislators, summer, 1978.

46. *Civil Rights Update* (U.S. Commission on Civil Rights), November 1978, p. 2.

47. Craig, *The Bracero Program*, pp. 142-43, 176-77.

48. John W. Sloan and Jonathan P. West, "The Role of Informal Policy Making in the U.S.-Mexican Border Cities," *Social Science Quarterly* 58 (September 1970):270-282; John W. Sloan and Jonathan P. West, "Community Integration and Policies Among Elites in Two Border Cities: Los Dos Laredo," *Journal of Inter-American Studies and World Affairs* 18 (November 1976): 451-74.

49. Reeves, "Mexican America," p. 8

50. A Chicano legislator in Texas manifested a similar confusion when he stated that he was opposed to Mexican illegal immigration even though his parents were illegal immigrants.

51. Norman H. Nie, Sidney Verba, and John R. Petrovik, *The Changing American Voter* (Cambridge: Harvard University Press, 1976), p. 104.

52. When asked what were the principal issues facing the Chicano community, over sixty Hispanic political appointees in Washington, D.C. and legislators in Texas responded by identifying these problem areas. Not one raised immigration or any international issue.

53. Herschelle Sullivan Challenor, "The Influence of Black Americans on U.S. Foreign Policy Toward Africa," in Abdul Aziz Said, ed., *Ethnicity and U.S. Foreign Policy* (New York: Praeger, 1977), p. 140.

54. Eduardo Peña, LULAC President, *Rocky Mountain News*, 4 May 1979.

15
Notes on an Interpretation of the Relations Between the Mexican Community in the United States and Mexico

Juan Gómez-Quiñones

International politics is not confined to the actions and interactions of nation-states; other actors are involved. The prevailing view in international relations studies claims statehood or sovereignty as the criterion for an international actor. However, transnational relations are not only those actions that are judged "significant" by major state players. Also included are transactions across state boundaries that have political significance to non-state actors involved and that impact on political international relations, such as the activities of international corporations, foundations and agencies.

Minority groups, although not organized into states or centralized political organizations, are nonetheless engaged in international politics. Minority groups are not limited to just domestically oriented activities; they have engaged in a diversity of transnational interactions. Negative claims about the legitimacy or soundness of these actions are meaningless given the fact that the actions have been continuous, diverse, and widespread.

Several questions must be raised: In what ways, under what conditions and to what extent does international politics affect

---

Juan Gómez-Quiñones is Professor of History and Director of the Chicano Studies Research Center, University of California, Los Angeles. He is the author of *Sembradores—Ricardo Flores Magón y el Partido Liberal Mexicano: A Eulogy and Critique; The Development of the Mexican Working Class North of the Rio Bravo;* and many other works on Chicano history.
© 1983 by Juan Gómez-Quiñones.

minority groups? In what ways, under what conditions, and to what extent do minority groups transcend domestic political systems and venture into nondomestic, i.e., transnational or international ones? The answers to these questions have implications for governmental policy decisions and minority political actions.

The status and experience of minorities cannot be understood by focusing solely on the domestic relation between minority groups and the majority population. Nondomestic trends, relations, and actors often influence what minorities do, how majorities act toward and perceive minorities, and how relationships develop between them. For some immigrant and minority groups, positive identification with and purposeful political actions towards their homelands served as important focal points to sustain collective activities and collective group identity. At times, this has been the case for Mexican Americans in the United States. This minority has been impacted on by larger forces at work in the international arena.

By the late seventies, even disdainful observers had to concede that the Mexican American community could play a role in the evolving relations between Mexico and the United States. Actually, since 1848, Mexico-related issues have been of concern to the Mexican American community. Through time, an interaction took place within a historical, political, and economic context between the two countries involving a non-state minority in transborder political activity.

The politics of the Mexican American community has had an international dimension because of the history, spatial relations, cultural ties, demographic increase, and the integral economic relationship between Mexico and the United States. This dimension can be called Pan-Mexican relations. Despite the political incorporation and economic integration of Mexican territories and peoples into the United States system, influences and contacts continued substantially in many socioeconomic aspects, as well as in the political life of the Mexican people living north of the political boundary.

This interaction was based on the cultural and social nexus between the Mexican American community and Mexico and was expressed through a perceived political-ideological community of interests. Through the decades, these connections increased in complexity. The historical presence within the U.S. of a large

Mexican population with continuing transnational ties, and the economic structure shared by Mexico and the United States, form the material basis for the interaction within this binational community, particularly in regions of northern Mexico. Mexican people north of the Rio Bravo were not wholly assimilated into the generalized Anglo-American culture of the United States. Ideologically, Mexicans north of the Bravo, while under the hegemony of the United States political system, existed as an identifiable subordinate sector of the population. On occasion, Mexicans in this country extended their political activity to political developments in Mexico.

Despite oppression, Mexicans north of the Bravo tried to use the political process to defend the rights of a particular Mexican social strata in Mexico, or of the Mexican community in general. Individuals, interest groups, and the community in the north maintained contacts, interests, and participation in the Mexican states' political process. Political contacts and activities occurred at informal and governmental levels. Their activities were directed at (1) receiving assistance from Mexico in defense of Mexican people living under the domination of the United States; (2) participating in Mexico's political ideological struggles; (3) combined actions to have an impact on both United States and Mexican policies; (4) acting in the defense of the sovereignty of Mexico. These four major forms of Mexican American political-ideological activities have been interdependent and have interpenetrated each other in political practice. They are part of Mexican American participation in the United States political-ideological process and are affected by the local political context in which they take place. They are also affected by the tenor of U.S. and Mexican administrations, as well as by the overall tenor of their relationship. On either side of the boundary, during political crisis, these political and ideological contacts crystallized and assumed definite organizational forms. Some defined the ideological and programmatic content involving broad sectors of the Mexican community on both sides of the frontier. Concurrent with this crystallization process, polarization, based on real and perceived political and ideological differences, also occurred because of the differing socioeconomic interests of the various class strata of the population on both sides. Nevertheless, over time and with the demographic increase of the Mexican community, the range and density of the relationship has strengthened throughout the twentieth century.

Internal and economic crisis and foreign policy considerations of both Mexico and the United States, as well as the cultural and political militancy of Mexicans in the United States, linked activity between Mexicans on both sides of the border through institutional and informal channels. A political relationship between the U.S. Mexican community and Mexico has always existed and intensified during specific periods. Prior to 1848, Mexicans across the Bravo, from Texas to California, were directly involved in Mexico's internal political process and in disputes between Mexico and the United States. After 1848, a linkage occurred and recurred at times of crisis and political mobilization: during the French intervention, the struggle against Díaz, the Plan de San Diego, the depression of the thirties, up to the activity from the late sixties through the eighties.

From 1848 until recently, political groups often had mutually supportive ties with the Mexican consulates. Throughout the latter half of the nineteenth century, Mexican consulates were present and active in the Southwest. Conflict was widespread in Mexico and the provinces annexed to the United States for a good part of this period. In response to this conflict, Mexican consulates played a modest political role by seeking to protect the Mexican community in the United States and to encourage trade. From the nineteenth to the mid-twentieth century, consulates were protective of Mexican civil and property rights.

Theft and violence perpetrated by Anglos, particularly along the border, affected Mexican Americans as well as Mexican nationals; and the Mexican government acted. The Mexican consul in San Francisco protested the punitive Foreign Miner's Tax of 1850 as a violation of the Treaty of Guadalupe-Hidalgo. In 1860, Andrés Treviño, the Mexican consul in Brownsville, Texas, expressed the view that harassment of Mexicans was economically motivated—Anglos wanted Mexican land. As Anglo persecution of Mexicans continued, the consulates sought to protect Mexicans from Anglo violence and supported the establishment of colonies in Mexico. Lands, funds, and transportation were obtained through the consulates, but with uneven success.

Through the 1850s and 1860s, sporadic expressions of concern for events in the Southwest were evident in Mexico. During the 1860s, occasional protests appeared in the newspaper *El Siglo*

Diecinueve against the persecution of Mexicans in the United States. Between 1855 and 1860, Mexican liberals spoke in behalf of Mexican Americans in the Southwest. During the constitutional convention of 1857 held in Mexico, delegates condemned the treatment of Mexicans in the United States and the violations of the Treaty of Guadalupe-Hidalgo. Prominent liberals such as Francisco Zarco, José María Mata, Benito Juárez, and Manuel Robles Pezuela on occasion singled out the grievances of Mexican Americans. Given Mexico's own travails between 1850 and 1860, it is noteworthy to find this limited expression of concern.

After 1848, mobilization on behalf of Mexico was among the first cross-regional political phenomena occurring within the Mexican American community. This mobilization had organizational and ideological impact. In the far north, Mexicans became increasingly concerned for the intensifying conflict in Mexico; first, in connection with the Liberal-Conservative struggle—the Wars of Reform, and later with the French Intervention. During the intervention, Mexicans in the United States who had been liberals prior to annexation now generally supported the legitimate Mexican government of President Benito Juárez (1858–1872). Mexican consular personnel and special commissioners were sent to the "Southwest"; in California and Texas in particular, they received the active support of Mexicans of all classes. Many Mexican Texans fought under General Cortina in Tamaulipas and the northeast. Cortina became the military governor of Tamaulipas and fought both the French imperialists and the Texas confederates in battles on both sides of the river.

Among the more prominent pro-Juarista Mexicanos in California were Augustín Aliviso, Víctor Castro, Silvo Pacheco, and Mariano Vallejo, whose son Uladislao fought as an officer in the Juarista army. Many of these men contributed substantial sums of money and were personally active in influencing popular opinion on behalf of the Juárez government. On more than one occasion, Romualdo Pacheco, the California secretary of state, persuaded state officials to protest the federal officials' seizure of arms shipments to Mexico. These actions were important to Mexico because, despite the United States' friendly neutrality, arms shipments were often stopped.

The *juntas patrióticas* or Juárez Clubs, organized by Plácido Vega and his agents throughout California, were especially important. Active branches of the *juntas patrióticas* existed in San

Francisco, Los Angeles, Jackson, San José, Marysville, Vallejo, Sacramento, Martínez, Greenwood, Hornitos, La Plancha, New Almadén, Sonora, San Pablo, Pinole, San Juan Bautista, and West Point. Support also came from other areas, such as Virginia City, Nevada. The clubs were active in raising funds, recruiting volunteers, locating arms for purchase and in organizing activities in support of the Mexican Republic. Besides the cities and towns, major support came from Mexicanos in the mining districts, many of whom joined the Mexican clubs. Arms purchased with the contributions of the Mexican people of California were sent from California to the Juárez forces on the west coast of Mexico. Scores of volunteer Mexicanos from the United States ultimately reached the front line in Mexico.

Particularly important in the Liberal-Conservative struggle for Mexican public opinion in the United States were Spanish-language newspapers in the Southwest. In San Francisco, two of the major Spanish-language newspapers were pro-Juárez: *El Mundo Nuevo*, edited by José María Vigil, and *La Voz de Méjico*, edited by Pedro Macillas. The third, *Eco del Pacífico*, was owned by a Frenchman, E. Derbes, and was strongly pro-imperialist and anti-Juárez. Newspapers and journalists played a role in informing the Spanish-speaking community of the progress in the struggle. They carried advertisements for recruitment of volunteers and received letters from readers in California, and Virginia City, Nevada. The Mexican-French contest stimulated and further politicized the existing Spanish-language press.

Juntas patrióticas also worked to support Republican candidates in the United States elections because they were generally more favorable to the Juárez government. Mexican Republicans and patriots worked to bring out the Mexican vote for Lincoln in the 1864 election. Continued United States recognition of the government of Benito Juárez and identification of the Confederacy with the imperialist cause were important considerations for the Mexican voters. The death of Juárez in 1872 was commemorated with elaborate memorial services in the Mexican American communities.

After the French Intervention, concern and contact continued. During the administrations of Miguel Lerdo de Tejada (1872–1876) and Porfirio Díaz (1876–1880 and 1884–1911), the consular system was expanded and standardized even more. The Ministry of Foreign Relations during the Díaz regime sought to protect the rights of Mexicans in the United States, usually because of the impetus of Matías Romero, ambassador to the United States. This interest resulted in part from a justified indignation over the flagrant abuse of Mexicans in Texas, the reports of these abuses in the Mexican press, and the loss of status for Mexico these implied. This concern also stemmed from the overall strategy to reduce tensions with the United States which was sought in turn in order to increase United States commercial investments in Mexico. Nevertheless, in many incidents, Mexico forthrightly raised objections concerning the violence directed by U.S. citizens against Mexicans, the judicial mistreatments of Mexicans by officials and the courts, and the abuse of Mexican merchants and workers by private interests and public authorities. Sometimes, certain consuls were zealous in offering protection, others were not. During Romero's time, the ministry did not differentiate between Mexicans born in the United States or Mexico. For the most part, benign Mexican government interest, when it occurred, was frustrated and subordinated to larger policy objectives.

During the late nineteenth century, both conservative and liberal newspapers occasionally referred to the Mexican-United States War and to the travails of the Mexican American people who were now seen as the "México de afuera." The border was understood to be a sensitive region and the perils and consequences of immigration were pointed out. In turn, the press in the Southwest reflected the current trends in ideals and literature in Mexico. They often preferred to debate politics in Mexico rather than in the local area. Newspapers, immigration, a consular system, and a common interest in politics kept the communities in touch. The community referred to itself as "la colonia mexicana." Prominent Mexican American politicians of the late nineteenth century had contact with the Mexican government and with Mexico. Among these were Ignacio Sepúlveda, Romualdo Pacheco, and Reginaldo del Valle of California; Casimiro Barela of Colorado; Elfego Baca of New Mexico, and others. Later, Reginaldo del Valle was to be appointed United States presidential representative to meet with the Mexican factions during 1913–1914.

Politics along the border have persistently manifested close relations with events in Mexico. The political relationship between the Mexican communities and the Mexican government have changed from endorsement to opposition. In his bid for power, Porfirio Díaz had support, at first, along both sides of the border region. Later, the Texas border became a refuge for his opponents and was noted for the opposition movements. When forced into exile, Paulino Martínez, an uncompromising liberal, continued his opposition to Díaz from Laredo, Texas, by publishing the antigovernment *La Voz de Juárez*. Similarly, General Ignacio Martínez, exile resident of Brownsville, published a newspaper critical of Díaz and actually considered a rebellion depending on support from Mexican residents of Texas. In 1891, he was shot down by horsemen who fled to Nuevo Laredo. During the same decade, Francisco Ruíz Sandoval recruited fifty men for armed action in Mexico, but United States authorities arrested him and ten others. In the early 1890s, Catarino Garza tried to organize several revolts along the border. In Texas, efforts were made to defend Mexican exiles and immigrants from persecution and extradition. With the tolerance and sometimes active support of the United States government, the Díaz government countered opposition in the Southwest by subsidizing a press favorable to its policies, organizing public support, and increasing its vigilance of opponents. The consuls played an important role in these activities. New and traditional opposition was met by old and new forms of repression.

Throughout the nineteenth century, contacts and influences with Mexico by Mexican Americans increased and expanded. Letters and visits to the Mexican president or to government offices expressed grievances against land claims. In Mexico there was strong reaction to the burning and lynching of compatriots in the United States. Family and economic contacts with Mexico existed at the elite and popular levels. Immigration was continuous and became, by 1910, a matter of government concern as well as a topic of discussion for intellectuals. Veterans of labor struggles in Mexico traveled to the United States with their ideals and experience. Ideologically, political struggle and crisis in Mexico affected large sectors of the Mexican community to the north. Revolutionaries and the Mexican government competed for the loyalty and support of Mexicans north of the border. Such an example was the 1906 plan, which contained specific clauses addressed to the rights of Mexicans abroad. After the turn of the century

Mexican political exiles were increasingly active, and with the development of revolutionary organizations such as the Partido Liberal Mexicano (PLM), their influence expanded. Precursory armed efforts to spark the revolution took place along the border in 1906, 1908, and 1910, involving Mexicans from the United States. Mexicans north of the border were frequently active participants in the revolution to the south. In addition, many political clubs supporting the various factions of the revolution were organized in cities throughout the Southwest. The Southwest Spanish language press in particular became more active and polemical.

Through their many groups, the activities of Ricardo Flores Magón and the PLM were particularly influential among militant Mexicans. The rise of the PLM, led by Magón, represented a benchmark in the political history of the Mexican people in the United States and Mexico. The PLM was an international revolutionary, ideological, and clandestine party. It fought for the destruction of the Díaz regime in Mexico and of capitalism in general. The PLM had its base of operation and support in the Southwest. Many from the Mexican communities in the United States participated in it and in the diverse areas of radical activity which ranged from forming local PLM chapters, organizing newspapers, conducting propaganda and legal defense work, and raising funds, supplies, and weapons for revolutionary participation. These activities attest to the solidarity and extensive support of the PLM by the Mexican community in the United States. The PLM, however, suffered from the limitations of its anarcho-communistic ideology, an inability to stabilize its membership base, factionalism and, of course, intense persecution. PLM influence in Mexico and in the United States was visible through the 1930s.

The Mexican people in the United States provided a dynamic and broad base for exiled revolutionary leaders and propagandists. At the same time, the antithesis was true. Sectors of the Mexican population, with interests antagonistic to the majority of the revolutionary supporters, collaborated with the consular representatives of the dictatorship and later with other conservative factions. Local, state, and federal offices of the United States government also worked with these conservative Mexican factions to persecute Mexicans who supported the more radical factions. For several years the United States served as a base of operations for different groups during the revolution and all factions across the political spectrum organized in the Mexican American communities.

From 1910 to 1917, a main activity of Mexican radicals in the United States centered around the Mexican revolution. Throughout the period Mexican Americans supported a variety of the political groups, further complicating the community's internal politics. During these years there was contention not only between Mexicanos but also between Mexico and the United States. The United States engaged in harassment and armed aggression against Mexicans: the landing of troops at Veracruz and Tampico in 1914 and the United States Punitive Expedition into Mexico in 1916. Francisco Villa's raid on Columbus, New Mexico, was the sole Mexican retaliation. The administrations of Francisco Madero (1912-1913), Victoriano Huerta (1913-1914), and Venustiano Carranza (1916-1920) had correspondence and contact with individuals and groups within the Mexican American community. The Madero and Carranza administrations both took into account the protection of Mexicans abroad and the allocation of resources for their integration into Mexico if they desired.

During the Carranza Administration, the Plan de San Diego, 1915-1917, reflected international as well as local economic and cultural conflicts. Factions in Mexico were suspected of involvement, and Mexican army commanders were accused of giving sanctuary to "sediciosos," the armed adherents of the Plan. Whatever its origins, in south Texas, the Plan resulted in armed uprisings of Mexicans against Anglo ranchers and merchants, and a subsequent mobilization of thousands of troops and several companies of Texas Rangers to quell the rebellion and carry out repression against the Mexican community. Hundreds of Mexicans were killed and many driven from their land. This oppression, and the heightened repression of Mexican radicals during World War I, led to the decline of radical activity in the Mexican community of the United States. It signalled a change in the political climate.

Yet, interest was broader than political activity in support of a given faction; concurrently, attention was given to Mexican art, history, intellectual, and labor trends. During this period Mexican nationalism was prevalent. Given the hostility and the discrimination faced by Mexicans in the United States, Mexican nationalism in the United States was so marked that it seemed extreme to visitors from Mexico. Overt patriotic loyalty to Mexican holidays and symbols intensified despite the prediction of assimilation by sociologists and the daily work of Protestant missions and public schools to eliminate the Mexican culture. From 1910 through the 1930s, Spanish language journalism flourished and perhaps reached its greatest literary expression in the Southwest, particularly in the pages of *La Opinión* and *La Prensa*. The printed media and the radio relayed news from Mexico. Radio and periodicals made a special effort to do so because in large measure their popular appeal depended on it. Use of and access to the media were important to political activity, not only for information but for mobilization.

As consular activity intensified during the first decades of the twentieth century, so did political and labor organizing influences from Mexico during the twenties and thirties. The major expression of a continuing influence was José Vasconcelos's campaign in 1928 for the presidency of Mexico. Running on a nationalist program which, however, contained implicit reactionary planks favoring the Catholic Church, the wealthy, and ultimately foreign interests, Vasconcelos aroused interest and support among the Mexican people in the United States in part because he proposed the establishment of Mexican schools and cultural programs supported by the Mexican government.

Vasconcelos, while not yet proclaiming his candidacy, increased his public speaking tours from Anglo college audiences to audiences in Mexican communities throughout the United States. Simultaneously, he sought favor with wealthy Mexican exiles. He urged the voluntary repatriation of skilled exiles who would benefit the nation by their return. These persons were to be guaranteed liberty of religion, right to property, and the opportunity to work. These ideas appealed not only to the wealthy and middle class, but also to many average Mexicans in the United States, a significant proportion of whom were from the areas affected by the Cristero revolt, a religious and agrarian-inspired militancy against the government.

Vasconcelos condemned the treatment of Mexicans in the United States. In particular, he denounced the anti-Mexican immigration "Box Bill" calling for a restrictive quota, the exclusionist unions which supported its passage, as well as the cynicism of the United

States trade union movement with its emphasis on economic demands. Vasconcelos also denounced the violence and the lynching of Mexicans, especially perpetrated by the Ku Klux Klan, to which he compared the exclusionist unions. He emphasized the strong national identity of the Mexican people and the need to strengthen the cultural basis of the community. He advocated the establishment of Mexican schools and other cultural institutions to be funded for Mexican communities in the United States.

During August and September 1928, Vasconcelos visited San Francisco, Los Angeles, Santa Fe, El Paso, San Antonio, Corpus Christi, Laredo, El Valle, McAllen, and Brownsville. He drew large and enthusiastic audiences. A letter poll in the pro-Vasconcelos newspapers, *La Opinión* of Los Angeles and *La Prensa* of San Antonio, showed that Mexicans in the United States supported Vasconcelos because he (1) supported repatriation, (2) was an educator, (3) was not a millionaire or landowner, (4) brought Mexico international prestige, and (5) opposed military leaders and the use of military power. As mentioned, Vasconcelos appealed to many wealthy Mexican exiles, many of whom were associated with different political views, including ex-Porfiristas, ex-Carranzistas, and ex-Huertistas. Among the more prominent supporters was General Nicolás Rodríguez, the future leader of the Gold Shirts, a Mexican fascist group.

Vasconcelos clubs were organized throughout many of the major centers of Mexican population in the United States. Later, many were represented in the subsequent convention in Mexico City. Aspects of the platform which appealed directly to Mexicans north of the border included: (1) more consular protection, (2) patriotic and Spanish language educational programs, (3) repatriation to irrigated agricultural centers in Mexico, (4) demands for equal economic treatment and working conditions for the Mexican workers in the United States, (5) protection of Mexican women, and (6) restrictions by the Mexican government on the immigration rate of Mexicans to the United States. Vasconcelos himself was aware of the importance of Mexicans within the United States as a political base.

The political and ideological position and objectives of Vasconcelos and his major supporters were actually diverse and contradictory. While appealing for mass support of his ostensibly popular program, the Vasconcelos campaign contained strong reactionary aspects. Vasconcelos was committed to ending several of the progressive foreign policy and foreign business policies of the Obregonistas which Calles championed. These aspects indicated Vasconcelos's own subsequent move further to the right.

In respect to the Mexican people north of the Bravo, the campaign was a significant instance of ideological, political, and organizational contact and exchange with the Mexican political process. The fairly broad influence and mass following of the Vasconcelos movement north of the border can be attributed to the popularly emphasized progressive aspects of the Vasconcelos platform. His "revolucionismo" called for the defense of the political and economic rights and national identity of Mexicans within the United States. Vasconcelos's image of legitimacy and respectability, his renown as an educational reformer, and his international reputation as a respected intellectual contributed greatly to his attractiveness. Clearly, a major reason for Vasconcelos's relative acceptance at this time involved the diplomatic and economic conflicts between the United States government and business interests with the Obregonistas and the emerging Callistas. The fact remains that Vasconcelos had a popular following among many workers and persons of modest means in the community. Because of this, the consulates as government agencies sought to counteract the Vasconcelos campaign.

During the 1920s and 1930s, more than at any other time, the direction and quality of consular roles depended often on the individual consuls. The administrations of Obregón-Calles (1920–1924 and 1924–1928) and Cárdenas (1934–1940) were generally sympathetic to Mexican residents in the United States and to Mexican workers in particular, often taking specific steps to provide aid and assistance to Mexicans abroad through orders to consulates or by providing resources. If a consul acted negatively, the decision was less because of standing government policy and more the result of personal bias. The evolution of the consular role must be viewed in specific situations. Consulates were quite active in cultural, political, and labor situations, and their advice and leadership, for better or worse, were consistently sought. Their role and function had stabilized during the Porfiriato and re-stabilized after the erratic interim of the years of conflict. By

1930, Mexico had over fifty consular agencies in the United States. With the assistance of "abogados consultores" and "comisiones honoríficas," they were quite active and enjoyed respect and support. Although by regulation and the Havana Convention of 1928, they were empowered to intervene only on behalf of Mexican citizens, citizenship by consanguinity, *jus sanguinis*, had been argued and recognized for the protection of foreign born Mexicans. Mexican consular officials became involved in strikes, sometimes favoring the owners, at other times the workers.

Since the early 1900s, Southwest labor efforts in mining, agriculture, and manufacturing had been influenced in part by Mexican labor coming from Mexico. Mexican labor organizing took place across the Southwest. Trade union issues were emphasized by the organizers, i.e., wages, conditions of work, and right to unionization as well as community rights in general.

Spontaneous and organized labor activity linking Mexicans together in the United States occurred throughout the twentieth century among field workers, miners, railroad workers, etc. Activities of the early Confederación Regional Obrera Mexicana, and later the Confederación de Trabajadores de México, impacted on the United States. Efforts to organize the garment industry in Los Angeles stemmed from two concurrent events, one in part from Mexico. California Mexican workers took the initiative to organize themselves at a meeting of a federation of Mexican societies held in Los Angeles in November 1927. This led to the formation of the Confederación de Uniones Obreras Mexicanas (CUOM), an effort influenced structurally and ideologically by the Confederación Regional Obrera Mexicana. A general CUOM convention was called in May 1928 and twenty-one unions representing both agricultural and industrial workers attended. Emilio Mújica, a fraternal representative from CROM, attended and remained in Los Angeles to aid in organizing Mexican unions there. By 1933, the confederation had some ten locals remaining, for the most part agricultural; it generally stimulated unionism among Mexican workers at a propitious time. In addition to progressive labor and political influences, reactionary influences stemmed from Mexico.

During the late thirties, the fascist Unión Nacional Sinarquista exerted a limited but significant influence on Mexican communities throughout the United States. It advanced a program which cloaked corporate, state, Catholic, and fascist ideology with extreme demagogic nationalism and active defense of the Mexican community against national oppression. As a result, the sinarquistas were able to recruit hundreds of members and established an estimated fifty branches in cities throughout the United States. Given the extreme economic conditions and the severe national oppression among sectors of the Mexican community, particularly the bourgeoisie and Catholic elements, this was relatively easy. In effect, the sinarquistas favored corporate and racist interests, not those of the broad sectors of the community.

The first regional sinarquista group north of the Bravo was organized in Los Angeles, California, in November 1937, a short time after their organization was established in Mexico. By 1942, the sinarquistas claimed two thousand members in the United States. According to the U.S. Department of Justice, sinarquistas were organized into fifty branches centered mainly in California and Texas, with a major branch in Chicago, Illinois, and scattered groups in other states. Among the California and Texas branches were those located in Pasadena, San Fernando, San Bernardino, La Verne, Ontario, Watts, Belvedere, El Monte, Oxnard, Pomona, and Azusa, in Southern California; El Paso, McAllen, Mission, and Laredo, in Texas. Sinarquismo in the Southwest promoted a reactionary version of Mexican nationalism through exploitation of the issue of discrimination and defense of the rights of Mexican people. The highly organized and structured sinarquista movement in the United States, apparently receiving financial support from right-wing Anglo organizations, was directly linked to the political leadership of the movement in Mexico.

With the beginning of World War II, the sinarquistas were forced to register with the United States Department of Justice under the Foreign Agents Registration Act and were under surveillance by the FBI. As a consequence, the movement curtailed most of its public activities in order to avoid interference. Sinarquismo north of the boundary represented the reactionary extreme of the process of Pan-Mexican relations, and in the late thirties and early forties it exercised limited but significant influence over sectors of the Mexican community in the Unites States. Though sinarquismo employed the rhetoric of Mexican nationalism, it actually represented a contradiction to the actual interests of a community composed primarily of working people.

In the long run, the sinarquista movement allied with, and received financial and propagandistic support from historical exploiters, landed interests, the reactionary upper clergy, foreign capitalists, etc. Its appeal to some sectors of the general community must be attributed to the national oppression against Mexicans within the United States and the natural desire of the oppressed to seek an end to that domination. Much of its support obviously derived from sectors having a false consciousness shaped by Catholic dogmatism and elitism, as well as from limited sectors with class interests opposed to the majority of Mexican working people.

The extent of support sinarquismo may have received from conservative sources is reflected in the subsequent investigation by the California state legislature of sinarquismo's role in the infamous "Zoot Suit Riots" in 1942. These so-called riots consisted of attacks on Mexicans by soldiers and sailors with support from the police. At first, in California, particularly in the Los Angeles press, much was made of the supposed "fascist sinarquista" influence over the Mexican community. Later the blame was directed at alleged communist influence. Thus, sinarquistas were effectively whitewashed despite their anti-Allied propaganda in favor of anticommunism at a time when the communists were the strongest proponents of the ideological anti-fascist aspect of the war effort.

During the Zoot Suit Riots, the Mexican government's direct intervention protesting these anti-Mexican attacks helped end the persecution of Mexican youth. This intervention represented an active stance on the part of the Mexican government. The administration of Avila Camacho sent Ernesto Félix Díaz to Mexican communities in the United States to denounce the sinarquista movement which had supposedly surfaced during these incidents.

The following years of the forties and fifties were relatively weak political periods in the Pan-Mexican relations. Nevertheless, the bracero program, the deportation drives and other issues kept contact alive, as did cultural programs and visits by Mexican officials. These years witnessed a further elaboration and formalization of the celebration of the Sixteenth of September and the participation in it by the Mexican government. Significantly, Mexican film comedies, songs, a novel, a play featuring border life and acculturation themes were widely disseminated in Mexico. In turn, Mexican periodicals, records, and Mexico's film industry dramatically increased their United States sales. Through the forties and fifties, magazines and radio were important in communicating political information. Many Mexican Americans accepted as a fact of life community interest in Mexico, and some believed there would be equal interest in them from Mexico.

In the sixties, renewed efforts at strengthening Mexican ties took place. Rather quixotically, Reies López Tijerina and the Alianza sought support and information in Mexico for the New Mexico land grant issues. He was expelled by one administration and later welcomed by another. Because of organizational problems related to workers from Mexico and the constant apprehension of a renewed bracero program, the union of farm workers headed by César Chávez made early efforts towards dealing with agencies and unions from Mexico. There were also efforts to establish programmatic and personal ties in Mexico by members of the Chicano Student Movement and the Chicano studies personnel dating from 1968 and 1970, forerunners of efforts in the seventies. Cultural nationalism, indigenismo, and the romanticizing of the Mexican "Revolution" became common among activists of the sixties. However, the reality of conditions and public opinion in Mexico dispelled illusions of widespread interest about Mexican people north of the Rio Bravo. It simply was not great. Furthermore, within political circles in Mexico, apprehension existed concerning involvement with Mexican Americans.

On the other hand, the events of 1968 involving students, intellectuals, and the left in protests against the government in Mexico impelled students, professors, and activists to visit and seek support in the United States. There were progressive leaders and writers, as well as a few liberal government functionaries, who had an interest in the conditions of Mexican people in the United States. The early efforts, and the presence of some support in Mexico, began to have an impact upon strengthening relations between Mexican Americans and Mexico. The relations became much more visible from 1970 to 1976. An important base for linkage was strengthened when Mexican business interests came to realize the potential of the Latino market in the United States. Furthermore, a few conscientious Mexican educators in Mexico began to explore individual and program contacts as ways of enriching the educational mission of Mexican agencies. Efforts at communication coincided with the time during which the Mexican government also sought to pursue a more ambitious and diversified foreign policy.

More recently, the Mexican government began to show interest in this interaction because of pressures created by the undocumented worker question, problems along the border, economic-political crises, accentuating unemployment, and differences with United States foreign and economic policies as a national bourgeoisie struggled with a bourgeoisie manipulated by the United States. In the late sixties and seventies, a number of developments occurred which were important to this interaction. Previous political constraints operating on Mexican Americans weakened; they became a more viable political force; their economic, organizational, and ideological resources increased. In Mexico, interest developed about United States politics with greater concern for autonomy in relations with the United States. Both Mexico and the Mexican American community were affected by the greater and more complex cultural, social, and economic interaction across the border which occurred throughout the seventies.

Mexican government interest in Mexicans in the United States is not novel. As shown in the past, precedents have been set by administrations from Juárez to the present. Since the nineteenth century through the administration of López Portillo, Mexican administrations and political groups have expressed concern for immigration. From 1972 on, efforts at binational cooperation have been varied and have involved a range of constituencies and leadership; some have been more substantive than others; some have been opportunistic; others, principled. These efforts were conducted by Mexican government agencies or institutions and by progressive groups and individuals. Government efforts took the form of conferences, publications, sympathetic media coverage, academic scholarships for Mexicans in the United States, visits and meetings with this country's Mexican elected and appointed officials, with La Raza Unida party leaders, with the heads of important national Mexican American organizations. Some of these meetings involved Mexican presidents. The most formal structure of this exchange in Mexico was the establishment of the Comisión Mixta de Enlace, involving the Secretaría de Trabajo, one Puerto Rican and nine Mexican American organizations.

Equally significant have been the meetings and cooperative efforts among left progressive Mexican organizations from both sides of the border, particularly the Centro de Acción Social Autónoma (CASA) in the United States during the seventies. To date, the educational, cultural and media efforts have had the most positive and substantive results, while the solidarity efforts inspired by the undocumented worker issue the most general ones. Migrant workers, business and economic ties, political trends, recurring economic and political crises, political cooperation, and Mexican agency efforts have been key to succeeding developments. The process has been hindered and abated by certain objective political and economic circumstances.

Recent population growth, limited political representation, increased communication, a growing economic base, as well as greater knowledge and interest in public affairs, all bear potentially on the relations between the Mexican American community and Mexico. It is possible that by the twenty-first century, United States border states will be electorally dominated by Mexican American voters active in local, state, and federal politics and bureaus. Though political power is not axiomatically equivalent to population, or even voting strength, and though demographic shifts occurring in the United States may nullify Mexican American growth, surely the Mexican American community has wider political influence than before. This increased influence can be identified specifically at national, state, and local levels. Presently, there are hundreds of elected and appointed officials. During recent successive administrations, Mexican Americans have had direct access to the White House via executive branch offices or White House appointments. In 1980 in Texas, eighty-five county commissioners of Mexican descent were elected. At the 1980 Democratic Convention, there were five hundred Hispanic delegates, the majority of whom were Mexican American, a significant increase from the handful which attended the 1968 convention or the few dozen present at the 1972 convention. Political gains can be measured by the organization of the Labor Council for Latin American Advancement, a national organization of the AFL-CIO comprised of elected and appointed Latino labor leaders; and also the National Association of Latino Elected and Appointed Officials (NALEO), comprised of hundreds of persons across the country holding local, state, and federal office.

Apart from political data, there are social and economic indications of the importance of Mexican American growth that may bear on relations with Mexico. The Spanish-origin population growth per year is about 4 percent. In Texas and California, over 20 percent of the population is Spanish-speaking. In California, one out of five persons is of Hispanic descent (1980 census). Hispanics will eventually outnumber blacks in the United States by the end of the century. Apart from the growth in English language media communication targeted at Mexican Americans, in 1979 there were 58 newspapers and magazines with Spanish language usage and 450 radio and television stations with all or some Spanish language programming. Receipts from Mexican movies, records, and performances were at an all-time high, and these have been important to Mexico-based producers. Of 80,000 Hispanic-owned businesses, 60,000 were owned by Mexican Americans; between 1970 and 1977, a 150 percent increase occurred in the number of Latino families earning over $15,000 a year. Sales income for Latino-owned businesses increased 30 percent despite a recession; over 100 Latino firms had sales of $1 million yearly, and the largest had sales of over $50 million. During the seventies in California, for example, the combined income of approximately four million Mexican Americans was $7.7 billion; over 400,000 families were classified as middle class, with 30 percent of the community preferring to speak Spanish; 62 percent had traveled to Mexico; and 60 percent wanted to know more about politics in general. At one time, the importance of a Mexican American sales market was minimized, but during the late seventies, it received increasing attention. On the whole, the Mexican American population growth, political influence, and purchasing power are probably due to the United States native-born population, with immigration as an important contributing force. Immigration increases the numbers of communities and their rate of growth, speeding geographic distribution as well as contributing to the continuity of ties with Mexico.

In the seventies, Mexico-related issues and political processes became significantly important to some Mexican American political activists and a few organizations. By the late seventies, Mexico had a greater interest in Mexican Americans than had been the case in the sixties. During the administrations of Presidents Echeverría (1970–1976) and López Portillo (1976–1982), a series of overt initiatives occurred vis-à-vis the Mexican American community. These two successive administrations invested more attention and resources on Mexicans in the United States than any previous one. Also, during the term of President Carter, Mexican Americans were consulted regarding Latin American policy in general and Mexico in particular; several served as ambassadors in Latin America, one in Mexico.

How relations between Mexican Americans and Mexico, and their role in Mexico–United States relations, will evolve cannot be predicted. It may enhance the political stature of Mexican Americans, it may gain greater public recognition, and it may result in greater political and economic resources for Mexican Americans. Relations may also incur risks; some in Mexico and the United States view this interaction as negative. What basis could there be for either Mexico or the United States to include the Mexican American community in their relationship?

One can assume that the United States would benefit politically and economically from the gains accruing to the Mexican American community, an argument raised by other interest groups. Additionally, the United States may benefit from a constituency that offers informed personnel with strong visible ties to Mexico. Mexico may benefit from a United States lobby because United States domestic decisions affect it willy-nilly. Mexican Americans are the major constituency Mexico has on the immigration question and in defense of its interests in general and one not dependent on fear or money. Mexico needs a countervailing lobby to the hostile ones. The immediate gains from the continuing relationship are not specific. From Mexico's point of view, there are Mexican American sales and tourism, support for legal access to jobs by immigrants, and pressure on the United States for goals and positions of Mexico. A present concrete interest in common is the undocumented worker. Undeniably, strong bonds of affection and empathy are also felt by the majority of Mexicans in the United States for the welfare of the people in Mexico.

Mexican American interests to be served are support for civil rights, for its business sector as agents and importers, access to Mexican institutions of higher education and international attention. Education and culture seem the strong areas for positive development. General problems between Mexican American-Mexico relations are that the Mexican government would accept conditions vis-à-vis the United States that Mexican Americans would not, and that the Mexican government can negotiate unilaterally without Mexican Americans. Specifically, strong disagreement will emerge if a bracero-type program is revived. Overall, Mexican Americans would benefit from a strong Mexico, but Mexico's underdevelopment and dependency have not been an asset for Mexican Americans.

Overt intervention by Mexico in the political struggles of the Mexican American community has been exceptional. In foreign domestic affairs Mexican policy *is* of a noninterventionist nature. Mexico cannot criticize another country's domestic repression without subjecting itself to charges. And it is not going to risk its substantial and continuing relations with the United States because of Mexican Americans. Equally, Mexican Americans are not going to respond to Mexico simply because of cultural identification. Furthermore, any interaction will be affected by a limited antipathy between Mexicans and Mexican Americans, which does exist, as does the hostility of influential people in Mexico towards Mexican Americans. The public manipulation of commonly held cultural symbols by political leaders from either side of the border cannot be equated with effective political support. Although Mexico has the constitutional obligation to defend its citizens abroad, this does not apply presently to the majority of United States-born Mexicans. Further, Mexico may not need support while there is oil and economic growth. For the most part, relations between Mexican Americans and Mexico have actually been conducted by small groups of elites, whether conservative, liberal, or progressive, in behalf of modest, specific programs and projects without claim to popular mandate. However, it is the social-cultural reality of the masses of Mexican Americans that ultimately gives the efforts political validity. Yet, no central political voice or general coordinating body speaks for Mexican Americans. Nor is it likely that there will be, given the political and class contradictions and differences within the community; in fact, these are evident in relations with Mexico.

Thus, the future of these relations is problematic. Economic and political benefits are mixed. If ethnic impact on United States foreign policy is related to a group's importance as an organized pivotal voting bloc, its ability to contribute financially to a resource base, its ability to influence a major sector regarding labor or the media, and its ability to demonstrate group solidarity, then the Mexican American community has demonstrated real, although partial, success in relation to its own interests in the United States. This indicates that future success will widen and deepen, not recede; and surely the Mexican American community is as free as any other constituency to voice its concern about foreign policy. After all, United States foreign policy is influenced as much by ethnicity as by other factors.

In 1848, the main concern in the relations between Mexico and Mexican Americans was one of juridical rights, and one would have expected the relationship to wane. By 1980, the concerns in the relations were broad and diverse; further, the relations were stronger and more complex than before. Concurrently, Mexico–United States relations have grown in significance for the politics of the Mexican American community in ways quite different from the past. A study of that past confirms it.

16
Mexican Political Actors in the United States and Mexico: Historical and Political Contexts of a Dialogue Renewed

Carlos H. Zazueta

In the 1970s, groups representing Mexicans in the United States[1] initiated a dialogue with political actors in Mexico, most notably, with the Mexican government. This phenomenon has received much discussion from differing perspectives.[2] Some writers have speculated on the benefits—and perils—the future may hold for Chicano political actors in the event that the areas of exchange expand significantly. Others have worried about the potentially negative reactions of the U.S. government should the dialogue take the form of an alliance in specific issue areas. Still others have argued that Mexico should promote closer relations with Chicano organizations with the hope that the latter will become a "Mexican lobby" for Mexican foreign policy interests in Washington, D.C. Finally, some authors have merely attempted to describe a new phenomenon about which little is known and whose future seems uncertain.

All of these concerns merit careful study. A review of some of the literature suggests, however, that other questions of fundamental importance have been overlooked. One set of questions which has received little attention has to do with the historical

---

Carlos H. Zazueta is Research Associate at the Centro Nacional de Información y Estadísticas del Trabajo in Mexico City. He is the author (with César Zazueta) of *En las puertas del paraíso*, and other works on Mexican immigration and the Mexican-U.S. border. The author would like to thank Manuel García y Griego for prolonged discussions and extensive editing of this paper.
© 1983 by Carlos H. Zazueta.

and political contexts within which the dialogue is taking place. Another relates to Mexico's foreign policy concerns and style. This essay focuses on a few important questions in these two areas of concern.

The argument that follows is based on a series of interrelated hypotheses. First of all, the on-going political dialogue which was perceived to have begun in the 1970s is actually the *renewal* of an old dialogue between the government and its expatriates—the *México de afuera*. This dialogue has grown and contracted several times in the last century; what we see today is merely the rebirth of interest in this political dialogue. Second, the immediate precedent for the on-going dialogue can be found in the activities of the Mexican consulates in the U.S. Mexican communities during the 1920s and 1930s. Many of the issues involved, as well as the political environment in which the dialogue was conducted at that time, have parallels in the present political exchange. Third, some of the events that took place during the 1920s and 1930s suggest the constraints and possibilities of the current dialogue. Fourth, contrary to popular assumptions, Mexico cannot avoid the issues posed by this dialogue. Rather, it will have to develop policy responses, though in the short term, it has considerable latitude in formulating its policy choices. And finally, it would be in Mexico's best interest to expand the current dialogue significantly, particularly within its domestic political context, and Mexico would stand to gain by moving the dialogue from its current emphasis on symbolic communication to substantive areas.

The discussion of these hypotheses can be divided roughly into three sections. The first emphasizes history and argues that to some extent, the future will follow the patterns of the immediate and more distant past. The second focuses on a set of questions that fit loosely into the category termed "political contexts" or "environments." This discussion stresses the constraints on and the possibilities for the current dialogue. The concluding section summarizes some of these arguments. It also suggests a number of approaches that could be considered by the most significant political actor in the dialogue, the Mexican government. To be sure, significant interaction has taken place among Mexicans on both sides of the border not involving the government; notably among them business leaders, trade unionists, intellectuals, and leftist popular elements. Nevertheless, the present focus is on those exchanges involving the Mexican government.

THE HISTORICAL CONTEXT

The political dialogue often described as "beginning" in the 1970s is not new and therefore not an ephemeral event. Strictly speaking, the starting point for Mexican-Chicano relations can be found in the aftermath of the war with the United States, which officially ended with the signing of the Treaty of Guadalupe-Hidalgo in 1848. The treaty provided for the transmission of U.S. citizenship to those Mexicans that remained in the annexed territories presently known as the Southwest and who did not expressly declare "their intention to retain the character of Mexicans." From that time forward, the Mexican government has been concerned with how to respond to the *México de afuera*.[3] In these responses the Mexican government may not have been consistent, nor has its relationship with Mexican expatriates always been felicitous, but the exchange across the Mexico-U.S. border has nevertheless endured for more than a hundred years.

The fact that Mexican foreign policy made room for the *México de afuera* at various times since 1848 is significant for today's political dialogue. The types of policy responses that occurred in the past seem to have established a pattern influencing the options presently available. If this hypothesis is correct, an examination of past exchanges between Mexican state actors and Mexican nonstate actors north of the U.S.-Mexican border may shed light on what future constraints and possibilities may shape the course of the on-going dialogue.

Though distant in time, it is significant that during the process of negotiating the Treaty of Guadalupe-Hidalgo—an act imposed upon Mexico by the United States—the former refused to give up the inhabitants residing in the annexed territories. This was reflected in some of the provisions of the treaty itself and in the statement by Manuel de la Peña y Peña, provisional president of the republic at the time the Treaty was submitted for ratification by Congress:

> If it is true that we are giving up a fertile and beautiful part of our territory of large dimensions, together with all the necessary elements to establish flourishing states. . . . I want it to be recorded that my administration has devoted attention to the citizens [of the territories of Alta California and New Mexico]. I can assure you, gentlemen, that their plight has weighed heavily upon me during this negotiation. The extent of the territory being given up [to the United States] would even have been increased, had it been possible

to assure the freedom of the Mexican population [in the annexed territories].[4]

This statement not only reflects the views of a man leading his country in defeat, but gives expression to the more popular view, held for decades after the annexation, that Mexico had been forced to sell its citizens "as a flock of sheep" to the United States.[5]

The imposition of a boundary between Mexico and its old northern territories did not effectively separate the Mexican populations on each side of the border. The social intercourse established between segments of these population groups continued. More importantly, significant flows of Mexican migration to the northern territories did not stop in the mid-nineteenth century; rather they grew, and continue to this day. And even though the nineteenth-century Mexican population in the United States was subjected to enormous social and political pressures as a consequence of its annexation, to a large degree these communities retained their identity as a distinct nationality. Powerful social and political forces seem to have consolidated and expanded the social base of the Mexican communities during the second half of the nineteenth century, and as a result, important and durable links were forged between Mexicans north and south of the boundary.[6] This interaction of Mexican populations across the border through familial, friendship, cultural, and economic ties will be referred to as the "social dialogue" between the two populations. Much of the more articulated political dialogue between political actors has rested upon this diffuse social dialogue at various points since the nineteenth century.

This "social dialogue" laid the foundations for the sharing of common perceptions, aspirations, concerns, and—ultimately—identity, among Mexicans north and south of the boundary. They have often shared a common struggle to keep their national or group integrity and to oppose oppression and discrimination. As a result, on several historic occasions, Mexican groups north and south of the border have come to the defense of each other during crisis or when national or group dignity was threatened. Thus the political problems of Mexicans on one side of the border have often been important to Mexicans on the other side, and the social and political exchange among them has involved both symbolic and substantive issues.

These fundamental realities must also be considered in light of a mutual ambivalence that also dates from the time the territories were annexed. Because this essay focuses on political actors south of the Mexico–U.S. boundary, it will discuss the historic ambivalence of Mexicans toward the *México de afuera*—toward those outcasts who on various occasions were perceived as traitors, opportunists, and sell-outs. Although similarly negative perceptions existed among some Mexicans in the north, these will not receive as much attention in this essay. The mutual distrust and conflicts arising from these perceptions have affected Mexican policy responses to the *México de afuera* at various times, and undermined perceptions of shared commonalities.

This part of the essay deals with the activities of the representatives of the Mexican government vis-à-vis the communities of Mexican origin in the United States during the early part of this century. While exploring some of these activities, it may be helpful to keep a number of considerations in mind. The first is that the exchanges that took place between consular officials and the expatriate population, although important, were not the only relations that existed between the government and this community. The contacts between consuls and the Mexican community did not take place in a vacuum, and other actors had some influence on this relationship, though an elaborate discussion of these is beyond the scope of this paper. Moreover, with few exceptions, this exchange did not dominate the activities of the consular offices.[7] It appears that the relations between the consulates and the Mexican community as such were peripheral to the day-to-day concerns of each. By focusing on this specific set of activities, one runs the risk of overstating their importance as historical events. In conducting this study, the purpose is *not* to stress their importance but to draw some hypotheses from them for the current policy debate.

Finally, it is necessary to distinguish clearly between policy and practice in reviewing the history of Mexican consular relations with Mexicans in the United States. For the communities at the receiving end, the goals enunciated explicitly by the government were, of course, of less concern than the outcomes that took place in the day-to-day exchanges between them and the consulates. For the purposes of this analysis, however, both matter. Policies are important since they reflect political commitments that were acknowledged by the government in the past, and therefore underscore the Mexican perceptions of mutualities of interest and of the limits imposed upon the dialogue by domestic or foreign policy principles. Outcomes are also important because the gap between policy and practice has, in the past, reduced the meaningfulness of the political dialogue. This is significant for evaluating the credibility of the process.

The period for which documentation is most readily available, and central to this essay, is 1916-1930. What little research has been done for the later period suggests that some of the patterns and issues observed earlier repeat themselves. It is also evident that with the growth of a large Mexican-origin population lacking Mexican citizenship, the role and importance of the consulate in the community progressively diminished after World War II. So, while the earlier period is unique in some respects, it still affords some significant lessons for the renewal of dialogue at the present time.

Another set of considerations has to do with Mexico's particular style of conducting its foreign affairs. Traditionally, Mexico's foreign policy has been characterized as defensive and isolationist. Domestic and international factors have led to the establishment of this tradition. Domestically, Mexico has been a country of limited economic development, lacking a material basis for affecting outcomes in world politics. Internationally, Mexico's experience has been tragic. At mid-nineteenth century it lost more than half of its territory and tens of thousands of its citizens after a war with the United States. Since then, it has suffered a number of invasions and interventions by foreign powers—among them, the United States. These considerations help explain Mexico's traditional reluctance to take positions on some international issues, and why, on many occasions, it has appealed to the norms of international law in seeking a settlement of international disputes.[8]

In part because of its early experience with foreign intervention and its relative defenselessness, Mexico's foreign policy has been profoundly shaped by its adherence to the principle of non-intervention in the internal affairs of other countries and its preoccupation with the defense of national sovereignty. Just as U.S. political leaders have stressed "democracy" as a sacred ideal for that country, Mexican leaders have evoked the principles of "non-intervention" and "sovereignty" to justify certain positions they have urged Mexico to take. An assertion of these principles has been perceived to be in the best interests of Mexico. This helps explain why they have been adopted by Mexico's public as its own, thus extending beyond the rhetoric of the diplomatic elite, and why with few exceptions the country has protested the intervention of foreign powers in the internal affairs of third countries—or sympathized with anti-colonialist and liberation movements asserting the self-determination of sovereign peoples.[9]

The present historical inquiry into the dialogue between the government and Mexicans in the U.S. goes back to the period when the goals of the Revolution were hammered out during the Constitutional Convention of 1916–17. In November 1916, Mexican diplomats were ordered to "use the full powers of their offices" to aid Mexicans in the United States.

> They were to visit jailed migrants and inform them of their rights under local law and see that those rights were respected. This was to be done by contacting police and court agencies to press for nondiscriminatory application of state and federal law, or, when funds were available, through legal representation.[10]

Months later, as the Constitutional Convention was debating what was to become Article 123, which regulated labor conditions, Mexican migration officials at the northern border were ordered to prevent the exit of any worker who did not have a signed, valid contract for employment in the U.S. in accordance with the provisions of the proposed article. Later in 1917, the Ministry of *Gobernación* instructed its migration officials to advise departing migrants to register with the nearest Mexican consul at their destination to facilitate the enforcement of their contracts.[11]

The consuls themselves became more active in defending what they believed to be the interests of Mexican workers in the United States. One became involved in a protracted labor dispute with Spreckles Sugar, eventually resolved with the negotiation of a more favorable contract for the workers.[12] Also in that year, the Ministry of Foreign Relations protested to the U.S. government the ill treatment of Mexican laborers at the hands of U.S. employers who were not fulfilling their contracts, and the lack of remedies to these problems in U.S. immigration procedures.[13] Apparently the consulates were most effective when they opposed the conscription of Mexican nationals into U.S. military service during World War I. Some consular officers argued cases before local draft boards, others before U.S. authorities. The Mexican Embassy protested the forcible induction of Mexican citizens into the U.S. Army.[14]

Mexican protests of ill treatment in the U.S. were based not only upon official perceptions of an obligation to protect the interests of Mexican citizens, but also upon Mexican public opinion with respect to the emigration of laborers. The Mexican public reacted strongly against news that its countrymen were the victims of racially-motivated violence and job abuses in the U.S.; it was outraged by stories that circulated about Mexicans being lynched by mobs in Texas and elsewhere. At the same time, the Mexican public perceived emigration as a symptom of what was wrong with the country or of the travails of the revolution. These perceptions had political salience throughout this period, and the government often reacted to abuses suffered by its citizens abroad not only out of a sense of duty but also because inaction would be criticized at home.

Thus, in 1919, presidential candidate Alvaro Obregón drew attention to the plight of migrants leaving for the U.S. when he "railed at the spectacle of freight cars full of Mexicans being taken by labor recruiters from Nogales, Sonora, 'like penned cattle.'"[15] Months later, "a spokesman for the Secretary [of *Gobernación*] indignantly denied the government had been indifferent to the fate of expatriates." An editorial published in *Diario Oficial* in March, 1920, reaffirmed government intentions to protect Mexican workers in the United States.[16]

Mexican public opinion was opposed to emigration, but it appears to have been ambivalent about the reasons why emigrants left their homeland. One view lamented the hardships suffered by the migrants at home and abroad. In the statement previously cited, candidate Obregón went on to say:

> To go to a foreign country men have to sell their sleeping roll, a burro, and even the beams of their home for firewood, attracted by the sweet promises of the labor recruiters. When they return, there is no longer sleeping roll, nor burro, nor home.[17]

Others saw the emigrants as traitors to the nationalist cause, as workers who had deserted Mexico for the U.S. "just when their own nation was in need of their labor and support. . . ."[18] According to the second view, emigrants were opportunists who went to the U.S. to cash in on the available opportunities there, while leaving others in the country behind to solve the problems posed by the Revolution.

By 1920, Mexico's concern with non-intervention issues had had a visible effect upon the execution of policy in the consular protection of Mexicans in the United States. During the Carranza administration, at the same time that the consuls were reporting home the ill treatment of Mexicans in the north, the consulates were cautioned "to admonish braceros to avoid confrontations with the police, courts, and local citizens" in the United States. They were urged not to act as strikebreakers nor to participate in work stoppages against employers, since such activities "inevitably led to many arrests and abuses by local police. . . ."[19]

A specific instance of this non-interventionist approach to safeguarding Mexican interests abroad can be found in a 1917 strike by 9,000 Mexican mining workers against copper companies in southern Arizona. The local consul:

> . . . was ordered by the Secretary of Foreign Relations not to interfere in any way with the course of the strike. He was, instead, to tell all Mexicans to obey all applicable laws, to help those who ran afoul of the law, and to make certain that the constitutional rights of each arrested Mexican were respected in conformity with local custom.[20]

Thus, while Mexican policy was designed to protect the interests of citizens abroad, this protection was limited by the principle that the consulate should not question the legal norms—nor the local political authorities—of a particular jurisdiction.

Perhaps because Mexico was sensitive to U.S. intrusions on its own territory in the name of protecting the interests of its citizens, it explicitly sought to promote good relations with the U.S. by adhering to the principle of non-intervention when acting as an advocate for its citizens in the north. "Non-intervention" seems to have been interpreted to mean the respect of the sovereignty of U.S. law within its territory, as well as the respect of the established order—even if they were unjust. Migrants were urged to register with the nearest consulate to facilitate consular intervention in the event it became necessary. But they were also advised to obey all laws and to stay out of trouble.[21]

In summary, by 1920 the scope of the responsibilities of Mexico's revolutionary regime toward the *México de afuera* appears to have been established. This responsibility had been acknowledged, and both a symbolic and substantive dialogue between the consulates and Mexican expatriates became a political reality. However, the relationship was not free of ambivalent attitudes, nor were the efforts of the consuls in defense of Mexicans free of constraints, real or perceived. However, it seems clear that a mutually beneficial political dialogue had been established.

The dialogue was to get its first serious test during the 1921-22 depression in the United States, a time of severe crisis in the expatriate communities of the north. As early as the fall of 1920, tens of thousands of Mexican emigrants were out of work and going hungry. Added to the pain of depressed socioeconomic conditions, Mexicans were persecuted in many communities as the cause of local unemployment or as unfair competition with unemployed "white" workers. Workers in Arizona threatened to go on strike if legislation was not passed to restrict Mexican immigration. In Oklahoma, Mexicans were accused of being "cheap laborers" and were threatened with having their houses burned to the ground if they did not leave. In New York, San Antonio, and Dallas, labor unions expressed hostile attitudes or took actions against Mexican laborers in the vicinity.[22] In one Texas rural community in 1921, night horsemen rode into the Mexican barrio and destroyed the property of residents, an unmistakable message that they were not welcome.[23]

Because of the severe economic downturn, and reinforced by the hostility of local U.S. communities during a time of acute job competition, thousands of workers started the return trip to Mexico. Mexican northern border towns became congested with unemployed repatriates, many without the means to continue the trek to their homes in the interior, and some so impoverished they were dying of hunger. Many in the capital city, however, did not immediately perceive the mass return flow as a consequence of an economic decline in the U.S. and initially attributed it to the fact that Obregón's revolt against Carranza had ended and that peace was apparently being restored to Mexico.[24]

The situation of the laborers contracted by the Arizona Cotton Growers Association in 1920-21 is illustrative of the problems Mexicans faced at the time in the U.S., and suggestive of the perceptions and responses of the newly-installed Obregón Administration.

The Cotton Growers Association had sent agents to recruit 13,000 workers from Mexico during the temporary admissions program of World War I, with promises of a good wage, stable employment and paid return transportation. However, these representations turned out to have been false. The growers, through their agents, had recruited more workers than necessary. As a result of the economic downturn, by the end of 1920 conditions worsened and the growers refused to pay for return transportation.[25] In the spring of 1921, the situation got desperate.

> Mexican consuls charged that as many as 800 Mexican cotton pickers were left destitute by farmers in one Arizona county alone. Many laborers had never been compensated for their work, and a considerable number had been paid with bad checks. Some workers claimed that employers had deducted transportation fees from wages but then failed to provide them with railroad tickets.[26]

Thus by the spring of 1921, the thousands of Mexicans who had been stranded by their employers in Arizona, and who had waited out the winter in expectation of renewed seasonal employment, found themselves in a difficult situation when they learned that the acreage to be cultivated had diminished drastically.[27]

The Arizona State Federation of Labor, which called the condition of the Mexican workers a "disgrace," reportedly set up bread lines to feed 900 of them each day. They demanded that the U.S. government deport them. The Bureau of Immigration, however, "steadfastly maintained that it was the responsibility of the growers, not the federal government, to return the penniless Mexicans to their homeland."[28]

President Obregón sent representatives to threaten the cotton employers with measures which would prevent Mexican workers from going to work there in the future if they did not arrive at some agreement on what do to about the situation. Finally, agents from the Mexican consulate, the governor of the state of Arizona, and the growers arrived at an agreement which, in the view of the Mexican government, would satisfactorily resolve the problem of the affected workers. They waited for a month, but the growers simply ignored the agreement. In the end, the Phoenix consul was authorized to spend $17,000 in food and lodging for workers, and the Secretary of Foreign Relations was ordered to provide free transportation home for all who expressed the desire to be repatriated from the area. An additional thousand dollars was spent on food for the repatriates while they waited at a border port before going home.[29]

From the very beginning, the responses of the Mexican government to the 1921 crisis involved the highest levels of government and included several ministries. The Ministry of Foreign Relations sent instructions to the consuls in the U.S. indicating that they should do what they could to assist Mexicans seeking to return to their homeland. The President allocated an initial sum of 25,000 pesos and created a department within the Ministry with the exclusive responsibility of managing the repatriation of Mexicans from the United States. The Ministry of *Gobernación*, in addition to assuming responsibility for the repatriates once they were at the border, began a propaganda campaign within Mexico dramatizing the effects of the U.S. economic crisis and exhorting would-be emigrants to stay home. Obregón declared optimistically, "The government shall spend all that is necessary to repatriate unemployed Mexicans in the United States."[30]

In response to the 1921–22 crisis the government created three new consulates (in Oklahoma, Idaho, and Alaska) to address the problem of destitute migrants in those parts of the country. Elsewhere, Mexican consuls interceded with local authorities to provide the railroad fares to return the unemployed workers and even paid for the installation of soup kitchens. In Philadelphia, 120 workers that had been recruited and then abandoned by the Pennsylvania, Baltimore and Ohio Railroads were given a small subsistence by the Mexican government.[31] The mayor of Fort Worth, Texas, wrote Obregón that the city's charities had spent all their money helping indigent Mexicans in the wake of the depression. Obregón responded by sending $5,000 to replenish the city's fund.[32]

Though the Mexican government was the most visible, it was not the only actor involved in providing repatriation assistance at this time. In Laredo, Mexican mutual-aid societies comprised of immigrants organized dance parties and bullfights to raise money for the assistance of those most in need. Local women's organizations put together public skits and concerts for the same purpose.[33] In Ciudad Juárez, the state government distributed food among the penniless migrants, many of whom were returning to their homes in the interior without any outside assistance at all.[34]

The 1921–22 repatriations reaffirmed a tacit acceptance, on the part of the Mexican government, of its responsibility toward the Mexican community in the United States. Here the definition of "mutual interest" was not particularly different from that employed before, except that it was made more credible by the expenditure of considerable financial resources for a regime which itself was in financial straits. This, of course, gave the "dialogue" some meaning, and it explains why throughout the 1920s and early 1930s migrants often turned to the consulates with the hope that they could solve their problems.

In other respects, the response by the Obregón Administration of the stranded migrants in the U.S. was not particularly different from what other administrations gave their citizens within Mexico who had suffered disaster. Thus, the mutualities of interest here need to be considered in a Mexican domestic context, almost as if the U.S.–Mexican boundary did not exist.

Even during this crisis, some ambivalence toward the emigrants resurfaced not only in the popular press but in official, internal correspondence. On the one hand, the plight of destitute Mexicans in the U.S. evoked compassion and indignation at the abuses suffered at the hands of U.S. employers and the discrimination and hostility from "Anglo" communities. On the other, emigrants were sometimes viewed as traitors to the Revolution, as foolish wanderers who should have known better than to think of the U.S. as a promised land, or as opportunists looking for a free ride home.

Reflecting this ambivalence, Mexico City newspapers reported in the spring of 1922 that the unemployed repatriates in Mexico were returning to the United States. The government renewed its propaganda campaign in the newspapers, admonishing would-be emigrants that U.S. employers were unscrupulous and did not comply with the labor contracts they promised.[35] At the same time, the migration officials of *Gobernación* at the northern border were ordered to verify the emigrants' labor contracts, and to prevent their departure unless the contracts were duly signed and notarized and the employers had deposited a sum to pay for the return of the workers. The latter provision had the purpose of assuring that if the workers were to suffer a situation similar to that of 1921, they could be repatriated at the employer's expense. However, there is no record that this policy was ever enforced.[36]

In the aftermath of the 1921-22 depression, the consulates in the United States became consistently more involved in protecting the rights of Mexican workers in the U.S., though the efforts expended were less costly and more diffuse. Indicative of this change, and of the interest of the government in consolidating consular efforts with respect to the *México de afuera*, is the replacement of the *Ley Orgánica del Servicio Consular Mexicano* of November 1911, and the directives of 1916 and 1917 with a new law, the *Ley Orgánica del Cuerpo Consular Mexicano* and its regulations, promulgated on January 9, 1923.[37] This change officially recognized what the consulates had been doing on an ad hoc basis, and formally established a policy which gave renewed emphasis to "protect the interests and rights . . . of Mexican citizens abroad."[38]

As early as 1922, the consuls were ordered to census the Mexican population in their jurisdictions so that they could report to the Ministry of Foreign Relations the dimension of the tasks before them. It appears that because the emigrants were fearful of what the data might be used for, and because the resources allocated to the effort were limited, the results of this project were not satisfactory.[39] Later in the twenties, the consulates were advised to collect such data anew, and lacking a census, they were to inquire into the number of Mexicans working in specific industries such as steel, railroads, and agriculture.[40] Nevertheless, the personnel to do this was limited, considering that the consular corps—51 in 1920—had only grown to 60 in 1929. Though the scale of the efforts that the consulates could undertake was obviously limited by its reduced personnel and scarce resources, the policy directives were explicit: "Each case of denial of due process involving a Mexican citizen had to be accurately recorded and promptly reported to Mexico City for proper action. With the aid of the new workers' organizations [such as the *comisiones honoríficas*], consuls now had a steady stream of information and could offer no excuses for dereliction of duty."[41]

Examples of consular actions designed to protect the rights of Mexican citizens or to protect them from ill treatment are not hard to find during this period, though such efforts did not always meet with success. In 1921, a Mexican citizen was sent to the electric chair, notwithstanding the efforts of the local consul to establish the fact that the accused was mentally incapacitated at the time the crime was committed.[42] In 1922, at the height of the post-war depression vigilantes took a Mexican awaiting trial in a Weslaco, Texas jail and summarily hanged him. A Mexican consul complained to the Texas governor, the embassy in Washington protested to the State Department, and the governor finally sent one hundred law enforcement officers to Weslaco to apprehend the perpetrators.[43] In 1923, the Mexican Embassy formally complained to the Pennsylvania governor that Mexican residents in a community in that state were being expelled from their homes because of rioting there.[44] In 1924 the Mexican consul in Gary, Indiana, was "instrumental in halting local police from making arrests each time a crime occurred in [Mexican] neighborhoods."[45] In 1929 the Phoenix, Arizona consul complained to the Santa Fe Railroad about the sanitary facilities provided by the company which were for "white men only."[45]

During the years following the depression of 1921-22, the consuls emphasized work-related and social problems in connection with their *labor de protección*. Workers who had entered without an immigration visa faced the greatest difficulties. Because of their illegal status they risked deportation by U.S. immigration authorities, particularly during times of high unemployment. They were frequently put in jails where they had to share cells with prisoners accused of murder and other serious crimes, and they were the victims of unscrupulous labor contractors. Frequently, undocumented workers were expelled without collecting their wages, and some would be separated from their families in the United States as a consequence of deportation. From the point of view of the Ministry of Foreign Relations, these were the most serious issues involved in the *labor de protección*.[47]

Much of the consuls' labor was to disseminate information and advice to those who sought them out. The purpose of this advice was to forewarn the emigrants about the various kinds of abuse that took place. Some consulates were busy throughout the 1920s preparing and distributing flyers and making announcements through the local press. Among other things, agricultural workers were advised to ask for labor contracts in writing, with a description of the type of work to be undertaken, the length of the work day and the wage rate, and they were urged to send these contracts to the nearest consulate so that the latter might be in a position to protect their interests.[48]

A less time consuming, but no less significant area of concern was securing payment for workers who had suffered work-related accidents. According to records of the Ministry of Foreign Relations, the consuls made significant progress in this area, and by the late 1920s practically all of the cases that had been handled had been resolved in the workers' favor.[49]

Despite such optimistic views of what the consulates were doing, it is evident that their activities were limited by the scarcity of resources and government revenues during the 1920s. As one report put it in 1929,

> [e]very year, our government has spent the entire amount budgeted for the repatriation and protection of Mexicans abroad, and tried to spend it as wisely as possible, given that the amount—only $20,000.00 per year—is actually very little. Care has to be exercised to secure the greatest possible benefit in all of those cases that may present themselves in the course of a year. . . .[50]

What became apparent by the mid-1920s was that protection had been given a higher priority than repatriation. It was less expensive and more useful since repatriates would return to the U.S. later in any event. Also evident by the mid-1920s was a more active involvement by the consulates' auxiliary groups—the *comisiones honoríficas* and the *brigadas Cruz Azul*. All of this may explain why with such a small budget, the consulates were able to provide limited assistance to 50,000 Mexicans in the U.S. in 1928–29.[51]

These auxiliary groups were involved in a wide range of activities, such as providing free medical supplies for the sick within certain consular jurisdictions. The need for this service is more evident when one considers that U.S. immigration laws excluding immigrants "likely to become a public charge" prohibited the distribution of medical assistance to immigrants with less than five years' residence.[52]

To provide some of these services, and to overcome the barrier of limited resources, some consuls occasionally organized community fund-raisers such as dances, *kermesses*, public lectures, skits and *veladas*.[53] These activities brought the consuls and local community groups closer together, and often made the consul an important figure in the local community. The funds raised were destined to provide food, shelter, and in some cases, return transportation for unemployed and indigent Mexicans.[54]

Much of the cost of the repatriations organized by the consuls during the mid-1920s was not borne by the national treasury; the same is true for the repatriates of the 1930s. The financial support and involvement of the *comisiones honoríficas* and auxiliary mutual-aid societies were crucial. This seems to have been in part due to the lessons learned from the Obregón repatriations by a frustrated ministry which was only beginning to understand the migration process.

> The emigration of Mexicans to the United States is that [problem] which causes the most headaches for the consulates . . . since most of our workers leave the country, enticed by labor contracts which are, in general, unjust, onerous, or do not provide sufficient guarantees for our countrymen.[55]

As the volume of emigration grew throughout the 1920s, it became a symbol of humiliation and subordination to the United States.[56] Gradually, the Mexican government recognized that it had no control over the process, and began to emphasize the "management" of the political problem it represented through the use of immigrant organizations in the U.S., with no serious attempts to repatriate migrants. One official of the Ministry of Foreign Relations was quoted, for example, as saying that government efforts to repatriate emigrants were backfiring and that they actually encouraged further emigration. Thus, he argued, the suspension of repatriation at government cost in 1926 "would surely" reduce emigration.[57]

The perception that emigration reflected poorly upon Mexico, and the on-again-off-again tensions in U.S.–Mexican relations during the twenties were also at the root of efforts by the consuls to encourage patriotic celebrations and to make public displays of nationalism.[58] The political symbolism of emigration was aptly captured by José Vasconcelos in a speech in Chicago in 1929, when he was running against the official party's candidate for president of Mexico:

> Mexicans, let us never forget or cease to show interest in our country and in the land in which we first saw the light of day. For if we are here working hard and suffering, it will not always be so. We are but the children of Israel who are passing through our Egypt here in the United States doing onerous labors, swallowing our pride, bracing up under the indignities heaped upon us here. If we expect to return and escape all this, as all good Mexicans ought to,

then we should show interest in the affairs of our country from this Egypt of ours.[59]

The symbolic value of emigration to the U.S. had by no means disappeared in the late 1920s. Vasconcelos in 1929, like Obregón ten years earlier, demonstrated that the issue was politically important for Mexicans.[60]

During the late 1920s, emigrants saw the Mexican consuls in some communities as a source of limited protection. It is difficult to judge the success of their efforts. Some authors attribute the low rate of naturalization of Mexican immigrants in the U.S. to the fact that keeping their Mexican citizenship kept open the possibility of petitioning the consulate for assistance when all else failed.[61] As one Mexican community newspaper in Chicago in 1926 put it,

> [w]hile the Department of State at Washington is demanding guarantees for its citizens in Mexico, we are being made the victims of the police in Chicago and other cities.[62]

Evidently, other agencies of the U.S. government could not be counted on to provide Mexicans with assistance. While the limited assistance of the consuls may not have been the most important reason for the low naturalization rate of Mexican emigrants, clearly, in some communities and at certain times, the consulate was the most visible symbol of protection.

Though surprising in retrospect, consular activities were not entirely limited to Mexican-born persons in the United States. To begin with, the Mexican definition of citizenship included those persons born outside of Mexico of Mexican-born parents. Such persons, also U.S. citizens by birth, were therefore dual nationals, and when the consulates extended protection to Mexican communities it was often assumed that all were Mexican citizens— either by birth or derivation. Because the proportion of third-generation or more distant descendants of Mexican immigrants was small, this assumption had a ring of truth. Apparently no one questioned consular activities affecting non-Mexican citizens of Mexican origin. To be sure, it was difficult to distinguish between Mexican citizens and others of Mexican origin since both groups lived in the same communities and shared the same problems. When consular officials were called upon to address a specific issue, such distinctions—even when they could be made—were often ignored. School segregation was typical. "Anglos" were separated from "Mexicans" in some communities, irrespective of place of birth. Thus, consular efforts to prevent this type of discrimination evidently benefited "Mexicans," whatever their citizenship.[63]

When citizenship and place of birth became more salient variables in Mexican domestic politics—in part because of contemporaneous State Department pressure in behalf of U.S. citizens with property in Mexico—these gradually acquired more significance in consular activities in the U.S. as well. This, together with the norms established by international conventions on the scope of consular activities in host countries, may explain a more evident reluctance by Mexican consulates to get involved in matters not directly related to the interests of Mexican citizens in the late 1920s and early 1930s. It is telling that in 1928 in Texas, "discrimination was so intense that some American-born Mexicans, according to one observer, had gone to Mexican consulates to become citizens of Mexico."[64] One might conclude from this that although there were *formal* policy constraints upon the consuls' activities vis-à-vis persons who were not Mexican citizens, an *informal* practice of being involved with the *México de afuera* existed, even when citizenship criteria were not met, because some important foreign (or domestic) policy objectives were at stake.

This practice was recognized by officials at the Ministry of Foreign Relations. One view officially proposed in 1940—though apparently not acted upon for the reasons cited earlier—suggested that Mexico extend the recognition of its responsibility toward noncitizens of Mexican origin:

> Mexico has left a deeply-rooted ethnic group in its train in the southern part of the United States—a group which must be heeded and whose welfare must be considered. The vestiges of *la raza* dispersed throughout the territory after the dismemberment of Mexico have been painfully joined by successive waves [of immigrants] pushed out of Mexico by its civil wars and the vicissitudes of its economy. The objective of this . . . is not to go into the causes of this persistent exodus, nor to go into an elaborate examination of whether or not the great mass of Mexicans resident in the south of the U.S. still conserves, from a strictly legal point of view, Mexican citizenship. Our fundamental purpose is to make note of the fact

that this large group of persons exists, and that Mexico has the unavoidable duty of addressing its most urgent and constant needs.[65]

This view, foreshadowing the discussion of Mexico's responsibility to Chicanos in the 1970s and 1980s, was expressed at a time when Mexico least needed to consider the emigration of its citizens to the U.S., a fact which makes it more significant. By 1940, several hundred thousand Mexican emigrants—and their U.S.-born families—returned to Mexico. The population left in the U.S. was a "hard core" of Mexican-origin residents committed to residing permanently in the United States. Two years later, however, Mexico found it politically advantageous to negotiate a contract labor program that would send hundreds of thousands of Mexicans for temporary work in the United States over a period of two decades. In that context, the 1940 proposal appears to have been forgotten.

In the aftermath of the Great Depression, and particularly after the oil expropriation of 1938, Mexico acquired a certain degree of self-confidence in its foreign relations. During World War II it negotiated a framework for settling the claims arising from the oil expropriation and other outstanding issues. It also moved toward a more independent foreign policy vis-à-vis the United States. Mexican public opinion, according to one author, evolved since World War II and

> has become accustomed to a healthy nationalism and to see Mexico take certain positions which demonstrate a measure of independence with respect to the United States, at least to the extent that they compare favorably with those taken by most Latin American governments. Thus, the effect of past attitudes has been transformed into a new premise for the nation's foreign policy.[66]

During the decades following the oil expropriation, Mexico followed a path in international affairs relatively independent from the United States—though still subject to certain constraints—a course taking it somewhat out of its isolationist tradition. In doing so it reaffirmed its commitment to non-intervention and self-determination as cornerstones of its foreign policy. Moreover, the role of the consulates in defending the interests of Mexican expatriates and in providing limited leadership in the Chicano community was scaled back and forgotten.[67] By the 1950s then, the political dialogue that had peaked in the 1920s and 1930s seems to have faded.

This historical overview reveals that the political dialogue between the Mexican government and Mexicans in the U.S. was very much alive in the early part of this century, and that to a great extent it was mutually beneficial. Mexicans in the north received limited assistance, particularly during times of crisis, and with the support of mutual-aid societies this assistance made it easier to weather their harsh existence in the United States. Through the consuls the Mexican government occasionally provided leadership. Through its embassy, its formal protests of discrimination and ill treatment, the government sometimes opened the doors of local U.S. officials and employers to the benefit of Mexican workers. More frequently, the consulate provided a stimulus for self-help within the community and a beacon for Mexicans away from home who, like "children of Israel," were passing through their "Egypt" in the United States. The dialogue of the 1920s and 1930s seems to have been exceptional but important.

By the same token, the government received some intangible benefits from this activity. The revolutionary regimes of the postwar were struggling throughout the 1920s to consolidate their hold on the country and battling the U.S. State Department over recognition and the enforcement of various provisions of the 1917 Constitution. As several actions by the government during the 1920s show, it was sensitive to the domestic criticism that not enough was being done to protect the rights of Mexican citizens abroad, and it was astute enough to recognize the legitimizing function of certain activities which protested the violations of those rights or which served to defend the nation's dignity before the United States. Then as now, symbolic responses were significant.

The basis for defining mutualities of interest was that of a responsibility—the obligation of a paternalistic government—to provide for its citizens, be they at home or abroad. One could argue that the consulates acted according to their perceptions of what their responsibilities were to Mexican expatriates. This included ensuring that their rights in the U.S. were protected under U.S. law, negotiating labor contracts for some workers consistent with Mexican law, and insuring that indigent, unemployed Mexicans had some means of survival—preferably at the expense of the employer, local government or local mutual-aid society, but if necessary, at the expense of the Mexican government. These perceptions define mutualities of interest in terms of the responsibility of a government to its citizens and constituencies.

A number of characteristics of this dialogue during the 1920s bear some discussion. First, it was overtly a dialogue between a government and its citizens. Whenever non-Mexican citizens were affected by consular activities it was a by-product of this dialogue. Thus, though cutting across an international boundary, the dialogue was essentially an exchange within the Mexican domestic political context. Second, the dialogue took place between a highly organized state actor and a diffuse set of nonstate actors. Under these circumstances, the government had more of an impact on the direction of the dialogue than did the weak and scattered organizations of Mexicans in the United States. This made the extent and tone of the dialogue dependent on governmental response to demands by Mexicans at home and abroad. Since the government lacked an established framework for these relations, a substantial basis of mutual interest existed only when the chief executive assigned a high priority to this area—such as during Obregón's time—or when individual consuls provided exemplary service.

A third characteristic is that the resources—political, financial, and administrative—spent by the government on the exchange with Mexicans in the north came out of the same pot as the resources spent on addressing the problems of the south. Given the severely limited resources of the government in this period, this led to competing interests between some Mexicans in the south and the north, which resulted in negative attitudes in the south about the expatriates. Thus, the ambivalent Mexican attitudes of the literate public in Mexico City and government officials to the emigrants prevented the expansion of the political dialogue and provoked mixed government responses, particularly in the execution of policy, to the dialogue.

Finally, the means of communication used by the expatriates to request assistance—and by the government to explain why it was being provided—was heavily laden with symbols evoking images of the Revolution, national dignity, and a sense of mission. It is no accident that the consulates were, and continue to be, at the center of activities during Mexican patriotic holidays. Indeed, repatriation policies were initially couched as an invitation for the prodigal sons to come home. Thus, protection, repatriation and dialogue were all part of a process which involved both substantive and symbolic exchanges.

POLITICAL CONTEXTS

To understand the dynamics of the renewed dialogue between Mexican and Chicano political actors one must recognize that the dialogue takes place simultaneously in three different political contexts: the U.S. domestic, U.S.-Mexican bilateral, and the Mexican domestic political environments. These contexts are mutually exclusive only in a semantical sense. Issues arise in one context which have currency in another. Still, distinguishing between them is useful because the rules of political behavior are different among them, and certain issues can be addressed better in one context than in another.

The first context, the U.S. domestic political environment, is where the most important issues for Mexican political actors in the U.S. arise, and where the outcomes are most meaningful. Chicano actors, who have increasing influence within the United States, have recently looked to Mexico as a potential ally in their struggle over important issues in the U.S. domestic political context. Mexican responses to overtures in these areas have been cautious and noncommittal. To the extent that the dialogue takes place within a context where the Mexican government's interests are only marginally involved and where the issues are clearly internal U.S. matters, Mexican responses will be muted or restrained. Significant Mexican responses to broaden the dialogue will face here their more serious constraints.[68]

In the second context, the binational political environment, Chicano groups are one among many U.S. nonstate actors who share interests with the Mexican government and who may play a significant role in U.S.-Mexico relations. Here, significant Mexican interests are at play in a government-to-government relationship, and issues, such as immigration and U.S. treatment of Mexican nationals—be they documented or not—are likely to be important to Chicano political actors and those in Mexico, including the Mexican government. In this area, Chicano political actors may be as important as U.S. oil companies are in energy matters to Mexico.[69]

In the last context, the Mexican domestic political environment, Mexicans in the U.S. are one more political actor with which the Mexican government has to deal in its own domestic politics. In this sense, Mexicans in the U.S. have pressed certain claims upon the government as any other Mexican constituency might—the difference being that geographically, this group has been outside of Mexico's borders. The dialogue described earlier took place in this context—the government was petitioned to respond, not as an outside agent in an internal U.S. matter or as an ally in a bilateral government-to-government issue, but as the ultimate problem-solver responsible for acting in behalf of its people. Mexican policy responses in this context have been varied, but most "interventionist" positions by the Mexican government in the U.S. can be characterized as actions which the government perceived to be in response to—or an extension of—domestic political concerns.

As has been pointed out, many issues salient to this dialogue arise in one environment but have implications in another. One example might be the protection of the rights of Mexicans in the United States. From the perspective of the Mexican political actors north of the boundary, such activities arise within a U.S. domestic context and a local struggle for civil rights. From the Mexican government's perspective such actions arise within the bilateral and the Mexican domestic context. In the former sense, protection of Mexican nationals abroad is an activity provided for by reciprocal agreements and international treaties, and such protection may serve important Mexican foreign policy objectives. In the latter sense, such activities respond, as they did in the 1920s, to domestic political pressure. Protecting Mexicans from abuse in the U.S. was a symbolic defense of national dignity as well as a concrete action designed to further the welfare of specific individuals; thus, it served a legitimation function for the government.

The migration of Mexican workers to the United States is an example of a related issue which cuts across domestic and international political environments. Three sets of actors—the U.S., the Mexican government, and the Mexican community north of the U.S.-Mexico border—have a high stake in this area, particularly in U.S. policy responses. Mexican actors in the north are likely to be concerned about possible punitive responses by the

United States to immigration in general and to undocumented migration in particular. The Mexican government is likely to be concerned about extremist policies in either direction, though for different reasons. The U.S. government is faced with the necessity of making *some* tangible response in an area where opposition groups have stalemated any change in policy for several years.[70] To implement a response it will have to hammer out a consensus policy within the U.S. domestic context, which means that it will consider strategies where one set of actors north of the border is used to neutralize a set of actors south of the border, or vice versa. In this case what is domestic politics for Mexicans residing in the U.S. and international relations for Mexico, is both for the U.S. government.

Thus, "political context" is useful in considering the course that the Mexican–Chicano dialogue may take. Based upon the previous historical analysis, one may hypothesize that salient issues arising as Mexican *domestic* or *bilateral* questions, are likely to receive some government response. Less salient issues, perceived to be internal U.S. matters, are more likely to be avoided or ignored.

Perhaps most important and least understood is the Mexican domestic political context. Significant responses by Mexican political actors are likely to be strongly conditioned by the perceptions, operating assumptions, and expectations that arise in that context. Several important short-term obstacles to broadening the dialogue can be located in this context. One of these is a negative perception by Mexicans about Chicanos. It may be appropriate to single out the attitudes of those Mexicans south of the border who are in policy-making positions within the government, i.e., an elite within Mexico. While apparently no systematic research has been done on these attitudes, the anecdotal information available suggests that some of the same class biases that Mexican elites have expressed toward their poorer countrymen have been reproduced in their contacts with Chicanos in Mexico. While this argument is merely speculation at this point, the reactions expressed by some Chicano intellectuals evidently based upon their experiences in Mexico would lead one to state this as a working hypothesis.[71]

Such views find a parallel among other broader segments of the Mexican population which link the Chicano with the bracero, the migrant and the *pochos* (a pejorative term which refers to the Anglicized Mexicans residing along the northern border with the United States):

> In the popular mind the bracero is transformed to the pocho, the outcast, an almost always ridiculous figure that speaks both languages badly and who will never be respectable in either [society]. When, in the early forties the California pachucos are persecuted . . . almost no one hears about it in Mexico. A group of Mexico City students causes a disruption at the U.S. Embassy in protest. But this is the exception. The more common view is an indifference before the outcasts, who—in the style of a familiar metaphor—are accused of trading their country for a bowl of beans.[72]

While this kind of image is breaking down in Mexico (indeed, the author whose essay is quoted above is a Mexican intellectual criticizing stereotypes of Mexicans in the U.S.) it must be noted that such images still persist. As was noted in the earlier historical discussion, these views are the product of an ambivalence toward the migration process itself. While it is difficult to assess the importance of this ambivalence as an obstacle, and while such views may not shape the *formulation* of Mexican policy toward Chicanos in the future, they will influence the *execution* of such policies, particularly in the short term.

Another obstacle arises from the different ways in which Mexicans and Chicanos perceive themselves and each other. A Mexican intellectual who has made some important contributions on this subject, writing about Chicanos for a Mexican audience, notes:

> The term "Chicano" is not unanimously accepted by the entire population of Mexican origin in the United States. For those who call themselves Chicanos, the term has an eminently political connotation, which reflects a political commitment in a struggle against "Anglo" oppression . . . Chicano is juxtaposed with . . . "Anglo." . . . To be considered "Chicano" by those who identify themselves as such, the country of birth is not relevant.[73]

This author contrasts this self-perception with what he considers to be the dominant view of Chicanos held in Mexico:

> Chicanos continue to be perceived in Mexico within the formalistic context of their place of birth. An extension of this formalism constitutes the mistaken political notion that the world of the

Chicanos is just as foreign to us [Mexicans] as anything else that we identify as alien.[74]

Considering the two views expressed above, the "Chicano" population is defined in ethnic and political terms on the one hand, and in legal, or citizenship terms, on the other. In the first case, the term refers to a group sharing a common ethnic and historical origin at the same time that it defines a set of individual political actors. What gives this group cohesiveness is a common origin and an opposition to its political subordination. In the second case, while this self-definition of Chicanos ignores citizenship and place of birth issues, the manner in which the population in Mexico defines *itself*—and others—generally treats these as important variables. It should surprise no one that citizenship distinctions have become important in a country which underwent a social revolution that was in part a reaction to foreign domination, and in a society which experienced foreign intervention—much of it from the United States—as a consequence of the claims made upon Mexico by foreigners living within its borders.[75] In the concrete case of persons of Mexican origin in the U.S., these distinctions are artificial and perhaps not functional, but they are made nevertheless.

Past discussions of this subject have often assumed that because of such obstacles, and given the historic ambivalence about the Mexican population in the north, the Mexican government can easily ignore the concerns of Mexicans in the U.S., be they Mexican citizens or not. According to this view, the dialogue has few, if any, possibilities.[76] In the short term, the Mexican government can probably avoid the issues posed by this dialogue, though there are arguments which suggest that it *should not* avoid them. But those that stress the constraints on the dialogue ignore a number of reasons why, in the medium and long term, the Mexican government *cannot* avoid the issues posed by the political dialogue. One of these is that, as demonstrated by history, the dialogue is not new—it is not a conjunctural event. The political conditions that have given it life and vitality have fluctuated throughout the decades, but they have not and are not likely to disappear. The forces that have drawn Mexicans as political actors together for the last hundred years or so cannot be merely wished away, and a dialogue—however limited—will continue.

Further, this on-going political dialogue rests upon a more diffuse, but enduring "social dialogue." The consolidation of a permanent Mexican population in the U.S. with a strong current of social and economic ties to Mexico resulted in a particular set of durable non-state relations across the boundary. The relations between these particular non-state actors—like those of other such actors—are largely out of Mexican and U.S. government control. But as in the more general problem, to the extent that these non-state relations impinge upon state-to-state relations or domestic state policy, they will require policy responses by the government involved, be it Mexico or the United States.

Another reason why Mexico cannot avoid continuing the political dialogue with Chicano organizations and with Mexicans in the U.S. is that the latter have emerged as significant political actors in the U.S. domestic, and to a lesser extent, international context. Some of these groups will look to the Mexican government and to Mexican groups as possible allies or opponents while seeking to affect outcomes in a U.S. domestic political environment. Some Chicano groups will try to influence Mexican policy responses with respect to issues that Mexico faces in its bilateral relations with the United States. Other political actors in the U.S. will be sought by Mexican political groups as allies in Mexican *domestic* political conflicts.

In these three contexts—U.S. domestic, Mexican–U.S. bilateral and Mexican domestic political environments—Chicano groups will become increasingly important actors in the years ahead. Even if they had no substantial social links with Mexicans south of the border, and even if no history of political exchange between the government and Mexicans north of the boundary existed, Mexico would still have to contend with Chicano groups as political actors in their own right. In this respect, Mexicans in the United States are becoming significant players in a context where the Mexican and U.S. "domestic" political environments are becoming internationalized.

Finally, at the same time that one considers the obstacles to dialogue, one must also recognize that the dialogue itself is in the process of changing the images associated with Chicanos in Mexico. One indicator of that is the development of a "dialogue" through the Mexican news media, especially in Mexico City, between Chicano political actors, their organizations and leaders, and the Mexican public. Since the mid-1970s, a number of Chicano spokespersons have had regular access to the Mexican media to give *their* side of the story on the coverage of many events in the U.S. reported in Mexico. A perusal of the major dailies in Mexico City and of national magazines reveals that they "discovered" Chicanos during the 1970s, and that their social conditions, struggles, hopes and public views have received largely favorable attention in Mexico. While exposure has not altered the perception by some Mexicans of this population as one belonging to the United States, it has brought out the manifestations of Mexican cultural traits in this U.S. population group, and the "social dialogue" that it maintains with Mexicans to the south has itself broadened into public discussion. Mexicans who are not directly connected with the migration process have become aware that a significant contingent of Mexicans reside in the north—some of Mexican and others of U.S. citizenship. Moreover, as in the case of the emigrants in the 1920s whose plight in the U.S. had political salience in the Mexican domestic context, the Mexican public has identified with the struggles of the Chicanos in the United States. Many of the symbols having currency then—the defense of Mexican national dignity, the protection of rights, the maintenance of a national identity, even repatriation—are important in this dialogue.

There are other indications that this dialogue has acquired legitimacy within the Mexican domestic political context. One of those can be found in some statements made by President López Portillo when he reported to the Mexican people what had been accomplished during his September, 1979 meeting with then-President Jimmy Carter:

> At the impassioned request of our Chicano brothers, I told the President of the United States that we viewed with great alarm that human rights were being denied them in the areas of education, health and legal protection; that we found it unacceptable for two civilized peoples to confuse immigration with labor rights, much less with human rights. This declaration [on my part] was accepted. We stand behind our Chicano brothers and we stand behind our undocumented citizens. . . .[77]

While this statement could be criticized as being merely rhetorical, it has real consequences, such as that of shaping Mexican public opinion—or the approaches taken by Mexican policy makers—

toward the Chicanos in the United States as a group distinct from Mexican migrants. It also conveys an image of solidarity—one that Mexico traditionally reserves for other Latin Americans fighting for freedom and self-determination.

One might ask if the traditional style of Mexican diplomacy, characterized by isolationsim, adherence to non-intervention, and concerns about U.S. government responses to this dialogue, will not serve as formidable constraints impeding the further development of this political dialogue. The historical overview presented earlier would seem to suggest that just as there are some compelling forces likely to maintain the dialogue in the future, others will place barriers beyond which the dialogue cannot expand.

A significant new development during the 1970s was that Mexico adopted a more active foreign policy, one which broke with the traditional mold of foreign relations. This is important for the Mexican-Chicano dialogue since it is likely to encourage a revision of past approaches to this and other foreign policy considerations. Two processes—one structural and economic, the other geopolitical—have altered, perhaps irreversibly, the traditional underpinnings of Mexico's relations with the rest of the world. In the first place, Mexico's economic development model seemed to have run out of steam during the Echeverría Administration, and almost simultaneously, Mexico rediscovered oil in abundance. Both events have forced the country to rely more heavily on foreign trade in effecting its economic recovery and in preparing national development plans under a new framework. In the process, Mexico has discovered that a nation cannot count on a plan for conquering export markets and be a significant oil producer, and at the same time remain isolated from the world and from world politics.

In the second place, events and processes just outside of Mexico's borders both to the south and to the north have heightened its sensitivity to relations with its neighbors. To the south, Central America seems to have entered a process of dramatic change. This, and the fact that Mexico's petroleum deposits lie near its southern boundary have accelerated the development of a more aggressive policy on events in those countries. To the north, Mexico is troubled by what has been perceived to be a qualitative leap in its strategic importance to the United States as a consequence of the discovery of new oil during a global energy crisis.

All of these processes converged during the 1970s to thrust Mexico as a more aggressive political actor onto the world stage. This was explicitly recognized by President López Portillo in an address before an assembly of the Ministry of Foreign Relations.

> We used to be a nation which stressed the principle of non-intervention; we were a country whose foreign policy revealed our preoccupation with decolonization and with securing independence from foreign pressures. More recently, we have undertaken a more active foreign policy to effect results outside our borders that we could not combat from within.[78]

While this statement signaled a more assertive and interventionist tone in foreign policy, it did not represent an explicit abandonment of the principles of non-intervention or of the defense of national sovereignty.[79]

In summary, the political environments within which Chicano–Mexican relations find expression are in a state of flux. Chicano political actors are flexing their muscles in all three "contexts," a fact that cannot be ignored by other actors in these arenas. Mexico's recent responses to these actors have permitted the dialogue to be renewed—and be re-established largely within the Mexican domestic political environment. Finally, Mexico's current approach to foreign relations, specifically with the United States, also seems to have significant new elements. All of these factors suggest that the possibilities for expanding the dialogue are opening rather than closing. That in itself is significant. But while change is slow, and so many political variables seem to be changing at once, it is difficult to predict the direction of the dialogue between Mexican political actors south and north of the U.S.–Mexican border. In part this difficulty resides in the fact that a coherent policy by any significant group of political actors has been lacking.

SOME FINAL CONSIDERATIONS

This essay suggests that Mexican and Chicano political actors are being drawn together to renew a political dialogue which, largely symbolic at this point, is nevertheless real and likely to be enduring. Moreover, in the medium to long term, the issues posed by this dialogue would seem to be unavoidable.

The preceding analysis sketched some of the factors that will shape this dialogue in the future. Even this brief examination of the topic reveals that the forces and processes determining the outcome of this political exchange are many and complex. The most important appear to be historical precedent; the changing political priorities and objectives of the principal actors; the commonalities that the communities of Mexicans in the north and south have shared with each other, as well as their mutual ambivalence; Mexico's adherence to the foreign policy principles of nonintervention and self-determination. The maturity reached by Chicano actors in recent years as well as the movement toward a more activist Mexican foreign policy are variables which seem likely to accelerate the renewal of the dialogue and to push it toward new frontiers.

Given this kaleidoscopic view of the process, predicting the future course of the dialogue is problematic. Because the dialogue is not new, because it rests upon a prior "social" and "cultural" dialogue between Mexicans on each side of the Mexican-U.S. boundary, and because of the political realities affecting the actors, it is clear that the dialogue will continue. Nevertheless, conflicts, misunderstandings, ambivalence, and lapses in communication will continue.

If this analysis is correct, then it is up to both sets of actors to channel their dialogue into constructive areas where mutual benefits will be realized and conflicts reduced and managed. Because the Mexican government is the actor with the greatest resources and organizational capacity, a greater share of the responsibility for supporting the dialogue should fall upon it. But what can it do to help develop this dialogue in a constructive manner? There are many possible answers but only a few alternatives will be explored.

One possibility is to continue with the same ad hoc approach that has been followed in the last few years. Were this to occur one might expect more scholarships for Chicanos to study in Mexican institutions, an increased distribution of Spanish-language and Mexican cultural materials for institutions in the United States, more invitations for Chicano leaders to visit Mexico and participate in domestic and international forums in various capacities. But this will continue to occur even if the government does not actively support it.

In this regard, the media—particularly the Mexican news print and electronic media—are likely to play an important role. Communication and mutual comprehension are severely lacking. Chicano political actors have, through the positions they have taken, often communicated a conditional support of Mexican policies and positions vis-à-vis the United States. Yet, because a thorough familiarity with Mexican foreign policy formulation and the domestic political process is lacking in the U.S., some actors have at times unintentionally promoted policies obviously offensive to Mexico. For instance, some Chicanos have publicly supported the North American Common Market idea, apparently unaware that such a policy is perceived in Mexico as largely advantageous to U.S. multinational corporations, being opposed by virtually every important political group in Mexico—except for some elements of its business sector.[80] Similarly, Mexican officials have in the past shown their ignorance about the diversity of political views in the Chicano community. A broader exchange of information would allow the players to know each other better, and would serve to promote a more constructive political exchange.

Along these same lines, Mexico could also consider sending personnel and resources to Chicano communities in the United States, just as they have to several Central American countries, to provide various forms of technical assistance and training. The precise areas in which such exchanges could take place need to be mapped out, taking both the needs of Mexicans in the north and the resources of Mexicans to the south into consideration. By the same token, Mexico has certain needs, particularly in skilled personnel, which will go unfulfilled as its economy grows in the years ahead. The foreign recruitment of such personnel for a limited number of temporary and permanent positions is a foregone conclusion. Tapping the Mexican community in the U.S. to fill some of those needs would appear to be a natural policy to follow.

To a certain extent, much of the dialogue's content in the future will resemble that of the immediate past. However, in the opinion of this writer, a framework going beyond the current ad hoc approach and addressing the issues posed by this dialogue head on is lacking. Also lacking is an explicit recognition that the Mexican domestic context is the political environment in which the dialogue has flourished most successfully. In the past, Mexico has acknowledged historic responsibility to its nationals—including dual nationals—in the United States, and at times the dialogue between the government and its expatriates has been meaningful and mutually beneficial. More recently, Mexico has acknowledged an historic responsibility to the peoples of the Central American nations—to peoples linked to it by history and geography, even though they are not Mexican citizens. What is needed is a framework within which Mexico explicitly accepts an historic responsibility for the descendants of its expatriates in the United States, be they Mexican citizens or not. Within this framework the government would formally recognize what in fact has occurred informally—Chicano groups have been addressed largely as if they were one more Mexican (domestic) constituency.

It would appear that the case for Mexico's acceptance of this responsibility is compelling. Mexico has some legitimate interests in the United States, particularly in protecting those of its citizens. These citizens have historically been tied to the Mexican-origin population. They are members of the same families, live in the same communities, share an ethnic identity and experience the same economic and political subordination in the United States that Mexican citizens have historically faced. More importantly, Chicano political actors have been involved in a number of issues of concern to Mexico, such as immigration, where they continue to fight political battles for Mexican citizens—particularly undocumented citizens. Some have done so for altruistic reasons, but many out of self-interest—the violation of the rights of Mexican citizens in the U.S. also harms the rights of Mexican-origin persons in that country, many of whom are several generations removed from Mexico.

Accepting an historic responsibility for Mexican-origin persons in the U.S. would mean, for want of a better term, the promotion of a "special relationship" with Chicano groups in the United States. This relationship is "special" now only in the sense that the dialogue is being renewed and that some exchange—much of it symbolic—has taken place. It could become a more substantive relationship were Mexico to promote a more active policy with significant material exchanges as has occurred with Mexico and some groups in Central America. Accepting an "historic responsibility" in this sense could mean that Chicanos or Chicano groups get preferential treatment in any of a number of areas—immigration, employment in Mexico, concessions of various types. Accepting the "special relationship" idea would mean that Chicanos —according to some acceptable criterion—would no longer be considered foreigners in Mexico and would be invited to participate in many areas of its national life.

Adopting a domestic political framework for the promotion of the dialogue is one possibility. Another possibility would entail emphasizing the mutualities of interest that Mexico shares with Chicano political actors in specific issue areas within a bilateral political context, such as the protection of the rights of undocumented Mexicans in the United States. A review of recent events involving the struggle to protect those rights—denouncing the violations of due process by local authorities, filing lawsuits to prevent unconstitutional searches during deportation raids, collecting the wages of deported migrants, prosecution of wage and fair labor standards violations and legal defense of the right of undocumented school-age children to enroll in public schools—demonstrates that in many of these areas, domestic U.S. groups, many led by Chicanos, are at the forefront. By contrast, Mexican consulates have not been given the personnel or resources necessary to become more active in areas such as these.[81] In any event, these are concrete areas where a constructive expansion of the dialogue might take place.

Mexican political actors in the south should be mindful that whether mutual areas of interest are promoted or not, Mexican political actors in the north can either work in alliance with or in opposition to what could be common political objectives. Because conflict among them would limit possibilities for expanded dialogue, it should be managed with care, and steps should be taken to reduce its likelihood. In this respect, it would be helpful if such actors—particularly the government—consulted Chicano groups in the U.S. to see how they might be affected by some Mexican policy responses to U.S. initiatives. To do so would build a relationship that does not rest on good will alone.

Notes

1. The term "Mexicans in the United States" is used to refer to all Mexican-origin persons in the U.S. regardless of citizenship. Another term used is "Mexicans north of the (U.S.-Mexican) boundary," to distinguish it from Mexicans south of the same. When the term "Chicano" is used, it refers to the subgroup of Mexicans north of the border who do not have Mexican citizenship.

2. See, e.g., Rodolfo O. de la Garza, "Demythologizing Chicano-Mexican Relations," in Susan Kaufman Purcell, ed., *Mexico–United States Relations*, Pro-

ceedings of the Academy of Political Science 34 (1981):88-96; Israel Galán, "Los chicanos, el petróleo mexicano y una alianza posible," in David Barkin et al., *Las relaciones México-Estados Unidos* (México: Editorial Nueva Imagen and Universidad Nacional Autónoma de México, 1980) vol. I, pp. 245-249; José Angel Gutiérrez, "Chicanos and the Mexican President, 1972-1980," paper presented at Mexico-United States Relations FIPSE Project, Santa Monica, Calif., April 1981 (Los Angeles: UCLA Chicano Studies Research Center, forthcoming); Georgie Ann Geyer, "Are Mexico and Chicanos Trying to Use Each Other?" in *Los Angeles Times*, 6 March 1978, Part II (Editorial Pages); Stanley R. Ross, "Introduction," in Richard D. Erb and Stanley R. Ross, eds., *United States Relations with Mexico: Content and Context* (Washington, D.C.: American Enterprise Institute for Public Policy Research, 1981).

3. The first official response perhaps was the government preparations for the evacuation—or "repatriation"—of its citizens from the newly conquered territories occupied by the United States; Luis G. Zorilla, *Historia de las relaciones entre México y los Estados Unidos de América, 1800-1958* (México: Editorial Porrúa, 1965), vol. I, pp. 259-273.

4. Secretaría de Relaciones Exteriores and Secretaría de la Presidencia, *México a Través de los Informes Presidenciales; la Política Exterior* (México: Talleres Gráficos de la Nación, 1976), vol. 3, p. 56.

5. Carey McWilliams, *North From Mexico: The Spanish-speaking People of the United States* (Westport, Conn.: Greenwood Press, 1968), p. 103.

6. The nineteenth century themes of conquest, the retention of a distinct ethnic identity by Mexican communities in the U.S., the retention of ties to Mexico, and the consolidation of Mexican communities in the U.S. as identifiable social and economic groups run through much of the vast literature on the subject. Even though the historical basis for the "social dialogue" is an important thesis for the argument developed in this paper, it cannot be discussed here. A sampling of pertinent titles might include: Albert Camarillo, *Chicanos in a Changing Society; from Mexican Pueblos to American Barrios in Santa Barbara and Southern California, 1848-1930* (Cambridge, Mass.: Harvard University Press, 1979); Agustín Cue Cánovas, *Los Estados Unidos y el México olvidado* (México: B. Costa-Amic, 1970); Raúl A. Fernández, *The United States-Mexico Border; a Politico-Economic Profile* (Notre Dame: University of Notre Dame Press, 1977); Mario T. García, *Desert Immigrants; the Mexicans of El Paso, 1880-1920* (New Haven: Yale University Press, 1981); Richard Griswold del Castillo, *The Los Angeles Barrio, 1850-1890; A Social History* (Berkeley: University of California Press, 1979); David Maciel and Patricia Bueno, eds., *Aztlán: historia del pueblo chicano (1848-1910)* (México: Secretaría de Educación Pública, 1975) [Sepsetentas, 174]; David J. Weber, ed., *Foreigners in their Native Land; Historical Roots of the Mexican Americans* (Albuquerque: University of New Mexico Press, 1973).

7. The reader should be aware that there is some debate on this point. The evidence suggests that at times commercial matters dominated the activities of the consulates, or even justified the creation of new offices while at other times, their relations with the local Mexican-origin population. Reports by Mexican government officials in 1885, for example, argued that the "presence of a large *colonia mexicana* . . . was enough to justify the establishment of a Los Angeles consulate regardless of commercial considerations." See Francisco Enrique Bal-

derrama, *In Defense of La Raza: The Los Angeles Mexican Community, 1929-36* (Tucson: The University of Arizona Press, 1982). One author has argued that notwithstanding commercial interests (p. 496), "From the nineteenth century until recently the consulates were at the center of the sociocultural activity in the Chicano community"; see Juan Gómez-Quiñones, "Piedras contra la luna; México en Aztlán y Aztlán en México: Chicano-Mexican Relations and the Mexican Consulates, 1900-1920," in James W. Wilkie et al., *Contemporary Mexico; Papers of the IV International Congress of Mexican History* (Berkeley and Mexico City: University of California Press and El Colegio de México, 1976). Another argued that the overriding concern in establishing the consulates in the Southwest, particularly during the nineteenth century, was commercial. According to this view, factors such as the protection of the interests of the Mexican government, or of its citizens in the U.S. were secondary. See Lourdes Urbina, "La política consular mexicana de protección en los Estados Unidos, 1920-1977," licentiate thesis in progress, Departamento de Relaciones Internacionales, UNAM, México, D.F., p. 11. Moreover, the creation of new consulates often responded to strong political concerns. Such seems to have been the case with the establishment of the New Orleans consulate, which was conceived "as a listening post for the purpose of gathering information on the trends and activities of the southern population in the United States. . ." See Secretaría de Relaciones Exteriores, *Los primeros consulados de México, 1823-1872*, Colección del Archivo Diplomático Mexicano, Tercera Epoca (México: Talleres Gráficos de la Nación, 1974), p. 27. In the research for this essay, it appears that with the exception of the years 1921-22, and possibly 1917-18 and 1929-36, the consulates were primarily involved in activities outside of those which brought them in contact with the Mexican expatriate community.

8. Perhaps the most comprehensive analysis of contemporary Mexican foreign policy can be found in Mario Ojeda, *Alcances y límites de la política exterior de México* (México: El Colegio de México, 1976).

9. An analysis of the underpinnings of the principle of non-intervention is beyond the scope of this paper. A reader not familiar with Mexican history should note that it has constituted an important—if not central—element of Mexican foreign policy from the beginning of the country's existence as a nation-state. It was expressed as early as the 1820s and 1830s when Mexico abstained from participating in the independence of Guatemala and Chiapas, and when it faced encroachments in the north during the Texas rebellion. See Secretaría de Relaciones Exteriores and Secretaría de la Presidencia, *México a Través de los Informes*, vol. 3. Cf: Jorge Castañeda, *México y el orden internacional*, 2nd edition (México: El Colegio de México, 1981), p. 189.

10. Lawrence Cardoso, *Mexican Emigration to the United States, 1897-1931; Socioeconomic Patterns* (Tucson: University of Arizona Press, 1980), p. 65.

11. *Ibid.*, p. 64.

12. *Ibid.*, p. 67.

13. Dispatch from Garza Pérez to Fletcher, reproduced in George C. Kiser and Martha Woody Kiser, *Mexican Workers in the United States; Historical and Political Perspectives* (Albuquerque: University of New Mexico Press, 1979), p. 15.

14. Cardoso, *Mexican Emigration*, pp. 68-69.

15. *Ibid.*, p. 58.

16. *Ibid.*, p. 59.

17. Quoted in Cardoso, *Mexican Emigration*, p. 58.
18. *Ibid.*
19. *Ibid.*, pp. 65-66.
20. *Ibid.*, p. 67.
21. *Ibid.*, p. 66.
22. Mercedes Carreras de Velasco, *Los mexicanos que devolvió la crisis, 1929-1932* (México: Secretaría de Relaciones Exteriores, 1974), p. 47.
23. Lawrence Cardoso, "La repatriación de braceros en época de Obregón, 1920-1923," in *Historia Mexicana* 26 (April-June, 1977):580.
24. Carreras de Velasco, *Los mexicanos que devolvió la crisis*, pp. 46-47.
25. Cardoso, "La repatriación," pp. 585-586; Mark Reisler, *By the Sweat of Their Brow; Mexican Immigrant Labor in the United States, 1900-1940* (Westport, Conn.: Greenwood Press, 1976), p. 49.
26. Reisler, *By the Sweat of Their Brow*, pp. 49-50.
27. *Ibid.*, p. 49; Cardoso, "La repatriación," pp. 484-586.
28. Reisler, *By the Sweat of Their Brow*, p. 50.
29. Cardoso, "La repatriación," p. 586.
30. Carreras de Velasco, *Los mexicanos que devolvió la crisis*, p. 47; Zorrilla, *Historia de las relaciones*, vol. 2, p. 373.
31. Reisler, *By the Sweat of Their Brow*, pp. 55, 50.
32. Cardoso, "La repatriación," p. 582.
33. Carreras de Velasco, *Los mexicanos que devolvió la crisis*, pp. 47-48.
34. *Ibid.*, p. 48.
35. Cardoso, "La repatriación," pp. 590, 591.
36. *Ibid.*, p. 592.
37. Urbina, "La política consular mexicana de protección," p. 11; Cardoso, *Mexican Emigration*, p. 106.
38. Secretaría de Relaciones Exteriores, *La Migración y Protección de Mexicanos en el Extranjero* (México: Imprenta de la Secretaría de Relaciones Exteriores, 1928), p. 9.
39. *Ibid.*, pp. 9-10.
40. Secretaría de Relaciones Exteriores, *Memoria de Agosto de 1929 a Junio de 1930* (México: Imprenta de la Secretaría de Relaciones Exteriores, 1930), p. 1731.
41. Cardoso, *Mexican Emigration*, pp. 106-107.
42. Zorrilla, *Historia de las relaciones*, vol. 2, p. 373.
43. Cardoso, *Mexican Emigration*, p. 114.
44. *Ibid.*
45. *Ibid.*, pp. 114-115.
46. *Ibid.*, p. 114.
47. Secretaría de Relaciones Exteriores, *La migración y protección*, pp. 21-30.
48. Urbina, "La política consular mexicana de protección," pp. 58-59.
49. Not surprisingly, employers sought to delay the payment of indemnification as much as possible. For a discussion of consular activity and goals in this area, see Secretaría de Relaciones Exteriores, *Memoria de agosto de 1928 a julio de 1929* (México: Imprenta de la Secretaría de Relaciones Exteriores, 1929), p. 1579.
50. *Ibid.*, p. 1585.

51. *Ibid.* An editorial in a major Mexico City newspaper in 1931 argued that Mexican consular offices in the U.S. "required additional funds and support from the home government in order to provide adequate legal protection for the Mexicans who were 'so exploited and reviled' . . ." Quoted in Abraham Hoffman, *Unwanted Mexican Americans in the Great Depression; Repatriation Pressures, 1929-1939* (Tucson: University of Arizona Press, 1974), p. 134.

52. Secretaría de Relaciones Exteriores, *Memoria, 1928-29*, p. 1783.

53. *Ibid.*

54. Secretaría de Relaciones Exteriores, *Memoria de agosto de 1932 a julio de 1933* (México: Imprenta de la Secretaría de Relaciones Exteriores, 1933), p. 217.

55. Carreras de Velasco, *Los mexicanos que devolvió la crisis*, p. 51; citing the *Memoria* of 1926-27 of the Ministry of Foreign Relations.

56. "The doleful caravan of northward-bound braceros had reduced Mexico to the status of an 'exporter of human meat' for the United States . . . a member of the federal Chamber of Deputies spoke for the majority of Mexican revolutionaries when he wrote that all of the nation's wars meant little when compared to the shame of the losses incurred through emigration." Cardoso, *Mexican Emigration*, p. 104.

57. Quoted in Carreras de Velasco, *Los mexicanos que devolvió la crisis*, p. 52.

58. *Ibid.* Consuls engaged in activities to conserve the "patriotic spirit" of Mexicans in the United States.

59. Quoted in Reisler, *By the Sweat of Their Brow*, p. 115.

60. In this vein, one may note that in the year 1927-28, the Ministry of Foreign Relations published an official report on the *labor de protección* it had undertaken in the U.S. and Guatemala. Repatriation was considered to be one element of protection, "without the necessity of promoting it." See Carreras de Velasco, *Los mexicanos que devolvió la crisis*, p. 51.

61. Reisler, *By the Sweat of Their Brow*, pp. 111, 113. Reisler cites Emory Bogardus and Paul Taylor in developing these arguments.

62. Quoted in *Ibid.*, p. 110.

63. Secretaría de Relaciones Exteriores, *Memoria, 1932-33*, p. 217. "Another remarkable dimension of protectionism as carried out by Mexican consuls in the United States," wrote Arthur F. Corwin, "has been the defense of Mexican nationals, and even Mexican Americans, against discrimination and segregation in schooling, housing, and social services . . ." See "Causes of Mexican Emigration to the United States: A Summary View," in *Perspectives in American History* 7 (1973):608.

64. Reisler, *By the Sweat of Their Brow*, p. 125, note 105.

65. Ernesto Hidalgo, *La protección de mexicanos en los Estados Unidos* (México: Secretaría de Relaciones Exteriores, 1940), p. 3. This view was in keeping with the relatively interventionist activities of the consuls in the 1930s. Most notably, they were involved in the organization and negotiation of agricultural labor strikes in which Mexican workers—regardless of citizenship—were involved. The role of the consuls has been viewed both as an asset and as a detriment to the organizing efforts of the workers. In most cases the consuls acted in what they perceived to be the best interests of the workers, although this perception may not

be shared in all cases by other observers, including this writer. Largely they worked for short-term bread-and-butter solutions to the labor problems faced by such workers, and partially because of that they frequently found themselves in conflict with more radical groups also involved in organizing Mexican agricultural labor at that time. While the results of their activities were mixed, it is fair to say that the consuls frequently became involved in these activities, notwithstanding the fact that they consciously perceived them to be internal matters of the United States. See Reisler, *By the Sweat of Their Brow*, pp. 235–246; Secretaría de Relaciones Exteriores and Secretaría de la Presidencia, *México a Través de los Informes*, vol. III, pp. 355–356; Secretaría de Relaciones Exteriores, *Memoria, 1932-33*, p. 231; Balderrama, "En defensa de la raza;" Devra Ann Weber, "The Organizing of Mexicano Agricultural Workers: Imperial Valley and Los Angeles, 1928–34, Oral History Approach," *Aztlán; Chicano Journal of the Social Sciences and the Arts* 3 (Fall 1972):307–337; Ronald W. López, "The El Monte Berry Strike of 1933," *Aztlán; Chicano Journal of the Social Sciences and the Arts* 1 (Spring, 1970): 101–112.

66. Jorge Castañeda, "En busca de una posición frente a Estados Unidos," in Centro de Estudios Internacionales, *Visión del México contemporáneo* (México: El Colegio de México, 1979), pp. 111–112.

67. A scathing and well-documented indictment of the inaction of the Mexican consulates with respect to braceros imported under contract to work in the U.S. during the 1950s was written by Ernesto Galarza in 1956. See his "Trabajadores mexicanos en tierra extraña," *Problemas Agrícolas e Industriales de México* 10 (January–March and April–June, 1958):1–84.

68. In the view of this writer, much of the current debate about the viability of the dialogue incorrectly assumes that the exchange largely takes place within the U.S. domestic political context.

69. This context emphasizes the mutualities of interest of the Mexican government and of Mexicans in the U.S. as *political actors*. The implications of this, which cannot be discussed here, are: (a) that Mexicans in the U.S. can act as a "lobby" for Mexico in some areas or can affect political outcomes within a U.S. domestic context related to issues which are salient to Mexico in its relations with the United States; and (b) that the Mexican government can use its position as a sovereign to leverage favorable outcomes from the U.S. government for Mexicans in the U.S. through government-to-government channels.

70. The last major change in immigration legislation affecting Mexico was passed in the closing session of Congress in 1977, and was slipped in with a number of last-minute bills which were not examined closely. Thus, every western hemisphere country was placed under a numerical limitation of 20,000 quota immigrants annually, a move which had been averted by opponents of immigration restriction for Mexico since the death of the "Box Bills" in the 1920s.

71. Remarks to this effect were made by Ralph Guzmán during an oral presentation titled "Chicanos and U.S.–Mexican Relations," made at Third College, University of California at San Diego, 7 October 1981. Other views by Chicano intellectuals corroborate this. See Gómez-Quiñones, "Piedras contra la luna," p. 494; de la Garza, "Demythologizing Chicano–Mexican Relations," p. 91.

72. Carlos Monsiváis, "From the Halls of Montezuma," in *Sabado* (supplement to *Uno Más Uno*) 116, 26 January 1980, pp. 5, 6. Monsiváis is obviously referring to the perception of Mexican migrants and Chicanos by Mexican non-

migrants. Cf. Carlos Monsiváis, "The Culture of the Frontier: The Mexican Side," in Stanley R. Ross, ed., *Views Across the Border* (Albuquerque: University of New Mexico Press, 1978), pp. 63-64.

73. Jorge A. Bustamante, "Chicanos: biografía de una toma de conciencia," in *Cuadernos Políticos* 6 (October-December, 1975):26.

74. *Ibid.*, p. 25.

75. The U.S. has intervened in Mexican internal affairs since the nineteenth century. Some of the military and political interventions are chronicled in Gastón García Cantú, *Las invasiones norteamericanas en México* (México: Ediciones Era, 1971). For examples of U.S. efforts to pressure Mexico so that it would not enforce its 1917 Constitution because doing so would harm the property rights of U.S. businesses, see Lorenzo Meyer, "El primer tramo del camino," in Centro de Estudios Históricos, *Historia General de México* (México: El Colegio de México, 1976), vol. IV, pp. 147-153.

76. For one articulation of this view, see de la Garza, "Demythologizing Chicano-Mexican Relations," pp. 88-89, 95-96.

77. "Ningún enclave militar en otro país: JLP," *Uno Más Uno* 2 October 1979, pp. 1, 6.

78. "La política exterior dejó ya de ser defensiva: JLP," *Uno Más Uno* 12 February 1980, pp. 1, 6.

79. In the same article cited above, López Portillo is quoted as saying: " 'We should note, with pride, that all of Mexico's governments since Independence—even those that could be repudiated for their domestic policies—have maintained a consistent foreign policy which traditionally has been defensive and lately come to be more active . . . I believe that the latter approach is complementary to the former. It is a vital and active expression of the same policy, and therefore represents continuity, a new approach vis-à-vis different circumstances . . .' "

80. A set of bold proposals recently presented by a Chicano political figure is an example of this. (See Mario G. Obledo, "Mexamerica: An Open Border," presentation made before the Southwest Border Regional Commission, San Diego, Calif., 2 May 1980, especially pp. 9-10.) The Common Market idea is but one of the proposals suggested therein which would be patently objectionable to most Mexican political actors in the south. Others include the proposal that the U.S. and Mexican military forces be joined together, that the instruction of English and U.S. history be mandatory in Mexican schools, and that Mexico give preference to U.S. direct investment above that from other countries. Apart from whether such proposals would be acceptable to others in the U.S., or whether the governments involved could actually implement them, their formulation reveals a lack of awareness of Mexican foreign and domestic policy principles and political realities. To get some sense of how widespread the negative reaction to the Common Market idea is in Mexico, for example, see "Mercado común México-Canadá-Estados Unidos?" *Foro Político y Polémico*, 13 April 1981, no. 34, Supplement to *El Día* (Mexico City). One can observe that although not always for the same reasons, political parties and groups ranging from one extreme to the other reject the plan unanimously.

81. For a number of reasons that are not immediately apparent, Mexican consulates are now *less* active in protecting the rights of Mexicans in the United States than they were in the 1920s. Chicano organizations and others in the U.S. have largely supplanted such efforts. The decision of a federal judge in Houston

ordering that undocumented school children be allowed to enroll in Texas public schools is but a recent illustration of this. An important Mexico City newspaper editorialized that this ruling had been achieved thanks to efforts by Chicano groups, and criticized the Mexican government for its inaction. "It is evident," stated the editorial, "that there are Chicanos who are assisting Mexican citizens in ways that not even their government or countrymen have acted." See "Triunfo chicano en favor de México," *Uno Más Uno*, 25 July 1980, p. 3.

Bibliography

GENERAL FRAMEWORKS: CONFLICT AND CONVERGENCE

Several citations in this section of the bibliography also address the more specific topics dealt with in other sections.

Asociación Nacional de Universidades de Enseñanza Superior. *Estudios fronterizos: Reunión de universidades de México y Estados Unidos, ponencias y comentarios.* México, 1981.
Baird, Peter, and McCaughan, Ed, eds. *Beyond the Border: Mexico and the U.S. Today.* New York: North American Congress on Latin America, 1979.
Ball, George W. *Diplomacy for a Crowded World.* New York: Little, Brown and Co., 1976.
Barkin, David, et al. *Las relaciones México-Estados Unidos.* Vol. 1 México: Editorial Nueva Imagen, 1980.
Brown, Lyle, C. "The Politics of United States-Mexican Relations: Problems of the 1970s in Historical Perspective." In *Contemporary Mexico*, edited by James W. Wilkie, Michael C. Meyer, and Edna Monzón de Wilkie. Berkeley: University of California Press, 1976, pp. 471-493.
Brown, Lyle C., and Wilkie, James W. "Recent United States-Mexican Relations: Problems Old and New." In *Twentieth-Century American Foreign Policy*, edited by John Braeman and Robert H. Bremmer. Columbus: Ohio State University Press, 1971, pp. 378-419.
Castañeda, Jorge. "Revolution and Foreign Policy: Mexico's Experience." *Political Science Quarterly* 78 (1963):391-417.
———. "En busca de una posición ante Estados Unidos." *Foro Internacional* 19 (1978):292-302.
———. *México y el orden internacional.* 2d ed. México: El Colegio de México, 1981.
Centro de Estudios Internacionales. *Continuidad y cambio en la política exterior de México.* México: El Colegio de México, 1977.
Centro de Estudios Internacionales. *Lecturas de política exterior mexicana.* México: El Colegio de México, 1979.
Cline, Howard. *The United States and Mexico.* 3d ed. New York: Atheneum, 1976.
Council for Inter-American Security. *Mexico 2000: A Look at the Potential of Modern Mexico.* Washington, D.C., 1980.

González Salazar, Roque. *La frontera del norte: integración y desarrollo.* México: El Colegio de México, 1981.
Lozoya, Jorge, and Estévez, Jaime. *Latin America and the New International Economic Order.* New York: Pergamon Press, 1980.
Manning, Bayless. "The Congress, the Executive, and Intermestic Affairs: Three Proposals." *Foreign Affairs* 55 (1977):306–324.
McBride, Robert H., ed. *Mexico and the United States.* Englewood Cliffs, New Jersey: Prentice-Hall, Inc., 1981.
Meyer, Lorenzo, and Vázquez, Josefina Zoraida. *Mexico and the United States.* Chicago: University of Chicago Press, forthcoming.
Ojeda, Mario. *Alcances y límites de la política exterior de México.* México: El Colegio de México, 1976.
Pellicer de Brody, Olga. "Mexico in the 1970s and Its Relations with the U.S." In *Latin America and the United States: The Changing Political Realities*, edited by Richard Fagen. Stanford: Stanford University Press, 1974, pp. 314–333.
———. "Veinte años de política exterior mexicana 1960–1980." *Foro Internacional* 21 (1980):149–160.
Peñaloza, Tomás. "La formulación de la política exterior en los E.U. de América y su impacto sobre México." *Foro Internacional*, 18 (1977): 10–31.
Rangel, Carlos. "Mexico and Other Dominoes." *Commentary* 71 (1981): 2–33.
Redclift, Michael, and Redclift, Nennecke. "Unholy Alliance." *Foreign Policy* (Winter, 1980–81):111–133.
Ross, Stanley R. *Views Across the Border: The United States and Mexico.* Albuquerque: University of New Mexico Press, 1978.
Schmitt, Karl M. *Mexico and the United States, 1828–1973: Conflict and Coexistence.* New York: John Wiley, 1974.
Shafer, Robert Jones, and Mabry, Donald. *Neighbors: Mexico and the U.S., Wetbacks and Oil.* Chicago: Nelson-Hall Publishers, 1981.
Silvert, Kalman H., et al. *The Americas in a Changing World: A Report of the Commission on United States–Latin American Relations.* New York: Quadrangle/The New York Times Book Co., 1975.
Simmons, Marlise; Smith, Peter H.; Fagen, Richard R. "Mexico." *The Wilson Quarterly* (Summer 1979):117–153.
Singh, Jyoti Shankar. *A New International Economic Order: Toward a Fair Redistribution of the World's Resources.* New York: Praeger, 1977.
Smith, Peter H. *The Labyrinths of Power: Political Recruitment in Twentieth-Century Mexico.* Princeton: Princeton University Press, 1979.
———. *Mexico: The Quest for a Policy.* New York: Foreign Policy Association, 1980.

Southern California Research Council. *Mexico and Southern California: Toward a New Partnership.* Claremont, Calif.: Pomona Colleges, 1981.
Stevens, Evelyn P. *Protest and Response in Mexico.* Cambridge, Mass.: The M.I.T. Press, 1974.
U.S. Congress. *Recent Developments in Mexico and Their Implications for the United States: Hearings Before the Subcommittee on Inter-American Economic Relations of the Joint Economic Committee.* Washington, D.C.: Government Printing Office, 1978.
Wyman, Donald L. "Dependence and Conflict in U.S.-Mexican Relations, 1920-1975." In *Diplomatic Disputes: U.S. Conflict with Iran, Japan, and Mexico,* edited by Robert L. Paarlberg. Cambridge, Mass.: Center for International Affairs, Harvard University, 1978.
Zorilla, Luis G. *Historia de las relaciones entre México y los Estados Unidos de América, 1800-1958.* 2 vols. México: Editorial Porrúa, 1965.

MEXICAN PETROLEUM

Castillo, Heberto. *Pemex Si, PUESA No.* México: CISA (Revista *Proceso*), 1981.
Centro de Estudios Internacionales. *Las perspectivas del petróleo mexicano.* México: El Colegio de México, 1979.
Fagen, Richard R. "Mexican Gas: The Northern Connection." In *Capitalism and the State in U.S.-Latin American Relations,* edited by Richard R. Fagen. Stanford: Stanford University Press, 1979.
Grayson, George W. *The Politics of Mexican Oil.* Pittsburgh: University of Pittsburgh Press, 1980.
Kraft, Joseph. "The Mexican Oil Puzzle." *The New Yorker,* 15 October 1979, pp. 150-181.
Mancke, Richard B., ed. *Mexican Oil and Natural Gas: Political, Strategic, and Economic Implications.* New York: Praeger Publishers, 1979.
Meyer, Lorenzo. *Mexico and the United States in the Oil Controversy, 1917-1942.* Austin: University of Texas Press, 1977.
Pazos, Luis. *Mitos y realidades del petróleo mexicano.* México: Editorial Diana, 1979.
Pellicer de Brody, Olga. "U.S. Concerns Regarding Mexico's Oil and Gas: Evolution of the Debate, 1977-1980." Working Papers in U.S.-Mexican Studies, no. 10. La Jolla, Calif.: Program in U.S.-Mexican Studies, University of California, San Diego, 1981.
Powell, Richard. *The Mexican Petroleum Industry: 1938-1950.* New York: Russel & Russell, 1972.

Proceso. México frente a Estado Unidos: petróleo y soberanía. México: Editorial Posada, S.A., 1979.
Rippy, Merrill. *Oil and the Mexican Revolution.* Leiden, Netherlands: E.J. Brill, 1972.
Ronfeldt, David, et al. *Mexico's Petroleum and U.S. Policy: Implications for the 1980s.* Santa Monica: Rand Corporation, 1980.
Tello, Carlos, and Reynolds, Clark W., eds. *Los relaciones México-Estados Unidos.* México: Fondo de Cultura Económica, 1981.
U.S. House of Representatives Subcommittee on Investigations and Oversight and the Subcommittee on Science, Research and Technology, Committee on Science and Technology. *U.S.-Mexico Relations and Potentials Regarding Energy, Immigration, Scientific Cooperations and Technology Transfer.* Washington, D.C.: U.S. Government Printing Office, 1979.
Williams, Edward J. "Oil in Mexican-U.S. Relations: Analysis and Bargaining Scenario." *Orbis* 22 (1978):201-216.

TRADE RELATIONS

Aspra, L. Antonio. "Import Substitution in Mexico: Past and Present." *World Development* 5 (1977):111-123.
Barkin, David. "Mexico's Albatross: The U.S. Economy." *Latin American Perspectives* 2 (1975):48-63.
Bennett, Douglas, and Sharpe, Kenneth. "Agenda Setting and Bargaining Power: The Mexican State vs. the Transnational Automobile Corporations." *World Politics* 32 (1979):57-89.
Bergsten, C. Fred. "Coming Investment Wars?" *Foreign Affairs* 52 (1974): 135-152.
Bhagwati, Jagdish N., ed. *The New International Economic Order: The North-South Debate.* Cambridge, Mass.: The MIT Press, 1977.
Ceceña, José Luis. *México en la órbita imperial: Las empresas transnacionales.* México: Ediciones "El Caballito," 1970.
Clement, Norris, and Green, Louis. "The Political Economy of Devaluation in Mexico." *Inter-American Economic Affairs* 33 (1978):47-76.
Comercio Exterior. "Mexico's Foreign Trade in 1978 and Future Prospects." *Comercio Exterior de México* (May 1979):128-133.
———. "A Dilemma for the Mexican Economy: Growth or Development." *Comercio Exterior de México* (August 1978):315-322.
Domínguez, Jorge I., ed. *Mexico's Political Economy: Challenges at Home and Abroad.* Beverly Hills: Sage Publications, 1982.
Green, Rosario. *El endeudamiento público externo de México, 1940-1973.* México: El Colegio de México, 1976.
———. "Mexico's Public Foreign Debt, 1965-1976." *Comercio Exterior de México* (January 1978):17-24.

Hansen, Roger D. *The Politics of Mexican Development.* Baltimore: The Johns Hopkins Press, 1971.
King, Timothy. *Mexico: Industrialization and Trade Policies Since 1940.* London: Oxford University Press, 1970.
Looney, Robert E. *Mexico's Economy: A Policy Analysis with Forecasts to 1990.* Boulder, Colo.: Westview Press, 1978.
de la Madrid, Malpíca. *¿Qué es el GATT?* México: Editorial Grijalbo, S.A., 1979.
Navarrete, Jorge. "The Foreign Trade of Mexico: Imbalance and Dependence." *Comercio Exterior de México* (January 1976):25–33.
Pellicer de Brody, Olga. "U.S. Trade Policy Toward Mexico: Are There Reasons to Expect Special Treatment?" Working Papers in U.S.-Mexican Studies, no. 9. La Jolla, Calif.: Program in United States-Mexican Studies, University of California, San Diego, 1981.
Poder Ejecutivo Federal. *El Plan Global de Desarrollo, 1980–1982.* México: El Gobierno Mexicano, 1980.
Poulson, Barry W., and Osborn, T. Noel, eds. *U.S.-Mexican Economic Relations.* Boulder, Colo.: Westview Press, 1979.
Reynolds, Clark. *The Mexican Economy: Twentieth-Century Structure and Growth.* New Haven: Yale University Press, 1970.
———. "Why Mexico's 'Stabilizing Development' Was Actually Destabilizing (With Some Implications for the Future)." *World Development* 6 (1978):1005–1018.
Schlagheck, James L. *The Political, Economic, and Labor Climate in Mexico.* Philadelphia: The Wharton School, University of Pennsylvania, 1977.
Tello, Carlos. *La política económica en México, 1970–1976.* México: Siglo Veintiuno Editores, 1979.
Vuskovic, Pedro. "Latin America: Crisis of Development Pattern and Its Political Implications." *Comercio Exterior de México* (January 1976): 34–45.
World Bank. *Special Study of the Mexican Economy: Major Policy Issues and Prospects, 1977–82.* 2 vols. Washington, D.C.: The World Bank, 1978.

MIGRANT WORKERS

Bustamante, Jorge A. *Espaldas mojadas, materia prima para la expansión del capital norteamericano.* México: El Colegio de México, 1975.
———. "U.S. Immigration Policy: A Mexican Perspective on President Reagan's Proposal." U.S.-Mexico Project Series 4. Washington, D.C.: Overseas Development Project, 1982.
Cardoso, Lawrence A. *Mexican Emigration to the United States, 1897–1931.* Tucson: University of Arizona Press, 1980.

Carreras de Velasco, Mercedes. *Los mexicanos que devolvió la crisis, 1929-1932.* México: Secretaría de Relaciones Exteriores, 1974.
Cornelius, Wayne A. "Mexican Migration to the United States." In *Mexico-United States Relations,* edited by Susan Kaufman Purcell. New York: The Academy of Political Science, 1981.
―――. "Immigration and U.S.-Mexican Relations." Working Paper No. 1. La Jolla, Calif.: Program in U.S.-Mexican Studies, University of California, San Diego, 1981.
―――. "The Reagan Administration's Proposals for a New Immigration Policy: An Assessment of Potential Effects." *International Migration Review* 15 (1981):760-778.
Corwin, Arthur, ed. *Immigrants-and Immigrants: Perspectives on Mexican Labor to the United States.* Westport, Conn.: Greenwood Press, 1978.
Cross, Harry E., and Sandos, James A. *Across the Border: Rural Development in Mexico and Recent Migration to the United States.* Berkeley: Institute of Governmental Studies, University of California, Berkeley, 1981.
Dinnerstein, L.; Nichols, R.L.; and Reimers, D.M. *Natives and Strangers: Ethnic Groups and the Building of America.* New York: Oxford University Press, 1979.
Galarza, Ernesto. *Merchants of Labor: The Mexican Bracero Story.* Santa Barbara, Calif.: McNally & Loftkin, 1964.
García, Juan Ramón. *Operation Wetback: The Mass Deportation of Mexican Undocumented Workers in 1954.* Westport, Conn.: Greenwood Press, 1980.
García y Griego, Manuel. "The Importation of Mexican Contract Laborers to the United States, 1942-1964." In *The Border That Binds: Mexican Immigrants and U.S. Responsibility,* edited by Peter G. Brown and Henry Shue. Totowa, N.J.: Rowman and Littlefield, 1982.
―――. "La comisión selector, la administración Reagan y la política norteamericana sobre indocumentados; un debate en transición." In *México-Estados Unidos: 1982,* edited by Lorenzo Meyer. México: El Colegio de México, forthcoming.
Gómez-Quiñones, Juan. *Development of the Mexican Working Class North of the Rio Bravo.* Los Angeles: UCLA Chicano Studies Research Center, 1982.
Hewlett, Sylvia Ann. "Coping with Illegal Immigration." *Foreign Affairs* 60 (1981-82):358-378.
Hoffman, Abraham. *Unwanted Mexican Americans in the Great Depression: Repatriation Pressures, 1929-1939.* Tucson: University of Arizona Press, 1974.
Kiser, George C., and Kiser, Martha Woody, eds. *Mexican Workers in the United States: Historical and Political Perspectives.* Albuquerque: University of New Mexico Press, 1979.

López, Gerald P. "Undocumented Mexican Migration: In Search of a Just Immigration Law and Policy." *UCLA Law Review* (1981):615-714.
Louv, Richard. *The Mexican Migration: Southwind.* San Diego: The San Diego Union, 1980.
MacCain, Johnny. "Contract Labor as a Factor in U.S.-Mexican Relations, 1942-1947." Ph.D. dissertation, University of Texas, Austin, 1970.
Portes, Alejandro, ed. "Illegal Mexican Immigrants to the United States." *International Migration Review* 12 (Winter 1978).
Reisler, Mark. *By the Sweat of Their Brow: Mexican Immigrant Labor in the United States, 1900-1940.* Westport, Conn.: Greenwood Press, 1976.
Ríos-Bustamante, Antonio, ed. *Mexican Immigrant Workers in the United States.* Los Angeles: UCLA Chicano Studies Research Center, 1981.
Teitelbaum, Michael S. "Right vs. Right: Immigration and Refugee Policy in the United States." *Foreign Affairs* 59 (1980):21-59.
U.S. Commission on Civil Rights. *The Tarnished Golden Door: Civil Rights in Immigration.* Washington, D.C.: U.S. Government Printing Office, 1980.
U.S. Select Commission on Immigration and Refugee Policy. *Immigration Policy and the National Interest.* (Several volumes including *Final Report, Staff Report,* and *Appendices*) Washington, D.C., 1981.
Weintraub, Sidney, and Ross, Stanley R. *The Illegal Alien from Mexico.* Austin: Mexico-United States Border Research Program, University of Texas, Austin, 1980.

CHICANOS AND THE BINATIONAL RELATIONSHIP

Acuña, Rodolfo. *Occupied America: A History of Chicanos.* New York: Harper and Row, 1981.
Balderrama, Francisco Enrique. *In Defense of La Raza: The Los Angeles Mexican Consulates and the Mexican Community, 1929-36.* Tucson: The University of Arizona Press, 1982.
Cué Canovas, Augustín. *Los Estados Unidos y el México olvidado.* México: B. Costa-Amic, 1970.
de la Garza, Rodolfo O. "Chicano-Mexican Relations: Issues, Actors, and Possible Directions." In "Mexico-U.S. Relations." Los Angeles: UCLA Chicano Studies Research Center, forthcoming.
———. "Demythologizing Chicano-Mexican Relations." In *Mexico-United States Relations,* edited by Susan Kaufman Purcell. New York: Academy of Political Science, 1981.
Galán, Israel. "Los chicanos, el petróleo mexicano y una alianza posible." In *Las relaciones México-Estados Unidos,* vol. I by David Barkin et al. México: Editorial Nueva Imagen, 1980.

García, Mario T. *Desert Immigrants: The Mexicans of El Paso, 1880-1920.* New Haven: Yale University Press, 1981.

Gómez-Quiñones, Juan. *Sembradores—Ricardo Flores Magón y el Partido Liberal Mexicano: A Eulogy and Critique.* Los Angeles: UCLA Chicano Studies Research Center, 1973.

―――. "Piedras contra la luna: México en Aztlán y Aztlán en México: Chicano-Mexican Relations and the Mexican Consulates, 1900-1920." In *Contemporary Mexico,* edited by James W. Wilkie, Michael C. Meyer, and Edna Monzón de Wilkie. Berkeley: University of California Press, 1976.

López, Hank Enrique. "Back to Bachimba." In *The Chicano: Mexican-American Voices,* edited by Ed Ludwig and Jamez Santibañez. Baltimore: Penguin Books, 1977.

Maciel, David, ed. *La otra cara de México: El pueblo chicano.* (México: Ediciones "El Caballito," 1977.

Nostrand, Richard Lee. "The Hispanic-American Borderland: A Regional, Historical Geography." Ph.D. dissertation, University of California, Los Angeles, 1969.

Raat, W. Dirk. *Revoltosos: Mexico's Rebels in the United States, 1903-1923.* College Station: Texas A&M University Press, 1981.

Rosenbaum, Robert J. *Mexicano Resistance in the Southwest.* Austin: University of Texas Press, 1981.

Said, Abdul Aziz. *Ethnicity and U.S. Foreign Policy.* New York: Praeger, 1977.